D1602592

French and Spanish Records
of Louisiana

French and Spanish Records
of Louisiana

A Bibliographical Guide to
Archive and Manuscript
Sources

Henry Putney Beers

Louisiana State University Press

Baton Rouge and

London

Designer: Barbara Werden
Typeface: Linotron Palatino
Typesetter: G&S Typesetters, Inc.
Printer: Thomson-Shore, Inc.
Binder: John H. Dekker & Sons, Inc.

Library of Congress Cataloging-in-Publication Data

Beers, Henry Putney, 1907—
   French and Spanish records of Louisiana.

   Bibliography: p.
   Includes index.
   1. Louisiana—History—To 1803—Sources—Bibliography.
2. Spaniards—Louisiana—History—Sources—Bibliography.
3. French—Louisiana—History—Sources—Bibliography.
I. Title.
Z1289.B44   1989   [F372]   016.9763   88-13619
ISBN 0-8071-1444-8 (alk. paper)

The paper in this book meets the guidelines for permanence
and durability of the Committee on Production Guidelines
for Book Longevity of the Council on Library Resources. ∞

To Charles Beers,
my bachelor uncle,
who financed my education

Contents

ፊ

V / *The Records of Arkansas*

Preface

This book presents a history and description of the French and Spanish records of colonial Louisiana. Although most of the settlements in that colony were in what became the state of Louisiana, others under the governance of Louisiana were located in what became Mississippi, Alabama, Missouri, and Arkansas. The French and Spanish officials of Louisiana at New Orleans, Baton Rouge, Natchitoches, Natchez, Mobile, St. Louis, and other places accumulated records that are important for the history of those places and for the concerns of the people who lived there. Under the terms of the treaties with the United States that transferred sovereignty over the colony, records of an administrative character were carried off to France and Spain and deposited in their colonial archives. Records relating to the property and personal concerns of the colonists remained in the colony. Papers of officials, military officers, clergymen, businessmen, and others containing communications from government officials that have been acquired by nongovernmental repositories are also described.

Each part of this book presents a brief account of the history and government of a region, a history of the procurement of reproductions of the records that were taken away to France and Spain, and an account of the compilation and publication of selections of these materials. Also presented are descriptions of materials that remained in the hands of officials or found their way to unofficial repositories. The records of local jurisdictions that remained in the custody of officials in parishes in Louisiana and in counties elsewhere are also detailed. Other chapters on land records describe the procedures under which grants were made by the French and Spanish officials and the documentation that resulted from the procedures adopted by the United States Congress for legitimatizing the grants. The Catholic priests who established churches in Louisiana introduced the practice of keeping registers of births, marriages, and burials—

a practice that had long been followed in Europe and that resulted in the accumulation of records valuable for information regarding individuals.

This book is based primarily on data in a wide variety and quantity of published books and articles. In addition, many repositories have supplied information in letters, lists, and copies of catalog cards. Acknowledgment is due them and numerous individuals whose communications are cited in footnotes.

For a helpful reading of the manuscript and assistance in proofreading and indexing, I am indebted to my wife, Dr. Dorothy D. Beers, retired professor of history at American University.

I

The Records of Louisiana

1

🕭

The French Regime

The Spanish and French explored Louisiana, but it was the French who finally occupied it. Early in the sixteenth century Alonso Alvarez de Piñeda explored the coast of the Gulf of Mexico and found the mouth of the Mississippi River, and Pánfilo de Narváez led an expedition inland from the coast of Florida. In 1541–1542 Hernando de Soto, the governor of Cuba, and a large body of soldiers explored the lower part of Louisiana, crossed the Mississippi, and descended that river. After Louis Jolliet and Père Jacques Marquette reached the upper Mississippi River from Canada in 1673, Robert Cavelier, Sieur de la Salle, travelling from the same colony, descended the Mississippi to its mouth in 1682, taking possession there in the name of the French king. La Salle failed in an attempt to establish a post at the mouth of that river in 1685, but his lieutenant, Henri de Tonti, erected a trading post near the mouth of the Arkansas River in 1686. Known as the Arkansas Post, it was the first settlement in the lower Mississippi Valley. The permanent settlement of the Gulf Coast began in 1699 with the founding by Pierre Le Moyne, Sieur d'Iberville, of Fort Maurepas at Biloxi, near the present Ocean Springs, Mississippi. Here was located the seat of government of French Louisiana until its removal to the Mobile River, where Jean Baptiste Le Moyne, Sieur de Bienville, erected Fort Louis in 1702. The outpost of the French to the west, Natchitoches, was established between 1712 and 1714 by Captain Juchereau St. Denis. For protection against the Indians, Bienville constructed Fort Rosalie (Natchez) on the Mississippi River in 1716. New Orleans, which became the capital of Louisiana in 1723, was founded by Bienville in 1718, and Baton Rouge originated as a fort in 1719. By exploring and occupying Louisiana, the French forestalled attempts by the Spanish and English to occupy the interior of the continent.[1]

1 / Alexander De Conde, *This Affair of Louisiana* (New York, 1976), 4–13.

The bounds of Louisiana as claimed by the French covered much of the Mississippi Valley and amounted to one-third of the present area of the United States. To the eastward the French claimed the land as far as the English colonies on the Atlantic coast and the Spanish settlement at Pensacola; westward, as far as the Red River, beyond which were the Spaniards. To meet the demands of the Company of the West, the Illinois settlements were incorporated into Louisiana by royal ordinance on September 27, 1717. The Illinois country continued to be governed as a part of Louisiana during the remainder of French rule in the Mississippi Valley, but the authorities there received instructions on occasion from the governors of Canada.[2]

From the date of the establishment of the colony of Louisiana in 1699 until 1712, its government was military in character, administered by the commanding officer at Biloxi. That officer exercised military and administrative authority and performed judicial and legislative functions. The *commissaire ordonnateur* or commissioner of finance, the first of whom was appointed in 1704, was in charge of finance, justice, and the police. He acted as the auditor, treasurer, storekeeper, and general manager of the colony.[3]

From 1712 to 1731, Louisiana was a charter colony. The grant to Antoine Crozat in 1712 placed in his hands direction of the affairs of the government of Louisiana. The civil government of Louisiana dates from this year, when the Crozat grant established the *coutume de Paris*, the chief codification of French law, as the fundamental law of the colony. To administer this code, there was formed on December 23, 1712, the Superior Council, consisting of the governor, the commissioner, the commander of the royal troops, two elected members, the attorney general, and a clerk. Besides having judicial power, the Superior Council possessed authority to make local or police regulations, to issue decrees, and to register notarial acts. By the edict of September 18, 1716, the Superior Council was constituted a permanent body. As it was the only court in Louisiana in the beginning, it decided cases of local occurrence upon evidence submitted by the commandants. The first attorney general arrived in 1719.[4]

In 1717 Crozat surrendered his charter and control of the colony of

2 / Clarence W. Alvord, *The Illinois Country, 1673–1818* (*The Centennial History of Illinois*, Vol. I) (Springfield, 1920), 151, 169, 191.

3 / Henry P. Dart, "The Legal Institutions of Louisiana," *Southern Law Quarterly*, III (November, 1918), 247–48.

4 / James D. Hardy, Jr., "The Superior Council in Colonial Louisiana," in John F. McDermott (ed.), *Frenchmen and French Ways in the Mississippi Valley* (Urbana, 1969), 87–88.

Louisiana, and its trade passed to the Company of the West (also known as the Mississippi Company), which was headed by John Law, a Scottish economist who had launched the Banque Generale in France. Complete government authority, including the right to name superior councilors, governors, commanders of troops, and judges, the right to grant land, and the right to erect churches and appoint clergy, was bestowed upon this company. The Company of the West soon became part of the Company of the Indies, an amalgamation of other companies taken over by Law. Under the company's management Louisiana increased in population and developed agriculture and lumbering. The company failed, however, in its attempt to exploit its monopoly in Louisiana because of the competition of traders from the neighboring Spanish and English colonies, and in 1731 it surrendered its charter.[5]

From 1717 to 1731, affairs in Louisiana were managed by arrangements between the French government and the Company of the West and the Company of the Indies. The companies' affairs were regulated by decrees emanating from the Conseil de la Marine. The French government provided annual subsidies for the support of garrisons and fortifications and for presents to the Indians. Early in 1718 Jean Baptiste Le Moyne, Sieur de Bienville, was appointed commandant general. He and the commissioner were designated as an administrative council to take care of the political, military, and commercial affairs of the colony. This council also had the function of deciding all disputes, lawsuits, and differences among the inhabitants of the colony.[6]

In administering the colony and serving as a court of justice, the Superior Council, which continued to function after 1718, was guided by the *coutume de Paris*—the codified customary law—and the king's statutes. In interpreting the law the council was advised by the attorney general, who also assisted the citizens in preparing their cases. The Superior Council considered both civil and criminal cases, and in its legislative capacity it adopted regulations on local affairs. French law required that property transfers, procurations, marriages, and wills be notarized and filed with the notary. The clerk of the council served as its notary, sat with it, and recorded and processed its decrees. A sheriff enforced the council's orders and judgments and conducted auction sales. In 1722 a councilor for religious affairs was added to the Superior Council. By 1725 the distinction between the administrative council and the Superior Council had disappeared.

5 / De Conde, *Louisiana*, 13–14; *Dictionary of National Biography*, II, 672–73.

6 / Jerry A. Micelle, "From Law Court to Local Government: Metamorphosis of the Superior Council of French Louisiana," *Louisiana History*, IX (Spring, 1968), 99.

The trading activities of the Company of the West were conducted at Nantes and those of the Company of the Indies at Lorient, and there such records as had been accumulated relating to Louisiana remained after the severance of the company's connection with Louisiana in 1731. About 1748 most of the records of accountability, the ship logs, and the commercial correspondence were removed to Paris. Upon the dissolution of the Company of the Indies in 1770, its establishment at Lorient and its records were delivered to the agent of the Ministère de la Marine. During the revolutionary period in 1793, a fire destroyed part of the naval arsenal and a considerable quantity of the registers, papers, and parchments stored there. The remaining records were placed in a storehouse there. At different times during the next sixty years, the Ministère de la Marine reclaimed portions of the records of the company, and quantities of other records regarded as useless were thrown out to reduce the congestion. When placed under the care of the *commissariat général* of the archives of the arsenal in 1853, the remaining records of the company were deposited in the attics of various government offices, where they could be neither properly guarded nor searched. Most of these records were placed in better quarters in 1866, but an inventory of the records published in 1913 showed them to be insufficient for a general history of the Company of the Indies because of the many gaps.[7]

Accountability, armaments, and commercial relations were found to be the most important subjects covered by the records; material on the policy of the company and on its administration and exploitation of the colonies was almost completely lacking. Pierre Heinrich, who evidently examined the records shortly before the inventory, thought they were of some value for the administrative history of the company after 1750 but of very little value for the history of the activities of the company in Louisiana. While investigating the archives in Paris for the Carnegie Institution of Washington in 1911, Waldo G. Leland located in the Archives Nationales 108 cartons of documents relating to the Company of the Indies and its Louisiana affairs. After examining at the Ministère de la Marine a catalog of the records of the Company of the Indies at Lorient, Leland journeyed to Lorient late in the summer of 1922 to look at those records. With the aid of a manuscript inventory, he located papers relating to Louisiana, including ship papers, muster rolls, lists of passengers, a list of voyages made by vessels of the company, registers of contracts with per-

---

7 / Albert Legrand, "Inventaire des archives de la Compagnie des Indes," France, Comité des travaux historiques et scientifiques, *Bulletin de la section de géographie*, XXVIII (1913), 160–251.

sons engaging for service in the colony, accounts of advances made to sailors, final accounts of individual sailors and officers, death certificates, certificates of identity, receipts for material, and orders for transportation.[8]

Although Louisiana was managed by charter companies during the years 1712–1731, the principal records for that period are those of the French government in Paris. As for other periods of the history of French Louisiana, the most valuable records are those in the Archives des Colonies and the Archives de la Marine. The *correspondance générale* (series C13A) of the Archives des Colonies contains letters from the directors of the Company of the Indies, from the councilors charged with conducting the affairs of the colony, and from the controller general of finances. Two miscellaneous volumes of this series contain documents concerning the posts of Louisiana. In the archives of the Ministère de la Marine, the minutes of the Conseil de la Marine, the correspondence between the Ministère de la Marine and the intendants and commissioners of the ports of Lorient, Port-Louis, Nantes, Rochefort, Le Havre, St. Malo, and Brest, and various personnel records are useful for Louisiana. In the archives of the Ministère des Affaires Étrangères are memoirs by Antoine Crozat, Hubert, Charles Le Gac, and Bienville.[9]

In January, 1731, the Company of the Indies, having failed to develop the colony, surrendered its charter to the Crown. Étienne de Périer continued as commandant until the arrival of Bienville in 1733, and Edme Gatien de Salmon was appointed *commissaire ordonnateur* in May, 1731, to succeed Jacques de la Chaise. Although it was intended to have a subordinate role, the Superior Council continued as the actual governing body of the colony. From this time until the transfer of sovereignty to Spain in 1769, Louisiana remained a royal colony.[10] French officials during the intervening years included the governor, the *commissaire général de la marine* (who was also the intendant and the first judge of the Superior Council), the acting *commissaire de la marine* (who was also the acting intendant and the second judge of the Superior Council), the councilor assessor, the keeper of the king's warehouse in New Orleans, the *procureur général*, the councilor assessor and acting *procureur général*, the town major of New

8 / W. G. Leland Report, March–April, 1911, September 6–30, 1922, Carnegie Institution of Washington, Department of Historical Research, Correspondence. Since I used this file, it has been consolidated with the papers of John Franklin Jameson and transferred to the Manuscript Division of the Library of Congress.

9 / Waldo G. Leland, John J. Meng, and Abel Doysié, *Guide to Materials for American History in the Libraries and Archives of Paris, Volume II, Archives of the Ministry of Foreign Affairs* (Washington, D.C., 1943), *passim*.

10 / Micelle, "Law Court," 104, 107.

Orleans, the royal notary, the sheriff and crier of the Superior Council, the attorney for vacant estates, the secretary of the governor, and the clerks or secretaries of the Superior Council.[11]

The most extensive government operation in Louisiana was the military establishment. At its head was the governor, who was responsible to the Ministère de la Marine in Paris, who directed the administration of the colonies for the king. The colony was garrisoned by *troupes de la marine* and Swiss mercenaries, who were assigned to military posts at New Orleans, Mobile, Fort de Chartres, and elsewhere. The posts were palisaded stockades for protection against the Indians, for the conduct of relations with them, and for trade. Besides subordinate officers in charge of the troops, the military force included engineers, surgeons, and storekeepers.[12] The engineers prepared plans for forts, inspected their construction, and conducted surveys preparatory to military campaigns.[13] Pierre le Blond de la Tour designed a plan for the city of New Orleans that was laid out by his assistant, Adrien de Pauger, in 1721. A reproduction of this plan and a later plan of 1725 have been published.[14] These posts became permanent settlements, for they were located at strategic points to control the Indians, to establish a chain of communication with Canada, and to prevent foreign intrusion.

For the same reasons a number of other forts were established among the Indian nations. Fort Toulouse was constructed by Bienville on the Alabama River in 1714 in the area occupied by the upper Creeks. Fort Pierre was founded near the mouth of the Yazoo River in 1715. A campaign against the Chickasaws in 1736 saw Fort Tombecbé built on the Tombigbee River and Fort Assumption constructed at the Chickasaw Bluffs on the Mississippi River, where La Salle had erected Fort Prudhomme in 1682 and where later the city of Memphis would develop. Not long after the founding of New Orleans, a pilot station and military work came into existence near the mouth of the Mississippi River. Closer to the capital, another settlement was made at English Bend, where Fort Ste. Marie was maintained. Above the capital, some of John Law's immigrants found a home on what became known as the German Coast. Years later, exiles

11 / *Louisiana Historical Quarterly*, XXVI (January, 1943), 169–70, where the names of the incumbents are given.

12 / David Hardcastle, "The Military Organization of French Colonial Louisiana," in William S. Coker (ed.), *The Military Presence on the Gulf Coast; Proceedings of the Gulf Coast History and Humanities Conference, 7th, Pensacola, 1977* (Pensacola, 1978), 1–20.

13 / George C. H. Kernion, "Reminiscences of the Chevalier Bernard de Verges, an Early Colonial Engineer of Louisiana," *Louisiana Historical Quarterly*, VII (January, 1924), 56–86.

14 / Samuel Wilson, Jr., *The Capuchin School in New Orleans, 1725: The First School in Louisiana* (New Orleans, 1961), 12, 15.

from Canada settled on another stretch of the Mississippi River that became known as the Acadian Coast. During the 1750s there were garrisons at Pointe Coupee on the western bank of the Mississippi and Fort d'Ascension on the Cherokee River. Whether for military or other reasons, all of these places had origins with official connections, and their beginnings can be traced in the French archives.[15]

The first step toward the organization of local government was taken on September 5, 1721. For administrative and military purposes the colony was divided into nine districts, in each of which the governor designated commandants: New Orleans, Biloxi, Mobile, Alibamons, Natchez, Yazoos, Natchitoches, Arkansas, and Illinois. The districts were grouped into four general commands: New Orleans, consisting of the districts of New Orleans, Natchez, Yazoos, and Natchitoches, under the commandant general; Biloxi, under the lieutenant general; Arkansas and Illinois, under a lieutenant of the king; and Mobile and Alibamons, also under a lieutenant of the king. The duties of the officers in charge of the commanderies were to make yearly inspections of plantations, supervise cultivation, conduct censuses, and organize the militia.[16]

At the time the United States took possession of Louisiana in December, 1803, all the archives of the colony for both the French and Spanish periods then in New Orleans were in the possession of Pedro Pedesclaux. He was custodian of the records as a result of having purchased in 1787 for $25,000 the offices of clerk and notary of the government, recorder of mortgages, and clerk of the Cabildo.[17] Soon after taking possession of the offices on March 14, 1788, he saved the public archives from destruction while suffering the loss of his own property during the great fire of March 21. Other notarial records were in the custody of Carlos Ximenes, secretary to the intendant. Pierre Clément de Laussat, the French commissioner for the transfer of Louisiana, issued a decree on November 30, 1803, as a result of which seals were placed on the offices containing the notarial and judicial records in the charge of Pedesclaux and Ximenes.[18] Commissioners appointed by the municipal council undertook but did

15 / Pierre Heinrich, *La Louisiane sous la Compagnie des Indes, 1717–1731* (Paris, 1908), *passim*; H. Mortimer Favrot, "Colonial Forts of Louisiana," *Louisiana Historical Quarterly*, XXVI (July, 1943), 722–54.

16 / Heinrich, *Louisiane*, 82; Charles E. A. Gayarré, *History of Louisiana* (1854–66; rpr. New York, 1972), I, 273.

17 / Petition of Peter Pedesclaux to the president, April, 1804, in Clarence E. Carter (ed.), *The Territory of Orleans, 1803–1812* (Washington, D.C., 1940), 236–38. Vol. IX of *The Territorial Papers of the United States*. 26 vols.

18 / Message to the Legislature, May 26, 1806, in Dunbar Rowland (ed.), *Official Letter Books of W. C. C. Claiborne, 1801–1816* (Jackson, Miss., 1917), III, 311–12.

not complete an inventory of the records. They placed the judicial records in separate packets and sealed them.

When William C. C. Claiborne, the American commissioner for the transfer, arrived in New Orleans, he found Pedesclaux's office closed and Pedesclaux himself vested with no appointment under Laussat.[19] As a result of the representations of the Spanish officials and several citizens who recommended Pedesclaux as a worthy and capable man, Claiborne appointed him to the offices of recorder of mortgages and notary on January 2, 1804. In a petition addressed to Governor Claiborne in April, 1804, Pedesclaux pointed out that the cession of the country had ended his hopes of reimbursing himself for the purchase price of the offices he had held, as the only ones left to him, since the establishment of American government, were those of recorder of mortgages and notary. He asked that either his former offices be restored to him, if consonant with the principles of American government, or he be reimbursed the sum paid for the same and that the right to hold public auctions for the sale of real or personal property be returned to him. His petition was forwarded to the president, who decided not to interfere in the matter.

It took several years to straighten out this situation. An act of the Legislative Council of the Territory of Orleans passed on March 5, 1805, authorized the governor to appoint a person to take charge of all the public papers, documents, records, and notarial acts in the possession of Carlos Ximenes and also to appoint a person to take charge of all the records in the office of Pedro Pedesclaux, which had been sealed up by order of Laussat.[20] Claiborne commissioned Estevan de Quiñones as keeper of records on March 12, 1805, and authorized him to receive possession of the records in the office of Carlos Ximenes, a transfer that appears to have been effected.[21] Claiborne addressed a message to the legislature on May 26, 1806, in which he pointed out that it had been difficult to ascertain from the wording of the act of the late legislative council whether it included all the documents in the possession of Pedesclaux, except his notarial acts, at the time his office was sealed according to the decree of Laussat, or whether the act extended only to the packets of judicial records on which seals had been placed.[22] He added that the records in Pedesclaux's possession were important, as they embraced title papers

19 / Claiborne to the president, April 27, 1804, in Louisiana Territory Papers, General Records of the Department of State, Record Group 59, National Archives.

20 / Orleans Territory, Acts, 1804–1805 (New Orleans, 1805), 80–83.

21 / Claiborne to Richard Relf and [blank], March 12, 1805, in Carter (ed.), Territory of Orleans, 416.

22 / Rowland (ed.), Official Letter Books, III, 311–12.

for much valuable property. The legislature passed an act on June 3, 1806, that authorized Pedesclaux to remove, in the presence of two members of the city council, the seals on the papers referred to in the act of March 5, 1805 (that is, the judicial papers).[23] Pedesclaux was to hold the records in his office for the use of any persons interested therein. This act actually repealed that part of the act of March 5, 1805, referring to Pedesclaux. He remained custodian, therefore, of both the judicial and notarial records that he had kept as a Spanish official. For some years he continued to serve as a notary public and to provide attested copies of the colonial documents in his custody.[24]

In succeeding years other members of the Pedesclaux family had custody of these records. Upon being informed that a great number of ancient titles of land from 1702 to 1771 and sundry other papers and documents affecting the rights of property were in the custody of Philip Pedesclaux, notary for New Orleans, the Louisiana legislature passed an act on April 7, 1826, providing for the indexing of the records and for their arrangement and storage in chronological and alphabetical order in cedar boxes.[25] This work was to be completed within a year by Felix Percy, and the index was to be delivered to Pedesclaux.

From the hands of another Pedesclaux these records passed in 1860 to the Louisiana Historical Society. Originally established in 1836, this society was revived by Charles Gayarré and others in 1860 and incorporated by the legislature. It was domiciled in Baton Rouge, where a room in the new state capitol was assigned for its use. On March 12, 1860, the Louisiana legislature resolved "that all the old Notarial and Colonial Records, touching the early history of Louisiana, now in the hands of H. Pedesclaux and Octave de Armas, notaries public of the city of New Orleans, be delivered to the State Librarian, whose duty it shall be to deposit the same in the room in the Capitol set apart for the Historical Society of the State."[26]

The next stage in the history of these records is not clear. They are said to have been carried off by Union soldiers during the Civil War and later returned to Baton Rouge through the assistance of Lyman Draper, secretary of the Wisconsin State Historical Society.[27] The Louisiana Historical Society, which had expired during the Civil War, was revived by

23 / Orleans Territory, *Acts*, 1806, p. 72.

24 / Louisiana Historical Quarterly, XX (1920), 910–11.

25 / Louisiana, Laws, Statutes, etc., *Acts of the Legislature*, 1826, pp. 176, 178.

26 / Louisiana, *Acts*, 1860, p. 95.

27 / Grace King, "The Preservation of Louisiana History," *North Carolina Historical Review*, V (October, 1928), 366.

William Preston Johnston, president of Tulane University in New Orleans from its renaming in 1884, and others. The Society held its meetings at Tulane, and here Professor Alcée Fortier reported in 1893 upon the judicial records that were then at the University.[28]

The establishment of the Louisiana State Museum resulted from efforts of the Louisiana Historical Society beginning in 1898. Its early promotion was connected with the celebration of the centennial of the Louisiana Purchase. The state legislature passed an act on July 10, 1900, to create a state museum for the purpose of preserving documents and relics relating to Louisiana that were being dispersed and lost.[29] As no appropriation was made, however, this act was ineffective. Following the Louisiana Purchase Exposition of 1903, however, the Board of Curators of the State Museum took up the matter of the preservation of the exhibits provided by the state of Louisiana with the Louisiana Purchase Exposition Commission. Louisiana State University was also interested in obtaining the exhibits. The commission, however, decided to rent a building in New Orleans, and on May 3, 1905, the exhibits were opened to the public on the Carondelet side of the lower floor of the Washington Artillery Hall. Through the continued efforts of the Louisiana Historical Society, the legislature passed an act on July 11, 1906, giving the Louisiana State Museum the function of caring for historical material relating to Louisiana, including historical documents belonging to the state.[30]

Both the Louisiana State Museum and the Louisiana Historical Society were provided with permanent homes in the Cabildo and the neighboring Presbytère by an ordinance of the New Orleans city council on June 30, 1908.[31] The Presbytère was a brick structure that had been purchased by the city of New Orleans from St. Louis Cathedral in 1853. Since the transfer of New Orleans to American possession, these buildings had been in continuous use as city and state offices. Owing to the delay in the completion of the new courthouse building, the Louisiana Historical Society was unable to occupy the Cabildo and the State Museum the Presbytère until 1910, and the removal of the exhibits was not completed until January 1, 1911. Several months were required for remodelling and repair-

28 / Alcée Fortier, "Report of Prof. Fortier," *Louisiana Historical Society Publications,* I (1895), 4.

29 / Louisiana State Musuem, *First Biennial Report, 1906–1908* (New Orleans, 1908), 7–8, 17.

30 / Louisiana, *Acts,* 1906, pp. 311–12.

31 / Henry P. Dart, "The Archives of Louisiana," *Louisiana Historical Quarterly,* II (October, 1919), 360.

ing the Cabildo, which was restored to its original lines. The Department of History of the state museum was finally opened on April 17, 1911. Its chief collection was the judicial records of colonial Louisiana. These and other valuable documents were kept in steel vaults on the ground floor of the Cabildo.

Since the transfer of the judicial records to the Louisiana State Museum, much has been done to facilitate their use for research purposes. During 1914–1915 William Price, an expert translator who had assisted Reuben G. Thwaites on *Jesuit Relations,* was employed jointly by the museum and the Louisiana Historical Society to arrange and index the records.[32] Publication of a calendar entitled "Records of the Superior Council of Louisiana" was begun in the *Louisiana Historical Quarterly* in January, 1917. Installments of the calendar are preceded by lists of the names of officials in office at the time. In 1920, Henry P. Dart, a well-known New Orleans lawyer who had become interested in the records through his studies of the legal history of Louisiana, secured the financial support of William Ratcliffe Irby for the continuation of the indexing and translation of the judicial records.[33] An Archives Department was established under the charge of Dart. Heloise H. Cruzat and Laura L. Porteous were employed to translate the French and Spanish records, respectively, and Mrs. Cruzat undertook the preparation of the calendar of the French records. On July 1, 1926, the Louisiana State Museum took over this work, which has been continued to the present time. Because of omissions and errors in the Cruzat calendar, the state museum about 1974 undertook a recalendaring that by 1982 had reached the year 1727. An index of the chronological list of the translations has been published.[34]

The Superior Council records, 1714–1769, encompassing 11,748 items, document the official and personal transactions of the French period.[35] The judicial papers concern civil and criminal cases, including murder cases, maritime cases, land suits, settlements of estates and orders and

32 / William Price, "Work of Indexing Louisiana Black Boxes," *Louisiana Historical Society Publications,* VIII (1914–15), 7.

33 / Henry P. Dart, "The Index to the French and Spanish Archives of Louisiana," *Louisiana Historical Quarterly,* X (July, 1927), 407–408.

34 / Mrs. Fred O. James, "Index to French and Spanish Translations of Original Documents from Louisiana State Museum Library, New Orleans," *New Orleans Genesis,* I–IV (1962–65); Mrs. Edwin X. de Verges, "The French and Spanish Colonial Archives of Louisiana," *New Orleans Genesis,* IV (January, 1965), 6–8.

35 / Alice D. Forsyth and Ghislaine Pleasonton, *Louisiana Marriage Contracts: A Compilation of Abstracts from the Records of the Superior Council of Louisiana during the French Regime, 1725–1758* (New Orleans, 1980).

decisions relating thereto, and documents relating to land transactions. The extensive variety of documents includes appointments, auction sales of ships' property, bills of exchange, business papers, commissions of officials, certificates of notaries, contracts, correspondence of officials, deliberations of family meetings, inquiries, inventories of estates and plantations and of various kinds of property, investigations, leases of property, manumissions of slaves, marriage contracts, militia meeting notices, mortgages, orders of the king and the Superior Council, partnership agreements and contracts, petitions for various actions, powers of attorney, procurations, promises to pay, promissory notes, ratifications of the exchange of lots, receipts, reports of appraisers on the value of property, reports of the proceedings of the Superior Council, reports on various subjects, sales of property documents, renunciations, slave emancipations, statements, successions, summonses connected with various actions, surgeons' reports, testimonials on character, testimony, and wills. The judicial proceedings contain extensive social, economic, and biographical data on the people of Louisiana.

Many documents from the Superior Council records, edited by Dart and translated by Cruzat, have been published in the *Louisiana Historical Quarterly*, as the index to that periodical shows. A sampling of documents from the records of the Superior Council and the Cabildo, with translations, has also been published.[36]

The Superior Council records and other colonial records of Louisiana are now in the Old United States Mint, 400 Esplanade Avenue, a building given to the state of Louisiana by the federal government in 1966. After the preparation of quarters in the Mint building, the records that had been in the Presbytère, one of the buildings of the Louisiana State Museum, were moved to the Mint in January, 1982. There they are kept in a fire-proof vault on the third floor, where there are also administrative offices, a reading room, and a stack area. The custodial part of the Louisiana State Museum has been known since 1977 as the Louisiana Historical Center.

The calendar of the Superior Council records published in the *Louisiana Historical Quarterly* is of great importance for research in Louisiana history and genealogy. It is not complete, however, because some documents had not been found at the time the calendar was done, and the original records are in such poor condition that they are unavailable for

36 / Boyd Cruise, *The Louisiana Historical Quarterly (Indexes), Index to the Louisiana Historical Quarterly*, [vols. 1–33, 1917–50] (New Orleans, 1956); Henry P. Dart (ed.) and Heloise H. Cruzat (trans.), "The Cabildo Archives—French Period," *Louisiana Historical Quarterly*, III–IV (January–October, 1920; April–July, 1921).

research.[37] A microfilm of the records that was prepared in the 1950s is in the Howard-Tilton Memorial Library of Tulane University, and the negative microfilm is in the Louisiana State Museum Library.[38] An agreement made later between the state museum and the state archives provided for the restoration and microfilming of the Superior Council records.[39] A grant of $43,000 was obtained in 1977 from the National Endowment for the Humanities and the Rockefeller Foundation for microfilming the records of both the Superior Council and the Spanish Cabildo.[40] The translation of the Superior Council records has been started.

Another index to the Superior Council records is the index to the Black Books in the Louisiana State Museum Library. This index is contained in ninety-four black looseleaf notebooks that are referred to as the "Black Books."[41] The entries in these books appear alphabetically by name and give the document number, the date, the document title, and a brief description. Although somewhat more complete than the Cruzat calendar, the entries contain misdatings, misfilings, and poor translations. This index has been published in *New Orleans Genesis*.[42] An alphabetical card index to biographical data in the Superior Council and other colonial records is also in the Louisiana State Museum Library. These cards contain digests of genealogical data and index numbers.

By the Treaty of Paris of February, 1763, concluding the Seven Years' War, France surrendered her empire in North America, giving up New France and the region east of the Mississippi River to Great Britain while ceding New Orleans and the region west of the Mississippi to Spain. Louisiana was recompense to Spain for the loss of Florida, which passed into the hands of the British as payment for the restoration of Havana.[43]

On April 21, 1764, the French government instructed Jean Jacques Blaise d'Abbadie, who had been appointed director general and commandant of the colony in 1763, to collect all the papers and documents relative to the finances and the administration of the colony and to trans-

37 / Winston De Ville, "Manuscript Sources in Louisiana for the History of the French in the Mississippi Valley," in John F. McDermott (ed.), *The French in the Mississippi Valley* (Urbana, Ill., 1965), 220.

38 / Connie G. Griffith, "Collections in the Manuscript Section of Howard-Tilton Memorial Library, Tulane University," *Louisiana History*, I (Fall, 1960), 326.

39 / A. Otis Hébert, Jr., "Keeping Louisiana's Records," *McNeese Review*, XVIII (1967), 30.

40 / Society of American Archivists, *News Letter*, November, 1977, p. 13.

41 / De Ville, "Manuscript Sources," 220–21.

42 / Mrs. Fred O. James, Mrs. Larry J. Dupuy, and Irene Owen, "Index to Black Boxes," *New Orleans Genesis*, IV–XVI (September, 1965–January, 1977).

43 / De Conde, *Louisiana*, 29.

port them to France in order to settle accounts.[44] Papers especially concerning the government of the colony either as to the territory and its limits or to the Indians and the different posts were, however, to be delivered to the Spanish. After d'Abbadie's death in February, 1765, Charles Philippe Aubry assumed control of military affairs and Nicolas Denis Foucoult became commissioner. In March, 1766, Antonio de Ulloa arrived in Louisiana to take control of the colony for Spain but did not do so because he lacked sufficient military backing.[45] In 1767 he did take control at Balize and some other posts. Finally on August 18, 1769, General Alexandro O'Reilly arrived with soldiers and occupied New Orleans.

The French representatives who remained in Louisiana after the colony passed into the hands of the Spanish concerned themselves with the French archives. The settlement of the French accounts was undertaken by Bobé Descloseaux, who had recently become commissioner of finance in Foucoult's place. When Aubry sailed for France with other officials and soldiers in November, 1769, on the *Père de Famille*, he took with him certain papers relating to the accounts. On February 17, 1770, as it attempted to enter the mouth of the Garonne to reach Bordeaux, the vessel was wrecked, and the papers and most of the passengers, including Aubry, were lost.[46] Other accounts were shipped in May, 1770, on the *La Chetis* to La Rochelle.[47] Chauvet du Breuil, *clerc de la marine* in Louisiana, reached Bordeaux about September, 1772, with seven cases containing storekeepers' accounts for the years 1757 to 1767.[48] Descloseaux finally embarked with nearly all the remaining accounts of the colony in August, 1772, on the *Marie Thérèse*. On the voyage to Port-au-Prince, the ship, the passengers, and the documents were lost.[49] Four years previously, however, minutes pertaining to the accounts had reached France. Only a portion, therefore, of the papers relating to the accounts reached France, and the records remaining in Louisiana were principally those relating to property and legal matters concerning the colonists.[50]

44 / Alcée Fortier, *A History of Louisiana* (New York, 1904), I, 143.

45 / De Conde, *Louisiana*, 30–31.

46 / Gustavus Devron, "Two Original and Newly-Found Documents of the Departure, Shipwreck and Death of Mr. Aubry, the Last French Governor in Louisiana," *Louisiana Historical Society Publications*, II (1897), 29.

47 / Descloseaux in the minister of the colonies, June 16, 1770, France, Archives des Colonies, C13A50:32, Archives Nationales, Paris (Transcript in the Library of Congress).

48 / Nancy Maria (Miller) Surrey (ed.), *Calendar of Manuscripts in Paris Archives and Libraries Relating to the History of the Mississippi Valley to 1803* (Washington, D.C., 1926–28), II, entries 1553, 1557.

49 / Baron Marc de Villiers du Terrage, *Les Dernières années de la Louisiane française: Le Chevalier de Kerlérec, D'Abbadie, Aubry, Laussat* (Paris, [1904]), 353.

50 / Paul Roussier, "Les Origines du Dépôt des Papiers Publics des Colonies: Le Dépôt de Rochefort (1763–1790)," *Revue de l'histoire des colonies françaises*, XVIII (1925), 28.

For many years some archives of Louisiana were kept in a depot of colonial archives at Rochefort, France. Among these were probably such records of accounts as reached France. After the Seven Years' War, French soldiers and refugees from Canada and Louisiana were repatriated at La Rochelle and Rochefort, which served as ports of entry for the colonies.[51] In March, 1765, a Dépôt des Papiers Publics des Colonies was established at Rochefort under Gui-Louis Haran, a *clerc de la marine*, as keeper of the archives received from the colonies. The Louisiana archives at this place in 1776 filled two closets and comprised books, portfolios, and other papers. Many colonial records are believed to have been destroyed in a fire at Rochefort in 1786. Early in 1790, following the death of Haran, part of the colonial archives at Rochefort were shipped to Versailles, where all the archives relating to the colonies were to be concentrated under the Ministre de la Marine. Some Louisiana archives appear to have been among those transferred.[52] In 1837 the archives of the lost colonies were removed from Versailles to the Ministère de la Marine et des Colonies. The archives in the custody of that ministry were separated into the Archives de la Marine and the Archives des Colonies in 1884. In 1911 the Archives des Colonies were finally transferred to the Archives Nationales.

Such papers as the French governors of Louisiana had in their possession at the conclusion of their terms of office were evidently carried off by them and have since largely disappeared. The papers of the Sieur de Bienville are believed to have been destroyed.

A surviving collection is that of the Marquis de Vaudreuil (Pierre de Rigaud de Vaudreuil), who served as governor from 1743 to 1752. In June, 1755, the same month in which the marquis began officiating as governor general of New France, his brother, François Pierre Rigaud de Vaudreuil, who had with him the marquis' Louisiana papers, was captured by the British on the French ship *L'Alcide* and imprisoned at Halifax. There he was joined by fellow prisoner Thomas Pichon, who had served as the Marquis de Vaudreuil's secretary while Vaudreuil was governor of Louisiana. The governor's brother turned the papers over to Pichon in the hope that they would reach France. Pichon, however, was then a British spy and on reaching England delivered the papers to Lord Loudoun, who had been appointed British commander-in-chief in North America. In 1923 the Henry E. Huntington Library and Art Gallery at San Marino, California, bought the papers of Lord Loudoun and with them acquired the papers of the Marquis de Vaudreuil.[53] The Vaudreuil papers, 1742–1753,

51 / Joseph E. Roy, *Rapport sur les archives de France relatives à l'histoire du Canada* (Ottawa, 1911), 433–34.
52 / Surrey (ed.), *Calendar of Manuscripts*, entry 1660.
53 / Stanley M. Pargellis and Norman B. Cuthbert, "Loudoun Papers: (a) Colonial,

containing 383 items, consist of correspondence between the governor and officials of the French government, correspondence with members of his family and friends in Canada, and correspondence with commandants and priests at forts and trading posts in the Mississippi Valley. A published calendar of the three letterbooks, June, 1743–March, 1753, provides a useful tool for using the collection.[54] Additional papers of Vaudreuil are said to have been burned during the Franco-Prussian War of 1870–1871 to prevent their falling into the hands of the Germans.

A collection of the papers of Louis Billouart, Sieur de Kerlérec, who served as governor from 1753 to 1763, was located by Marc de Villiers du Terrage in the archives of the Département de Finistère.[55] He also used family papers but did not give their location. The correspondence of Kerlérec, from August 23, 1758, to October 17, 1759, containing twenty-eight items, has been reported to be in the library of the port of Toulon, and it includes letters from the officer of the garrison of Mobile.[56] Some Kerlérec documents of 1761 are in the possession of the Louisiana Historical Society. Documents originating with French governors, including commissions, letters, orders, and proclamations, are in the Louisiana State Museum. That repository also has official French laws, orders, and regulations, from 1690 to 1729, in two volumes.

The Superior Council records are the most valuable records for the French period. These documents reveal the operations of the charter companies and the royal government and of their military and civilian representatives throughout the Mississippi Valley. Business, industrial, maritime, agricultural, commercial, naval, slave-trading, and privateering activities are revealed in these records. Biographical and family data, as well as data on immigration and the spread of settlements, are available in the records. Relations between the colonists and officials and between missionaries and the Catholic Church are disclosed. Papers on the collection of debts, successions, and inventories of estates contain much social, economic, biographical, and architectural data. Unfortunately, neither the authors of general histories of Louisiana nor the historians of

---

1756–58, (b) French Colonial, 1742–53," *Huntington Library Bulletin*, no. 3 (February, 1933), 104–107.

54 / Bill Barron (ed.), *The Vaudreuil Papers: A Calendar and Index of the Personal and Private Records of Pierre de Rigaud de Vaudreuil, Royal Governor of the French Province of Louisiana, 1743–1753* (New Orleans, 1975).

55 / David M. Matteson, *List of Manuscripts Concerning American History Preserved in European Libraries and Noted in Their Published Catalogues and Similar Printed Lists* (Washington, D.C., 1925), 150.

56 / Villiers du Terrage, *Louisiane française*, vi, 358.

parishes and localities have made adequate use of the Superior Council records. These records are also the primary source of data on special subjects that have yet to be investigated.

By the Treaty of Paris of 1783 concluding the Revolutionary War, Great Britain ceded to the United States eastern Louisiana between the Mississippi River and the Appalachians, south of the Great Lakes, setting the southern boundary at the 31st parallel.[57] The Anglo-Spanish treaty did not define the boundary but stated that the Spanish were to retain West Florida, so the Spanish claimed the land north to a line running east from the junction of the Yazoo River with the Mississippi, or 32°26', to which the British had extended West Florida in 1764. This disputed area, or Yazoo strip, was inhabited by powerful Indian tribes over whom the Spanish sought, by means of treaties and the promotion of trade, to extend their influence in order to use them as a barrier against the Americans.

Spanish policy in Louisiana and the Floridas during this period was aimed at containing the aggressive American frontiersmen, whose settlements had already crossed the Appalachians but had not yet reached the Mississippi or the region that is now Alabama and Mississippi.[58] To the Spanish, the Floridas were the bulwark of the far richer province of New Spain. By intrigue with the leaders of the trans-Appalachian American settlements and by encouraging the immigration of Americans to Louisiana, the Spanish endeavored to weaken the Americans and to strengthen themselves.

Spanish influence in what became the American South was further implemented by the establishment of military posts in the Indian country. In 1790 the old French Fort Tombecbé was reconstructed on the Tombigbee River and named San Estevan de Tombecbé (Fort Tombigbee, St. Stephens).[59] The Spanish moved westward in the next year and on the east bank of the Mississippi at the mouth of the Yazoo located Fort Nogales (Walnut Hills, Vicksburg). Following a treaty at Fort Nogales with the Choctaw and Chickasaw tribes, in 1793, Fort Confederation was erected on the Tombigbee River above its junction with the Black Warrior, and Fort San Fernando de las Barrancas (Chickasaw Bluffs, Memphis) was built on the Mississippi.[60] The last two named forts were north of 32°26', within American territory.

57 / De Conde, *Louisiana*, 38–39.

58 / Arthur P. Whitaker, *The Spanish-American Frontier, 1783–1795: The Westward Movement and the Spanish Retreat in the Mississippi Valley* (Boston, 1927), 17, 34ff.

59 / Peter J. Hamilton, *Colonial Mobile: An Historical Study Largely from Original Sources, of the Alabama-Tombigbee Basin and the Old South West* . . . (Boston, 1897), 316.

60 / Whitaker, *Spanish-American Frontier*, 24, 54, 58, 169, 178, 214–16.

It was not until the threat of a war with England that the Spanish were induced to conclude the Treaty of San Lorenzo on October 27, 1795, by which the southern boundary of the United States was set at the 31st parallel. The agreement also allowed free navigation of the Mississippi River and the right of deposit at New Orleans. Owing to changed circumstances in Europe, the posts north of the agreed-upon line were not evacuated until 1798; then, too, the running of the boundary was undertaken. Negotiations that had been under way in Madrid culminated in the secret treaty of October 1, 1800, by which Spain retroceded Louisiana to France. Before Napoleon's plans to occupy Louisiana were effectuated, however, a treaty was signed at Paris on April 30, 1803, by which the United States purchased the territory for eighty million francs.[61] According to its second article, "The Archives, papers & documents relative to the domain and Sovereignty of Louisiana and its dependances will be left in the possession of the Commissaries of the United States, and copies will be afterwards given in due form to the Magistrates and Municipal officers of Such of the said papers and documents as may be necessary to them."[62] The French commissioner, Pierre Clément de Laussat, took over New Orleans on November 30, 1803.[63] After an interval of twenty days, during which Laussat acted as governor, the sovereignty of Louisiana was transferred on December 20 at New Orleans to the United States commissioners, William C. C. Claiborne and General James Wilkinson. In the following month they occupied the Government House (Cabildo). President Thomas Jefferson had informed Claiborne on July 18, 1803, that "the government and public property, archives &c of Louisiana are to be delivered up to us immediately after the exchange of ratifications."[64]

Pierre Clément de Laussat, the French commissioner for the reception of Louisiana from the Spanish, had arrived in New Orleans on March 26, 1803, and left that place on April 21, 1804. During that period he corresponded with Duc Denis Decrés, Ministre de la Marine, and with Spanish and American officials. Some Louisiana matters were terminated at Martinique, where he served as prefect after his departure from Louisiana.

Negotiations for the delivery of the archives were carried on by Laussat, who had instructions from the king of Spain, dated October 15,

61 / De Conde, *Louisiana*, 171ff.

62 / David Hunter Miller (ed.), *Treaties and Other International Acts of the United States of America* (Washington, D.C., 1931–48), II, 500.

63 / Arthur P. Whitaker, *The Mississippi Question, 1795–1803: A Study in Trade, Politics and Diplomacy* (New York, [1934]), 250.

64 / Carter (ed.), *Territory of Orleans*, 5.

1802, that directed the Spanish officials, after evacuating the posts of Louisiana and New Orleans, to "cause to be collected all the papers and documents relating to the royal treasury and to the administration of the colony of Louisiana in order to bring them to Spain for the purpose of settling the accounts; delivering nevertheless to the governor or other French officer commissioned to take possession, all those which may be related to the limits and boundary of said territory, as also those which relate to the savages, (Indians) and other places, taking receipts for the whole for your discharge."[65]

The American commissioners gave their attention to this matter and reported on December 27, 1803, that Laussat had assured them that the documents were being arranged for delivery. Although he had transferred authority to United States officials, Laussat had not yet received the archives from the Spanish commissioners who remained in New Orleans after the change of sovereignty. The American commissioners were requested on January 21, 1804, to designate two persons to arrange with Citizens Henri Daugerot and Jean Paul Blanque, appointed for the purpose by Laussat, for the delivery of the archives of the government and the papers relating to concessions. Major Decius Wadsworth and Daniel Clark were thereupon appointed commissioners to receive the archives. Some of the records were received shortly afterwards and were placed in the Government House, which had been turned over to the United States earlier that month. On February 7, the delivery of certain land records was reported. The remaining public archives were received in the following month, according to the commissioners' report, which, however, did not specifically describe the records. They were deposited in a room on the ground floor of the Cabildo, where they were kept secure by a guard of regular soldiers supplied by the garrison in the city. Their duties supposedly completed, Laussat sailed for Martinique and Wilkinson for New York in April, 1804.[66]

65 / Joseph M. White (ed.), *A New Collection of Laws, Charters, and Land Ordinances of the Governments of Great Britain, France and Spain . . . Together with the Laws of Mexico and Texas on the Same Subject* (Philadelphia, 1839), II, 191.

66 / Correspondence between American officials and between them and Laussat, January–February, 1804, on the delivery of the records is in James A. Robertson (ed.), *Louisiana under the Rule of Spain, France, and the United States, 1785–1807, as Portrayed in Hitherto Unpublished Contemporary Accounts* (Cleveland, 1911), 243, 290, and in Carter (ed.), *Territory of Orleans*, 111–12, 155–56. Unpublished correspondence between Laussat and Claiborne and Wilkinson is in the Orleans Territory Papers, General Records of the Department of State, RG59, NA. An inventory of the papers transferred, February 6, 1804, is listed in Roscoe R. Hill, *Descriptive Catalogue of the Documents Relating to the United States in the Papeles Procedentes de Cuba Deposited in the Archivo General de Indias at Seville* (Washington, D.C., 1916), xxxvii.

The government of the newly acquired territory remained in Claiborne's hands. On October 3, 1803, he had been commissioned to act as temporary governor until Congress made further provision. The Territory of Orleans was established on March 26, 1804, and Claiborne was commissioned as governor on December 12 of that year. James Brown became the first secretary of the territory on October 1 but left the position on December 11 to assume that of district attorney. He was succeeded on the following day by John Graham, who served until 1807. Among the duties of the secretary was the care and preservation of the records of the territory.

After taking control from the Spanish on November 30, 1803, at New Orleans, Laussat dissolved the Spanish Cabildo and appointed in its place a city council of ten members. Étienne de Boré was appointed mayor and Pierre Derbigny secretary.

Records concerning the government of New Orleans and Louisiana during the Laussat period, kept for many years in the city hall, were transferred in 1946 to the New Orleans Public Library. A journal of the proceedings of the city council, dating from November 30, 1803, is available in French and in an English translation. Documents and letters of Laussat and of the Spanish commissioners, November 30, 1803, to March 31, 1804, are contained in one volume and include public notices and proclamations. The volume has been translated into English. The letters of Laussat and the proclamations of Laussat and of Claiborne, November 30, 1803, to March 31, 1804, one volume, and a census of New Orleans, 1804, also in one volume, are in French. The French versions of the city council proceedings, the documents and letters of Laussat, and the printed broadsides issued by Laussat are available in the Microfilm Collection of Early State Records of the Library of Congress.[67]

After terminating his career as a colonial official, Laussat deposited his papers in the family home, the Chateau de Bernadets, located near the city of Pau in the Pyrenees region of southern France. He sprinkled the containers with cayenne pepper to preserve the papers from rot and vermin. In 1929 a descendant, Antoine du Pre de Saint-Maur, inherited the chateau and in a tower discovered the Laussat papers in dusty canvas boxes.[68] In that year Saint-Maur met André Lafargue of New Orleans,

67 / The titles are from copies of catalog cards supplied by Collin B. Hamer, Jr., head of the Louisiana Division of the New Orleans Public Library, with a letter of August 13, 1983, in Henry P. Beers Correspondence.

68 / Robert D. Bush, "Documents on the Louisiana Purchase: The Laussat Papers," Louisiana History, XVIII (Winter, 1977), 105.

then visiting France, and promised to send him copies of the Laussat documents. When Lafargue later received the copies, he published a list of them.[69] In 1972 the Laussat papers were rediscovered at the Chateau de Bernadets by Sister M. Bernardo Pastwa while she was doing research in France. Besides two volumes concerning Louisiana, there were four on his political career and a copy of his memoirs, which had been published in an edition of one hundred copies at Pau in 1831.[70] In 1975 the Laussat papers, 1756–1835, containing several hundred items, were acquired by the Historic New Orleans Collection through the efforts of Mr. and Mrs. Ernest C. Villeré on behalf of Kemper and Leila Williams, founders of the collection.[71]

Other documents relating to Laussat are in repositories in the United States and France. His correspondence with Claiborne and Wilkinson, the United States commissioners, concerning the transfer of Louisiana is in the Orleans Territory papers in the General Records of the Department of State (Record Group 59) in the National Archives. Correspondence and other documents from that source have been published.[72] Letters written by Laussat to the Ministre de la Marine and some of his decrees and proclamations are also in print.[73] Lists of printed issuances by Laussat before the transfer of Louisiana to the United States have been published, in part from copies of the decrees supplied by André Lafargue.[74] A collection of transcripts of Laussat documents, 1803–1804, sixty-eight items, from the Archives Nationales and the Bibliothèque Nationale in Paris is in the New Orleans Public Library, Louisiana Department.[75] A smaller collection of Laussat papers, 1803–1804, with nineteen items, is in the Howard-

69 / André Lafargue, "Pierre Clément de Laussat, Colonial Prefect and High Commissioner of France in Louisiana: His Memoirs, Proclamations and Orders," *Louisiana Historical Quarterly*, XX (January, 1937), 159–82.

70 / Pierre Clément de Laussat, *Memoirs of My Life to My Son During the Years 1803 and After, Which I Spent in Public Service in . . . the United States*, ed. Robert D. Bush, trans. Agnes-Josephine Pastwa (Baton Rouge, 1978), xix. An earlier translation had been prepared by Henri Delville de Sinclair, with English translations of Laussat letters from materials in the Howard-Tilton Library of Tulane University.

71 / Bush, "Laussat Papers," 104.

72 / Robertson (ed.), *Louisiana under the Rule of Spain*; Carter (ed.), *Territory of Orleans*.

73 / Robertson (ed.), *Louisiana under the Rule of Spain*, II, 27–60.

74 / Douglas C. McMurtrie, *Early Printing in New Orleans, 1764–1810, with a Bibliography of the Issues of the Louisiana Press* (New Orleans, 1929), 61–62; Douglas C. McMurtrie, *Louisiana Imprints, 1768–1810; in Supplement to the Bibliography in "Early Printing in New Orleans"* (Hattiesburg, Miss., 1942).

75 / U.S. Library of Congress, *The National Union Catalog of Manuscripts*, 1959/61 (Ann Arbor, Mich., 1962); 1962 (Hamden, Conn., 1964); 1963/64–84 (Washington, D.C., 1965–84).

Tilton Memorial Library of Tulane University.[76] Letters and other documents concerning Laussat's activities in Louisiana are in Marc de Villiers du Terrage's book.[77]

76 / Connie G. Griffith, "Summary of Inventory: Louisiana Historical Collection," *Louisiana History*, IX (Fall, 1968), 365.

77 / Villiers du Terrage, *Louisiane française*, 397–428.

2

$\partial \mathbf{a}$

The Spanish Regime

Louisiana was divided between Great Britain and Spain as a result of the French and Indian War. In a secret agreement made in November, 1762, France ceded the Isle of Orleans, which included New Orleans, and that part of French Louisiana west of the Mississippi River to Spain. In the Treaty of Paris of September 3, 1763, ending the Seven Years' War, that part of Louisiana east of the Mississippi was ceded to Great Britain. Antonio de Ulloa, who had been appointed governor and captain general of Louisiana, reached New Orleans with a small military force in March, 1766. He decided not to take formal possession immediately and arranged with Charles Philippe Aubry, the acting French governor, that he continue in charge with the Spanish assuming the expenses. Discontent among the French colonists over Spanish sovereignty exploded into a revolt in the fall of 1768. On August 18, 1769, General Alexandro O'Reilly with a large body of Spanish troops took formal possession of Louisiana.[1] He issued ordinances on the government of the colony, declared the French Black Code the law of the colony, and on December 1, 1769, installed Luis de Unzaga y Amezaga as governor.

The Spaniards utilized the opportunity afforded by the American Revolutionary War to recover the Floridas. The declaration of war against England by Spain on May 8, 1779, and the latter's recognition of American independence on the following August 19 was followed by the Spanish conquest of West Florida. This victory was accomplished by Bernardo de Gálvez, the brilliant, young, and energetic governor of Louisiana, who captured Fort Bute on the Iberville River (Bayou Manchac) and Baton

---

1 / William J. Eccles, *France in America* (New York, 1972), 216–245.

Rouge in September, 1779.[2] Because of the fall of Baton Rouge, Fort Panmure at Natchez was surrendered on October 5, 1779. Gálvez completed
the conquest of West Florida by taking Mobile on March 14, 1780, and
Pensacola on May 9, 1781. Through these victories Spanish control was
extended over the area that the British had consolidated in 1763 into the
province of West Florida and that previously had been part of French
Louisiana.

West Florida from the time of its conquest until the cession of Louisiana in 1803 was governed as a part of Louisiana. Immediately after the
capture of Baton Rouge, Natchez, and Mobile, Governor Gálvez appointed commandants for those places. In 1781 a lieutenant governor was
designated for Pensacola, to which Mobile and later Fort St. Stephens became subordinate. On occasion, however, the lieutenant governor corresponded directly with the captain general at Havana and received orders
in the same way. The influx of Americans into the region around Natchez
so increased its population that in 1789 the Natchez-Baton Rouge district
was formed into a separate lieutenant governorship. Not far away from
Baton Rouge, south of the Iberville River, the new settlement of Galveztown was founded in 1778.[3] The orbit of Natchez lay west of the Pearl
River while that of Pensacola extended from the Pearl River to some un-
marked point east of St. Marks.

The governor of Louisiana was subordinate to the captain general of
Cuba in political and military matters, but in connection with certain important subjects he could correspond directly with the Spanish court.[4]
The annual subsidy for the support of the government of Louisiana, as
well as that of Cuba, came from the viceroyalty of New Spain, of which
the captaincy general of Cuba was a dependency. The authority of the
intendant of Cuba was extended by the crown over the treasury of Louisiana in 1776.[5] Consequently, the archives of Cuba and Mexico, as well as
those of Spain, contain materials relating to the administration of the
province of Louisiana.

The governor was the supreme military and civil official of the province. He exercised legislative power by issuing ordinances, regulations,
and instructions. In his civil capacity he was also concerned with the municipal affairs of New Orleans and with the administration of justice. As
head of the military forces of the province, he was responsible for its defense and security and for the maintenance of discipline among the

2 / John W. Caughey, *Bernardo de Gálvez in Louisiana, 1776–1783* (Berkeley, 1934), 149.
3 / *Ibid.*, 159, 212, 79–81.
4 / Clarence H. Haring, *The Spanish Empire in America* (New York, 1947), 26.
5 / Lillian E. Fisher, *The Intendant System in Spanish America* (Berkeley, 1929), 15.

troops. He managed Indian affairs, issued orders to officers commanding outlying posts and districts, and regulated the affairs of the militia. Prior to the appointment of an intendant, he was involved in the management of the royal treasury and afterwards sometimes functioned as the intendant. He was instructed to promote immigration and agriculture and to enforce regulations governing commerce, including the suppression of smuggling. A secretary attended to the clerical details of the governor's office and took care of the records. Other officials included a treasurer, an assessor, and a prosecuting attorney.[6] The Spanish kept voluminous records on good quality paper that has been well preserved. The governor in New Orleans kept copies of communications sent to subordinates in the colony, to the captain general in Cuba, and to officials in Spain.

As the commander of the military forces in the province, the governor had charge of the regular Spanish troops, the militia, and a small number of naval vessels. Consisting of infantry, cavalry, artillery, and engineers, the regular troops were posted in widely scattered garrisons extending from St. Marks in East Florida to St. Louis in Upper Louisiana. These detachments were under commandants who were subject to the orders of the governor and the lieutenant governors of Louisiana. Financial matters pertaining to the army were the concern of an accountant of the army. A small squadron of galleys that operated along the Gulf Coast and on the Mississippi River under the command of Pierre G. Rousseau was also under the governor's authority.[7] The formation of militia companies consisting of both white and colored men was instituted by General O'Reilly.[8] Companies were organized in later years wherever new settlements were founded. The infantry and cavalry companies of the militia came under the authority of the local commandants, but their officers received appointments from the governor. The military budget of Louisiana also covered the pay of Indian commissioners, agents, and interpreters, whose activities in keeping the Indians loyal to Spain supplemented those of the commandants and the lieutenant governors. Gifts to the Indians were also dispensed and accounted for by the military department.

At the time of the Spanish occupation of Louisiana, the position of intendant was just being established in the Spanish colonies in America.

6 / Caughey, *Gálvez*, 68–69; Whitaker, *The Mississippi Question*, 30.

7 / Jack D. L. Holmes, *Gayoso, the Life of a Spanish Governor in the Mississippi Valley, 1789–1794* (Baton Rouge, 1965), 255, 162–63, 245.

8 / W. James Miller, "The Militia System of Spanish Louisiana, 1769–1783," in William S. Coker (ed.), *The Military Presence on the Gulf Coast; Proceedings of the Gulf Coast History and Humanities Conference, 7th, Pensacola, 1977* (Pensacola, 1978), 36–63.

Several officials concerned with finances, including a commissary of war and a military intendant, a royal comptroller, and a treasurer, accompanied Governor Ulloa to Louisiana and remained there after his departure. These positions were continued after the establishment of Spanish authority, but an intendant was not appointed until 1780. The first appointment of an intendant in the colonies was that at Havana in 1764, and in the following decade this official became concerned with the supervision of the finances of Louisiana.[9] When a new comptroller was appointed in Louisiana in 1770, the governor was made the superior and instructed to combine with his powers the powers of the intendant.[10] The former treasurer, Martin Navarro, was designated as intendant in 1780 and made subordinate to the governor. Chiefly a fiscal officer, he was concerned with collecting and disbursing the revenues of the province. The duties of the intendant as prescribed by law on December 4, 1786, were much broader than those granted him at first in Louisiana and were concerned with the administration of justice, the police, the treasury, and military matters, and they included the promotion of economic affairs and the improvement of local administration.[11] From 1788 to 1793 the governor of Louisiana also served as intendant.

As the duties of the intendant increased, he came to head a department of the provincial government independent of the governor's authority. A number of the most important officials of the colony became subordinate to the intendant: the comptroller kept accounts concerning expenditures, the treasurer functioned as a cashier, and the interventor superintended public purchases and bargains. The administrator in charge of the custom house in New Orleans, established in June, 1785, was also subject to the intendant. After 1798, when the power to make grants of land was transferred from the governor to the intendant, the latter official controlled the surveyor general. The intendant was assisted by a secretary and an auditor or assessor who was his legal adviser. The intendant's tribunal was concerned with revenue and admiralty cases.

Regulations for the conduct of the commerce of the posts in Louisiana and West Florida were issued by the Spanish crown in accordance with mercantilist principles that required the control of commerce for the benefit of Spain. By royal decree on March 23, 1768, trade in both Spanish and foreign goods and products was permitted between authorized ports

9 / Fisher, Intendant System, 9.
10 / Jo Ann Carrigan, "Government in Spanish Louisiana," Louisiana Studies, XI (Fall, 1972), 216.
11 / Fisher, Intendant System, 97–135, contains an English translation.

of Spain in Spanish vessels, free of export duty in Spain and of import duty in Louisiana. In Louisiana an official of the royal treasury was required to receive the register for the ship's cargo, to issue return receipts or certificates testifying to the unloading of the cargo, and to furnish a list of cargo and money taken on in Louisiana, along with a formal declaration stating that they were products of that colony. Foreign goods and products could be taken to Louisiana only through ports of Spain, where duty was paid upon their introduction. Trade did not prosper under this regulation, for the people of Louisiana were used to French products, and indirect importation made these goods too expensive. Consequently, another decree, on January 22, 1782, permitted for a period of ten years direct commerce between New Orleans and Pensacola and French ports where Spanish consuls resided.[12] The goods and products so transported, except slaves and staves of the barrels and casks, were subject to import and export duties of 6 percent. To collect the foregoing duty and the 2 percent duty imposed on Spanish goods exported to Havana and other Spanish possessions in the Indies, customs houses were to be established at New Orleans and Pensacola. The customs officials were also to certify the invoices of cargoes submitted to them by the captains of ships. Since a tariff schedule had to be approved by the crown beforehand, the customs service was not established at New Orleans until June, 1785. The regulations of 1782 were renewed and extended by a royal order on June 9, 1793.[13] At Pensacola the governor, acting as subdelegate of the intendant of Louisiana, supervised the customs service, a function performed in Mobile by the commandant.

The administration of justice in the province was in the hands of several courts. In the principal court of the colony, the governor sat as the sole judge and was assisted by a legal adviser (the auditor or the assessor).[14] The ordinary *alcaldes* were local judges for the city of New Orleans and its dependencies. In civil cases the jurisdiction of the governor's court and that of the ordinary *alcaldes* was concurrent, but the governor supervised the latter court and other officials having judicial power. Appeals could be made from both of these courts to the *cabildo*. The ecclesiastics came under the jurisdiction of the ecclesiastical judge,

12 / Lawrence Kinnaird (ed.), *Spain in the Mississippi Valley, 1765–1794* (Washington, D.C., 1949), I, 45–50, II, 1–5.

13 / Arthur P. Whitaker (ed.), *Documents Relating to the Commercial Policy of Spain in the Floridas, with Incidental References to Louisiana* (De Land, 1931), 227 n. 37, 177–84.

14 / Henry P. Dart (ed.), "Civil Procedure in Louisiana Under the Spanish Regime as Illustrated in Loppinot's Case, 1774," *Louisiana Historical Quarterly*, XII (January, 1929), 34.

who was the vicar general of the province. Appeals could be carried from the provincial courts to the *audiencia* of Santo Domingo in ordinary cases or to the governor at Havana in the cases of those having privileges, and from these tribunals appeals could go to the King.[15] Since the clerk of the governor's court was also the clerk of the *cabildo*, the judicial records were kept together. This clerk also acted as a notary; consequently, the judicial records also include some notarial acts.

Concerning the notary public, the laws of Spain stated as follows:

> By a notary public is meant a person skilled in writing: there are two kinds of notaries. The first, they who draw up the privileges and other instruments of writing, issuing from the king's court; the second, they who execute acts of sale, purchase, and the contracts or agreements which men enter into, in towns and cities. The good they do is very great, when they faithfully discharge the duties of their offices: for by them the necessary business of the kingdom is executed, and dispatched; and through them the remembrance of things past is perpetuated in the minutes preserved in their registers, and by the acts they execute.[16]

Notaries public were required to be men of good repute, to write well, to be knowledgeable in the notarial art, and to conserve secrecy. Notaries were enjoined to keep registers of the acts they drew up so that if the acts were lost or if doubt should arise in regard to them, recourse could be had to the register.

Notaries functioned throughout Louisiana in accordance with the customs of their ancient profession. Besides the notary of the cabildo, there was at New Orleans another notary who accumulated a separate body of notarial acts. A schedule promulgated by Governor O'Reilly in November, 1769, prescribed fees to be charged by notaries for a sitting in the city and a sitting in the country, for opening wills, and for copying various documents, including decrees, provisions, leaves of writing, dispatches, exemplifications of acts, bills of sale of slaves, sales of personal property, simple bonds, and bonds with mortgage, receipts, and agreements. The employment of the notary's services was made obligatory for certain documents by a proclamation of Governor Unzaga on November 3, 1770, which, in pointing out the necessity for preventing fraud and malpractices, stated that "no person, whatever be his or her rank or con-

15 / Haring, *Spanish Empire*, 86.
16 / Louis Moreau Lislet and Henry Carleton (trans.), *The Laws of Las Siete Partidos, Which Are Still in Force in the State of Louisiana* (New Orleans, 1820), 244.

dition, shall henceforth sell, alienate, buy, or accept as a donation or other wise, any negroes, plantations, houses and any kind of sea-craft, except it be by a deed executed before a Notary Public; to which contracts and acts of sale and alienation shall be annexed a certificate of the Registrar of Mortgages; that all other acts made under any other form shall be null and void."[17] The Spanish notary operating under the civil law was a more important official than his counterpart under the common law of the English colonies and American states, for only writings executed by him and witnessed were regarded as authentic acts. The notary's services were required in all transactions demanding care and certainty, and his acts covered all kinds of business and personal dealings, including contracts, agreements, settlements of estates, and last wills and testaments.[18]

The recorder of mortgages kept a record of mortgages given for the security of payments for personal property, slaves, or vessels, for a house, plantation or other real property. Upon the payment of prescribed fees, he issued certificates of mortgages.

After the transfer of Louisiana to Spain, the occupation of the outlying districts was initiated by Governor Antonio de Ulloa, but the full establishment of Spanish control had to await the coming of General Alexandro O'Reilly. Ulloa spent most of his time while in the colony at Balize, the pilot station at the mouth of the Mississippi, which he rebuilt in 1767–1768 on an island on the northeast pass of the river. A Spanish detachment reached the mouth of the Missouri River in September, 1767, and later posts were built on both sides of the river.[19] Early in 1768, Captain Alexandre de Clouet was placed in command of the Arkansas Post. To control the mouth of the Mississippi River, Governor François Hector Carondelet constructed Fort San Felipe at Plaquemines and Fort Bourbon across the river.

After studying the situation for over a year, Governor O'Reilly decided in February, 1770, that effective administration would be promoted by the designation of lieutenant governors for the Illinois and Natchitoches districts and local commandants at other places.[20] He appointed local commandants, all of whom were Frenchmen, at the following places: half the German Coast, including the parish of St. Charles; the other half of the German Coast, including the parish of St. Jean Baptiste; Pointe

17 / Gayarré, *History of Louisiana*, III, 631.

18 / Edgar Grima, "The Notarial System of Louisiana," *Louisiana Historical Quarterly*, X (January, 1927), 76.

19 / Louis Houck (ed.), *The Spanish Regime in Missouri* (Chicago, 1909), I, 35, 39, 49–52.

20 / Kinnaird (ed.), *Spain in the Mississippi Valley*, I, 157.

Coupee, Opelousas; Iberville Coast as far as Ascension Parish; Fourche de Chetimachas, including the parish of Ascension; Kabahanosse, including the parishes of St. James, Rapides, and Ste. Geneviève.[21] In each district the governor appointed a commandant, a judge, and a number of *syndics*. The judges exercised civil and criminal jurisdiction; the *syndics* functioned like justices of the peace.

The outlying districts taken over or developed by the Spaniards were governed by commandants appointed by the governor. In the larger places the commandants were officers of either the army or the militia who functioned as both military and civil commandants. Separate officials served as civil commandants and militia officers in smaller places. As chief police officer, the commandant was responsible for maintaining peace and order and for inspecting the passports of travelers to see that no persons took up residence without the written permission of the governor. He conducted relations with the Indians, issued to them their annual presents, and licensed Indian traders. As trade with the English and the Americans was forbidden, he regulated the affairs of local merchants and endeavored to suppress smuggling. In the administration of justice, he dealt with disputes over contracts, attachments, and judgments and decided cases involving sums of not over one hundred dollars. When cases involved larger amounts, he collected evidence and submitted it to the governor. He could inflict corporal punishment only on slaves. When he imprisoned persons, he had to submit reports on those cases to the governor. In his notarial capacity he registered sales of slaves and land, handled sales of property, prepared inventories of the estates of intestates, and executed judgments. Some districts had civilian notaries who acted with the commandants in notarial matters, served as clerks, and had charge of local records. In places having garrisons, the commandants acted as subdelegates of the intendant. The responsibility for enforcing the land regulations to which reference has been made was chiefly that of the commandant or of the *syndic*.

The *syndics* or justices of the peace occupied an important local role. They were appointed in the outlying settlements of the various districts under whose commandants they officiated. A decree issued by Governor Carondelet in 1792 provided for the appointment of *syndics* and another issued in 1795 regulated their duties. Unlawful acts, including seditious discourses, were to be reported to the *syndics*, who were to investigate and submit information to the commandant for his action. The *syndics*

21 / Melvin Evans, *A Study in the State Government of Louisiana* (Baton Rouge, 1931), 13–14.

were to be responsible for the general police and security of their districts, the repair of bridges, roads, and levees, the general inspection of coasters and passengers, the management of Negro camps, and the security of horses and cattle from theft by the Indians. In administering justice the *syndics* were authorized to take cognizance of matters involving sums not over ten piasters; the others were to be referred to the commandants, who were to handle only cases under fifty piasters in amount.

One phase of the commandant's duties that is of interest to the present-day researcher is his administration of records. In the instructions issued by Governor O'Reilly on February 17, 1770, to the lieutenant governor of Spanish Illinois, the latter was directed to utilize every opportunity to write to the governor reporting on everything that occurred at his post.[22] Besides maintaining a correspondence, the lieutenant governors and commandants submitted reports on soldiers, musters of militia companies, censuses of inhabitants in the different districts, and reports on grain harvested and furs secured. The statistical reports of products soon covered as well the quantities of lead mined. From the Natchez district came reports on the amounts of tobacco grown. With the development of the colony, both this district and Spanish Illinois prepared reports on immigrants from the United States. Inventories of the records that accumulated at the posts were prepared when transfers of command occurred.[23]

Such were the provincial officials and their duties, the governmental organs and their functions, the political subdivisions of the province and their officials, and the regulations under which they operated and the places in which they operated. A proper understanding of the records requires some prior knowledge of these subjects. Most of these topics still need investigation, for which the records can be a valuable resource.

On November 25, 1769, Governor O'Reilly abolished the French superior council and established a city council or *cabildo*, which was the customary local governmental body of Spanish America. The *cabildo* was primarily a municipal council for New Orleans, and it possessed administrative, legislative, regulatory, and judicial powers. It consisted of six councilors (*regidores*) who were appointed by the governor. The *cabildo* elected annually two ordinary *alcaldes* or judges, who sat with the *cabildo*, an attorney general, and a treasurer. Laws for the government of the colony were issued from Spain, from the captain-general of Cuba, from

---

22 / Houck, *Spanish Regime in Missouri,* I, 82.

23 / Numerous inventories are listed in Hill, *Descriptive Catalogue,* xxxiv–xxxix, and a few are published in Houck (ed.), *Spanish Regime in Missouri,* I, 126–30, 258–64, II, 261–67.

the Cuban administrative council, and from the governor. In its administration of the affairs of the city, the *cabildo* adopted ordinances for the public welfare, examined the accounts of the city steward, maintained public works, superintended public expenditures, required sureties of the governor, imposed and collected taxes, examined the sureties of the depositary general and the receiver of fines, and supervised the sale of public offices.[24]

Certain offices were distributed among the councilors. The provincial *alcalde* mayor had jurisdiction over crimes committed in the country outside cities and towns and over the apprehension of fugitives from city justice and runaway Negroes. The *alguacil* mayor functioned as the sheriff and chief of police. He appointed the jailor who was in charge of the city prison. The depositary general had charge, on behalf of the various tribunals, of deposits of money, real estate, land, slaves, bonds, and notes. The other councilors served as the receiver of fines and the royal standard bearer. The appointed attorney general functioned as the chief law officer.

The judges elected by the *cabildo* had first cognizance of civil and criminal cases arising in *alcalde* courts in New Orleans and the principal towns of the province involving not more than twenty piasters. Minor criminal cases were decided verbally, but in cases of greater importance, the judges met in chamber and their proceedings were recorded. The judges, assisted by constables, were responsible for preventing disorders at night. They were also to detect and punish public offenses under the law. The *cabildo* had cognizance of appeals in civil cases from sentences of either the governor or the judges involving sums not exceeding 90,000 maravedis. Cases could be appealed to the *audiencia* at Santo Domingo and after 1781 to the superior court at Havana.[25]

The clerk or notary (*escribano*) of the *cabildo* was responsible for preserving in his archives all the papers concerning the *cabildo*, its cases, and its trials. He kept a record of the proceedings and decisions of the *cabildo*'s sessions and preserved the originals of all decrees, royal provisions, and dispatches addressed to that body. He recorded in separate books the bonds and deposits of both the depositary general and the receiver of fines, who also kept their own records. He preserved original patents and commissions of trusteeships and their sureties and recorded them. In an-

24 / Ronald R. Morazán, "The Cabildo of Spanish New Orleans, 1769–1803: The Collapse of Local Government," *Louisiana Studies*, XII (Winter, 1973), 589–93; Carrigan, "Government in Spanish Louisiana," 217–21.

25 / Morazán, "The Cabildo," 589.

other book he inscribed mortgages upon contracts. For copies of documents from the files, he could charge only prescribed fees.

By order of Governor O'Reilly a city hall that became known as the Cabildo was built on the Place d'Armes (later Jackson Square) in 1769–1770.[26] The *cabildo* met in the new building until 1788 when that structure and many others in New Orleans were destroyed by fire; luckily, the council's records were saved from destruction. A new town hall was started in 1795, and the *cabildo* began meeting in a chamber on the second floor in 1799. This building also became known as the Cabildo and was occupied by government offices until 1910 when, upon the completion of a new courthouse, it was transferred to the care of the Louisiana State Museum.[27] The Museum installed exhibits on the Cabildo's second floor, and the Louisiana Historical Society also occupied quarters in the building.

The judicial records of the *cabildo*, August 18, 1769, to December 31, 1803, comprise 4,395 items in the Louisiana State Museum. They consist of civil and criminal suits containing a wide variety of documents arising from the trial of the cases before the *cabildo* and relate to most aspects of the life of the colony.[28] The documents concern the settlement of estates, family relationships, business and economic matters, agriculture, land ownership, slaves, commerce and shipping, plantations and other property, governmental activities, and the practice of medicine. Many samples of the documents in the judicial records have been printed in the *Louisiana Historical Quarterly;* these samples are listed in the index to that periodical under inventories of estates, marriage contracts, mortgages, suits, trials, and wills.[29]

Various steps have been taken to further the use and preservation of the Spanish records. In 1919 the arrangement of these records was undertaken in preparation for the publication of a calendar in English. Laura L. Porteous prepared an index that has been published.[30] The entries in the index show the date, an identification of the case, the number of pages in the documents, short abstracts of the case, and sometimes original notes. Handwritten slips for a continuation of the calendar to 1803 are in the

26 / Samuel Wilson, Jr., and Leonard V. Huber, *The Cabildo on Jackson Square: The Colonial Period, 1723–1803, The American Period, 1803 to the Present* (New Orleans, 1970), 13–15.

27 / Louisiana State Museum, *Handbook of Information Concerning Its Historic Buildings and the Treasures They Contain,* by Robert Glenk (New Orleans, 1934), 13.

28 / *National Union Catalog of Manuscripts,* 76–1453.

29 / Cruise, *Louisiana Historical Quarterly Index,* 1917–50.

30 / A. Otis Hébert, Jr., "Resources in Louisiana Depositories for the Study of Spanish Activities in Louisiana," in John F. McDermott (ed.), *The Spanish in the Mississippi Valley, 1762–1804* (Urbana, [1974]), 28.

Laura L. Porteous Collection in the Louisiana State University Department of Archives and Manuscripts. A similar index-calendar for what are known as the "Black Books" in ninety-four ringbinders in the Louisiana State Museum has been published.[31]

Like the records of the French superior council, those of the Spanish *cabildo* are not available for research because of their poor condition. In the mid-1970s archivists began preparing the records for microfilming by removing scotch tape. The staff of the Louisiana State Museum also undertook to organize and recalendar the records.[32] Microfilming was done on 261 reels through grants that were received in 1977 from the National Endowment for the Humanities, the Rockefeller Foundation, and the state of Louisiana. The translation of the Spanish judicial records is under way.

At the time of the transfer of sovereignty in New Orleans, the records of the Spanish *cabildo* passed into the custody of the municipality of New Orleans.[33] After nearly a century and a half and with the quarters on the top floor of the city hall being considered unsafe for these valuable records, the city council—on the recommendation of the Bureau of Governmental Research and civic clubs, and with the library board's agreement—in 1946 adopted an ordinance authorizing the transfer of the records to the New Orleans Public Library.[34] Not, however, until 1958, when the completion of a new library building provided the necessary quarters, did the transfer become possible.[35]

The documents of the *cabildo* now in the Archives Department of the New Orleans Public Library include its records and deliberations from August 18, 1769, to November 18, 1803, in ten volumes.[36] These are minute books or a journal of the proceedings of the *cabildo*. A typescript and translation of the records and deliberations, prepared by Adolph Baun and Arthur Troncoso for the Federal Writers Project, is in the same repository. Microfilms of the typescript and of the translation, in three and

31 / James, Dupuy, and Owen, "Index to the Black Boxes."
32 / Newsnote in *American Archivist*, XXXVIII (January, 1975), 107–108.
33 / Society of American Archivists, *News Letter*, November, 1977, p. 13.
34 / John H. Jacobs, "Keeping Archives Widens Library Community Service," *Library Journal*, XLVII, June, 15, 1947, p. 950; Margaret Ruckert, "Archive Preservation in New Orleans," *Library Journal*, LXXXIII (July, 1958), 2000.
35 / Collin B. Hamer, Jr., "Recent Genealogical Acquisitions in the New Orleans Public Library," in *Eighteenth Annual Genealogical Institute Proceedings, 22 March 1975* (Baton Rouge, 1975), 16.
36 / A. Otis Hébert, "Resources in Louisiana Depositories," 30.

four reels, respectively, are in the New Orleans Public Library, Loyola University Library, Louisiana State Library, and St. Martin Parish Library, St. Martinville. In the late 1940s for a project sponsored by the University of North Carolina, William S. Jenkins and an assistant microfilmed the records of the *cabildo* and other Spanish and French records in New Orleans for the Library of Congress' Microfilm Collection of Early State Records.[37]

All the New Orleans records are now on microfilm, and researchers are required to use the film unless it is shown to be unsatisfactory. Security copies of the microfilm are in the Southern Vital Records repository in Flora, Mississippi, or, for those made by the Mormons, in their Utah repository.

Other records of the *cabildo* in the New Orleans Public Library include petitions, decrees, and letters, 1770–1799, in two volumes, with a typed English translation of Volume I, 1770–1772; a repertory or index of the records and deliberations of the *cabildo* and of the city council initiated by Pierre C. Laussat, 1769–1828, in one volume with an English translation; and a digest of the acts of the *cabildo*, 1769–1803, in a one-volume typescript, prepared by the Work Projects Administration in 1939.

Other Spanish documents in the New Orleans Public Library include: private dispatches of Governor Estevan Miró, 1784–1790; documents relating to the repair and enlargement of the jail, 1799–1803; census of New Orleans, November 6, 1791; miscellaneous Spanish and French documents, December 23, 1789, to January 30, 1816, in four volumes, with Spanish and English typescripts; documents concerning the estate and succession of Gilberto Antonio de St. Maxent, 1784–1803, in five volumes; proceedings instituted by Lorenzo Sigur against Doña Isabel Larroche concerning the settlement of certain accounts, 1795–1796; proceedings by Francisco Blache to execute the last will and testament of Luis Blondeau, 1799–1803, in one volume.[38]

Records of New Orleans are also in other repositories in Louisiana. City council records, 1770–1803, in two volumes, are in the Louisiana State Museum. About 1946 the Louisiana State University received a collection of miscellaneous records of the *cabildo* dating from 1765, and that repository also has a fifty-one-page document of the city treasurer's re-

37 / U.S. Library of Congress, Photoduplication Service, *A Guide to the Microfilm Collection of Early State Records, a Supplement* (Washington, D.C., 1961), 1–2, 62–68.

38 / Letter from Collin B. Hamer, Jr., Head, Louisiana Division, New Orleans Public Library, with reproductions of catalog cards, to Henry P. Beers, August 12, 1982, in Beers Correspondence.

ports, 1771? to December, 1787.[39] Tulane University Library has acquired, by gift and purchase from various sources, materials dating from 1770 relating to New Orleans.[40]

The Spanish officials—Governor Manuel de Salcedo, his fellow commissioner for the transfer of the province to France, the Marquis de Casa Calvo, and Intendant Juan Ventura Morales, and others—remained in New Orleans long after the delivery of the city to the Americans. During their sojourn as unwelcome guests in the capital, they proceeded to carry out the royal order of October 15, 1802, regarding the archives that directed them as follows:

> After the evacuation of said posts and city of New Orleans you [must] cause to be collected all the papers and documents relating to the royal treasury and to the administration of the colony of Louisiana, in order to bring them to Spain for the purpose of settling the accounts; delivering, nevertheless, to the governor or other French officer commissioned to take possession, all those which may relate to the limits and boundaries of said territory, as also those which relate to the savages (Indians), and other places, taking due receipts for the whole, for your own discharge.[41]

The Spanish succeeded under the very nose of the American governor in removing not only these administrative records but also others relating to property that according to the treaty should have been turned over to the Americans.

In a number of shipments made during 1804–1806, the administrative records of Spanish Louisiana were removed to West Florida, which still remained in Spanish possession, and later to the headquarters of the captain general at Havana.[42] The records of the governor's office were taken to Pensacola. In 1804, records of the comptroller's office (*contaduria*) and of the custom house were sent to Havana.[43] In preparation for his own departure from New Orleans, the intendant transferred other treasury records to Pensacola in 1805. Having been ordered out of New Orleans by Governor Claiborne, Morales embarked for West Florida early in 1806 with records of the intendancy. He landed at Mobile, but an order

39 / *Journal of Southern History*, XII (February, 1946), 141.
40 / *National Union Catalog of Manuscripts*, 1961, entry 377.
41 / White (ed.), *New Collection of Laws*, II, 191.
42 / Hill, *Descriptive Catalogue*, xv–xxii.
43 / *Ibid.*, xvi; Cuba, Archivo Nacional, *Catálogo de los Fondos de las Floridas* (Havana, 1944), xviii.

from Spain settling a dispute between him and Lieutenant Governor Vizente Folch y Juan designated him as intendant of West Florida and moved him to Pensacola.[44] For auditing purposes treasury records were sent from time to time in succeeding years from Pensacola to the tribunal of accounts and to the intendancy at Havana. The intendancy of West Florida was abolished in 1817, and early in 1818 Morales deposited papers of that office in the intendancy at Havana. In 1819 when the transfer of the Floridas impended, still other Louisiana and West Florida records went to Havana. Despite attacks by English corsairs and Argentine revolutionaries and storms at sea, most of the records transported to Havana survived and were placed in the archives there. Attempts made by the United States in later years to recover the records were unsuccessful.[45]

The administrative records of Louisiana and West Florida thus removed from American territory became part of the Cuban archives. When the Archivo General de Ministerio de Hacienda was established in 1840 in the Real Factoria, an old tobacco warehouse in Havana, the records from Louisiana and West Florida were soon assembled in a room of that repository.[46] These records were given their present organization in 1856–1857 in preparation for their transfer to the Archivo General de Cuba, which replaced the Archivo General de Hacienda. The new archive was housed in the old Convent of San Francisco, which was used as a custom house.

A royal order of March, 1883, directed the transfer of the records of Louisiana and the Floridas from Cuba to Spain.[47] After the receipt of further orders resulting from the captain general's failure to take action, measures were initiated for the removal of the records. For a year following June, 1888, thirteen shipments of records were made, each accompanied by checklists.[48] The documents were deposited in the Archivo General de Indias at Seville and, in accordance with Spanish archival practice, designated as the Papeles Procedentes de la Isla de Cuba or Papers from the Island of Cuba. After their receipt in the Seville repository, they had to be treated with benzine to kill the vermin.

44 / Duvon C. Corbitt, "The Administrative System in the Floridas, 1781–1821," *Tequesta*, I (August, 1942), 50.

45 / Brian E. Coutts, "The Cuban Papers," *Louisiana Genealogical Register*, XXVII (December, 1980), 358–59.

46 / Joaquin Llaverías y Martínez, *Historia de los archivos de Cuba* (Havana, 1942), 33, 35, 41, 42.

47 / Hill, *Descriptive Catalogue*, xi; Luis M. Pérez, *Guide to Materials for American History in Cuban Archives* (Washington, D.C., 1907), 3–4.

48 / Llaverías, *Historia*, 106–43, prints all of the inventories; Cuba, Archivo Nacional, *Catálogo*, xlv–lx, prints inventories for Louisiana and West Florida records only.

The Papeles de Cuba consist of the archives accumulated by the governor general and other officials of Louisiana and West Florida from 1761 to 1821. They comprise 2,375 *legajos*—bundles tied up in cardboard covers by ribbons—and hundreds of volumes, including letter books and account books, totaling millions of documents. These records include correspondence, reports from commanding officers of outlying posts, records of settlements made by immigrants, architectural plans, battle plans, accounts of gifts to Indians, hospital records, and supply schedules. Other records relating to individuals include censuses, lists of ships and crews, licenses, service and employment records, and lists of crown debtors.[49]

The voluminous Papeles de Cuba contain abundant data on a variety of subjects and are of paramount importance for the history of Louisiana in all its aspects, both at the capital and at outlying settlements. Details of life at those places—such as military and militia affairs, Indian relations and trade, smuggling, land transactions, relations with the English and Americans, exploration, religion, agriculture, the fur trade, and other subjects—are documented in these records. Available only recently to American investigators through reproductions in repositories in the United States, this wealth of material still largely awaits exploitation.

The classification given to the records in Cuba was retained by the Archivo General de Indias. The series relating to the United States includes West Florida, East Florida, Louisiana, New Orleans, and the captain general's office at Havana.[50] The 'last-named series contains correspondence with the governors of Louisiana and the Floridas, the commandant of Pensacola, other subordinate officials, and the Spanish government.[51]

At the time of the removal of the Louisiana and Florida records from Cuba to Spain, a few bundles were inadvertently left behind. Luis M. Pérez, an agent of the Carnegie Institution of Washington, surveyed the Archivo Nacional de Cuba during 1905–1906 in search of material relating to the United States. He found a quantity of Louisiana and Florida records for the years 1737 to 1823, consisting of correspondence of the governors and other officials and other documents relating to general administration, commerce, finances, trade, Indians, land concessions, the conquest of West Florida, censuses, letters from commandants of posts, customs tariff, and the sale, lease, and repair of state and church property.[52] Al-

49 / Hill, *Descriptive Catalogue,* xxix–xxxi; Coutts, "Cuban Papers," 356.
50 / Hill, *Descriptive Catalogue, passim.,* contains detailed descriptions of each series and of the *legajos* of which they are composed.
51 / Llaverías, *Historia,* 134–39; Pérez, *Guide,* 4.
52 / Pérez, *Guide,* 85–99; Roscoe R. Hill, *The National Archives of Latin America* (Cam-

though fragmentary in character, these records constitute important additional documents on Louisiana. The records of the intendancy in Havana were found to contain a file of royal decrees and orders dating back to the sixteenth century and dispatches sent by the intendants to the Spanish ministers that are important for financial, economic, and commercial matters. A calendar of the royal orders and decrees had already been published.[53] In the proceedings of the intendency are documents concerning the administration of the royal subsidy of Louisiana and the Floridas and the commercial relations between those provinces and Cuba.[54] A considerable quantity of the correspondence of the captain general dating from 1716 is still in the Cuban archives.

A subsequent reorganization of the Cuban archives produced a different arrangement of the Louisiana and Florida records. It rendered useless the archival references accompanying the description of those records in the guide by Pérez. His list has been reprinted, however, with updated references.[55] This new catalog is itself a more useful guide than the general description provided by Pérez, however, for the bulk of it is an alphabetical index to the individual documents in the collection, and the documents themselves are further indexed in a general index in the back of the volume. The *Catálogo* is more comprehensive than the list in Pérez, which covers only part of the material in the Archivo General de Cuba relating to Louisiana and the Floridas, more having been uncovered.

Another collection of documents on Spanish Louisiana is in the Bancroft Library of the University of California at Berkeley. These had been purchased by Hubert H. Bancroft, California historian and collector, from Alphonse L. Pinart, who had obtained them at Havana in the early 1880s. Pinart served as Bancroft's agent in acquiring historical materials in the West Indies and northern Mexico. These Spanish Louisiana records, 1764–1809, containing about nine hundred items, include correspondence, reports, printed pamphlets, and broadsides. The correspondence is that of governors and lieutenant governors with officials in Spain and with commandants of outlying posts in Louisiana. The papers are ar-

bridge, 1945), 44. See also Sociedad Colombista Panamericana, *Documents Pertaining to the Floridas Which Are Kept in Different Archives of Cuba. Appendix Number 1: Official List of Documentary Funds of the Floridas—Now Territories of the States of Louisiana, Alabama, Mississippi, Georgia and Florida—Kept in the National Archives* (Havana, 1945).
53 / *Boletin de Archivo Nacional*, vols. XIV–XXXVI.
54 / Pérez, *Guide*, 14, 19–20.
55 / Cuba, Archivo Nacional, *Catálogo*, lxiii–xcvi.

ranged by successive governors' administrations.[56] This collection, together with transcripts and photographic reproductions from Spanish archives in the Bancroft Library, forms the basis of Lawrence Kinnaird's *Spain in the Mississippi Valley* and was also drawn on by Abraham P. Nasatir for his compilation on the Missouri River.

56 / California, University, Berkeley, Bancroft Library, *A Guide to the Manuscript Collections of the Bancroft Library, Volume I, Pacific and Western Manuscripts, Except California* (Berkeley, 1963), 116–17.

3

৯৯

Archival Reproductions

The most important collections of records concerning the administration of the French colonies in Louisiana and elsewhere in North America are those preserved in archival repositories in Paris and in other places in France. The correspondence between colonial officials and the ministries in France is preserved in the archives of those ministries in Paris. The Archives des Colonies in the Archives Nationales in Paris contain the most important series relating to Louisiana. The letters and reports sent to officials of the French government in charge of the colonies and those officials' outgoing letters are on file there. The incoming letters and reports are classified as series C13A, Correspondance générale, Louisiane; letters, instructions, orders, and memoranda sent to officials in Louisiana comprise series B, Correspondance envoyée, Ordres du roi. Other series in the Archives des Colonies concern troops, personnel, accounts and finance, commercial companies, commerce, religious missions, passengers to the colony, and civil status. The Archives de la Marine contain correspondence with naval and port officers including those at Brest, Rochefort, and other ports having close connections with North America.[1] The Archives de la Marine also contain log books of naval vessels that voyaged to Louisiana and Florida during the period 1684–1788, giving data regarding their crews, cargoes, destinations, officers, and ports of embarkation.[2]

A variety of other finding aids are available to investigators interested in using the French archives. The chronological calendar by Nancy

1 / Henry P. Beers, *The French in North America: A Bibliographical Guide to French Archives, Reproductions, and Research Missions* (Baton Rouge, 1957), 12–23.

2 / France, Archives de la Marine, *Inventaire des Archives de la Marine: Service Hydrographique, sous-série 4 JJ (journaux de bord) déposée aux Archives Nationales* (Paris, 1963), 14–19.

Miller Surrey listing twenty thousand documents in Paris archives and libraries is still useful in locating materials on a variety of subjects. Other, more recently published, guides are available for the holdings of the Archives Nationales, for the colonial correspondence received from Louisiana (series C13A), for the correspondence sent to the colonies, and for the Service Hydrographique.[3] A listing of finding aids relating to the French archives is available in print.[4]

The Dépôt du Comité Technique de Génie has custody of records of the Corps of Engineers, including correspondence, memoirs, journals, histories, descriptions, and maps and plans of places, ports, and fortifications. In the Archives du Ministère des Affaires Étrangères are documents relating to the exploration, commerce, conduct of war, and general affairs of Louisiana. The various ministries all have materials of a geographic nature, including maps, charts, memoirs, correspondence, reports, and log books of navigators and explorers.[5] The Bibliothèque Nationale and other libraries in Paris have important and varied materials.[6]

French archives in Paris and elsewhere in France contain extensive materials relating to military and civilian personnel who served in Louisiana and colonists who settled there. These files are preserved in the Archives des Colonies, series D and E. Lists of passengers who were transported to Louisiana and censuses of settlements that developed there are in the Archives des Colonies, series G. Records relating to Frenchmen who emigrated to Louisiana and to Acadians who were transported from Canada to France and later removed to Louisiana are in repositories outside Paris. These records include departmental, municipal, notarial, port, and church archives, as well as the records of naval arsenals, chambers of commerce, church officials, and others.[7]

A historical account has been published of the activities of historians, state institutions and libraries, including the Louisiana Historical

3 / Surrey (ed.), *Calendar of Manuscripts;* France, Direction des Archives, *Guide des sources de l'histoire des États-Unis dans les archives françaises* (Paris, 1976); France, Archives Nationales, *Inventaire des archives coloniales: Correspondance à l'arrivée en provenance de la Louisiane, Tome I, (Articles C13A 1 à 37)* [1678–1762] (Paris, 1976).

4 / France, Ministère de la France d'Outre-Mer, Service des Archives, *Inventaire analytique de la correspondence générale avec les colonies, départ, série B (déposée aux Archives Nationales), I, Registres 1 à 37 (1654–1715)* (Paris, 1959).

5 / Jack D. L. Holmes, "Maps, Plans and Charts of Louisiana in Paris Archives: A Checklist," *Louisiana Studies,* IV (Fall, 1965), 200–21.

6 / Waldo G. Leland, *Guide to Materials for American History in the Libraries and Archives of Paris, Volume I, Libraries* (Washington, D.C. 1932).

7 / Beers, *French in North America,* 261–65; Jacques Levron, "Les Registres paroissiaux et d'état civil en France," *Archivum,* IX (1959), 55–100.

Society and the Library of Congress, in obtaining reproductions of materials in French archives relating to the Mississippi Valley.[8] In the early 1800s and for nearly a century after that, the copying was done in longhand transcripts, a slow method that resulted in many mistakes. The Library of Congress began using a photostat machine in 1911; then the inauguration of a large-scale copying program in Europe in 1927 funded by a Rockefeller Foundation grant introduced the microfilm camera, which facilitated the acquisition of a greater quantity of more reliable reproductions. In the 1930s and beginning again in 1948 with the resumption of copying following World War II, the Library of Congress continued to obtain reproductions from France on a smaller scale.[9]

In more recent years the Library of Congress has obtained other reproductions from French archives by utilizing the income from a grant made in 1925 by James B. Wilbur, a retired banker from Manchester, Vermont. In the summer of 1962 Daniel J. Reed, the assistant chief of the Manuscript Division, conferred with archivists and librarians in Europe with a view to furthering the procurement of reproductions. While in Paris he met Mrs. Ulane Z. Bonnel, an American woman who had graduated from West Texas State University at Canyon, Texas, served as a reserve officer in France during World War II, and in 1947 married Paul H. Bonnel, a medical officer in the French navy. After her appointment as the library's agent in December, 1962, her function was to conduct surveys in the Archives Nationales and to recommend materials for microfilming.[10] In September, 1963, James E. O'Neill was designated as the library's specialist on European manuscripts, with special responsibility for developing the French copying program—an assignment that resulted in the publication of a summary inventory.[11] During succeeding years the Library of Congress received extensive reproductions from the Archives des Colonies, the Archives de la Marine, the Service Hydrographique, and the Ministère des Affaires Étrangères.[12] By 1975 the acquisitions of microfilm included: 140 reels from the Archives de la Marine, series B1, B2, and B4; 69 reels from the Archives des Colonies, series

8 / Beers, *French in North America, passim;* Francis G. Henshaw, "A Brief History of the Library of Congress Microreproduction Projects," *National Microfilm Association Proceedings, 8th Annual Meeting, Washington* (1959), 221.

9 / Beers, *French in North America,* 219–26.

10 / Ulane Z. Bonnel, "La Déléguée à Paris: The Library of Congress Foreign Copying Program in France," *Library of Congress Quarterly Journal,* XXIII (July, 1966), 187.

11 / James E. O'Neill, "Copies of French Manuscripts for American History in the Library of Congress," *Journal of American History,* LI (March, 1965), 674–91.

12 / *National Union Catalog of Manuscripts,* 1967, entries 160, 162, 960, 961, 963, 964, 966.

C13A, C13B, and C13C; 13 reels from the Archives du Ministère des Affaires Étrangères, series Mémoires et documents, États-Unis, volumes 1–18, for 1780–1812; and 113 reels from the Correspondance politique, États-Unis, 1790–1829.[13] The Manuscript Division also has microfilm of the Archives du Directoire Executif, 1793–1812, 3 reels containing correspondence between the French agents in the United States and the Directoire, 1793–1798, and miscellaneous manuscripts, 1799–1813, relating to the cession of Louisiana and the financing of its purchase. The more recent acquisitions from the Archives des Colonies and the Archives de la Marine are noted in the Library's *Quarterly Journal of Current Acquisitions*.

The establishment of the Colonial Records Collection at the University of Southwestern Louisiana in 1967 by Glenn R. Conrad soon resulted in an extensive copying program in French archives. The first acquisition was a copy of the Library of Congress microfilm of materials in the Archives Nationales, 46 reels covering most of the materials listed in Nancy M. Miller Surrey's *Calendar*. In 1967 Conrad initiated talks that resulted in the formation of the Louisiana Colonial Records Project in which the participants were the Library of Congress, the University of Southwestern Louisiana, Loyola University of New Orleans, Memphis State University, and the Mississippi Department of Archives and History. The result was the acquisition by all five institutions of microfilm of all fifty-four volumes of the Archives des Colonies, C13A series, Correspondance générale, Louisiane, in 69 reels. Microfilm obtained from other French repositories concerns the emigration of Germans, Alsatians, and Acadians to Louisiana, and materials from the Archives de la Marine concern maritime matters.[14]

The Center for Louisiana Studies that was established at the University of Southwestern Louisiana in 1973 has continued to acquire reproductions of materials on the French in North America. It purchased from the Centre d'Études Acadiennes at the Université de Moncton, New Brunswick, copies of the French Archives des Colonies, series C11A, C11B, and C11C, consisting of correspondence from New France, Île Royale, Île St.-Jean, and Acadia. From the same repository it obtained 212 reels of microfilm of the Archives des Colonies, Ordres du Roi, series B, containing instructions from French ministers to colonial officials throughout North America. From the Library of Congress were obtained copies

13 / U.S. Library of Congress, Manuscript Division, *Manuscripts on Microfilm: A Checklist of the Holdings in the Manuscript Division*, by Richard B. Bickel (Washington, D.C., 1975), 22–24.

14 / Carl A. Brasseaux, "The Colonial Records Collection of the Center for Louisiana Studies," *Louisiana History*, XXV (Spring, 1984), 182–83.

of the Moreau de Saint-Méry Collection of the Archives Nationales, consisting largely of the Louisiana Superior Council minutes, 1714–1765, and copies of memoirs on Louisiana. From the McGill University collection of microfilm from the Archives Départementales de la Charente Maritime were obtained copies of materials on trade between La Rochelle and New France and Louisiana. In 1974 it obtained fifty-four volumes on microfilm of the C13A subseries of the Archives des Colonies, containing the correspondence of French colonial personnel in Louisiana. Reproductions from the État Civil section of the Archives Nationales, volumes 412 and 463–65, contain most of the documentation on the German emigration fostered by John Law. From the Archives du Ministère des Affaires Étrangères, the Center obtained 6 reels of microreproductions from the memoirs and documents series on Louisiana affairs in the eighteenth century.[15] These acquisitions by the University of Southwestern Louisiana make up the largest collection of primary materials on French activities in North America of any repository in the United States.

Another Louisiana repository that has obtained reproductions from the French archives is the Historic New Orleans Collection. Alfred E. Lemmon of that repository made arrangements with the Archives Nationales for microfilming while he visited Paris in 1983–1984. From the Archives des Colonies 68 reels of microfilm have been obtained from series C13A, volumes, 1–54, C13B1, and C13C, volumes 1–5, consisting mainly of letters received by the Secretaire d'État de la Marine from Louisiana from 1678 to 1767. From the records of the Dépôt des Fortifications des Colonies in the same repository were obtained microfilm copies of documents and photographs of maps and plans, 141 items concerning New Orleans, Balize, Natchez, Mobile, Dauphin Island, and Biloxi. A smaller number of reproductions of maps of Louisiana and plans of forts and buildings are from the Moreau de Saint-Méry Collection in the Archives Nationales.[16]

Another large collection of microfilm from French archives is that of the Genealogical Society of the Church of Jesus Christ of Latter-Day Saints. In order to enable families to prepare ancestral and other genealogies for religious purposes, the society has been engaged for years in obtaining microfilm of church and other records in repositories in the United States, Europe, Latin America, and the Far East. After completing arrangements with the director of the Archives de France, the society be-

15 / *Ibid.*, 184–89.
16 / Letter from Alfred E. Lemmon, with lists, to Henry P. Beers, April 16, 25, 1985, in Beers Correspondence.

gan microfilming parish records in 1959 and later extended the microfilming to registers of civil status.[17] The church registers date from the sixteenth and early seventeenth centuries, and the registers of civil status were begun in 1792. Later the microfilming was extended to other materials, including censuses, emigration and immigration records, declarations of pregnancies, and other series. Positive copies of the microfilm were given to the French repositories where the microfilming was done, and the negative copies were deposited in the society's vault inside a mountain in Little Cottonwood Canyon, southeast of Salt Lake City. In that place, positive copies of the microfilm were made and cataloged. Eventually, the catalog entries will be computerized. Arrangements to use the microfilm can be made through the branch library of the Genealogical Society in Baton Rouge or at more than one hundred other branch libraries throughout the United States.

Microfilm of French archives is also held by other repositories. The Bancroft Library of the University of California at Berkeley has microfilm of French documents on Louisiana, 1741–1783, 704 exposures from the Bibliothèque Nationale and the Archives du Ministère des Affaires Étrangères. Twelve reels of microfilm of photostats from French and Spanish archives in the Library of Congress and the New York Public Library of documents on Louisiana, 1750–1780, are in the Stanford University Library. Microfilm from the French Archives des Colonies, series C13, in the Howard-Tilton Memorial Library of Tulane University numbers fifty-one reels. The Public Archives of Canada also have microfilm of correspondence relating to Louisiana in the Archives des Colonies.[18]

Some of the Acadians who were expelled from Canada in the 1750s were transported to English colonies on the Atlantic seaboard while others were carried to England and to France, where they were settled in French ports and remained until their return to Canada or their departure for Louisiana in the 1780s. Under French law, record was made locally of births, marriages, and deaths that occurred among the Acadians while they were domiciled in France. Milton P. Rieder, Jr., of Metairie, Louisiana, did some research in the archives of French ports and towns; he later engaged researchers to continue these investigations and received from them a great deal of material from archives in Paris and from the archives of ports, towns, and naval districts. Using the data thus obtained, he published lists of Acadians who were transported to England and later

17 / C. Russell Jensen, *Preliminary Survey of the French Collections* (Salt Lake City, 1980), xiii.

18 / Canada, Public Archives, *Union List of Manuscripts in Canadian Repositories* (Ottawa, 1975), 424–27.

removed to France and of others who were carried directly to French ports, and rolls of Acadians living in French towns.[19] An earlier publication of Rieder's contains lists of the crews and passengers of seven ships that carried Acadians from France to Louisiana in 1785.[20] These lists, published from copies obtained from the archives at Nantes and Brest, show the names of family members registered for the voyage, their ages, relationships, the places they came from, their occupations, and the names of ship officers. The 1,574 Acadians who were transported to Louisiana were given land along the Mississippi and the Bayou Lafourche in an area that became the parishes of Ascension, Assumption, Lafourche, and Terrebonne.

In the late 1970s Albert J. Robichaux, Jr., of Louisiana, researched the registers in the archives of the *départements* of Île-et-Vilaine and Côtes-du-Nord, where Acadians had settled. He published English transcripts of the records of marriages in a number of the towns in the *départe-ment* of Île-et-Vilaine.[21] In another book he gives texts of about eight hundred marriages, baptisms, and burials that occurred between 1777 and 1785 from the registers of eleven churches in and around Nantes.[22] Later Robichaux published additional genealogies on Acadians in France based upon researches in French departmental archives in Île-et-Vilaine, Côtes-du-Nord, Morbihan, and Loire-Atlantic and municipal archives at Nantes.[23] Parts 1 and 2, pages 1–820, of his three-part publication contain abstracts of marriage records, and part 3, pages 821–1182, contains abstracts of Acadian marriages in France.

Most of the records accumulated by French and Spanish officials who served in Louisiana and West Florida were shipped away when those possessions were transferred to the United States. In 1804–1805 records of the *contaduria*, the New Orleans custom house, and the treasury were transported to Havana or Pensacola.[24] Inventories of the shipped records of the

19 / Milton P. Rieder, Jr., and Norma G. Rieder (comps. and eds.), *The Acadians in France, 1762–1776. Volume I, Rolls of the Acadians Living in France Distributed by Towns for the Years 1762 to 1776. Volume II, Belle-Isle-en-Mer Registers, La Rochelle Papers. Volume III, Archives of the Port of Saint Servan* (Metairie, La., 1967–73).

20 / Milton P. Rieder, Jr., and Norman G. Rieder (comps.), *The Crew and Passenger Registration Lists of the Seven Acadian Expeditions of 1785* (Metairie, La., 1965).

21 / Albert J. Robichaux, Jr., *Acadian Marriages in France, Department of Îlle-et-Vilaine, 1759–1776* (Harvey, La., 1976).

22 / Albert J. Robichaux, Jr., *The Acadian Exiles in Nantes, 1775–1785* (Harvey, La., 1978).

23 / Albert J. Robichaux, Jr., *The Acadian Exiles in Saint-Malo, 1758–1785* (Eunice, La., 1981).

24 / Roscoe R. Hill, *Descriptive Catalogue of the Documents Relating to the History of the United States in the Papeles Procedentes de Cuba Deposited in the Archivo General de Indias at Seville* (Washington, D.C., 1916), xvi–xviii.

different offices were prepared; other inventories were also prepared for the shipped records of interior posts.[25] These records and others created by Spanish officials who were concerned with the administration of the colonies were eventually deposited in various Spanish archives. The principal such repositories were the Archivo General de Indias at Seville, the Archivo General de Simancas, and the Archivo Histórico Nacional at Madrid. In the Archivo General de Indias, the sections containing documents for the United States include (I) Audiencias, (II) Indiferente General (general miscellaneous), (III) Ministerio de Ultramar (Ministry of the Colonies), (IV) Papeles de Estado (state papers), (V) Patronato Real (royal patronage), and (IX) La Contaduria (Office of the Controller). The Archivo General de Simancas contains records of the departments of the Spanish government, including the secretariat of state (custodian of the records of the crown) and the secretaries of war, navy, and finance, and colonial records brought back to Spain. In the Archivo Histórico Nacional, the pertinent documents are the Papeles de Estado (state papers). Other repositories in Madrid having Hispanic-American materials include the Biblioteca Nacional, Real Academia de la Historia, Biblioteca del Palacio Real, Museo Naval, Biblioteca Central Militar, Archivo del Servicio Histórico Militar, and the Archivo Central de Marina, Archivo General de Ministerio de Hacienda, Museo de Ciencias Naturales, the Ministerio de Asuntos Exteriores, and the Archivo General Militar de Segovia. Registers of births, marriages, and burials that were kept by Catholic churches in Spain contain information about the origins of persons who emigrated to Spanish America. Descriptions of materials in Spanish archives with citations to published and manuscript catalogs, guides, inventories, and indexes are in print.[26]

The Carnegie Institution of Washington, which had been founded in 1902 with an endowment from Andrew Carnegie, a wealthy Pennsylvania industrialist and philanthropist, created a Department of Historical Research in 1903 to undertake the investigation of materials in European archives relating to the history of the United States. Under the skillful

25 / *Ibid.*, xxxvii–xxxix.
26 / Ernest J. Burrus, S. J., "An Introduction to Bibliographical Tools in Spanish Archives and Manuscript Collections Relating to Hispanic America," *Hispanic American Historical Review*, XXXV (November, 1955), 443–83; Jack D. L. Holmes, "Maps, Plans and Charts of Louisiana in Spanish and Cuban Archives: A Checklist," *Louisiana Studies*, II (Winter, 1963), 183–203; Eric C. Beerman, "A Check-list of Louisiana Documents in the Servicio Histórico Militar in Madrid," *Louisiana History*, XX (Spring, 1979), 221–22; Gilbert C. Din, "Sources for Spanish Louisiana," in Light T. Cummins and Glen Jeansonne (eds.), *A Guide to the History of Louisiana* (Westport, Conn., 1982), 127–38.

direction of John Franklin Jameson, former head of the department of history at the University of Chicago, agents of the institution began investigating the archives of the countries of western Europe that had colonized and administered the regions in North America that became the United States.[27] After spending the summer of 1905 investigating archives at Simancas, Madrid, and Seville, William R. Shepherd prepared a guide that supplied preliminary information on materials pertaining to the United States in the archives of those places.[28]

For the task of investigating the Papeles de Cuba in the Archivo General de Indias at Seville, Jameson selected Roscoe R. Hill, a former student of his at Chicago and of Shepherd's at Columbia, who had recently been a teacher in Matanzas, Cuba.[29] Hill spent the period from January, 1911, to April, 1913, at this task and engaged several clerks to prepare calendar cards for individual documents.[30] During his investigations Hill identified the various series concerning Louisiana and West Florida and obtained descriptive information regarding their contents.[31] He examined 934 bundles relating wholly or partly to the United States, took notes for a general descriptive inventory and prepared an itemized list of documents in some 143 bundles considered to be the most important.[32] After his return from Spain and while he was on the faculties of Columbia University and the University of New Mexico, he completed the *Descriptive Catalogue of the Documents Relating to the United States in the Papeles Procedentes de Cuba . . . at Seville* that was published by the Carnegie Institution in 1916. The card calendar that was prepared during his mission in Seville is in the Manuscript Division of the Library of Congress.

In 1914 Jameson arranged with Francis S. Philbrick, a law professor at Northwestern University who had worked in and had copying done in the Archivo General de Indias in Seville in 1909–1910 and again in the summers of 1912 and 1913, to supervise the copying of the dispatches of the Spanish governors of Louisiana to the captains general of Cuba,

27 / Beers, *French in North America*, 186–88.

28 / William R. Shepherd, *Guide to the Materials for the History of the United States in Spanish Archives (Simancas, the Archivo Nacional, and Seville)* (Washington, D.C., 1907).

29 / Jameson to Hill, May 18, 1910, Jameson to Waldo G. Leland, July 20, 1910, Carnegie Institution of Washington, Department of Historical Research, Correspondence. This file contains other letters of Hill concerning his work in Spain and his later work on the catalogue.

30 / Hill, *Descriptive Catalogue*, xxiv; Roscoe R. Hill, *American Missions in European Archives* (México, D.F., 1951), 41.

31 / Hill, *Descriptive Catalogue*, xii–xiii.

32 / Carnegie Institution of Washington, *Report of the Department of Historical Research* (Washington, D.C., 1905–29), 1913, p. 152.

1766–1792.[33] The photographing was done by the Señores Hijos de Pérez Romero and was continued in 1915 under the supervision of Mrs. Adolph Bandelier, who with her husband had been obtaining copies of documents relating to New Mexico. Sets of the three thousand photographs were obtained and distributed to the following institutions: Harvard University Library, New York Public Library, Hispanic Society of America in New York, Library of Congress, Howard-Tilton Memorial Library of Tulane University, Louisiana State University Library, Newberry Library, University of Illinois Library, Missouri Historical Society, Wisconsin State Historical Society, and one private individual.[34] The University of Illinois Library also has typed copies of documents in the Archivo General de Indias relating to the administration of the provinces of Louisiana and Florida from 1746 to 1820, totaling 1,114 pages, and other compilations on the government and administration of Louisiana and Florida from 1765 to 1800 in 940 pages, and the history of Louisiana, Florida, and the Mississippi Valley from 1730 to 1800.

In the 1930s the Survey of Federal Archives in Louisiana, under the direction of Stanley C. Arthur, Louisiana historian, prepared translations of the dispatches of the Spanish governors of Louisiana, 1766–1792, from the Carnegie Institution photographic copies in the Howard-Tilton Memorial Library and from photostatic copies of the Baron de Carondelet's dispatches and the confidential dispatches of Bernardo de Gálvez, 1770–1781, borrowed from the Library of Congress.[35] Sets of the translations are in the National Archives, the Department of Archives and Manuscripts of the Louisiana State University, and the Louisiana State Museum Library.[36] An authority on Louisiana history considers the translations to be of in-

33 / Letters of Francis S. Philbrick to Henry P. Beers, June 27, July 15, 1949, in Beers Correspondence; Carnegie Institution, Report, 1914, p. 163.

34 / Hill, American Missions, 44; Carnegie Institution, Report, 1917, p. 152. The set in the New York Public Library is in thirty volumes, totaling 2,989 pages, with a one-volume calendar.

35 / Survey of Federal Archives, Louisiana, Dispatches of the Spanish Governors of Louisiana (1766–1792) New Orleans, 1937–38; Survey of Federal Archives, Louisiana, Confidential Dispatches of Don Bernardo de Gálvez, Fourth Spanish Governor of Louisiana, Sent to His Uncle Don José de Gálvez, Secretary of State and Ranking Official of the Council of the Indies [1777–1782] (New Orleans, 1937–38); Survey of Federal Archives, Louisiana, Dispatches of the Spanish Governor of Louisiana. Messages of Francisco Luis Hector, El Baron de Carondelet, Sixth Spanish Governor of Louisiana, 1792–1979 (New Orleans, 1937–41).

36 / The titles of these transcriptions are in the bibliography of this book. A list of the individual volumes in the set in this repository is in Brian E. Coutts and Merna Whitley, "An Inventory of Sources in the Department of Archives and Manuscripts, Louisiana State University, for the History of Spanish Louisiana and West Florida," Louisiana History, XIX (Spring, 1978), 249.

ferior quality, necessitating the use by serious scholars of the original photostats or microfilm.[37] A reproduction of the index that accompanied the translations has been published.[38]

In 1905 Herbert Putnam, the Librarian of Congress, launched a program for obtaining copies of documents from the archives of Spain and other European countries. In 1915 the Library of Congress joined a cooperative program for which William E. Dunn, who had been an instructor in Latin American history at Stanford University, secured transcripts from the Archivo General de Indias. When he left Seville in the summer of 1916, Dunn arranged for copyists to continue their work. The library also obtained copies from that place through Charles H. Cunningham, a University of California fellow, and Irene A. Wright, a young American woman who had lived in Spain for several years doing research for Roland C. Conklin of New York and working on her own history of Cuba.[39] By 1927 the library had received several thousand pages of transcripts from the Archivo General de Indias and the Archivo General de Simancas. Frederick B. Acosta, a Spanish historical scholar, was employed for several months in 1923 to arrange and catalog the copies.

In order to inaugurate a large-scale operation in European archives, in 1927 the Library of Congress sought and obtained from John D. Rockefeller, Jr., a grant of $450,000, to be expended over a period of five years.[40] Samuel F. Bemis, a history professor at George Washington University who had worked in the Archivo Histórico Nacional in Madrid in 1924 and 1925, was selected as general director of the undertaking, which became known as Project A. Management of the project in Washington was placed in the Manuscript Division, of which John Franklin Jameson became director in 1928. After doing some preliminary work in Washington, Bemis embarked for Europe in the fall of 1927, making arrangements in the different countries for operations of the library's representatives. Lansing B. Bloom of the University of New Mexico was the first of the library's agents in Spain. He was succeeded in the fall of 1928 by Roscoe R. Hill, who made his residence at Seville for the two-year apointment. In turn he was succeeded by Charles C. Griffin, Elizabeth H. West, who had recently worked on a calendar of the Spanish archives of New Mexico in the Library of Congress, and Irene A. Wright. When Bemis returned to teaching in the fall of 1929, his successor as general director was Worth-

37 / Review by Jack D. L. Holmes in *Louisiana History*, XVII (Spring, 1976), 216.
38 / Stanley C. Arthur, *Index to the Dispatches of the Spanish Governors of Louisiana, 1766–1792* (New Orleans, 1975).
39 / Hill, *American Missions*, 66–67, 89.
40 / *Ibid.*, 71–72; Henshaw, "Microreproductions Projects," 220.

ington C. Ford, a former head of the Division of Manuscripts of the Library of Congress and recently retired editor for the Massachusetts Historical Society. Ford remained in charge of the library's European operations until June 20, 1935.

The reproductions relating to Louisiana and West Florida obtained by the Library of Congress under Project A were chiefly from the sections Audiencia and Papeles de Cuba in the Archivo General de Indias.[41] These reproductions include the correspondence of governors and intendants of Louisiana with the captains general of Cuba, government officials in Spain, and subordinate military and civil officials in Louisiana.[42] Other reproductions were largely from the Archivo Histórico Nacional at Madrid and the Archivo General de Simancas and mainly concern diplomatic relations between the United States and Spain.[43] The Manuscript Division arranged the transcripts and photographic copies according to the original archival provenance; consequently, the previously cited guides by Shepherd and Hill can readily be used. Positive enlargements of the microreproductions were made in order to facilitate their use by researchers.

In later years the Library of Congress obtained additional reproductions from the Papeles de Cuba on a much smaller scale by using the James B. Wilbur fund. The copying was supervised by Irene Wright until the outbreak of World War II forced the suspension of work in 1940. A grant of $65,000 from the Rockefeller Foundation in 1956 enabled the Library of Congress, in cooperation with the American Historical Association, to utilize the services of Fulbright fellows in obtaining reproductions of documents and unpublished inventories and catalogs.[44] By 1975 the microfilm reproductions in the library from the Papeles de Cuba included 26 reels of positive microfilm and 257 negative microfilm reels.[45]

In judicial matters Louisiana was under the jurisdiction of the Audiencia of Santo Domingo after 1768, and materials in its archives relating to Louisiana are significant for the province's history.[46] Photostats and transcripts relating to Louisiana, 1521–1813, were obtained in the 1930s from the Audiencia records in the Archivo General de Indias. From the Papeles de Estado in the Archivo Histórico Nacional at Madrid, there are 46 reels of positive microfilm and 270 reels of negative microfilm. The Li-

41 / Hill, *American Missions*, 79.
42 / U.S. Library of Congress, *Annual Report of the Librarian of Congress* (Washington, D.C., 1866–1980), 1932, p. 67.
43 / *Ibid.*, 1934, p. 42, 1935, p. 40, 1936, p. 41.
44 / Henshaw, "Microreproduction Projects," 226.
45 / Library of Congress, *Manuscripts on Microfilm*, 61.
46 / Shepherd, *Guide*, 11, 63–65, 71–73.

brary of Congress has not published a detailed guide to its holdings of reproductions from the various Spanish archives. Memphis State University has copied the microfilm in the Library of Congress and in other places. In the early 1970s the University of West Florida at Pensacola obtained xerographic copies of the photostats of the Papeles de Cuba in the Library of Congress.

Louisiana institutions have also obtained large quantities of reproductions from Spanish archives. A commercial mission to Spain in 1959 by Charles Nutter on behalf of International House of New Orleans resulted in that organization's promoting the procurement of copies of documents on Louisiana, a project in which Loyola University of New Orleans was enlisted.[47] The Reverend Ernest J. Burrus, S. J., of the Institutum Historicum Societatis Iesu, in Rome and St. Louis, directed the project until ill health forced him to relinquish the task to the Reverend Charles E. O'Neill, S. J., of Loyola University. The documents selected for microfilming were from the Archivo General de Indias, Audiencia de Santo Domingo, Section Five, which contains a large quantity and variety of documents on Spanish Louisiana and Mississippi that had not then been reproduced.[48] The microfilm was deposited in Loyola University Library in New Orleans, which makes them available for research but cannot loan them or make copies. A catalog of the collection published in 1968 facilitates use of the 140,000 pages in the collection.[49] This collection of Spanish documents, 1762–1810, in 234 reels, consists of correspondence from Spanish officials in colonial Louisiana to officials in Spain.

In 1977 after receiving a grant from the National Endowment for the Humanities, Louisiana State University and Loyola University launched a project for microfilming the entire collection of the Papeles de Cuba. Paul E. Hoffman of Louisiana State University proposed the undertaking and after consultation with Father O'Neill learned that Loyola had been considering a similar undertaking. Work began in 1977, under the direction of Father O'Neill and Professor Hoffman, with the employment of some Spanish clerks in the Archivo General de Indias to reorganize the papers within the *legajos* and to stamp them with numbers in order to make them easier to find and to keep them in order. The first shipment of accounts, other fiscal records, and other materials was received early in

47 / Louisiana Historical Association, *News Letter*, I, no. 3 (July 1, 1959).
48 / William S. Coker, "Research in the Spanish Borderlands: Mississippi, 1779–1798," *Latin American Research Review*, VII (Summer, 1972), 42–43.
49 / José de la Peña y Cámaro, *et al.*, *Catálogo de documentos del Archivo General de Indias (sección V, Gobierno, Audiencia de Santo Domingo) sobre la época española de Luisiana* (New Orleans, 1968).

1979.[50] By the end of 1982, about 400 of the 570 *legajos* concerning Louisiana had been restored to proper archival order or found to be properly organized. A catalog index of the collection will be prepared by Professor Hoffman. Arrangements were made with the Centro Nacional de Microfilm of Madrid for microfilming the 118 reels of the Documentos de Luisiana y Florida Occidental, 1762–1819. The documents microfilmed have been entitled "Cargos, datas, cuentas y asientos de Luisiana y Florida, Occidental." In 1983, when the Historic New Orleans Collection assumed financial support for the project, Alfred E. Lemmon of that institution met with colleagues at Loyola University and Louisiana State University and made trips to Spain in 1983 and 1984. Under arrangements then made, microfilming continued in the Papeles de Cuba.

The Louisiana State University Department of Archives and History also has smaller collections of microfilm from the Papeles de Cuba. These include a collection of 12 reels obtained by Jack D. L. Holmes of the University of Alabama at Birmingham on colonial Louisiana and a copy of the 12 reels of the Stetson Collection on Spanish Louisiana and West Florida of the Florida State Historical Society.[51]

Smaller collections of transcripts and photostats from Spanish archives have been obtained by other institutions, but they have been superseded by the more voluminous and reliable collections of microreproductions mentioned above. W. W. Pierson, of the history department of the University of North Carolina, obtained from 1924 to 1927 photostats relating to Florida and Louisiana from the Archivo General de Indias, the Archivo Histórico Nacional, and the Archivo General de Simancas.[52] Arthur P. Whitaker spent two years as an Amherst College fellow in the 1920s obtaining photostats and typescripts of Spanish documents in the Archivo Histórico Nacional and the Archivo General de Indias relating to the Old Southwest, which were then deposited in the McClung Collection of the Lawson McGhee Library at Knoxville, Tennessee. Abraham P. Nasatir of the University of California, San Diego, made a specialty of French and Spanish activities in the upper Mississippi and Missouri River valleys. During several trips abroad he amassed a collection of 200,000 pages of transcripts and photostats. As a Native Son of the Golden West fellow in 1924–1925 and again in 1934–1935 as a Social Science Research Council fellow, he collected copies of documents in France

50 / A list of the *legajos* with titles is in Coutts, "Cuban Papers," 364–66, where there is also a chronological list of censuses of Louisiana and West Florida (1766–1820), 267–68.

51 / Cummins and Jeansonne (eds.), *Guide to the History of Louisiana*, 155.

52 / Hill, *American Missions*, 112; Historical Records Survey, North Carolina, *List of the Papeles Procedentes de Cuba in the Archives of the North Carolina Historical Commission* (Raleigh, 1942).

and Spain. Nasatir's collection was eventually deposited in the Bancroft Library of the University of California at Berkeley.[53]

In the late 1970s microreproductions were also obtained by the Center for Louisiana History of the University of Southwestern Louisiana for its Colonial Records Collection. Arrangements were made with the Archivo General de Indias for microfilming the commandants' reports in the Papeles de Cuba, *legajos* 186–221. These reports were arranged alphabetically by name of post and chronologically thereunder. After the pages of the reports were numbered, they were sent to the Centro Nacional de Microfilm at Madrid for microfilming. The great bulk of the material and the labor involved in restoring the order of the papers delayed the completion of this project until late 1978. Work was then undertaken on the correspondence of the Spanish governors, intendants, and other officials, which was arranged by author in order of rank and chronologically thereunder.[54] The Center also has microfilm of the letters in the Carondelet papers at the Bancroft Library of the University of California. Microfilm of late-eighteenth-century census reports on Louisiana settlements from the Audiencia de Santo Domingo papers, *legajos* 2529–2689, in 140 reels, and of governors' and intendants' reports for 1766–1771 and 1785 concerning Spain's early administration of Louisiana, the war for North American independence, the New Orleans rebellion of 1768, and Acadian immigration were also obtained from the Archivo General de Indias.[55]

Reproductions from the Papeles de Cuba in the Archivo General de Indies are also in other institutions. Photographic reproductions in the Howard-Tilton Memorial Library of Tulane University number twenty-five volumes. Microfilm of papers of Juan Ventura Morales relating to the Ouachita district are in the Northeastern Louisiana University Archives at Monroe, Louisiana. Other microreproductions from the Papeles de Cuba, in 277 reels, are in the John Brister Library of Memphis State University, where there are also 4 reels from the Council of the Indies on the Louisiana governors and 16 reels from the Archivo General de Simancas, Guerra Moderna, on the military.

While in Spain in 1983 and 1984 arranging for the continuation of microfilming in the Papeles de Cuba in the Archivo General de Indias in Seville, Alfred E. Lemmon of the Historic New Orleans Collection made arrangements at eight other repositories for the microfilming of materials

53 / Abraham P. Nasatir, *Spanish War Vessels on the Mississippi, 1792–1796* (New Haven, 1968), v; Beers, *French in North America*, 120–21.

54 / An abstract of this correspondence is being published: Carl A. Brasseaux, "Official Correspondence of Spanish Louisiana, 1770–1803," *Revue de Louisiane*, VI– (Winter, 1977–).

55 / Brasseaux, "Colonial Records Collection," 185–86.

relating to Louisiana. From the Archivo General de Indias was received microfilm of 295 maps and plans relating to Louisiana. Documents from the Servicio Histórico Militar, Madrid, in 4 reels, relate to defense, boundaries, reaction to the Louisiana Purchase, and West Florida, 1721–1824. Documents from the Museo Naval, Madrid, in 1 reel, relating to navigation, boundary lines, commerce, and descriptions of Spanish colonial Louisiana, 1766–1830, include documents by José de Evía, others relating to the Baron de Carondelet, a report by Carondelet on the defense of the territory, documents on immigration policy, and Estevan Miró's description of Louisiana. A collection of documents on the history of Louisiana, 1768–1801, in 2 reels, from the Biblioteca Nacional, Madrid, concerns Spanish administrative policy. A small collection of documents from the Biblioteca del Palacio Real, Madrid, in 2 reels, concerning Louisiana relates largely to commerce. Documents relative to the boundary between Texas and Louisiana in 2 reels are from the Real Academia de la Historia. Lists of the items in the collections described above are in the Historic New Orleans Collection. Reproductions of maps and plans were also obtained from the Servicio Histórico Militar, the Archivo del Museo Naval, and the Servicio del Ejercito.[56]

The largest collection of microfilm from the Papeles de Cuba in the Archivo General de Indias at Seville in the southeastern part of the United States comprises 421 reels and is in the P. K. Yonge Library of Florida History at the University of Florida at Gainesville. The calendaring of these documents was started in 1974 with the aid of grants from the National Endowment for the Humanities.[57]

When the archives of Louisiana and West Florida were shipped from Havana, Cuba, to Spain in 1888–1889, eight bundles were left behind in the Archivo Nacional de Cuba.[58] These records have remained in that repository and consist of documents of 1765–1818, including appointments, censuses, correspondence, customs tariffs, decrees, inventories of stores, memorials, proclamations, regulations, and a copybook of letters sent by Governor Carondelet, from January 8, 1792, to May 31, 1796. Other documents concern the settlements of the Baron Felipe de Bastrop and Abraham Morehouse on the Ouachita. West Florida documents, 1806–1810, concern a conflict between Vizente Folch and Juan Ventura Morales,

56 / Letters from Alfred E. Lemmon to Henry P. Beers, accompanied by copies of the lists, April 16, 27, 1985, in Beers Correspondence.
57 / Michael V. Gannon, "Documents of the Spanish Florida Borderlands: A Calendaring Project at the University of Florida," William and Mary Quarterly, XXXVIII (October, 1981), 718–22.
58 / Pérez, Guide, 77, 85–99, 105.

the smuggling of Negroes into Baton Rouge, and the West Florida Republic of 1810. Following the removal of the Archivo Nacional de Cuba from Castillo de la Fuerza to the Cuartel de Artilleria in 1906, the archives were reorganized in a systematic manner by the director, Joaquin Llaverias, making it easier for researchers to use them.[59] A finding aid that was published later contains a list of documentary series.[60]

Reproductions from Cuban archives relating to Louisiana are in a number of repositories. Elizabeth H. West, chief of the archives division of the Texas State Library, on a visit to Havana in 1914 obtained copies of letters of Bernardo de Gálvez on thin paper. She had these reproduced by the blueprint process and sold copies to the Library of Congress, the State Library of California, the Wisconsin State Historical Society, and the Newberry Library. The Edward E. Ayer Collection of the Newberry Library has typed copies of letters of Bernardo de Gálvez to José de Gálvez, 1777–1781, and to officials of West Florida. Beginning in the 1930s, Duvon C. Corbitt searched the Cuban archives for documents, which he published, on the activities of the Spanish on the Georgia-Florida frontier.[61] The library of the National Archives in Washington received in 1946 an extensive series of photostatic copies of documents in the Cuban archives relating to Louisiana and the Floridas, 1778–1820, including correspondence of officials, royal orders and proclamations, and instructions to officials.[62] Transcripts in the Manuscript Division of the Library of Congress include selections from the Florida series, *legajos* 1, 2, and 4, and royal orders, volumes 284 and 286, and the letter book of Bernardo de Gálvez. That repository also has a book of royal decrees, 1764–1790, of 141 pages.

Institutions in the United States having reproductions from French and Spanish archives and other interested institutions should sponsor the preparation of a union catalog of such reproductions. This catalog would enable researchers to find out where such reproductions are and would prevent further duplication of holdings.

59 / Duvon C. Corbitt, "Señor Joaquin Llaverias and the Archivo Nacional de Cuba," *Hispanic American Historical Review*, XX (May, 1940), 283–86.
60 / Sociedad Colombista Panamericana, *Documents Pertaining to the Floridas*.
61 / Duvon C. Corbitt, "Exploring the Southwest Territory in the Spanish Archives," *East Tennessee Historical Society Publications*, XXXVIII (1966), 109–18.
62 / Cuba, Archivo Nacional, "Inventario de las copias fotostáticas."

4

Documentary Publications

Affairs in French Louisiana were governed by ordinances issued by the king and decrees of the council of state. The Black Code promulgated in 1685 for the government of Negro slaves was enforced in both French and Spanish Louisiana and subsequently by the state of Louisiana until the Civil War. A copy of the code printed in Paris in 1735 is in the Biblioteca Parsoniana, formerly in New Orleans, now at the University of Texas. The same repository has *ordonnances du roi*, January 17, 1730–December 19, 1734, May 25, 1745–December 1, 1759; *arrêts du conseil d'état du roi*, February 7, 1730–October 15, 1759, February 9, 1765, December 14, 20, 1786; *déclarations du roi*, November 22, 1730, September 27, 1732, May 6, 1733, May 15, 1756, August 9, 1776; *reglements du roi*, June 22, 1733, August 23, 1739, September 22, 1748, June 26, 1756; and royal ordinances signed by the king, 1678–1776. Microfilm copies of these issuances were obtained by the Library of Congress from the collection in the Biblioteca Parsoniana.[1] The Louisiana archives collection in the Bancroft Library of the University of California also includes printed documents that have been removed from the collection and catalogued separately. A compilation of official French laws, orders, and regulations, 1696–1739, in two volumes, is in the Louisiana State Museum. A compilation of regulations, edicts, and decrees, published in Paris in 1765, was translated by the Survey of Federal Archives in Louisiana and copies were deposited in the Louisiana State University Department of Archives and Manuscripts and in the National Archives.[2]

In the nineteenth century, individuals were more active than govern-

1 / Library of Congress, *Microfilm Collection, Supplement*, 9, 23–25. For information regarding other publications including French administrative acts, see Beers, *French in North America*, 23–25.

2 / Survey of Federal Archives, Louisiana, Collection of Regulations, Edicts, and De-

ments in publishing compilations of documents relating to the Mississippi Valley. Joseph M. White, a Pensacola lawyer who had served as a member of the board of land commissioners in West Florida, was an early investigator. At the request of the United States attorney general, he made a compilation of French and Spanish ordinances affecting land titles in Florida and Louisiana that was published.[3] After two visits to Paris in the 1830s when he collected additional documents from the French archives, he published an enlarged collection.[4] Benjamin Franklin French, a Virginian who lived in Louisiana during the period 1830–1850, continued after moving to New York in 1850 the publication of a collection of documents made up largely of reprints and translations that had already appeared in French editions.[5] During a long term of employment with the Archives de la Marine et des Colonies in the Ministère de la Marine, Pierre Margry gathered from those archives material pertaining to North America. A six-volume compilation of French documents published by Margry contains in volumes I through III papers relating to La Salle and his discoveries in the Mississippi Valley and in volumes IV and V letters and reports of Iberville and Bienville, the colonizers of Louisiana.[6] Smaller numbers of the letters of governors Louis Billouart Kerlérec, Jean Jacques d'Abbadie and Charles Philippe Aubry are in the appendix of the work on those men by Marc de Villiers du Terrage.[7] Besides the French archives, the author used Kerlérec family papers in the Archives of the Département de Finistère. Chapters of the history by Villiers du Terrage on d'Abbadie, Aubry, and Pierre Clément de Laussat contain reproductions of some of their letters. Other letters of Kerlérec from August, 1753, to February, 1755, are in another compilation.[8]

---

crees Concerning the Commerce, Administration of Justice and the Policing of Louisiana and the French Colonies in America with the Black Code (Typescript; Paris, New Orleans, 1940).

3 / Joseph M. White (ed.), *Spanish and French Ordinances Affecting Land Titles in Florida and Other Territory of France and Spain, February 13, 1829*, in *House Documents*, 20th Cong., 2nd Sess., No. 121, reprinted in *American State Papers, Public Lands, (1789–1837)*, ed. Walter Lowrie and Matthew St. Clair Clarke (Washington, 1860), V, 631–774.

4 / White (ed.), *New Collection of Laws*.

5 / Benjamin F. French (ed.), *Historical Collections of Louisiana, Embracing Translations of Many Rare and Valuable Documents Relating to the Natural, Civil and Political History of That State* (New York, 1846–53); Benjamin F. French (ed.), *Historical Collections of Louisiana and Florida, Including Translations of Original Manuscripts Relating to Their Discovery and Settlement, with Numerous Historical and Biographical Notes* (New York, 1869, 1875). Both compilations were reprinted in New York by the AMS Press, 1976.

6 / Pierre Margry (ed.), *Découvertes et établissements des français dans l'ouest et dans le sud de l'Amérique Septentrionale (1614–1754): Mémoires et documents originaux* (Paris, 1876–86).

7 / Villiers du Terrage, *Louisiane française*.

8 / Theodore C. Pease and Ernestine Jenison (eds.), *Illinois on the Eve of the Seven Years' War, 1747–1755* (Springfield, Ill., 1940), 822–927, *passim*.

Of all the Gulf Coast states that were colonized by the French, only Mississippi published an extensive collection of documents from the French archives on its colonial period. Louisiana never had an organization strong enough to undertake the task. Alabama established a Department of Archives and History before Mississippi did, but it was never successful in acquiring the funding for undertaking a program of publishing documents on the colonial period. Since the capital of Louisiana was at Mobile until 1723 and what became Mississippi and Alabama was governed from New Orleans thereafter, documents on those states also concern Louisiana.

Besides the five-volume documentary compilation published by the Mississippi Department of Archives and History, smaller compilations on Mississippi have also been published. One of the compilers of that collection, using other transcripts in the same department, published a small collection of translations of documents relating to the regime of Antoine Crozat in Louisiana. It includes instructions to Governor Antoine de La Mothe Cadillac and Commissioner Duclos and their correspondence with the French government.[9] A report from Louisiana to the Company of the Indies is also in print.[10] Memoirs by the Reverend François Le Maire, the chaplain at Fort Louis at Mobile, supply data on life and occupations at that post and the surrounding country.[11] A memoir by Charles Le Gac, a director of the Company of the Indies, concerns events during his stay in Louisiana from 1718 to 1721.[12]

To regulate affairs in Louisiana during the Spanish rule, the governor, intendant, and superior council issued decrees, proclamations, ordinances, and regulations in broadside form. Many of these issuances have found their way into American libraries and archives. Bibliographies of the titles with repository locations of the issues during the late French years, the Spanish period, and the short Laussat period are in print.[13] The

9 / Albert G. Sanders (trans.) and Henry P. Dart (ed.), "Documents Concerning the Crozat Regime in Louisiana, 1712–1717," *Louisiana Historical Quarterly*, XV (July, 1932), 589–609; XVI (April, 1933), 293–308; XVII (April, July, 1934), 268–93, 452–73.

10 / Heloise H. Cruzat (trans.), "Louisiana in 1724: Banet's Report to the Company of the Indies, Dated Paris, December 20, 1724," *Louisiana Historical Quarterly*, XII (January 1929), 121–33.

11 / Jean Delanglez, S. J. (trans. and ed.), "M. Le Maire on Louisiana [January 15, 1714]," *Mid-America*, XIX (April, 1937), 124–54; Jean Delanglez, S. J. (ed.), "Mémoire [by François Le Maire] sur la Louisiane, 1717," *Revue d'histoire de l'Amérique française*, III (June, September, December, 1949), 94–110, 256–69, 423–46.

12 / Charles Le Gac, *Immigration and War: Louisiana, 1718–1721, from the Memoir of Charles Le Gac*, trans. and ed. Glenn R. Conrad (Lafayette, La., [1970]).

13 / McMurtrie, *Early Printing in New Orleans*; McMurtrie, *Louisiana Imprints*; Douglas C. McMurtrie, *Denis Braud, imprimeur du roi à la Nouvelle Orleans* (Paris, 1929). Titles of a few

United States government has reprinted Spanish and French ordinances affecting land titles.[14] Official acts of Louisiana printed before 1801 are in the Readex Microprint edition of early American imprints, published by the American Antiquarian Society. A collection of manuscript ordinances relating to Louisiana and other French colonies in America, 1678–1776, in the Biblioteca Parsoniana is in the Microfilm Collection of Early State Records in the Library of Congress. In the same collection is microfilm of broadsides of 1764–1782; broadsides of 1795–1803 are in various repositories.[15]

Compilations of English translations of Spanish documents relating to Louisiana have been published by a number of American scholars. A small collection assembled by Edmund C. Burnet from Spanish archives, the East Florida papers in the Library of Congress, and reproductions from Mexican archives includes correspondence of officials of Spanish Louisiana.[16] James A. Robertson brought together from repositories in the United States a collection of documents relating primarily to the transfer of Louisiana to the United States. Besides correspondence of Spanish officials, it includes letters between the French commissioner Laussat and Spanish and American officials, and between Laussat and Duc Denis Decrés, the French Ministre de la Marine.[17] Another important compilation of documents is that on Athanase de Mézières, the Spanish commandant at Natchitoches, edited by Herbert E. Bolton mainly from transcripts of documents in the Papeles de Cuba, the H. H. Bancroft Collection at the University of California, and the diocesan archives at San Antonio. Containing the correspondence of Mézières, the governors of Louisiana, and others, the compilation is significant for information about Indian trade and relations, the promotion of peace among the Indian tribes, agriculture, hunting, the control of trade, and exploration.[18]

Braud imprints not listed by McMurtrie are in Darnell Roaten, "Denis Braud: Some Imprints in the Bancroft Library," *Bibliographic Society of America Papers*, LXII (1968), 252–54.

14 / Matthew St. Clair Clarke (comp.), *Laws of the United States, Resolutions of Congress under the Confederation, Treaties, Proclamations, Spanish Regulations, and Other Documents Respecting the Public Lands* (Washington, D.C., 1828); *American State Papers, Miscellaneous Affairs (1789–1823)*, ed. Walter Lowrie and Matthew St. Clair Clarke (Washington, D.C., 1834); *American State Papers, Public Lands*, V, 631–774; White, *New Collection of Laws*.

15 / U.S. Library of Congress, "Codes and Compilations," in *A Guide to the Microfilm Collection of Early State Records* (Washington, D.C., 1950), 9, 62–63, 66–68.

16 / Edmund C. Burnet (ed.), "Papers Relating to Bourbon County, Georgia, 1785–1786," *American Historical Review*, XV (October, 1909, January, 1910), 66–111, 297–353.

17 / Robertson (ed.), *Louisiana Under the Rule of Spain*.

18 / Herbert E. Bolton (trans. and ed.), *Athanase de Mézières and the Louisiana-Texas Frontier, 1768–1780. Documents Published for the First Time, from the Original Spanish and French Manuscripts, Chiefly in the Archives of Mexico and Spain* (Cleveland, 1914).

Other historians with academic connections who specialized in the history of the Spanish in Louisiana have published collections of documents on a variety of subjects. A compilation of documents from the Archivo General de Indias and the Archivo Histórico Nacional edited by Arthur P. Whitaker shows changes that were made in the conduct of commerce in the provinces during the years 1778–1808.[19] In 1937 the editor of the East Tennessee Historical Society suggested to Duvon C. Corbitt, who was then connected with Candler College at Marianao, Cuba, that he undertake the preparation of the reproductions from the Spanish archives that had been deposited by Whitaker in the McClung Collection of the Lawson McGhee Library in Knoxville for inclusion in the society's *Publications*.[20] Thus began a long-lived project in which Corbitt, who was later connected with Columbia College in South Carolina and Asbury College in Wilmore, Kentucky, was associated with Roberta D. Corbitt, a professor of languages at the same institutions. The collection includes the correspondence of governors and other officials of Louisiana related to their efforts to sustain the Spanish claims to the region south of the Ohio River and east of the Mississippi. Corbitt also published another series of Louisiana documents obtained from the Archivo Nacional de Cuba.[21] Corbitt's collection consists of correspondence between Spanish officials and Panton, Leslie and Company and Alexander McGillivray.

Lawrence Kinnaird, professor of history at the University of California at Berkeley, using original Louisiana documents that had been purchased by Hubert H. Bancroft from Alphonse L. Pinart, the collector, and selected documents from the Bancroft Library's transcripts and photographic reproductions from Spanish archives, published an extensive collection of documents relating to Spain in the Mississippi Valley.[22] Besides correspondence, reports, and instructions on a variety of subjects, the collection includes censuses, acts of possession, lists of inhabitants, appointments, lists of trade goods, instructions to commandants, petitions, proclamations, and statements of crops produced. Two additional volumes for the years 1794–1805 were planned but have never been published. The royal patents raising Bernardo de Gálvez to a dukedom are printed with English translations, largely from reproductions in the His-

19 / Whitaker, *Commerical Policy of Spain in the Floridas*.
20 / Duvon C. Corbitt (ed.), and Roberta D. Corbitt (trans.), "Papers from the Spanish Archives Relating to Tennessee and the Old Southwest, 1783–1800," *East Tennessee Historical Society Publications*, nos. 9–50 (1937–78).
21 / Duvon C. Corbitt, "Papers Relating to the Georgia-Florida Frontier, 1784–1800," *Georgia Historical Quarterly*, XX–XXXV (1936–51).
22 / Kinnaird, *Spain in the Mississippi Valley*.

toric New Orleans Collection.[23] The patents recite his wartime achievements and provide a genealogical survey of his family.

A number of other compilations supply collections of documents in Spanish only. A compilation by Manuel Serrano y Sanz contains accounts, diaries, letters, and memoirs of the years 1762–1794 by some of the principal officials of the time.[24] Drawing upon numerous collections both in the United States and in other parts of the Americas, Jack D. L. Holmes has provided a collection of documents by important figures, largely for the later years of Spanish Louisiana, accompanied by biographical sketches and maps.[25] Holmes has also published a collection of documents on the charting of the coast of the Gulf of Mexico by the royal naval pilot.[26] Documents relating to the independence movement in the United States are presented in a volume by Parificación Medina Encina.[27]

The French and Spanish practice of taking censuses has left many enumerations of population that are useful for genealogy and local history. A number of early censuses of Louisiana from 1706 to 1741 have been reproduced from transcripts in the Louisiana Historical Society. Included are censuses of Natchitoches, New Orleans and neighboring places, Natchez, Dauphin Island, Mobile, and Pascagoula.[28] Enumerations of the numbers of people in the early settlements of Louisiana have been published from copies obtained from the Archives Nationales, Archives des Colonies, G1 and G13C. These include New Orleans and vicinity (1721, 1727, 1732), Cannes Brulées to the Tunica villages (1722), German villages (1724), New Orleans to the German villages (1722), Dauphin Island, Mobile, and Pascagoula (1725), Louisiana (1726), landowners (1731), and children baptized at New Orleans (1728, 1729).[29] A 1731 census of inhabitants on both sides of the Mississippi above and below New Orleans, includ-

23 / Ralph L. Woodward, Jr. (trans. and ed.), *Tribute to Don Bernardo de Gálvez* (New Orleans, 1979).

24 / Manuel Serrano y Sanz, *Documentos históricos de la Florida y la Luisiana, siglos XVI al XVIII* (Madrid, 1912).

25 / Jack D. L. Holmes (ed.), *Documentos inéditos para la historia de la Luisiana, 1792–1810* (Madrid, 1963).

26 / Jack D. L. Holmes (ed.), *José de Evía y sus reconocimientos del Golfo de México, 1783–1796* (Madrid, 1968).

27 / Parificación Medina Encina, *Documentos relativos a la independencia de Norteamérica existentes en archivos españoles, Vol. I, Archivo General de Indias, sección de gobierno, años 1752–1822* (Madrid, 1976).

28 / Jay K. Ditchy (trans.), "Early Census Tables of Louisiana," *Louisiana Historical Quarterly*, XIII (April, 1930), 205–29.

29 / Glenn R. Conrad (comp. and trans.), *The First Families of Louisiana* (Baton Rouge, 1970).

ing the German Coast, gives the last name of the settler along with the quantity of land and the last name of the person from whom it was purchased.[30] Another compilation contains a list of census tables with places of pubication and reproduces twenty-eight early censuses for Fort Maurepas, Biloxi, Fort Louis at Mobile, New Orleans, and along the banks of the Mississippi River.[31]

Some censuses of settlements during the Spanish period are also in print. Lists of Acadians at different settlements in Louisiana for the years 1758–1788 and lists of Acadian families who left France for Louisiana in 1785 include some for Fort Toulouse, Kabahanosse, St. Gabriel, Baton Rouge, and Natchez.[32] Another collection shows, for settlers along the Bayou Lafourche in Ascension Parish, information on family members, arpents of land owned, and numbers of domestic animals for several years between 1770 and 1798.[33] Both compilations are indexed by name. A study of the population of Louisiana based upon reports in Spanish archives presents data from seventy-four full and partial population reports from sixteen communities of Louisiana and West Florida.[34] A list of the censuses with title and date is in print.[35]

Passenger lists of immigrants transported to Louisiana are another valuable source for genealogists. An attempt to publish a complete compilation of such lists for the years 1717–1732 includes lists of civilians, military officers, and soldiers, with citations to the sources in the Archives des Colonies.[36] A list of passenger lists shows the names of the vessels, their captains, their ports of departure, the names of passengers with their occupations, and the names of concessionaires and the number and type of persons in their parties.[37] Other early passenger lists reproduced from copies in the Louisiana Historical Society supply the names of persons transported to Louisiana on several ships by the Company of

30 / Irna A. Centanni and Sidney L. Villeré, "Early Census of the Louisiana Province," *New Orleans Genesis*, V (June, September, 1966), 221–25, 349–51, VI (January, 1967), 35–41.

31 / Charles R. Maduell, Jr. (comp. and trans.), *The Census Tables for the French Colony of Louisiana from 1699 through 1732* (Baltimore, 1972).

32 / Jacqueline K. Voorhies (comp. and trans.), *Some Late Eighteenth-Century Louisianians: Census Records of the Colony, 1758–1796* (Lafayette, La., 1973), 421–528.

33 / Albert J. Robichaux, Jr. (comp., trans., and ed.), *Louisiana Census and Militia Lists, 1770–1789, Volume I, German Coast, New Orleans, Below New Orleans and Lafourche, Volume II, Colonial Settlers Along the Bayou Lafourche* (Harvey, La., 1973–74).

34 / Antonio Acosta Rodríquez, *La población de Luisiana española (1763–1803)* (Madrid, 1979).

35 / Jack D. L. Holmes, "A New Look at Spanish Louisiana Census Accounts: The Recent Historiography of Antonio Acosta," *Louisiana History*, XXI (Winter, 1980), 77–86.

36 / Conrad (comp. and trans.), *First Families of Louisiana.*

37 / Neil J. Toups, *Mississippi Valley Pioneers* (Lafayette, La., [1970]), 23–127.

the West. These lists contain the names of company officials and clerks, military officers, soldiers, and their wives, concessionaires to whom land grants had been given, miners, tobacco workers, and servants.[38] Another publication contains the names of German and Swiss immigrants who early in 1721 embarked on five ships from the port of L'Orient for Louisiana to work for the Company of the Indies.[39] The names of the numerous places from which these passengers were recruited are shown, and the volume is indexed by names of persons and places. A passenger list of the *Beaumont*, which transported Acadians from Nantes to Louisiana in 1785, shows the names by families, giving the name of the husband, his occupation, and the names of his wife and children and their ages.[40] A list of ninety persons transported to Louisiana for settlement on the grants of Bastrop and Morehouse in the district of Ouachita shows the names and ages of all members of the families.[41]

Rosters of the soldiers and the recruits, sometimes accompanied by their wives, transported to Louisiana have been published.[42] A number of ship lists, which usually contain personal information about the passengers and sometimes their accompanying wives, have been published.[43] Passenger lists of volunteer recruits from the Canary Islands are also in print.[44] A roll of the French soldiers who sailed on the *Touneur* from La Rochelle in 1751 contains the names of 160 men and their wives.[45]

Lists of military personnel who served in Louisiana are also in print. An alphabetical list of troops gives personal and service information.[46] Another general roll of French troops, 1720–1770, shows the disposition of many of the soldiers who arrived in the colony during the years

38 / Albert L. Dart (trans.), "Ship Lists of Passengers Leaving France for Louisiana, 1718–1724," *Louisiana Historical Quarterly*, XIV (October, 1931), 516–20, XV (January, July, 1932), 68–77, 453–67, XXI (October, 1938), 965–78.

39 / Alice D. Forsyth and Earline L. Zeringue (comps. and trans.), *German "Pest Ships,"* 1720–1721 (New Orleans, 1969).

40 / Harold Préjean, "The Passenger List of the *Beaumont*," *Attakapas Gazette*, VIII (December, 1973), 165–73.

41 / Luis M. Pérez, "French Immigrants to Louisiana, 1796–1800," *Southern History Association Publications*, XI (March, 1907), 106–12.

42 / Winston De Ville, *Louisiana Colonials: Soldiers, and Vagabonds* (Baltimore: Genealogical Publishing Co., 1963).

43 / Winston De Ville, *Louisiana Recruits, 1752–1758: Ship Lists of Troops from the Independant* [sic] *Companies of the Navy Destined for Service in the French Colony of Louisiana* (Cottonport, La., 1973).

44 / Sidney L. Villeré, *The Canary Islands Migration to Louisiana, 1778–1783. The History and Passenger Lists of the Isleños Volunteer Recruits and Their Families* (New Orleans, [1971]).

45 / Winston De Ville (trans.), "French Soldiers in Louisiana—1751," *Louisiana Genealogical Register*, XV (September, 1968), 85–87.

46 / Winston De Ville, *Louisiana Troops, 1720–1770* (Fort Worth, [1967]).

1717–1732.[47] A list of French officers of 1750 is printed from Governor Vaudreuil's papers.[48] Lists and muster rolls of militia, 1765–1789, for New Orleans, the German Coast, Opelousas, Attakapas, Pointe Coupee, St. Louis, and Fort San Carlos Principe de Asturias are in print.[49] Another compilation contains an alphabetical list of service records of the Louisiana infantry regiment, showing for each serviceman his name, date of service, archival repository, date and place of birth, age, marital status, rank, and regiment. Service sheets of militiamen in the same compilation show name, dates of service, place of birth, and age.[50] Besides the censuses referred to above Albert J. Robichaux, Jr., obtained from the Archivo General de Indias in Seville copies of militia lists of 1770–1785 that he published. These include militia lists of New Orleans for 1770, the German Coast for 1770, and the parish of St. Charles des Allemands for 1785.[51] An Attakapas militia list of 1785 is also in print.[52]

With the assistance of Irene A. Wright, Charles Robert Churchill, who became president of the Louisiana Society of the Sons of the American Revolution in 1916, obtained materials from the Papeles de Cuba in the Archivo General de Indias relating to men who served under General Gálvez in the Spanish-English war of 1779–1783 in Louisiana, Alabama, and Florida.[53] Copies of the microfilm are in the Howard-Tilton Library of Tulane University, the Louisiana State University Library, and the Stephens Library of the University of Southwestern Louisiana. Typescripts of the compilation are in the Howard-Tilton Library, the D.A.R. Library in Washington, D.C., the Louisiana State Library, and the Library of the S.A.R., Louisiana Division. Lists of men prepared from the Churchill materials by Louis C. Landry, Jr., are published for the Acadian Coast, Attakapas, Iberville, and Opelousas. Other excerpts from the Churchill materials supply the names of the servicemen in the different companies.[54]

47 / Conrad (comp. and trans.), *First Families of Louisiana*, 155–239.
48 / Winston De Ville, "Louisiana Officers in 1750," *Louisiana Genealogical Register*, XVII (December, 1970), 314, 321.
49 / Voorhies, *Some Late Eighteenth-Century Louisianians*, 89–161.
50 / Jack D. L. Holmes, *Honor and Fidelity: The Louisiana Infantry Regiment and the Louisiana Militia Companies, 1766–1821* (Birmingham, Ala., 1965), 89–161, 161–258.
51 / Robichaux, *Louisiana Census and Militia Lists*, 3–90.
52 / "Attakapas Militia List," *Louisiana Genealogical Register*, IX (September, 1962), 39–40.
53 / Jack D. L. Holmes, "The Historiography of the American Revolution in Louisiana," *Louisiana History*, XIX (Summer, 1978), 310 and n. 6.
54 / Louis C. Landry, Jr., "Louisiana Colonial Militia Lists," *Louisiana Genealogical Register*, IX (June–December, 1962), 20–25, 33–40, 51–54, X (March, 1963), 11–16. The Attakapas list is also in Mary E. Sanders, *Records of Attakapas District, La., 1739–1811* ([Lafayette, La.], 1962), 42–45. A roster of army regulars is in Charles R. Churchill, "The Gálvez Expedition, 1779–1783, Register of Infantry Regiment of Louisiana, Roster," *New Orleans Genesis*, XVI (September, 1976), 321–23; see also Pearl M. Segura, "Infantry Regiment of Louisiana. Book

Journals, diaries, memoirs, and narratives provide information supplementary to that found in official records and other sources. These accounts were written by army and navy officers, civilian officials, missionaries, priests, and other travelers. Some were placed in archives and manuscript collections and have been found and published. Some of these travel accounts were published soon after they were written, and of these some have been republished. Others remain preserved in archives and manuscript collections. These accounts are too numerous to be taken up individually, but information regarding them can be found in various bibliographies.[55] Numerous compilations of documents discussed in Henry P. Beers' *The French in North America* also contain journals. Other compilations of Spanish documents by Louis Houck, Lawrence Kinnaird, the Mississippi Department of Archives and History, and Abraham P. Nasatir also contain travel narratives. A collection by Newton D. Mereness contains a journal by Diron d'Artaguette, inspector general of Louisiana, for 1722 and 1723, a journal of Antoine Bonnefoy's captivity among the Cherokees, in 1741 and 1742, and De Beauchamps' journal of his journey to the Choctaws, 1746.[56] The titles of other more recently published travel accounts can be found only in general bibliographies, library catalogs, and publishers' catalogs. Less extensive is a historical account of the operations of Spanish war vessels on the Mississippi River, accompanied by diaries concerning their voyages by Pierre Rousseau, Juan B. Barnó Ferrúsola, and Manuel Gayoso de Lemos.[57] Captain Pierre Rousseau's log of the *Galiot* from January 5 to March 25, 1793, is also in print.[58]

---

of Life and Customs and Services of Commissioned Officers, First Sergeants, and Cadets of Said Regular Regiment up to the End of December of 1781," *Louisiana Genealogical Register,* VII (March–December, 1960), 9–12, 24–26, 41–43, 57–58, IX (March, December, 1962), 7–9, 55–56.

55 / Thomas D. Clark (ed.), *The Formative Years, 1527–1783: From the Spanish Exploration Through the American Revolution* (Norman, Okla., 1956) and *The Expanding South, 1750–1825: The Ohio Valley and the Cotton Frontier* (Norman, Okla., 1959). Vols. II and III of Clark (ed.), *Travels in the Old South: A Bibliography;* Bernard Faÿ, *Bibliographie critique des ouvrages français relatifs aux États-Unis (1770–1800)* (Paris, 1925); Robert R. Hubach, *Early Midwestern Travel Narratives: An Annotated Bibliography, 1634–1850* (Detroit, 1961); John F. McDermott (ed.), *Travelers on the Western Frontier* (Urbana, Ill., 1970); William Matthews, *American Diaries: An Annotated Bibliography of American Diaries Written Prior to the Year 1861* (Berkeley and Los Angeles, 1945); William Matthews, *Canadian Diaries and Autobiographies* (Berkeley and Los Angeles, 1950); Frank Monaghan, *French Travellers in the United States, 1765–1932: A Bibliography* (New York, 1961).

56 / Newton D. Mereness (ed.), *Travels in the American Colonies* (New York, 1916), 15–94, 239–55, 259–97.

57 / Nasatir, *Spanish War Vessels*, 149–341.

58 / Raymond J. Martínez, *Pierre George Rousseau, Commanding General of the Galleys of the Mississippi* (New Orleans, 1964), 46–74.

5

ફ

Manuscript Collections

Manuscript repositories in Louisiana and other places in the United States have numerous collections of papers that add significantly to the sources for the history of colonial Louisiana. The Louisiana State Museum, created by an act of the general assembly of the state in 1906, has extensive collections of published books, archives, transcriptions of archives, and manuscripts, in addition to museum objects. In 1977 the Louisiana Historical Center was created as the custodial department of the museum. A collection of Mississippi Valley French manuscripts, consisting of original documents on French colonial administration, includes decrees relative to the commerce of Louisiana in 1722, the *Code Noir* of 1724, and the letters patent issued to Antoine Crozat in 1712 and to the Company of the West in 1717. The correspondence of Charles Philippe Aubry, 1768–1769, in two volumes, relates to the period when he was acting governor of Louisiana. Nicolas Denis Foucoult's papers concern his participation with others in the rebellion against the government in 1768. Other items include documents relating to the de la Ronde family baptismal certificates. Materials relating to French and Spanish governors in several collections include commissions, orders, proclamations, and letters.[1] Other materials include reports by Echavarria, 1722, Bernardo de Gálvez, 1777, and Luis de Unzaga, 1772; Alexandro O'Reilly's orders relating to St. John the Baptist Church, 1770; a petition of P. Trepagnier to be relieved of military service, 1774; and a table of the Spanish military force in Louisiana and Florida, 1774. A collection of papers for 1765–1803 in the Louisiana State Museum includes junta items relating to the expul-

1 / Louisiana State Museum, *Biennial Report*, 1912–14, p. 76, 1914–15, pp. 39–40, 1926–27, p. 23, 1930–31, pp. 73–74.

sion of Antonio de Ulloa and others in 1769, an account of Alexandro O'Reilly's arrival, 1769, and other documents concerning Unzaga and Gálvez, 1770–1792.

Baron Joseph Xavier Delfan de Pontalba, a native of New Orleans, was educated in France, served there in the French army, and returned to Louisiana in 1782. He married in 1789 Jeanne Louise Le Breton, a niece of Celeste de Macarty Miró, the wife of Governor Estevan Miró. Madame Pontalba left New Orleans for Madrid in 1795 to be with Madame Miró, who had become ill following the death of her husband. Pontalba himself remained in Louisiana for a while longer. Letters written in journal form by him to his wife from February 24 to November 10, 1796, were preserved at the family home in Senlis, France. A translation of the 1796 letters was made by the Survey of Federal Archives from copies loaned by George C. H. de Kernion.[2] The Pontalba collection also includes twenty letters for 1792 and two for 1795; those for 1793–1794 have disappeared.

The papers of Governor Miró were preserved by his widow after his death and became part of the Pontalba family archives at Senlis, France. Transcripts of the Miró papers, 1787–1789, comprising fifty items, are in the Louisiana State Museum. Microfilm of Pontalba-Almonester-Miró papers, 1792–1796, in seven reels, is in the Louisiana State Museum. That repository also has the transcriptions and translations of the dispatches of the Spanish governors, 1766–1796, prepared by the Survey of Federal Archives. The James Wilkinson papers, containing eleven items, concern the Aaron Burr conspiracy and the Spanish in West Florida. Commissions, orders, proclamations, and letters of the governor of Louisiana are in other collections of papers in the museum. Other microfilm holdings include the records of Avoyelles Parish, 1793–1796, St. Charles Parish, 1740–1792, and St. Landry Parish, 1764–1793, in three reels, nine reels, and eight reels, respectively.

The Louisiana State Seminary, established at Pineville in 1860, moved in 1869 to Baton Rouge and was renamed the Louisiana State University and Agricultural and Mechanical College. Edwin A. Davis of the university's history department traveled around the state in the early 1930s collecting manuscripts for deposit at the university's library. In 1935 he was relieved of half his teaching duties and placed in charge of a Department of Archives and Manuscripts in the library. An act of the state legislature on July 7, 1936, authorized the university to receive and collect public records and documents and materials bearing on the history of the state.

---

2 / Survey of Federal Archives, Louisiana, The Letters of Baron Joseph X. Pontalba to His Wife, 1796 (Typescript; New Orleans, 1939).

Since that time the department has accessioned a variety of materials on the colonial period.

The department's principal collection on the French period is the writings of Jean Charles Pradel. He arrived in Louisiana as an army officer in 1713 and, except for visits to France during 1720–1722 and 1727–1728 to recover his health and other visits in 1731 and 1750, lived there until his death in 1764. He served in Upper Louisiana, at Natchez, and at New Orleans and acquired a plantation opposite New Orleans. He wrote many letters to relatives in Uzerche, Bas Limousin, France, describing conditions in Louisiana. The collection also includes an inventory of the property of Nicolas Denis Foucoult, 1769, and copies of materials on his life. These materials were turned over to A. Baillardel and A. Prioult, who used them to prepare a book on eighteenth-century Louisiana containing Pradel's letters from 1714, which provide descriptions of the military, civil, economic, and social life of the colony.[3] The collection was acquired by Louisiana State University.

Materials in the Louisiana State University Library on the Spanish period are more voluminous. The papers of governors include those of Bernardo de Gálvez, 1778–1781, in 70 items; papers of Estevan Miró, 1782–1791, in 8 items; papers of Francisco Luis Hector, baron de Carondelet, 1791–1796, in 28 items; Manuel Gayoso de Lemos letters, 1792–1799, in 42 items; memoir of Louis Milfort, 1775–1802; regulations and royal tariffs for the free commerce of Spain to Louisiana, 1778, in two volumes; Padre Antonio de Sedella letters, 1785–1816, and the constitution of the Charity Hospital at New Orleans, 1793; the papers of Manuel Lopez, 1802–1835, in 26 items, concerning the administration of the royal warehouse at New Orleans and his duties later as justice of the peace of East Baton Rouge Parish. Transcriptions of the documents of Nicolas Forstall, 1779–1795, in 2 items, concern his administration of the town of New Iberia, founded in 1779. Another collection consists of the papers of Captain Antonio P. Walsh, an officer in the Mississippi River squadron. The papers of William C. C. Claiborne, 1804–1805, 1812–1813, in two pieces, one volume, concern the period when he was governor of the Territory of Orleans and the state of Louisiana. The extensive Charles E. A. Gayarré collection, 1720–1895, in five volumes with 588 items, contains documents of earlier family members who held official positions under the Spanish government.[4]

---

3 / A. Baillardel and A. Prioult, *Le Chevalier de Pradel: Vie d'un colon français en Louisiane au xviiiᵉ siècle d'apres sa correspondance et celle de sa famille* (Paris, 1928).

4 / Coutts and Whitley, "Inventory of Sources," 213.

Tulane University, established in New Orleans in 1834, began collecting manuscripts about a hundred years later. The university completed a new fireproof library building in 1940 to house these historic manuscripts safely. A memoir by Charles Le Gac, who served as a director of the Company of the West in Louisiana from August, 1718, to March, 1721, supplies information on conditions in the colony. This document was one of the translations made by the Survey of Federal Archives. Several other early documents in the library, dated from 1682 to 1737, were also translated by the survey and were given the title "Louisiana Indian Miscellany."

The Favrots, father and son, served in the army in the Mississippi Valley in the eighteenth century. Claude Joseph Favrot took part in the campaigns against the Natchez and the Chickasaws and commanded Tunica, Pointe Coupee, Balize, Natchitoches, and Fort de Chartres. Pierre Joseph Favrot served at Arkansas Post and in Santo Domingo before going in 1772 to Rochefort, France, where he became a lieutenant attached to the garrison. In 1778, after obtaining a commission as a captain in the Spanish infantry regiment of Louisiana and changing his name to Pedro, he reported for duty to Governor Gálvez. He served successively at Baton Rouge, New Orleans, Mobile, again at New Orleans, and from 1792 to 1794 at Natchez and continued in the service of Spain until 1803.[5] The Favrot papers were stored in old trunks in the attics of successive generations of the family until they were deposited about 1910 in the Louisiana State Museum. The Favrot family papers, 1700–1897, comprise 909 items and include letters, diaries, pamphlets, military commissions, and orders. Pedro Favrot, while a young man in France in 1773, had collected copies of baptismal, marriage and burial records relating to his forebears; these records are also in the collection.

The Favrot papers were transferred in 1948 to the Howard-Tilton Memorial Library of Tulane University. The Favrot papers for 1669–1803, containing 825 items, comprise less than half the total collection, which extends to 1937. The Louisiana Historical Records Survey had begun transcribing the Favrot papers while they were still in the Louisiana State Museum, and this task was continued after the transfer to Tulane. Between 1940 and 1942, the Historical Records Survey issued seven volumes of transcripts in mimeographed form for the years 1695–1803.[6] These volumes constitute one of the most important collections of documents for

5 / Helen H. Parkhurst, "Don Pedro Favrot, a Creole Pepys, New Orleans, La.," *Louisiana Historical Quarterly*, XXVIII (July, 1945), 680–81.

6 / Historical Records Survey, Louisiana, Transcriptions of Manuscript Collections in Louisiana, no. 1, The Favrot Papers [1695–1769] (New Orleans, 1940–42).

colonial Louisiana, including letters from several Spanish governors and other officials. The official letters and military instructions in the Favrot papers, August 16, 1734–August 10, 1799, consisting of 104 items, are in the Microfilm Collection of Early State Records in the Library of Congress.[7] Also included are letters from governors Bernardo de Gálvez and the Baron de Carondelet and other officials, including the Chevalier de Kerlérec, Carlos de Grand Pré, Juan Ventura Morales, Andrés López y Armesto, José de Gálvez, and other prominent persons. The Rosemunde E. and Emile Kuntz Collection of French and Spanish manuscripts dating from 1655 was presented to Tulane University in 1954 by Felix H. Kuntz as a memorial to his parents. These manuscripts concern the families of Kernion, Bouligny, D'Auterive, d'Auberville, Maison Rouge, Coulanges, Grand Pré, Villemont, Villars, the governments of New Orleans and Louisiana, the Company of the Indies, and the revolution of 1768.[8]

Collections of other families' papers from the Spanish period are also at Tulane. Papers of Spanish governors include those of Estevan Miró, 1779–1791, containing 49 items; those of Bernardo de Gálvez, 1779–1781, containing 17 items; of Baron de Carondelet, 1793–1797, 85 items; and of Manuel Gayoso de Lemos, 1797–1799, 10 items. The papers of the Marquis de Casa Calvo, 1800–1803, contain 10 items and concern the period when he was acting governor of Louisiana following the death of Manuel Gayoso de Lemos in July, 1799, and later when he acted as commissioner for the transfer of Louisiana to the United States. The Montegut family papers include some documents of Dr. Joseph Montegut in his position as chief surgeon of the Spanish royal hospital at New Orleans and other papers of Joseph Montegut, Jr., who was secretary to the intendant in New Orleans.[9] The Bouligny-Baldwin papers, dating from 1710, include some of Francisco Bouligny, who was prominent in the government. There are also copies of the Survey of Federal Archives transcriptions and translations of the dispatches of the Spanish governors, 1766–1791, and microfilm of letters of the Baron Joseph Xavier de Pontalba to Governor Miró, 1792–1795, and to his wife, 1796. Another collection is the W. C. C. Claiborne papers, 1800–1818, with 18 items.

Besides materials described elsewhere in this volume, the New Orleans Public Library has other holdings. Miscellaneous Spanish and French documents, 1782–1816, in four volumes, and English typescripts of the same are useful for research in such topics as genealogy, Negro

7 / U.S. Library of Congress, *Microfilm Collection, Supplement*, 62.
8 / Guillermo Nañez Falcón (comp.), *The Rosemunde E. and Emile Kuntz Collection: A Catalogue of the Manuscripts and Printed Ephemera* (New Orleans, 1981).
9 / *National Union Catalog of Manuscripts*, 1964, entry 1212.

history, the cabildo, flood control, censuses, and other matters. During the French regime Gilbert Antoine de St. Maxent was a merchant in New Orleans and a militia officer; after participating in the Spanish campaign against Mobile, he became commandant of the militia in Louisiana.[10] Documents pertaining to the estate and succession of St. Maxent, 1784–1803, in five volumes, include inventories, wills, testimony, marriage records, acts of sale, and other papers concerning his estate and heirs.[11] Private dispatches of Estevan Miró are for the years 1784–1794. A census of November 6, 1791, in one volume, is also on microfilm. Other items include lawsuits, 1790–1800, in one volume; the proceedings by Francisco Blache to execute the last will and testament of Luis Blondeau, 1799–1803, in one volume, and the proceedings by Lorenzo Sigur against Isabel Larroche for the settlement of certain accounts, 1795–1796, also in one volume. The papers of William C. C. Claiborne, 1804–1814, containing 122 items, concern the period when he was governor of the Territory of Orleans and the state of Louisiana and include letters and messages from the mayor and city council of New Orleans, financial reports, bills, and communications from federal officials.[12]

The Historic New Orleans Collection, established in 1966 by General and Mrs. L. Kemper Williams to house their own art collection, opened in New Orleans in 1974 and also has acquired manuscripts as well as archival reproductions. These acquisitions include proclamations of General O'Reilly, September 11 and December 7, 1769, papers relating to the administration of Bernardo de Gálvez, 1782–1787, and papers of General Claude Victor, 1802–1804, containing thirty-eight items. The papers of General Victor, who had been designated by Napoleon to command the French occupying force, include papers of Decrés, minister of the French Navy, and Laussat, the French commissioner for the transfer of Louisiana to the United States.

Repositories outside of Louisiana also have manuscripts relating to the French and Spanish Louisiana regimes. A fifteen-page memoir on Louisiana, dated April 19, 1719, in the Bancroft Library of the University of California reports on the trade and organization of the colony at the time of the liquidation of Crozat's monopoly. An account of a voyage from La Rochelle to Louisiana in 1720 by the Sieur Fourcade, a surgeon, is in the repository of the Chicago Historical Society. The same repository

10 / James J. Coleman, Jr., *Gilbert Antoine de St. Maxent; the Spanish-Frenchman of New Orleans* (New Orleans, 1968), 81–82, 105, 111, 114.

11 / Information from copies of catalog cards of manuscript collections, supplied by the New Orleans Public Library, is in Beers Correspondence.

12 / National Union Catalog of Manuscripts, 1965, entry 1699.

has a journal of a trip by M. Régis de la Roullet in 1732 from Mobile to the Choctaw country and down the Pearl River to New Orleans. The society also has an extensive collection of James Wilkinson papers, 1779–1823, with 650 items, and in the Charles F. Gunther Collection are documents relating to the transfer of Louisiana in 1803. The Otto L. Schmidt Collection in the society's holdings contains a memoir by Le Page du Pratz, a contemporary patent under which La Salle explored the Illinois country, several letters of Henri de Tonti, and letters of Louis Jolliet to his family. The Edward Gay Mason Collection, also one of the society's holdings, contains unpublished documents relating to the Mississippi Valley signed by the governor of New France, by explorers of the Illinois country, and by the king of France and documents signed by Claude Jean Allouez, by Louis Jolliet, and by Robert Cavelier de La Salle.

The Edward E. Ayer Collection in the Newberry Library in Chicago also contains some memoirs relating to the Mississippi Valley. These include La Salle's account of the discovery of the Mississippi River in 1682 and his return to Quebec in 1683; a memoir by Jean Baptiste Le Moyne on the Indians of Louisiana, no date; a memoir by the Sieur de Beranger on surveys in Louisiana during the years 1697–1722; and Pierre Le Moyne's letter and journal of his voyage of 1698–1699 to Louisiana and his return to Rochefort. Other items include M. Roussel's journal of a voyage in 1718 and G. M. Butel Dumont's memoir of an engineer officer, no date.[13] The papers of Jean Frédéric Maurepas, comte de Phelypeau, 1731–1751, in three feet, in the Cornell University Library concern his activities as the French minister of the navy and the secretary of state and relate in part to American affairs.[14] Letters of members of the Maurepas family, 1720–1738, commenting on the administration of Louisiana are in the James Ford Bell Collection in the University of Minnesota Library. Correspondence of both French and Spanish governors of Louisiana is included in the papers of Major General Thomas Gage, commanding general of the British forces in North America, 1763–1773, in the William L. Clements Library of the University of Michigan. As the representative of Philadelphia merchants in Kentucky and as a U.S. Army officer after 1791 and the commanding general of the U.S. Army in the West after 1796, James Wilkinson engaged in intrigues with the Spanish governors in New Orleans, corresponding with and receiving payments from them. One small collection of Wilkinson letters, 1784–1811, containing 21 items, is in the holdings of the Kentucky Historical Society.

13 / Ruth L. Butler, *A Check List of Manuscripts in the Edward E. Ayer Collection* (Chicago, 1937), 33–36.
14 / *National Union Catalog of Manuscripts,* 1964, entry 956.

Although it had long had manuscripts in its custody, the Library of Congress did not have a manuscript division until 1897, when the library occupied a new building. As a federally operated repository, the Library of Congress has acquired manuscripts relating to all parts of the country—some by gift, others by purchase. In its Peter Force Papers is the Manning Ferguson Force Collection of papers relating to the exploration of the Mississippi River, 1678–1846, in one volume. The collection includes letters, patents, commissions, pamphlets, maps, and other papers. Items purchased at a Henkel sale in 1912 include Baton Rouge district land concessions, 1785–1798, in one volume, and regulations concerning general police, June, 1795, also in one volume. Other materials include Jean-Baptiste Bénard de la Harpe's *journal historique*, 1724; documents on French and Spanish management of Louisiana, 1731–1799; manuscripts of 1780 on Louisiana and Florida; surveyors' records, including correspondence of François Gonsolin, Louis LeBlanc, Carlos Laveau Trudeau, on the Attakapas district; a record book of Spanish land grants, 1785–1799, of 186 pages; a surveyor's notebook, 1795–1797; thirty-six manuscript plats for land grants located mostly in the Baton Rouge district; vital statistics from a Bible and other sources; and a few papers each for Bernardo de Gálvez, 1776–1786, and Manuel Gayoso de Lemos, 1794–1797; correspondence of American and French officials relating to the purchase of Louisiana, 1803–1804, in fifteen boxes, available on five reels of microfilm. The papers of Oliver Pollock, 1767–1788, containing about 290 items, include correspondence and accounts concerning his activities as an agent of the Continental Congress in New Orleans and Havana from 1775 to 1781 and his commercial dealings with merchants in Natchez, Pensacola, Philadelphia, and Richmond. Xerox copies of some of the Pollock papers are in the Louisiana State University Department of Archives and Manuscripts. The James Wilkinson papers, 1780–1824, with 29 items, include correspondence on affairs in the West with W. C. C. Claiborne, Caesar Rodney, Winthrop Sargent, Colonel Thomas H. Cushing, and others and an orderly book containing entries at Fort Washington at Cincinnati, New Orleans, and in Missouri and Mississippi.[15]

Other repositories also hold important materials relating to Louisiana. William C. C. Claiborne was appointed by President Jefferson on October 31, 1803, to serve as commissioner with General Wilkinson to receive Louisiana from the French. Designated on the same date as temporary governor of the Orleans Territory, Claiborne continued in office as

15 / U.S. Library of Congress, Manuscript Division, Dictionary Catalog of Collections (unpublished catalog in the library).

governor of the Louisiana Territory until 1817. His executive journals and letter books, 1798–1817, contained in fifteen volumes in the Mississippi Department of Archives and History include seven volumes relating to his services as governor of the Orleans Territory and the Louisiana Territory. Other correspondence and papers, 1801–1810, are in one box in the same repository, which has published a voluminous collection of his letters.[16] Albert Gallatin served as secretary of the treasury from 1801 to 1814. A collection of his personal and official correspondence and papers, 1780–1849, in twenty-eight feet and seventeen volumes in the New York Historical Society repository, includes material on the purchase of Louisiana and correspondence with many officials, including Claiborne and land officials. The same repository has a twenty-four-page document by M. Badins, 1803, supplying descriptive data on the Ouachita country.

Several collections in the New York Public Library concern Louisiana. That repository purchased in 1932 the letter books of John Fitzpatrick, 1768–1790, in three volumes; Fitzpatrick was a merchant at Manchac, Louisiana, who traded in slaves, tobacco, peltry, mules, and other items and who suffered depredations by both the Spanish and the Americans during the Revolution.[17] Other materials include some correspondence relating to John Law and his Mississippi scheme; M. Monteil's *journal de dépenses de la colonie de la Nouvelle Orleans*, 1766, in 174 pages; and James Wilkinson papers, 1777–1821, containing nineteen items.

Edward Alexander Parsons, a wealthy collector of New Orleans who purchased orientalia and classical and renaissance materials as well as incunabula, was also interested in documents and early manuscripts of Louisiana. Housed in his home at 5 Rosa Park, New Orleans, the collection became known as the Biblioteca Parsoniana. It includes appointments of officers in New Orleans by the Company of the Indies, documents and letters of French and Spanish governors, 1699–1803, royal decrees, orders, proclamations, and regulations, Governor O'Reilly's Black Code, Spanish royal orders, papers on Bernardo de Gálvez' expedition against Pensacola in 1781, governors' proclamations, a census of 1785, reports of the *alcaldes* of New Orleans, payrolls of the guard of the night watch, a register of chimneys in the Vieux Carré, letters of Padre Antonio de Sedella, a secret report on the Floridas made to Napoleon, a contract of marriage, sales of real property and slaves, and letters and documents of Kerlérec and Laussat.[18] The manuscript ordinances signed by the king of

16 / Dunbar Rowland (ed.), *Official Letter Books.*
17 / *National Union Catalog of Manuscripts,* 1969, entry 843.
18 / Historical Records Survey, Louisiana, *Guide to Manuscript Collections in Louisiana* (University, La., 1940), 1.

France, 1678–1776, and the Black Code published in Paris in 1735 have been microfilmed.[19] Parsons sold his collection to the University of Texas in 1958.

Another private collector opened the Thomas Gilcrease Institute of American History and Art in Tulsa, Oklahoma, in 1949. The people of that city voted a bond issue in 1954 to acquire the institute. Its extensive collection of books and rare documents includes materials on Spanish explorations, among which is the treaty negotiated by Governor Manuel Gayoso de Lemos with the Chickasaws and Choctaws at Natchez in 1792.

The papers of Daniel Parker, adjutant and inspector general of the U.S. Army, 1810–1845, in the Historical Society of Pennsylvania repository in Philadelphia include correspondence of Wilkinson, Claiborne, and other prominent persons connected with the affairs of Louisiana, Alabama, and the Floridas. Other papers concern the case of Wilkinson versus Daniel Clark, Louisiana merchant and territorial delegate, 1788–1808, containing three hundred items. Other Wilkinson items of the period 1789–1792 in the papers of Reed & Forde, Philadelphia merchants, concern trade on the Mississippi and in the Spanish country.[20] Additional correspondence of Albert Gallatin, 1801–1811, in three boxes, further documents his relations as secretary of the treasury with other officials. James Wilkinson papers, 1777–1821, with eleven items, are in the New York State Library in Albany, New York.

Guy Soniat du Fossat, on a visit to Paris in 1900, was invited by his cousin, Henri de Pousayues, a general in the French army, to visit the Chateau du Fossat, the family home on a stream called the Lot near the junction of the Garonne. The general opened rooms containing heirlooms of the family, among which were papers and documents pertaining to the American branch of the family. On a promise to return them, these papers were taken to New Orleans, where at the suggestion of Professor Alcée Fortier a historical narrative that was among the documents was translated.[21] Its author, Guy de Soniat du Fossat, had served in the French army in Louisiana from 1751, transferred to the Spanish service in 1767, and retired in 1772 to become a planter. François, a son who had also served as a Spanish officer, went to France upon the death of his uncle to take possession of the Chateau du Fossat.

19 / Library of Congress, *Microfilm Collection,* "Codes and Compilations," 9.
20 / Historical Society of Pennsylvania, *Guide to the Manuscript Collections of the Historical Society of Pennsylvania* (Philadelphia, 1949), entries 238, 466, 534, 541, 829.
21 / Guy Soniat du Fossat, *Synopsis of the History of Louisiana, from the Founding of the Colony to the End of the Year 1791* (1903; rpr. New Orleans, 1976).

6

こ▲

Parish Records

After the transfer of sovereignty over Louisiana at New Orleans on December 20, 1803, steps were taken by William C. C. Claiborne and General James Wilkinson, the American commissioners, to secure control of the forts and settlements at other places. This work was done with the cooperation of Pierre Clément de Laussat, who obtained the necessary orders from the Marquis de Casa Calvo and Governor Manuel de Salcedo to the commandants at the local posts. Early in December, 1803, Captain Nathaniel Leonard of the U.S. Army took possession of Forts Bourbon, St. Philip, and La Balize below New Orleans on the Mississippi River. In January, 1804, other posts and their archives were taken over at Attakapas and Opelousas by Lieutenant Henry Hopkins while ex-captain Ferdinand L. Claiborne, brother of Commissioner Claiborne, took over the post of Concord on the Mississippi River opposite Natchez. Lieutenant Joseph Bowmar reported from Fort Miró on the Ouachita River on April 15, 1804, that he had that day taken over from the Spanish commandant. The important frontier post of Natchitoches was surrendered to Captain Edward Turner on April 26.[1] In February, 1804, Dr. John Watkins of New Orleans was sent by Claiborne to reappoint the commandants of the posts on the Mississippi as far up as Baton Rouge as well as those west of the river or to replace them where reappointment was declined.[2]

---

1 / Robertson (ed.), *Louisiana Under the Rule of Spain*, II, 237; Winston De Ville, *Opelousas: The History of a French and Spanish Military Post in America, 1716–1803* (Cottonport, La., 1973), 85; Robert D. Calhoun, "A History of Concordia Parish, Louisiana," *Louisiana Historical Quarterly*, XV (April, 1932), 214–15; Joseph Bowmar to W. C. C. Claiborne, April 15, 1804, Edward Turner to W. C. C. Claiborne, May 1, 1804, in Carter (ed.), *Territory of Orleans*, 223–24, 238–39.

2 / Robertson (ed.), *Louisiana Under the Rule of Spain*, II, 309–22.

According to orders from their superiors at New Orleans, the Spanish commandants of these interior posts prepared inventories of the documents in their charge and turned over to their successors records relating to property, wills, marriages, and other personal interests of the inhabitants. Receipts for the archives were signed by the American officers.[3] Records that were retained by the Spanish, including orders, correspondence, etc., were transmitted to New Orleans and placed among the archives in the governor's office and therewith shipped out of Louisiana as described above. Inventories were also prepared of archives at Lafourche, New Orleans, and Plaquemine in 1804–1805. The records of Louisiana posts that were taken to New Orleans were shipped from that place to Pensacola during the period 1804–1806. Later the Louisiana records were shipped to Havana and remained part of the archives there until their removal in the 1880s to Spain, where they were placed in the Archivo General de Indias at Seville. The post records from 1765 to 1804 were kept with the records of the governors of Louisiana and were classified with them in *legajos* 1–227.[4] According to a list of June 25, 1805, there were fifty-two bundles of documents from the posts of Louisiana.

In 1805 the temporary arrangements for local government that had been set up by Claiborne were replaced by more regular institutions. Even before a legislative act provided for local government, some of the military officers who had taken over from Spanish commandants were replaced by civilian appointees. The Orleans Territory act of April 10, 1805, establishing a county system of government provided for the appointment of inferior courts, the judges of which were to record notarial acts and take custody of the local records that had been transferred by the Spanish commandants.[5] In appointing the local judges, Governor Claiborne instructed them to take over the records that had been in the charge of the local posts.

An act of Congress of March 26, 1804, divided the Louisiana Purchase into the Territory of Orleans and the District of Louisiana, the former lying south of the 33rd parallel of latitude (later the southern boundary of Arkansas).[6] Claiborne was inaugurated governor of the Territory of

3 / Hill, *Descriptive Catalogue*, xiii–xiv. Note 19 contains an inventory of documents of 1801–1804 that were transferred to Claiborne at Concordia, January 12, 1804, and an inventory of May 14, 1804, shows the types of documents that were retained by the Spanish at Iberville.

4 / Hill, *Descriptive Catalogue*, xxxvii–xxxviii, xv, xxviii.

5 / Robert D. Calhoun, "The Origin and Development of County-Parish Government in Louisiana (1805–1845)," *Louisiana Historical Quarterly*, XVIII (January–October, 1935), 79.

6 / U.S. Laws, Statutes, etc. *The Statutes at Large of the United States of America*, 1789–. Boston, 1845–51; Boston, 1855–73; Washington, D.C., 1875–. 2 *Statutes* 283.

Orleans at New Orleans on October 2, 1804, by James Pitot, mayor of the
city of Orleans, and was provided with a secretary, whose duty it was to
maintain and preserve the public records.

An act of the legislative council of the territory on April 10, 1805,
divided the Territory of Orleans into twelve counties called Orleans,
German Coast, Acadia, Lafourche, Iberville, Pointe Coupee, Attakapas,
Opelousas, Natchitoches, Rapides, Ouachita, and Concordia.[7] New officers were appointed to take the place of the Spanish officials.[8] The function of recording notarial acts was vested in the county judge, who also
became the custodian of the records taken over from the Spanish commandants. The act of March 31, 1807, however, created nineteen parishes
based upon informal colonial ecclesiastical parishes, a form of subdivision more familiar to the mostly Catholic residents of Louisiana.[9]

These parishes (rearranged in alphabetical order with numbers in-
dicating their sequence in the act) were as follows:

Parish	Seat
Ascension (7)	Donaldsonville
Assumption (8)	Napoleonville
Avoyelles (16)	Marksville
Baton Rouge (11)	Baton Rouge
Concordia (13)	Vidalia
Iberville (10)	Plaquemine
Lafourche (Interior) (9)	Thibodaux
Natchitoches (17)	Natchitoches
Orleans (1)	New Orleans
Ouachita (14)	Monroe
Plaquemines (3)	Pointe-a-la-Hache
Pointe Coupee (12)	New Roads
Rapides (15)	Alexandria
St. Bernard (2)	Chalmette
St. Charles (4)	Hahnville
St. James (6)	Convent
St. John the Baptist (5)	Edgar
St. Landry (18)	Opelousas
St. Martin (19)	St. Martinville

7 / Historical Records Survey, Louisiana, *County-Parish Boundaries in Louisiana* (New Orleans, 1939), 16–17. See p. 19 for a map of the Territory of Orleans, 1805–1806 showing the boundaries of the counties.

8 / A register of appointments made under the act of 1805 is in Carter (ed.), *Territory of Orleans*, 598–603.

9 / Historical Records Survey, Louisiana, *County-Parish Boundaries*, 17–20. This publication contains maps of the boundaries of the parishes formed in 1807 and in later years.

The parishes created in 1807 and others subsequently formed became the chief units of local government in Louisiana. The counties were retained only for the purposes of electing representatives to the state legislature and levying taxes. Under the parish system of government, the parish judges took over the duties of most of the county officials, including the notarial duties of recording deeds, mortgages, conveyances, and other acts and of preserving the local records.[10]

The country south of the Mississippi Territory between the Mississippi and the Perdido rivers had been claimed by the United States under the cession of 1803, but Spain had retained possession. When Americans living in the area captured Baton Rouge in 1810, President James Madison issued a proclamation on October 27 of that year taking control of that area for the United States and adding it to the Orleans Territory. Governor Claiborne issued a proclamation on December 22, 1810, establishing within the annexed territory the parishes of Feliciana, East Baton Rouge, St. Helena, and St. Tammany.[11] After the admission of Louisiana as a state in 1812, the parishes created in 1807 and 1810, many of which were extremely large—particularly those outside the southeastern part of the state—were subdivided and resubdivided until there was a total of sixty-four parishes.[12]

In March, 1936, a survey of parish archives of Louisiana was undertaken by the Historical Records Survey under the direction of Lyle Saxon, state director of the Federal Writers Project. He was succeeded in March, 1937, by John C. L. Andreassen, who had attended the graduate school of Louisiana State University. Survey workers investigated the archives in parish courthouses and prepared inventories that were issued in processed form during the years 1938–1942 to a limited number of libraries and government agencies outside Louisiana. Inventories for twenty parishes were issued before the termination of the project in 1942.[13] Research and inventory materials for the other parishes were deposited in the Louisiana Archives and Records Service, Office of the Secretary of State.[14] The Department of Archives and Manuscripts of Louisiana State University had been established in 1935 through the efforts of Edwin A. Davis, a member of the history department of the university. It was designated by

---

10 / Calhoun, "County-Parish Government," 88, 92–93.

11 / Ibid., 99–100.

12 / Alcée Fortier (ed.), Louisiana: Comprising Sketches of Counties, Towns, Events, Institutions, and Persons, Arranged in Cyclopedic Form (Atlanta, 1909), II, 290–91.

13 / Listed in Sargent B. Child and Dorothy P. Holmes, Bibliography of Research Projects Reports: Check List of Historical Records Survey Publications (Washington, D.C., 1943), 21–22.

14 / Loretta L. Hefner, The WPA Historical Records Survey: A Guide to the Unpublished Inventories, Indexes and Transcripts (Chicago, 1980), 17.

an act of the state legislature of 1936 as the official state repository and given authorization to receive records and documents and to make a survey of the official records of the state, its parishes, and other subdivisions.[15]

In 1954 the Louisiana legisature again authorized a survey of the state, parish, municipal, colonial, territorial, and federal records in the state to ascertain their condition, location, and availability. Andreassen was appointed director of the survey and Davis was designated as consultant. In conducting the survey of the parish archives between July, 1955, and January, 1956, Andreassen did not attempt to gather the detailed information that had been collected by the Historical Records Survey. His report supplies summary information regarding the parish archives and lists the Historical Records Survey inventories. Remnants of colonial records were found in Orleans and nineteen other parishes. In its *Report No. 2*, the Louisiana Archives Survey recommended the cleaning and lamination of the colonial and territorial archives, the microfilming of the records for central deposit, the preparation of accurate guides to the microfilm, and the preparation of name indexes to the records to facilitate their use for public and private research.[16]

The Louisiana State Archives and Records Commission was established by an act of July 10, 1956. It was empowered to appoint a professionally qualified director and an assistant director to head the State Archives and Records Service, which was given responsibility for promoting and improving records management among state agencies and subdivisions and for establishing and operating a records storage center.[17] Athough Governor Earl K. Long vetoed an appropriation made in 1956, John Andreassen served as a consultant in records management during 1956–1957. An appropriation was made in 1958, but Andreassen was dismissed on August 1, 1960, and replaced by a political appointee. The commission became the custodian of the records of Avoyelles Parish and in the 1960s published a series of *Calendars of Louisiana Colonial Documents*, including those for Avoyelles, St. Charles, St. Landry, and Opelousas parishes. Parish records accessioned later included some for Natchitoches, East Feliciana, and East Baton Rouge.[18] In 1975 an act of the legislature consolidated the Louisiana State Archives and Records Commission into

15 / A. Otis Hébert, "Keeping Louisiana's Records," 30.
16 / John C. L. Andreassen and Edwin A. Davis, *Louisiana Archives Survey Report No. 1, Survey of Public Records (Under Act No. 381, 1954)* ([Baton Rouge, 1956]), 289–389; John C. L. Andreassen and Edwin A. Davis, *Louisiana Archives Survey Report No. 2, Findings and Recommendations* ([Baton Rouge, 1956]), 9, 20.
17 / A. Otis Hébert, "Keeping Louisiana's Records," 33.
18 / Ernst Posner, *American State Archives* (Chicago, 1964), 126–27.

the Office of the Secretary of State, in which a full-time archivist was to be employed to develop an archival program in the state.

The parish records contain a variety of documents that are useful for research on numerous subjects. Most varied in content are the notarial acts, which include adjudications, claims contracts, conveyances, donations, declarations of insolvency, dissolutions of partnerships, family meetings, inventories of property, land grants, exchanges and sales, letters, manumissions, marriage contracts, nominations of tutors, partitions, petitions for tutors, procès-verbaux, procurations, promises to pay, quit claims, receipts, redemptions, releases, royal decrees, sales of real and personal property, settlements of debt, slave sales, successions, testaments, and wills.[19] The documents give the dates of their execution, the names of the principals, the witnesses, and the officer recording the act, the date recorded, and the signature of the recorder. Marriage contracts contain not only the names of the bride and groom but also the places of their nativity, the names of their parents and witnesses, the agreements regarding property, and the signatures of the principals, the witnesses, and the notary.

The variety of information supplied by the parish records is important for genealogy, biography, local history, and social and economic history, including agriculture, cattle raising, and property ownership. The Spanish had introduced cattle into the New World and, with them, the practice of using hot irons for marking them with brands in their hides in order to establish ownership and thus prevent rustling. As the references in the present volume testify, the value of the parish records has been discovered by genealogists but evidently not to the same extent by historians of localities in Louisiana.[20]

Several authors have used both civil and church records of Louisiana in preparing compilations useful for genealogical research. The work by Bona Arsenault is concerned with the Acadians. Concentrating upon southwest Louisiana, Donald J. Hébert's compilation provides an alphabetical list of names derived from church and civil records of thirteen parishes. Using the civil records, Nicholas R. Murray has published a computer index to marriage records of Ascension, Iberville, Lafourche, Pointe

19 / Glenn R. Conrad, *St. Charles: Abstracts of the Civil Records of St. Charles Parish, 1770–1803* (Lafayette, La., 1974), 1; Louisiana State Archives and Records Service, *Calendar of Louisiana Colonial Documents, Volume II, St. Landry Parish*, comp. Winston De Ville ([Baton Rouge], 1964), xi.

20 / Lauren C. Post, "Cattle Branding in Southwest Louisiana," *McNeese Review*, X (Winter, 1958), 101.

Coupee, St. Charles, St. John the Baptist, St. Martin, St. Mary, and West Feliciana parishes.[21]

When fires destroyed the early wooden courthouses of Louisiana, the parish records often went up in flames. It was not until 1840 that the legislature adopted an act requiring the construction of fireproof vaults for keeping the parish records safe.[22] How rigidly this legislation was enforced has not been ascertained. Even when vaults were built, some records were not kept in them. Little used records were stored in attics and basements, where they were damaged by dust, vermin, and water. Eventually more adequate structures of stone, concrete, and brick have provided safe storerooms and work rooms for the parish records.[23]

Microfilm of the parish archives of Louisiana is in a number of repositories. In 1961 the Genealogical Society of the Church of Jesus Christ of Latter-Day Saints began the most extensive microfilming program. The practice of the church photographers has been to microfilm marriage contracts, wills, censuses, administrations of estates, deeds, land records, powers of attorney, and military records. In Louisiana an exchange program has also been in effect under which negative microfilms, when available, were borrowed for copying. The negatives were inspected, used for the preparation of the desired number of positives, catalogued, and placed in the church library for the use of patrons. The original negative was placed in the church records vault, which is in a granite mountain twenty miles from Salt Lake City in Little Cottonwood Canyon. The natural temperature and level of humidity in the vault are close to ideal for the storage of microfilm. The clerks of court cooperated with the microfilming program and were furnished with free copies by the church. Copies are also available at the Louisiana State Library in Baton Rouge and at the New Orleans Public Library.[24]

The Louisiana section of the Louisiana State Library has purchased copies of the microfilm in order to make it available in one place in Louisiana; the state library lends the microfilm. Other copies for forty-two parishes are in the New Orleans Public Library. The St. Charles Parish

21 / Bona Arsenault, *Histoire et généalogie des Acadiens* ([Montréal], 1978); Donald J. Hébert, *Southwest Louisiana Records: Church and Civil Records of Settlers, Volume I, 1756–1810* (Eunice, La., 1974); Nicholas R. Murray, *Computer-Indexed Marriage Records* (Hammond, La., 1980–81).

22 / Calhoun, "County-Parish Government," 144.

23 / Carl A. Brasseaux, Glenn R. Conrad, and R. Warren Robison, *The Courthouses of Louisiana* (Lafayette, La., 1977), *passim.*

24 / Kent Rowsell, "Talk Given by Mr. Kent Rowsell, Field Operator for the Genealogical Society of the Church of Jesus Christ of Latter-Day Saints," *New Orleans Genesis,* VI (March, 1967), 100–102.

records were not microfilmed by the Mormons but have been copied by the Louisiana State Archives, and copies are available in the New Orleans Public Library. Copies of the microfilm can also be used at Latter-Day Saints genealogical libraries at Shreveport and Baton Rouge and at many other places throughout the United States, which will borrow them for a small fee from the genealogical department of the church at Salt Lake City. Computer terminals being installed in the branch libraries in the 1980s facilitate the procurement of family data from the vast microfilm holdings of the church archives, which have been placed in computer files. Microfilm of the colonial records of twelve parishes is in the Center for Louisiana History at the University of Southwestern Louisiana in Lafayette.

Ascension Parish (Donaldsonville). This parish in southeastern Louisiana on both sides of the Mississippi River was settled in the middle of the eighteenth century by French and Spanish immigrants who came directly from Europe. Soon after the arrival of the Acadians from Nova Scotia, that portion of the Mississippi became known as the Acadian Coast. When the upper part of the coast was set up as Ascension Parish in 1807, the seat was placed at Donaldsonville. Fires that destroyed the courthouse in 1846 and 1889 and a federal bombardment in 1862 may have destroyed some of the parish records.[25]

Records of Ascension Parish date from 1770; none are available for the French period. Microfilm of the conveyance records and the marriage records, with indexes, is in the New Orleans Public Library. Microfilm of the notarial records, 1770–1803, in five reels, is in the University of Southwestern Louisiana's Center for Louisiana History. Microfilm of the marriage records from 1787 and succession records is in the Louisiana State Library in Baton Rouge. In the same repository is a compilation by Sidney A. Marchand on pioneer settlers in the second Acadian settlement, Ascension Parish, 1772–1829, on one reel of microfilm. Marchand has published a list of the names of residents in 1770, a list of the names of persons born during the years 1772–1789, and information on the housing of Acadian exiles—all derived from the parish records. In another publication Marchand compiled a list of the first five hundred native-born citizens of Ascension Parish, with the names of their parents and their dates of birth. Sidney A. Marchand, Jr., presents in dictionary form another compilation of data on seven hundred of the original Acadian settlers of the parish derived from the paish records of 1770–1805. An index

25 / Sidney A. Marchand, *The Story of Ascension Parish* ([Baton Rouge], 1931), 20–21; Fortier (ed.), *Louisiana Sketches*, I, 354; Brasseaux, Conrad, and Robison, *Courthouses of Louisiana*, 35.

of marriages is arranged alphabetically by the names of males, with the dates of the marriages and the names of the brides.[26]

Assumption Parish (Napoleonville). In the middle of the eighteenth century, French settlers occupied locations along the Bayou Lafourche in south central Louisiana, where they were soon joined by some Acadians.[27] After the parish was created in 1807, the seat was located at Napoleonville. The records of Assumption Parish include original notarial acts from October 30, 1788, to 1804, arranged chronologically by date of filing. A record of conveyances of real and personal property, from March 1, 1786, to 1804, is arranged chronologically by date of instrument. *Hypothèques* or original mortgage acts encumbering real and chattel property, from October 6, 1789, to 1804, are arranged chronologically by date of act. Procurations, from January 27, 1792, to 1804, are original notarial acts passed before the commandant and are arranged chronologically by date executed. A conveyance record, from October 30, 1788, to 1804, contains a record of the acts of conveyance of real estate, slaves, and other property; a translation of this record was prepared in 1958–1960. Besides an old index of conveyances arranged alphabetically by the first letter of the individual's surname, there are modern permaflex indexes for vendors and vendees. A record of cattle brands begins August 26, 1789, and is arranged chronologically by date of record. Successions or probate case papers, from November 13, 1786, to 1804, are arranged in volumes chronologically by date of instrument and indexed by surname of deceased or estate. Marriage contracts, from November 18, 1789, to 1804, are arranged chronologically by date of instrument. Marriage licenses and certificates, also from November 18, 1789, to 1804, are arranged chronologically by date filed.[28] Microfilm of the marriage rcords with index is in the New Orleans Public Library. Microfilm of the notarial records in four reels is in the University of Southwestern Louisiana Center for Louisiana History.

Avoyelles Parish (Marksville). French traders settled in this parish in central Louisiana early in the eighteenth century and were soon joined by

26 / Marchand, *Ascension Parish*, 21–22; 71–81, 85–92; Sidney A. Marchand, *Acadian Exiles in the Golden Coast of Louisiana* (Donaldsonville, La., 1943), 71–81; Sidney A. Marchand, Jr., *An Attempt to Re-assemble the Old Settlers in Family Groups* (Baton Rouge, 1965); Nicholas R. Murray, *Ascension Parish, Louisiana, 1768–1899. Computer-Indexed Marriage Records* (Hammond, La., [1980?]).

27 / Fortier (ed.), *Louisiana Sketches*, I, 46.

28 / Historical Records Survey, Louisiana, *Inventory of the Parish Archives of Louisiana, No. 4, Assumption Parish* (Napoleonville) (Baton Rouge, 1942), 44–46, 49–51, 59, 63, 70–71, 95.

other Frenchmen who became stockmen.[29] Later in that century, Acadians, British, Americans, and Spaniards arrived in the area. Some years
passed after the parish was created in 1807 before it acquired land for a
courthouse in what became Marksville, where a circuit rider had previously held court.[30]

In 1961 the records of Avoyelles Parish for the colonial period were
transferred from the parish seat to the custody of the Louisiana State Archives and Records Commission at Baton Rouge. The collection had been
depleted in prior years by removals of the parish offices from one courthouse to another. The state archives arranged the records chronologically
and numbered and indexed them by personal name. They were found to
consist of 430 items for the years 1786–1803.[31] The collection contains a
variety of documents of cloth-content paper, including agreements concerning property boundaries, petitions of married persons for the separa-
tion of goods, letters to the commandant, petitions to the commandant
for the seizure of goods to pay debts, bonds, declarations regarding land,
petitions to the governor for land grants, petitions to make arrests, certificates regarding imprisonment, petitions regarding partnerships, inventories of goods, successions regarding property, governors' decrees, lists of
debts, responses of accused persons, communications regarding debts,
marriage contracts, inventories of personal property, certificates regarding land surveys, letters regarding debts, powers of attorney, petitions
regarding payment for land, mortgages, proceedings in suits, procès-
verbaux regarding arrests, sales of slaves, and dwellings, and criminal
suits.[32] The parish records also include a brand book, from April 1, 1785,
to 1809, giving the names of persons registering the brands, the dates on
which they registered, and the names of the clerks.[33] Microfilm of indexes
to notarial acts, 1786–1803, in three reels, is in the University of Southwestern Louisiana Center for Louisiana History. Microfilm of the
Avoyelles Parish records of 1793–1796, also in three reels, is in the Louisiana State Museum.

29 / Louisiana State Archives and Records Service, *Calendar of Louisiana Colonial Documents, Volume I, Avoyelles Parish*, comp. Winston De Ville ([Baton Rouge], 1961), xi.

30 / Brasseaux, Conrad, and Robison, *Courthouses of Louisiana*, 38.

31 / Louisiana Archives, *Calendar of Documents, Avoyelles Parish*. Gaps in the collection
exist for 1787–89 and 1801–1802.

32 / A translation of notarial acts of the parish, 1783–1812, is in Corinne L. Saucier, *The
History of Avoyelles Parish, Louisiana* (New Orleans, [1943]), 429–542. The author of this collection compiled a list of names found in the parish records that is published in the same volume, pp. 353–58.

33 / Alberta R. Ducote, "Mark and Brand Book I, Avoyelles Parish," *Louisiana Genealogical Register*, XVII (September, 1970), 254–56.

Concordia Parish (Vidalia). In 1798 when the Spanish withdrew from Natchez, José Vidal, who had been the commandant there, moved directly across the Mississippi River and established the post of Concordia, where Fort Panmure had been located.[34] When Concordia Parish was established in 1807, its seat was at Concordia, but an act of the Louisiana legislature on March 11, 1811, changed the name to Vidalia in honor of the former commandant.

Papers of José Vidal dating from 1797 in the Louisiana State University Department of Archives and Manuscripts include materials relating to land grants. Other Vidal papers, 1789–1809, in the Louisiana State Museum, include correspondence with Governor Gayoso de Lemos, Vizente Folch, and Daniel Clark.[35]

Robert D. Calhoun, the historian of Concordia Parish, assembled a collection of official documents and photostatic copies of documents on the parish that relates mostly to the years after 1805 but contains some materials of an earlier date.[36] The collection is in the Louisiana State University Department of Archives and Manuscripts. Footnotes in Calhoun's history cite a deed book, conveyance records, a probate record book, and a will book.

East Baton Rouge Parish (Baton Rouge). In 1718 in an effort to promote settlement on the east bank of the Mississippi, the Company of the Indies gave a grant of land to Diron d'Artaguette, and immigrants from France settled there.[37] A fort was built to control the Indians. Upon the conclusion of the Seven Years' War in 1763, the British acquired sovereignty in the region. After Spain became an ally of France during the Revolutionary War, Governor Bernardo de Gálvez of Louisiana captured Manchac, Baton Rouge, and Natchez in 1779; by the spring of 1781, the Spanish had won control of all of West Florida.[38]

When the Spanish conquered West Florida, they made arrangements for its government. Captain Pedro Favrot was made commander at Baton Rouge, and Carlos de Grand Pré was designated civil and military governor of the district, with his headquarters at Natchez. In 1779, West Florida

34 / Robert D. Calhoun, "A History of Concordia Parish, Louisiana," *Louisiana Historical Quarterly*, XV (January, 1932), 54; Fortier (ed.), *Louisiana Sketches*, I, 573.

35 / *National Union Catalog of Manuscripts*, 1978, entry 1271; Louisiana State Museum, *Biennial Report*, 1912–14, pp. 61–64.

36 / Historical Records Survey, Louisiana, *Guide to Depositories of Manuscript Collections in Louisiana* (University, La., 1941), 24.

37 / Fortier (ed.), *Louisiana Sketches*, I, 377.

38 / Caughey, *Gálvez*, 153–59.

was divided into the districts of Baton Rouge, Feliciana, St. Helena, and Chifonete (later called St. Ferdinand). After the transfer of the region north of the 31st parallel of latitude to the United States in 1798, Grand Pré's headquarters were shifted from Natchez to Baton Rouge. His authority extended over the region from the Mississippi River to the Pearl River.[39] Although the United States claimed the region south of the Territory of Mississippi as far east as the Perdido River under the Louisiana Purchase treaty of 1803 on the grounds that it had formed part of French Louisiana, it did not push this claim immediately following the acquisition of the country west of the Mississippi River.[40]

The activities of insurgent Americans, who entered West Florida after 1804 in increasing numbers, made life difficult for the Spanish officials and finally resulted in intervention by the United States government. By 1810, sentiment for independence had greatly strengthened; a movement for self-government was inaugurated in July, and in November the independent government of West Florida was launched under the governorship of Fulwar Skipwith.[41] It was but short-lived, however, for on December 7, Governor Claiborne seized St. Francisville, capital of West Florida, pursuant to President Madison's proclamation of October 27, in which he claimed the region as part of the Louisiana Purchase. On December 10, Baton Rouge was surrendered upon the arrival of Governor Claiborne, Governor David Holmes of the Territory of Mississippi, and Colonel Thomas Covington in command of a body of American troops. Claiborne, proceeding with the organization of the government of the region, added it to the Territory of Orleans. His proclamation of December 22, 1810, established in what had been West Florida the parishes of Feliciana, East Baton Rouge, St. Helena, and St. Tammany. An act of Congress of April 14, 1812, extended the eastern boundary of the Louisiana Territory to the Pearl River, thus annexing the Florida parishes to that territory.[42]

In 1918 the Library of Congress received by transfer from the Treasury Department, which had probably received them with land records many years earlier, records of the West Florida revolutionary convention and republic. These documents were later edited for publication by James A. Padgett and included the journal of the revolutionary conven-

39 / Dunbar Rowland, *History of Mississippi, the Heart of the South* (1925; rpr. Spartanburg, S.C., 1978), I, 289–94.

40 / Isaac J. Cox, *The West Florida Controversy, 1798–1813: A Study in American Diplomacy* (Baltimore, 1918), 340 ff.

41 / Rowland, *History of Mississippi*, I, 451–52.

42 / 2 *Statutes* 708–709.

tion at St. John's Plains, July 25 to August 29, 1810; the journal of the West Florida constitutional convention at St. Francisville, September 22 to October 28, 1810; the Senate journal, November 19 to December 10, 1810; the House journal, November 19 to December 10, 1810; miscellaneous documents, including accounts and vouchers concerning the business affairs of the convention and the legisature; a consolidated monthly report of the regiment in the service of the convention from September 11 to December 10, 1810, with names of officers and biographical data concerning them, and an inventory of the public property in the garrison at Baton Rouge. The Senate and House journals also contain footnotes supplying biographical data on their members.[43] The constitution of the West Florida republic has also been published from the copy in the Library of Congress.[44] Letters of members of the convention, convention orders, a report on military strength, and the addresses of Fulwar Skipwith, including one to the people of West Florida, have also been published from the manuscripts in the Library of Congress.[45]

A collection of documents relating to the West Florida republic, July 30–October 16, 1810, containing thirty-one items, has also been published. These documents include the declaration of independence, the constitution, and correspondence between officials of the republic and Governor Carlos DeHault DeLassus and U.S. officials. They were obtained by the editor of the collection from descendants of participants in the revolution and from the collections of the Louisiana Historical Society and the Howard-Tilton Memorial Library of Tulane University.[46]

Papers of the West Florida revolution, from 1810, 1816, and 1845, comprising fifteen items in the Louisiana State University Department of Archives and Manuscripts, include reports by Governor Carlos DeHault DeLassus, reports by the governor to representatives of the people of West Florida, reports by Colonel Philomen Thomas, commander of the fort at Baton Rouge, to the inhabitants of West Florida, and related papers.[47]

43 / Library of Congress, *Annual Report*, 1918, p. 42; James A. Padget (ed.), "Official Records of the West Florida Revolution and Republic," *Louisiana Historical Quarterly*, XXI (July, 1938), 685–805.
44 / James A. Padgett (ed.), "The Constitution of the West Florida Republic," *Louisiana Historical Quarterly*, XX (October, 1937), 881–94. The constitution is also published in Stanley C. Arthur, *The Story of the West Florida Rebellion* (St. Francisville, La., 1935), 69–88, along with a few other documents.
45 / James A. Padgett (ed.), "The West Florida Revolution of 1810, as Told in the Letters of John Rhea, Fulwar Skipwith, Reuben Kemper and Others," *Louisiana Historical Quarterly*, XXI (January, 1938), 76–202.
46 / John S. Kendall (ed.), "Documents Concerning the West Florida Revolution, 1810," *Louisiana Historical Quarterly*, XVII (January–July, 1934), 81–95, 306–14, 474–501.
47 / Coutts and Whitley, "Inventory of Sources," 247.

The original records of the Spanish government of West Florida, 1782–1794, 1799–1810, in eighteen volumes, 4 feet, 10½ inches, are in the East Baton Rouge Parish courthouse in Baton Rouge. Volume XIX contains documents of the years 1799–1816. Handwritten in Spanish, French, and English, these records are arranged chronologically. A separate index, 1782–1810, in two volumes, is arranged chronologically and alphabetically by names of persons. The collection contains both notarial acts and judicial proceedings and includes land and slave sales, wills, indentures, declarations, powers of attorney, mortgages, probate proceedings, marriage certificates, civil and criminal trials, and emancipations of slaves.[48] The Spanish West Florida Collection contains documents relating to all of the Florida parishes of Louisiana; consequently, the records of those parishes are minimal for the Spanish period. In the courthouse at Baton Rouge are also a small quantity of Spanish land grants and a survey of land belonging to Jonathan Smith dating from 1799. Microfilm of the Spanish West Florida records, 1782–1810, on thirteen reels, is in the Louisiana State Library, the Louisiana State University Library, Tulane University Library, the University of Southwestern Louisiana Center for Louisiana History, the St. Martin Parish Library at St. Martinville, Southeastern Louisiana University Library, Hammond, and the repository of the Genealogical Society of the Church of Jesus Christ of Latter-Day Saints.

Some aids to research in the Spanish archives of West Florida have been published. Mrs. Edwin A. Broders has prepared from the transcripts in the Louisiana State University Library an alphabetical name index with the page numbers in the eighteen volumes of the records. She has also prepared a list of the successions, giving the names by volumes with the page numbers. Data from the succession records are also in another publication. Indexed abstracts of the Spanish West Florida records prepared for the use of genealogists show names, dates, and family relationships and are numbered in order to facilitate searches. A census that has been published shows only the names of white males, though there were numerous slaves and freedmen.[49]

---

48 / Historical Records Survey, Louisiana, *Title-Line Inventory of the Parish Archives of Louisiana, Parts 1 and 2, Acadia Through Winn* (New Orleans, 1939), 3–4; Coutts and Whitley, "Inventory of Sources," 249. Inventories of 1781 and 1787 are printed in Historical Records Survey, Louisiana, *Favrot Papers*, II, 118–23, III, 101–106; and inventories of 1797 and 1808 are listed in Hill, *Descriptive Catalogue*, xxxvi, xxxviii.

49 / Mrs. Edwin A. Broders, "Index of Spanish West Florida Archives, East Baton Rouge Parish Courthouse," *Louisiana Genealogical Register*, XI–XVII (September, 1964–December, 1970); Mrs. Edwin A. Broders, "List of Successions Found in the Records of the Spanish West Florida Archives, East Baton Rouge Parish Courthouse," *Louisiana Genealogical Register*, XI (September, December, 1964), 42–44, 57–60; Clyde P. Young (comp.) and E. Russ Williams,

Work on the Spanish records of West Florida became a big project for the Survey of Federal Archives. During a personal examination of the records in 1936, Stanley C. Arthur, the director of the survey, found some damage to the records by termites. Responding to a recommendation from the East Baton Rouge Bar Association, the survey undertook in 1936 the transcription and translation of the records. Produced by a staff of translators, historians, and stenographers at Baton Rouge, the work was completed in November, 1939.[50] Copies were supplied to the clerk of the court at Baton Rouge, the National Archives Library, the Louisiana State University Library, and the Howard-Tilton Memorial Library of Tulane University. The eighteen volumes of transcriptions contain 6,584 pages. A transcription of the original Spanish index was also prepared in one volume.

In addition to these volumes, two volumes of translations and transcriptions have been made of the notarial acts of East Baton Rouge Parish. These cases, dating from 1799 to 1816, were the outgrowth of litigations begun in the Spanish period.[51] Sets of the translated volumes have been distributed as follows: three sets to Louisiana State University and one each to the National Archives; the Howard-Tilton Memorial Library; the clerk's office, District Court, Baton Rouge; the East Baton Rouge Bar Association; the clerk's office, St. Francisville, Louisiana; and Southeastern Louisiana University, Hammond. Two copies were retained by the Survey of Federal Archives office in New Orleans.

An index to the translations and typescripts of the Spanish West Florida records, originally prepared by the Survey of Federal Archives in 1937, was published nearly forty years later.[52] It indexes not only the eighteen volumes of records but also a nineteenth volume concerning the litigation of 1799–1816.

Jr. (ed.), *Succession Records of St. Helena Parish, Louisiana, 1804 Through 1854, Abstracted from the Original Files* (Bogalusa, La., 1966); Elizabeth B. Gianelloni, "Spanish West Florida Records: Index to Abstracts of Translations," *Louisiana Genealogical Register,* XVI–XX (December, 1969–December, 1973); Albert Tate, Jr., "Spanish Census of the Baton Rouge District for 1786," *Louisiana History,* XXIV (Winter, 1983), 70–84.

50 / Survey of Federal Archives, Louisiana, Archives of the Spanish Government of West Florida, a Series of 18 Bound Volumes of Written Documents Mostly in the Spanish Language Deposited in the Records Room of the 17th Judicial District Court, Baton Rouge, Louisiana (New Orleans, 1937–39).

51 / Survey of Federal Archives, Louisiana, Original Notarial Acts, Book No. 1, Bundles A, B, C, 1799 to 1816. Archives of the Spanish Government of West Florida, Vol. XIX, part 1, Translations and Transcriptions, Vol. XIX, part 2 (New Orleans, 1940).

52 / Survey of Federal Archives, Louisiana, *Index to the Archives of Spanish West Florida, 1782–1810* (New Orleans, 1975).

East Feliciana Parish (Clinton). Feliciana Parish, one of the West Florida parishes created in 1810, was divided by an act of the Louisiana legislature on February 17, 1824, into East and West Feliciana parishes. A wooden courthouse for East Feliciana Parish was built in 1825 on donated land in what became the town of Clinton.[53] The early courthouse was destroyed by fire in March, 1839, and was replaced in 1840 by a brick and wood structure, which in restored condition still serves.

Records of East Feliciana Parish in the Louisiana State Archives include a survey of land owned by William Stevens, 1791, and a list of private land claims, 1793–1814, in one volume.[54] Microfilm of the marriage and succession records is in the Louisiana State Library. The records concerning this parish during the Spanish period are included in those of East Baton Rouge Parish.

Iberville Parish (Plaquemine). The Iberville district, sixty miles above New Orleans on the east side of the Mississippi River, was settled by the French and Spanish. During the period 1765–1775 and in later years, immigrants from the Canary Islands and Acadians located in the area.[55] In 1779, English and American refugees from British West Florida settled at Galveztown near the confluence of the Amite and Iberville rivers.[56] When Iberville Parish was established in 1807, the seat of justice was initially at Galveztown, but in 1843 it was moved to Plaquemine. A hotel at Plaquemine was used as the courthouse from 1843 until 1848, when a new building was constructed. Another courthouse constructed in 1906 was remodeled in 1949.[57]

The records of Iberville Parish in the custody of the clerk at Plaquemine include notarial acts passed before judges Louis Dutiene and Nicolas Deverbois, April 16, 1770–March 28, 1798, in four volumes, 300 pages; notarial acts of Marco Diveless, August 3, 1787–August 4, 1804, in one volume, 150 pages; notarial acts passed before Francisco Rivas, May 14, 1798–April 17, 1804, in three volumes, 300 pages; and records of marriage contracts, 1770–1796, in one volume, 200 pages. An index volume, 1770–1802, of fifty pages, covers marriage contracts, sales, wills, inventories, and brands.[58] An inventory of the judge's office, 1770–1798, in one

53 / Brasseaux, Conrad, and Robison, *Courthouses of Louisiana*, 74.
54 / Coutts and Whitley, "Inventory of Sources," 223.
55 / Fortier (ed.), *Louisiana Sketches*, I, 550.
56 / Caughey, *Gálvez*, 79–81.
57 / Brasseaux, Conrad, and Robison, *Courthouses of Louisiana*, 90.
58 / The description is from a one-page inventory supplied to the author by Luther H. Evans, National Director of the Historical Records Survey, April 20, 1939, in Beers Correspondence.

volume, 50 pages, supplies a checklist of marriage contracts, sales of real and personal property, wills, and inventories. A book of brands begins on September 1, 1781, and gives dates and names of owners but no reproductions of brands. References have also been found to a conveyance record, a book of donations, and maps dating from the 1770s.[59] Indexes prepared by the Works Progress Administration covering suits, conveyances, marriages, and changes in the ownership of realty are also in the clerk of the court's office. Microfilm of conveyance records and marriage records dating from 1770 with indexes is in the New Orleans Public Library. Among the records held by the clerk of the court at Plaquemine are notarial acts of Galveztown. Microfilm of an index to the marriage records, 1770–1798, and of the succession records, 1777–1948, is in the Louisiana State Library. Microfilm of the notarial acts, 1770–1805, in eight reels, is in the University of Southwestern Louisiana Library. A published index to the marriage contracts contains alphabetical lists of names of grooms and brides, dates, names of parents, relationships of witnesses to the espoused, dowries, and occupations.[60]

Lafayette Parish (Lafayette). The earliest settlers in the Attakapas country of southwestern Louisiana were trappers, traders, ranchmen, and smugglers.[61] The population in 1769 included French Canadians and English traders from the Carolinas. Acadians who settled in this remote part of Louisiana became known as Càjuns, and they form a large part of the present-day population of the state.[62] Lafayette Parish was created by the Louisiana act of January 17, 1823, from the western part of St. Martin Parish.[63] Initially, the seat was at Pin Hook, but in 1824 Vermilionville was laid out on donated land in the eastern part of the parish. The name of the parish seat was changed in 1884 to Lafayette. Records of Lafayette Parish in the custody of the clerk of the court include notarial acts dating from 1779 and a conveyance book dating from 1799.[64]

59 / Sherburne Anderson (ed.), "Brand Books of Iberville Parish, Louisiana," *Louisiana Genealogical Register,* XI (June, 1964), 15–20; Albert L. Grace, *The Heart of the Sugar Bowl: The Story of Iberville* (Plaquemine, La., 1946), 236, 241.

60 / Mrs. Ben S. Konikoff, "Special Index for Special Marriage Contracts, Book #1, 1770–1798, Iberville Parish, Louisiana," *Louisiana Genealogical Register,* XXII (March, 1975), 55–61. See also Nicholas R. Murray, *Iberville Parish Louisiana, 1777–1900, Computer-Indexed Marriage Records* (Hammond, La., [1981]).

61 / Harry L. Griffin, *The Attakapas Country: A History of Lafayette Parish, Louisiana* (New Orleans, 1959), 12.

62 / Arsenault, *Histoire des Acadiens,* 189–98.

63 / Historical Records Survey, Louisiana, *County-Parish Boundaries,* 36.

64 / Historical Records Survey, Louisiana, *Inventory of the Parish Archives of Louisiana, No. 28, Lafayette Parish (Lafayette)* (University, La., 1938), 33–34.

Lafourche Parish (Thibodaux). This parish derived its name from Bayou Lafourche in southern Louisiana. The bayou was explored by Frenchmen, who, by the middle of the eighteenth century, were settling on its banks. The area was settled originally in the 1760s by Acadian refugees from Canada, who were joined by other Acadians from France in 1785. Late in the 1770s Canary Islanders brought over by the Spanish government were settled by Governor Gálvez at Valenzuela. Later other Spaniards and Americans settled in the area. The Lafourche district of the eighteenth century included what became Lafourche, Terrebonne, and Assumption parishes and the west bank of the Mississippi in Ascension Parish. After Lafourche Parish was set up on the Gulf Coast in 1807, the seat was located at Thibodauxville, which was later shortened to Thibodaux.[65]

The records of Lafourche Parish include probate case papers and documents dating from 1796, arranged numerically by docket number. A docket of inventories begins in 1796 and contains an alphabetical list of inventories ordered in probate proceedings by name of estate, showing the relationship to the survivor. Information concerning individuals derived from the parish records is presented in a volume that is useful for genealogical research. A volume of succession lists from the parish records for 1770, 1777, 1778, 1791, 1795, 1797, and 1798 contains records of inhabitants, land ownership, slaves, weapons, large and small cattle, as well as rice and grain production.[66]

Natchitoches Parish (Natchitoches). The post of St. Jean Baptiste was established on the site of Natchitoches by Louis Juchereau de St. Denis in 1714.[67] Located at the head of navigation on the Red River, it is the oldest permanent settlement in Louisiana. During his long command there, St. Denis promoted trade and friendly relations with the Indians and Spaniards in Texas. Athanase de Mézières, who served for many years as the commandant of the French post at Natchitoches, was appointed lieutenant governor there by Governor O'Reilly in 1769. In 1807 that post became the seat of Natchitoches Parish, which originally comprised all of northwestern Louisiana. Natchitoches has had several courthouses: an 1840 courthouse burned in the late 1850s; others were built in 1872, 1896, and 1939, with a courtroom annex added in 1959.[68]

65 / Fortier (ed.), *Louisiana Sketches*, II, 26, 528.
66 / Historical Records Survey, Louisiana, *Inventory of the Parish Archives of Louisiana, No. 29, Lafourche Parish (Thibodaux)* (Baton Rouge, 1942), 72; Donald J. Hébert, *South Louisiana Records: Church and Civil Records of Lafourche-Terrebonne Parishes, Volume I, 1794–1840* (Cecelia, La., 1978); Albert J. Robichaux, Jr. (comp., trans., and ed.), *Colonial Settlers Along Bayou Lafourche: Louisiana Census Records, 1770–1798* (Harvey, La., 1974).
67 / Fortier (ed.), *Louisiana Sketches*, II, 408.
68 / Brasseaux, Conrad, and Robison, *Courthouses of Louisiana*, 117–18.

The records of Natchitoches Parish in the office of the clerk of the court in the 1930s included conveyances on the sale of real and personal property, divisions of land, procurations, and donations from 1738, arranged chronologically, unindexed; mortgages, judgments, and marriage contracts, from 1716 on, chronologically arranged, unindexed; civil suit papers of the commandant, 1797–1804, arranged chronologically and numerically by suit numbers, unindexed; and private papers relating to the estates of St. Denis and his wife, 1773–1835, in one bundle. English abstracts of the marriage contracts, 1739–1803, show the names of the groom and bride, names of their parents, occupations of the groom and the groom's father and his nationality, place of residence of the parents, names of witnesses for the groom and the bride, information regarding dowries, and the signatures of the persons present, including that of the notary.[69] In the 1940s the Louisiana State University Library acquired Natchitoches records of 1734–1792, containing 124 items, from private sources. The materials in that repository include land grants and surveys. Transcripts of Mézières' letters, obtained from a Mexican repository, are in the University of Texas Library.

The Natchitoches records were microfilmed by the Genealogical Society of the Church of Jesus Christ of Latter-Day Saints. Later, a project for microfilming the Natchitoches records was arranged by the Louisiana State Archives, Northwestern State University, and the office of the clerk of the court in Natchitoches, and copies of the microfilmed records, 1732–1819, in twenty-five reels, were acquired by all of the parties.[70] The clerk of the court also has xerox copies for easier reference. Microfilm of the conveyance records is in the New Orleans Public Library. Microfilm of the marriage records is in the Louisiana State Library. Microfilm of the St. Denis papers is in the Louisiana State University Library. Transcripts of Natchitoches records, 1722–1781, are in the University of Texas Library. Typewritten transcripts of St. Denis papers, 1697–1728, in one volume, obtained from the Archives Nationales in Paris are also in the University of Texas Library.

Other original records of Natchitoches are in the Watson Library of Northwestern State University at Natchitoches. The Melrose Collection in that repository contains Natchitoches documents of the years 1730–1804, which are listed in a publication. There is also a fragment of a court

69 / Historical Records Survey, Louisiana, *Inventory of the Parish Archives of Louisiana, No. 35, Natchitoches Parish (Natchitoches)* (University, La., 1938), 46–47, 55, 70; Winston De Ville, *Marriage Contracts of Natchitoches, 1739–1803* ([Nashville?], 1961).

70 / Wade O. Martin, Jr., "Archives," in *Eighteenth Annual Genealogical Institute Proceedings, 22 March 1975* (Baton Rouge, 1975), 2–3.

record book beginning with page 258 and containing entries from May 4, 1799, to May 29, 1804. A tax list for 1793 contains the names of persons who were taxed for the work of the community.[71] Memoirs and relations of the post of Natchitoches, dated June 12, 1724, are in the Edward E. Ayer Collection of the Newberry Library.

Some of the Natchitoches documents have been published. Translations of documents of 1722–1760 include an account of St. Denis with the Company of the Indies, 1722–1760. A 1766 census is printed from a typescript in the Bancroft Library of the University of California. Documents on the succession of François Clauseau from the conveyance records at Natchitoches have been published. The texts of numerous Natchitoches censuses, militia rolls, tax lists, and delinquent tax rolls have been printed from the microfilm held by the University of Southwestern Louisiana. Since settlers east of the Sabine River, in what is now northwestern Louisiana, were included in the jurisdiction of Texas, censuses of Nacogdoches contain information regarding them. A March 1, 1790, census of Natchitoches has been published. A 1782 Natchitoches militia list has been printed from a reproduction in the Northwestern State University Library.[72]

Orleans Parish (New Orleans). An act of the Louisiana legislature of March 31, 1807, set up the city of New Orleans and its precincts as Orleans Parish.[73] In 1818 the limits of the city were expanded, and in 1852 that part of Jefferson Parish known as the city of Lafayette was added to Orleans Parish. The parish government was housed at first in the Cabildo but was later transferred to the Presbytère which was purchased from St. Louis Cathedral by the city in 1853.[74]

An act of the Louisiana legislature of March 28, 1867, established an

71 / Carolyn M. Wells, *Index and Abstracts of Colonial Documents in the Eugene P. Watson Memorial Library* (Natchitoches, La., 1980); Winston De Ville, "Natchitoches Tax List for 1793," *Louisiana Genealogical Register,* XXVII (September, 1980), 245–48.

72 / Germaine Portré-Bobinski (trans.), *Natchitoches: Translations of Old French and Spanish Documents* ([Rutland, Ill.], 1928); Katherine Bridges and Winston De Ville, "Natchitoches in 1766," *Louisiana History,* IV (Spring, 1963), 145; Carol Wells (trans. and ed.), "The Succession of François Clauseau," *Louisiana Studies,* XI (Spring, 1972), 70–83; Elizabeth S. Mills, *Natchitoches Colonials: Censuses, Military Rolls, and Tax Lists, 1722–1803* (Chicago, 1981), xiii; Henry P. Beers, *Spanish & Mexican Records of the American Southwest: A Bibliographical Guide to Archive and Manuscript Sources* (Tucson, 1979), 108, 110 and n. 24; Robert B. L. Ardoin, *Louisiana Census Records: Avoyelles and St. Landry Parishes, 1810 & 1820* (Baltimore, 1970), II, 141–50; Elizabeth S. Mills, "Natchitoches Militia of 1782," *Louisiana Genealogical Register,* XX (September, 1973), 216–18.

73 / Fortier (ed.), *Louisiana Sketches,* II, 274.

74 / Brasseaux, Conrad, and Robison, *Courthouses of Louisiana,* 120–21.

office of custodian of notarial records in the parish of Orleans whose duty it was to preserve the records of notaries who had ceased to function by reason of death, removal, or otherwise.[75] The records were to be preserved safely in a fireproof building, and copies of documents were to be supplied to those needing them. Before this time, the records had passed from one notary to another.[76] The notarial acts formerly in the custody of Pedro Pedesclaux were transferred by the Louisiana Historical Society to the custodian of notarial records. That official was provided with space in government buildings in New Orleans and for years was in the court-house completed in 1904. In 1959 the notarial records were transferred from the old civil courts buiding to the new civil courts building, in the New Orleans civic center adjacent to the city hall.[77]

The notarial records of New Orleans for the colonial period date from 1739. Those accumulated by Jean Baptiste Garic date from June 6, 1739, to September 23, 1779. Of the twelve volumes for Garic, eleven are for the years 1739–1766, and the other is for 1767–1779. These volumes have tables of contents at their beginnings. The volume for Charles J. Maison, July 8, 1766–April 13, 1769, has no table of contents. There are records for nine other notaries, but they are not bound separately; instead they are scattered in the records of other notaries and in miscellaneous record books.[78] Succession books, 1731–1792, in two volumes, contain papers relating to many prominent men of early Louisiana. In the 1930s the Work Projects Administration arranged the disorganized notarial records and bound them into volumes that were indexed. Abstracts of the notarial records that were kept by Estevan de Quiñones have been published. A list of the notarial achives has also been published. An index to Spanish notarial documents that covers 350 marriage contracts and 1,300 wills and testaments has been published.[79] A copy of the microfilm of the notarial records prepared by the Genealogical Society of the Church of Jesus Christ of Latter-Day Saints in the 1960s is in the New Orleans Public Library. Microfilm of the New Orleans notarial records, 1764–1803,

75 / Louisiana, Laws, Statutes, etc., Acts of the Legislature, 1867, p. 261; Grima, "Notarial System of Louisiana," 78.

76 / Louisiana Historical Association Newsletter, I, no. 12 (1959).

77 / De Ville, "Manuscript Sources in Louisiana," 218–19.

78 / Elizabeth B. Gianelloni, Love, Honor, and Betrayal: The Notarial Acts of Estevan de Quiñones, 1785–1786 (Baton Rouge, 1964–65).

79 / Rudolph H. Waldo, Notarial Archives of New Orleans Parish, 1731–1953 ([New Orleans, 1953]); Charles R. Maduell, Jr., Marriage Contracts, Wills, and Testaments of the Spanish Colonial Period in New Orleans, 1770–1804 ([New Orleans], 1969); Collin B. Hamer, Jr., "Library Additions, New Orleans Public Library [List of New Orleans Notarial Records Available on Microfilm]," New Orleans Genesis, XI (September, 1972), 406–409.

in forty-seven reels, is in the Colonial Records Center of the University of Southwestern Louisiana. Inventories of the notarial records of Carlos Ximenes, 1768–1770, and of Pedro Pedesclaux, 1770–1804, are in the Louisiana Room of the New Orleans Public Library. A list of sixty-one bundles that were missing in 1966 is in index volume number 61, labelled "N. Broutin (15) Marriage Contracts, Sundry Dispensations," referring to documents executed in Spanish between 1777 and 1806.[80] The list covers a variety of documents, including petitions to establish purity of blood, abjurations of the Protestant faith, suits to collect money, emancipation suits, successions, and suits for breach of promise to marry.

At the time of the transfer of sovereignty at New Orleans in December, 1803, Pedro Pedesclaux occupied the office of keeper of mortgages. Despite being removed from the office by Governor Claiborne in 1807, he continued to hold it and the records until the next year when, following a legal suit, he surrendered it together with the records.[81] The records passed into the custody of Peter L. B. Duplessis, Claiborne's appointee.[82] The keeper of mortgages at New Orleans was directed by an act of March 24, 1810, to send extracts of all mortgages in force in the six parishes of the territory to the respective parish judges.[83] The record of mortgages, March 15, 1788–August 3, 1805, in two volumes, contains abstracts of conventional mortgages on improved and unimproved land, slaves, boats, and cattle, showing the date recorded, the names of mortgagor and mortgagee, a description of the property mortgaged, the amount of the loan, the date of maturity, and the name of the notary before whom the mortgage was passed. The volumes were in poor condition at the time the Historical Records Survey examined them in the 1930s and were still in that condition when the Louisiana Archives Survey conducted its survey, twenty years later.

Ouachita Parish (Monroe). In 1785, Captain Juan Filhiol established a settlement on the Ouachita River in northeastern Louisiana that was soon given the name of Fort Miró.[84] It became the seat of Ouachita Parish in

80 / Grover Rees, "The Missing Sixty-One Bundles," *New Orleans Genesis*, V (January, 1966), 11–12.

81 / W. C. C. Claiborne to the president, May 19, 1807, June 28, 1807, in Carter (ed.), *Territory of Orleans*, 735, 746; Claiborne to the president, March 13, 1808, in Rowland (ed.), *Official Letter Books*, IV, 161–62.

82 / Carter (ed.), *Territory of Orleans*, 752, 825.

83 / Orleans Territory, *Acts*, 1810, p. 62.

84 / J. Fair Hardin, "Don Juan Filhiol and the Founding of Fort Miro, the Modern Monroe, Louisiana," *Louisiana Historical Quarterly*, XX (April, 1937), 465–66.

1807, but the name was changed to Monroe in 1819. Initially a very large parish, it was greatly reduced when other parishes were formed from it. The parish records were removed to save them from destruction when the frame and stucco courthouse was fired by federal troops in April, 1864. Another courthouse, built in 1868, was destroyed by fire in 1882. The present four-story structure was built of concrete and limestone in 1924.[85]

The records of Ouachita Parish consist of notarial acts, including conveyances, mortgages, and marriage contracts, 1785–1804, arranged chronologically, unindexed; powers of attorney from 1788; suits, acts, and miscellaneous records, 1789–1805, in the parish court suit papers, indexed in a separate volume; records of the French and Spanish commandants of the post of Ouachita, 1784–1805, including civil, criminal, and probate case papers.[86] Microfilm of the conveyance records is in the New Orleans Public Library. Microfilm of the marriage records is in the Louisiana State Library.

Papers of Juan Filhiol and his descendants, 1783–1876, containing sixty items, in the Library of Congress, Manuscript Division, include correspondence, orders, reports, a petition for a land grant that included Hot Springs, Arkansas, and a map.[87] The collection consists partly of transcripts and photocopies and is on microfilm. Some of the documents were published by J. Fair Hardin in his article on Filhiol, cited above. Reproductions obtained by Hardin from the Papeles de Cuba in the Archivo General de Indias, including an instruction of Governor Miró in 1783 and a copy of Filhiol's report on his exploration of the Arkansas country in 1786, are in the Louisiana State University Library. A list of the names of ninety French immigrants who settled in the Ouachita district shows the names and ages of the heads of families and of wives and children. A 1790 census of the Ouachita post is in print.[88] A Ouachita land record book, 1808–1832, in one volume, containing a record of sales of the estate of Abraham Morehouse and Andrew Y. Morehouse, settlers in the colonial period, is in the holdings of the Historical Society of Pennsylvania. Papers of Felipe E. N. Bastrop, 1796–1819, thirty-five items, in the Louisiana State University Department of Archives and Manuscripts include mate-

85 / Brasseaux, Conrad, and Robison, *Courthouses of Louisiana*, 124–25.

86 / Historical Records Survey, Louisiana, *Inventory of the Parish Archives of Louisiana, No. 37, Ouachita Parish (Monroe)* (Baton Rouge, 1942), 59–60, 75–77, 120; Margery Wright and Benjamin E. Achee, *Index of Ouachita Parish, Louisiana, Probate Records, 1800–1870* (Shreveport, 1969).

87 / *National Union Catalog of Manuscripts*, 1976, entry 158.

88 / Pérez, "French Immigrants to Louisiana," 106–13; Winston De Ville, "Census of the Ouachita Post in Louisiana: 1790," *Louisiana Genealogical Register*, XXIX (March, 1982), 21–24.

rials concerning land grants of Bastrop and others in the Ouachita River valley and contain letters exchanged between Bastrop and Governor Carondelet during 1796–1797.[89] The J. Fair Hardin Collection in the same repository contains materials relating to the Maison Rouge land claims in the same region.

Plaquemines Parish (Pointe-a-la-Hache). Established in 1807 from part of Orleans County, this parish is divided by the Mississippi River. The establishment of the parish seat was delayed for many years by a dispute over the site between residents of the east bank and those on the west bank. Finally in 1890 a courthouse was built at Pointe-a-la-Hache on the east side, fifty miles below New Orleans.[90] The records of Plaquemines Parish include notarial acts from August 20, 1792; notarial record index from 1792, arranged alphabetically by the first letter of the surname; and a book of wills, dated March 15, 1794.[91]

Pointe Coupee Parish (New Roads). Pointe Coupee, on the west bank of the Mississippi River, was settled early in the eighteenth century by French Canadians who came down the Mississippi from the Illinois country. Their numbers were increased by colonists brought over from France by large landowners. When the parish was set up in 1807, its seat was at Pointe Coupee, where predecessor regimes had been located.[92] After the destruction of the quarters there by fire, the seat was moved in 1848 to New Roads.[93]

Records of Pointe Coupee in the clerk's vault at New Roads include notarial acts beginning in the 1720s, recorded in numerical order in books; a chronological index from which the names of parties can be ascertained; another notarial acts file, dating from January 3, 1788, arranged numerically by file number and chronologically thereunder, with a separate alphabetical index; an index to conveyances from 1765; and a chronological listing of notarial acts from February 1, 1762.[94] Documents dated prior to 1762 are interfiled with those of later dates and are not in the index. About 1959 the old records were in fifteen leather volumes; five years later some were missing. Some notes made from the missing records, giving

89 / A. Otis Hébert, "Resources in Louisiana Depositories," 35.

90 / Brasseaux, Conrad, and Robison, *Courthouses of Louisiana*, 127.

91 / Historical Records Survey, Louisiana, *Inventory of the Parish Archives of Louisiana, No. 38, Plaquemines Parish (Point a la Hache)* (University, La., 1939), 91, 93, 128.

92 / Fortier (ed.), *Louisiana Sketches*, II, 314, 247.

93 / Brasseaux, Conrad, and Robison, *Courthouses of Louisiana*, 129.

94 / Historical Records Survey, Louisiana, [Inventory of Entries Covering the Colonial Records of Louisiana]. Typewritten inventory supplied to the author by the Survey in 1939, in Beers Correspondence.

the dates, the types of documents, and the names of the persons they relate to, have been published. A general census of the inhabitants of Pointe Coupee of December 20, 1745, shows the names of men and women, their ages, the numbers of children, slaves (black, red, and mulatto), farm animals, and arms, and the quantity of land occupied. An index to marriages compiled from the records in the courthouse includes the names of the parents. A Spanish census shows the names of the husband and the wife, the number and ages of sons and daughters, the quantity of land, and the number of slaves for each entry. A compilation relative to marriages is arranged alphabetically by the names of the husbands, with the date of the marriage and the name of the bride. A list of the names of the persons taking the loyalty oath to Spain in 1769 is in print. An oath of allegiance to the Spanish government taken by the inhabitants of Pointe Coupee and Fausse River before the commandant of the post, September 10, 1769, contains signatures or names with marks. Histories of 106 families of this parish are included in a history of the parish.[95] Microfilm of the parish civil records in ten reels is in the Colonial Records Collection of the University of Southwestern Louisiana.

Rapides Parish (Alexandria). Eary in the eighteenth century, French settlers located on the Red River on grants made by the Company of the West.[96] About 1723, the French established a post at the rapids of the Red River in central Louisiana above present Alexandria.[97] In 1807 Rapides Parish was created, with its seat at Alexandria. When the Union troops withdrew from that town on May 13, 1864, it was set on fire and most of the buildings, including those housing the government offices and their records, were destroyed.[98]

95 / De Ville, "Manuscript Sources in Louisiana, 225; Winston De Ville, "A Partial Calendar of Non-Extant Pointe Coupee Post Records, 1762–1769," *Louisiana Genealogical Register* XV (December, 1968), 129–38; Bill Barron (ed.), *Census of Pointe Coupee, Louisiana, 1745* (New Orleans, 1978), 3–34; Veneta de Graffenried Morrison (comp.), *Index—Early Marriages of Pointe Coupee, 1771–1843* (New Roads, La., [1971?]); Winston De Ville (ed.), and Mrs. Drouet W. Vidrine (trans.), "Spanish Census of Point Coupee—1766," *Louisiana Genealogical Register,* VII (September, December, 1960), 33, 55; Nicholas R. Murray, *Pointe Coupee Parish, Louisiana, 1763–1872. A Computer-Indexed Marriage Record* (Hammond, La., [1982]); "Loyalty Oath List for Pointe Coupee to the Government of Spain, 1769," *Louisiana Genealogical Register,* XI (March, 1964), 10–11; Henry P. Dart (ed.), "The Oath of Allegiance to Spain," *Louisiana Historical Quarterly,* IV (April, 1921), 205–15; Judy Riffel (ed.), *A History of Pointe Coupee Parish and Its Families* (Baton Rouge, 1983).

96 / Fortier (ed.), *Louisiana Sketches,* II, 346.

97 / G. P. Whittington, "Rapides Parish, Louisiana—a History," *Louisiana Historical Quarterly,* XV–XVIII (October, 1932–January, 1935); see especially XV (January, 1933), 30.

98 / Whittington, "Rapides Parish," *Louisiana Historical Quarterly,* XV, 567.

Red River Parish (Coushatta). This parish was formed from portions of older, neighboring parishes in northwestern Louisiana by act of the Louisiana legislature on March 2, 1871.[99] A courthouse for the new parish was erected at Coushatta. Research and inventory materials for this parish are in the Louisiana State University Department of Archives and Manuscripts. Some conveyance records on microfilm, dating from 1746, are in the New Orleans Public Library; microfilm of marriage records is in the Louisiana State Library.

St. Bernard Parish (Chalmette). The parish of St. Bernard, south of Orleans Parish on the Mississippi River, was settled early in the eighteenth century by colonists from France and Spain.[100] They obtained grants of land on which they raised food for the New Orleans market. Later in that century, Canary Islanders and Acadians arrived. Established as one of the original parishes in 1807, St. Bernard had its seat at the village of Violet until its removal in 1848 to a new courthouse at St. Bernard. A courthouse constructed at St. Bernard in 1880 was destroyed by fire in 1884. New courthouses were completed there in 1889 and 1915, but the removal of the seat to Chalmette was voted on in 1938, and in the next year a courthouse was finished there.[101]

Most of the records of St. Bernard Parish were destroyed in the courthouse fire in March, 1884. A volume of original notarial acts of commandant Pedro Denys de la Ronde, September 14, 1788–November 5, 1802, survives.[102] The volume includes mortgages, sales of land, property, and slaves, agreements, marriage contracts, leases, and donations. These acts were reassembled by the Historical Records Survey, placed in folders, and stored in the vault in the office of the clerk of the court. In 1981 a grant was made by the National Historical Publications and Records Commission for arranging, microfilming, and indexing these old acts.

St. Charles Parish (Hahnville). Early in the eighteenth century, German immigrants from Alsatia under the leadership of Charles Frederick D'Arensbourg, attracted by the publicity of the Company of the West, settled on the banks of the Mississippi River above New Orleans on what became known as the German Coast. In 1807 these settlements were set up as St.

99 / Hisorical Records Survey, Louisiana, *County-Parish Boundaries,* 86.
100 / Fortier (ed.), *Louisiana Sketches,* II, 404.
101 / Brasseaux, Conrad, and Robison, *Courthouses of Louisiana,* 138–39.
102 / Andreassen and Davis, *Louisiana Archives Survey,* 361; Historical Records Survey, Louisiana, *Inventory of the Parish Archives of Louisiana, No. 44, St. Bernard Parish (Chalmette)* (University, La., 1938), 50.

Charles Parish. The seat was at St. Charles Parish Courthouse, which was renamed Hahnville in 1872.[103] Notarial records of St. Charles Parish, 1740–1804, in thirty-five volumes, formerly in the office of the clerk of the court, have been transferred to the Louisiana State Archives. These records are arranged chronologically, but the Historical Records Survey reported gaps in the file for 1728–1739, 1759–1764, and 1768–1770. A one-volume index that extends to 1831 is available. A calendar of the earliest acts of the German Coast recorded by D'Arensbourg has been published.[104] Translations and abstracts of the notarial acts for 1770–1803, comprising 1,954 documents, have been published.[105] In preparing this compilation, Glenn R. Conrad placed the documents in proper order and found them in a fair state of preservation with little evidence of mutilation or abuse. He also noticed that the French scribes tended to Gallicize German names. Microfilm of the original acts of St. Charles Parish, 1740–1803, in thirteen reels, is in the University of Southwestern Louisiana Center for Louisiana History. Microfilm of those acts and of other records of St. Charles Parish is in the Louisiana State Museum, the Louisiana State Archives, the St. Martin Parish Library, and the New Orleans Public Library. Censuses of 1749 and 1766 of settlers on the banks of the Mississippi River have been published. A census of May 1, 1804, ordered by Governor Claiborne, has also been published. An index of marriage records by the name of the groom, with the date of marriage and the name of the bride, is in print.[106]

St. Helena Parish (Greensburg). One of the West Florida parishes created in 1810, this parish originally had its seat at Montpelier.[107] After the southern part of the parish was set aside as Livingston Parish by an act of the Louisiana legislature on February 10, 1832, a wooden courthouse was

103 / Fortier (ed.), *Louisiana Sketches,* I, 515.

104 / Historical Records Survey, Louisiana, *Inventory of the Parish Archives of Louisiana, No. 45, Saint Charles Parish (Hahnville)* (University, La., 1937), 40; Louisiana State Archives and Records Service, *Calendar of Louisiana Colonial Documents, Volume III, St. Charles Parish, Part I: The D'Arensbourg Records, 1734–1769,* comp. Elizabeth B. Gianelloni (Baton Rouge, 1967).

105 / Conrad, *St. Charles Abstracts.* A continuation arranged chronologically has been published: Glenn R. Conrad, *The German Coast: Abstracts of the Civil Records of St. Charles and St. John the Baptist Parishes, 1804–1812* (Lafayette, La., 1981).

106 / Yvette G. Boling, "The German Coast of Louisiana in 1749," *Louisiana Genealogical Register,* XXIX (December, 1982), 373–90; Gladys Hebert (ed.), and Sidney L. Villeré (trans.), *A Partial Colonial Census of Saint Charles Parish—Louisiana," New Orleans Genesis,* VII (January, 1968), 30–34; Sidney L. Villeré, "General Census of the First German Coast Province of Louisiana [May 1, 1804]," *New Orleans Genesis,* VI (September, 1967), 337–40; Nicholas R. Murray, *St. Charles Parish, Louisiana, 1771–1900. Computer-Indexed Marriage Records* (Hammond, La., [1981]).

107 / Fortier (ed.), *Louisiana Sketches,* II, 411.

erected at Greensburg near the geographic center of the parish.[108] The early courthouse was replaced by a brick structure in 1855 and then in 1938 by a concrete building. Records of this parish during the Spanish period are included in those of East Baton Rouge Parish.

St. James Parish (Convent). Small settlements that were made early in the eighteenth century along Lake Maurepas and the Mississippi River were greatly augmented in the 1760s by the arrival of Acadians, who settled on both sides of the Mississippi.[109] Located above the German Coast, these settlements became known as the Acadian Coast. Other Frenchmen from the Illinois country settled there late in the eighteenth century. This area, known as the second Acadian Coast, became St. James Parish in 1807 and included settlements on both sides of the Mississippi River. The parish seat was initially at St. James on the west side of the river, but in 1869 it was moved to a site on the east side of the river near the Convent of the Sacred Heart and became known as Convent from its proximity to that institution.[110]

Notarial acts of Miguel Cantrelle, the commandant, from January 9, 1782, to 1787, contain acts concerning the sale of real and personal property, mortgages, inventories, and family meetings. A file of miscellaneous documents that begins in 1750 includes civil and criminal suits, peace and bail bonds, and copies of wills. Microfilm of the original acts of St. James Parish, 1782–1787, on one reel, is in the University of Southwestern Louisiana Center for Louisiana History. Microfilm of marriage records is in the Louisiana State Library. Censuses of the inhabitants of Cabonocey on both banks of the Mississippi for April 9, 1766, September 14, 1769, and January 1, 1777, give the names and ages of members of families. The first two also give the number of slaves and the quantity of land, cattle, hogs, sheep, and guns. Lists of militia members for April 8, 1766, and January 23, 1770, are also published in the same book. A list of Acadians married during 1766–1768 shows the names of the groom and the bride and the date of the ceremony. Published abstracts of the records of 1782–1787 signed by Miguel Cantrelle contain land sales, slave sales, marriages and successions, wills, contracts for the exchange of property, auction sales, inventories of property, judicial sales of property, and naming of tutors of minors.[111] This compilation contains much information on people and is indexed by name.

108 / Brasseaux, Conrad, and Robison, *Courthouses of Louisiana*, 142–43.

109 / Fortier (ed.), *Louisiana Sketches*, II, 413; Lillian C. Bourgeois, *Cabonocey: The History, Customs and Folklore of St. James Parish* (New Orleans, [1957]), 8–14, 23.

110 / Brasseaux, Conrad, and Robison, *Courthouses of Louisiana*, 144.

111 / Historical Records Survey, Louisiana, *Title-Line Inventory*; Bourgeois, *Cabonocey*,

St. John the Baptist Parish (Edgard). This parish on the Mississippi River below New Orleans was settled by Germans in the middle of the eighteenth century. The settlement became known as the Second German Coast, and into it in 1766 came exiled Acadians, who in later years became known as Cajuns.[112] On March 31, 1807, the area between Lakes Maurepas and Pontchartrain and the Mississippi was set up as St. John the Baptist Parish. Its seat was initially at Lucy, but it was moved to Edgard in 1848. A two-story wooden courthouse, built there in 1847, was replaced in 1968 by a brick structure.[113]

The notarial records of this parish date from 1753; earlier records were kept by the commandant of the first German Coast (St. Charles Parish). The records for this parish are considered complete and well preserved. An abstract of the original acts of St. John the Baptist Parish in English is arranged, like the records themselves, in chronological order, but an alphabetical name index is provided. This compilation provides considerable information about the early families of St. John and their property and is accompanied by a partial genealogy of some of the families.[114] Microfilm of the original acts of St. John the Baptist Parish, 1770–1803, in eleven reels, is in the University of Southwestern Louisiana Center for Louisiana History.

St. Landry Parish (Opelousas). The Opelousas district, where a trading and military post was established about 1750, was settled by Acadians from Nova Scotia and France, by Americans, by settlers from Santo Domingo, and by others of various nationalities. The early pioneers were assisted by the government with grants of land and equipment to engage in farming and raising stock.[115] The post of Opelousas became the headquarters of the district under a French and later a Spanish commandant. When St. Landry Parish was established in 1807 with jurisdiction over much of southwestern Louisiana, Opelousas became the parish seat. For many years the records of the parish were stored in the attic of the courthouse at Opelousas in a "remarkable state of confusion."[116]

The notarial records of St. Landry Parish, 1764–1803, contain the

162–70, 173–79, 183–92; Eileen L. Behrman (comp.), *St. James Parish, Louisiana, Colonial Records, 1782–1787* (Conroe, Tex., 1980).

112 / Lubin F. Laurent, "History of St. John the Baptist Parish," *Louisiana Historical Quarterly,* VII (April, 1924), 319.

113 / Fortier (ed.), *Louisiana Sketches,* II, 414; Brasseaux, Conrad, and Robison, *Courthouses of Louisiana,* 146.

114 / Glenn R. Conrad, *Saint-Jean-Baptiste des Allemands: Abstracts of the Civil Records of St. John the Baptist Parish, with Genealogy and Index, 1753–1803* (Lafayette, La., 1972), 281–387.

115 / Griffin, *Attakapas Country,* 13.

116 / Louisiana Archives, *Calendar of Documents, St. Landry Parish,* ix.

usual variety of documents concerning the settlers in the area and their property. Two Louisiana investigators interested in genealogy located the marriage contracts while examining the records in 1959 and 1960 and published an abstract of their contents in English.[117] A chronological calendar of the records for 1764–1785 covering southwestern Louisiana provides abstracts of a wide variety of documents.[118] This calendar was reprinted in 1979 with a name and place index and with an additional part consisting of documents on microfilm that were not listed in the 1964 calendar. The plan to publish a similar calendar for the later years was dropped because the records remained in disorder. A guide to the St. Landry Parish records has been published. In 1961 the records of the parish were transferred to the Louisiana State Archives and Records Service in Baton Rouge, where better storage space was available. The repository has microfilmed the records. A brand book for the Opelousas and Attakapas districts, dating from 1760, with the names of owners, dates of registration, and reproductions of the brands is in the Stephens Memorial Library of the University of Southwestern Louisiana. The brand book has been microfilmed in 630 frames. A census of landowners for 1793 is in print, and a census of the inhabitants taken on May 28, 1796, is arranged by neighborhoods. An alphabetical list of the names of those who sold land during the years 1765–1805 is also in print.[119] A copy of the microfilm of the colonial records, 1764–1789, in seven reels, is in the Center for Louisiana History at the University of Southwestern Louisiana and at the Louisiana State Museum in New Orleans. The University of Southwestern Louisiana also has some papers on slave sales and land sales and other legal documents, 1786–1803, comprising seventeen items.

St. Martin Parish (St. Martinville). The earliest settlers in the Attakapas district of southern Louisiana in 1765 were Acadian refugees from Santo Domingo. Other early settlers were Canary Islanders and French émigrés. The military post established at Attakapas in 1769 became the seat of

117 / Jacqueline O. Vidrine and Winston De Ville (comps.), *Marriage Contracts of the Opelousas Post, 1766–1803* ([Ville Platte?], 1960).

118 / Louisiana Archives, *Calendar of Documents, St. Landry Parish.* The Louisiana Archives and Records Service has a typewritten index to this calendar.

119 / Louisiana, State Archives and Records Service, *Calendar of Documents of the Opelousas Post, 1764–1789*, comp. Arthur W. Bergeron, Jr. (Baton Rouge, 1979); Jacqueline O. Vidrine, *The Opelousas Post, 1764–1789: Guide to the St. Landry Parish Archives Deposited at Louisiana State Archives* (Baton Rouge, 1979); Lauren C. Post, "The Old Cattle Industry of Southwest Louisiana," *McNeese Review*, IX (Winter, 1957), 46 n. 8; Winston De Ville, "Land Census of the Inhabitants of the Opelousas, 1793," *Louisiana Genealogical Register*, VII (March, June, 1960), 8–9, 26–28; Winston De Ville, "Census of the Opelousas Post, 28 May 1796," *Louisiana Genealogical Register*, XIII (March, 1966), 7–8; Mrs. Joseph Ducote, "The Names of Those Who

Spanish authority in the district.[120] Initially covering a large area, the district included what became St. Martin, Iberia, Lafayette, St. Mary, and Vermilion parishes. In 1807, the Attakapas country was set up as the parish of St. Martin, with the seat at St. Martinville.

An examination of the parish records in the office of the clerk of the court in the 1960s disclosed them to be in remarkably good condition, without any significant gaps.[121] Notarial acts begin in 1760, are chronologically arranged by date of instrument, and are indexed in separate books. Among the acts are marks and brands for the period 1760–1770. Another set of books contains notarial acts dating from 1793, similarly entered but without an index. A daily book register of notarial acts begins in 1760. A file of marriage contracts dates from 1760, is arranged by date of ceremony, and is indexed by the names of both parties in separate volumes. A conveyance record-vendee from June 13, 1760, is arranged by first letter of the vendee's surname. A chronological record of marks and brands from 1761 is unindexed.[122] Microfilm of the parish records, 1760–1803, in eleven reels, is in the University of Southwestern Louisiana.

Several publications are useful for the work of genealogists and other researchers. English texts of the marriage contracts, 1760–1803, show the names of the notary or commandant, the groom, the bride, their parents, and witnesses. The entries sometimes also show the positions or occupations of the parents and the birthplaces of the groom and the bride. This compilation also includes an index to the names of the grooms and a 1774 census of Attakapas. Several lists compiled from the parish records are in another place. A list of marriages, 1760–1811, is arranged alphabetically by the groom's name and shows the date and the archival source. A list of marriages, 1774–1810, gleaned from other sources is similarly arranged. Included also is a list of estates and wills, 1760–1805, and a list of inventories, testaments, and miscellaneous instruments pertaining to heirship. This compilation contains about three thousand names of early settlers of the Attakapas district (the present parishes of St. Martin, St. Mary, Lafayette, Vermilion, and Iberia). Lists of militia that participated against the British during the Revolutionary War obtained by Charles R. Churchill from the Papeles de Cuba and a later list of 1792 are also in the same publication. An index to marriages arranged by the name of the groom and also showing the date of the marriage and the name of the bride is in

Sold Lands Situated in the Post of Opelousas [1765–1805]," *Louisiana Genealogical Register*, XIX (March, 1972), 82–85.

120 / Griffin, *Attakapas Country*, 22.
121 / De Ville, "Manuscript Sources in Louisiana," 227.
122 / Historical Records Survey, Louisiana, *Title-Line Inventory*.

print. A general census of 1774 gives the names of males and the numbers of children, farm animals, and slaves.[123]

St. Mary Parish (Franklin). This parish was created on April 17, 1811, from part of Attakapas Parish.[124] Court sessions were held at Franklin from 1811 to 1820, and in the latter year the state legislature designated that place as the parish seat. No inventory of the records of this parish has been published. An index of the marriage records includes data from 1739.[125]

St. Tammany Parish (Covington). This parish was created in 1811 from part of West Florida, which was annexed to the state in 1810. The parish court met at different places until an act of the legislature in 1818 resulted in the selection of Claiborne as the seat.[126] An act of February, 1829, changed the seat to Covington, where rented buildings were used until the courthouse authorized in 1839 was constructed. That courthouse was succeeded by a brick one in 1896 and a reinforced concrete building in 1959.[127] Records concerning this parish during the Spanish period are included in those of East Baton Rouge Parish.

West Baton Rouge Parish (Port Allen). Originally created in 1807 as Baton Rouge Parish, it comprised that part of the territory west of the Mississippi River formerly known as Baton Rouge.[128] After the acquisition of Baton Rouge in 1810, East Baton Rouge Parish was created, and the parish west of the Mississippi became West Baton Rouge Parish. The first courthouse was built at St. Michel, but it had to be abandoned because of the encroachment of the Mississippi River. Another courthouse was built at Port Allen, on the Mississippi River opposite Baton Rouge, where the latest one dates from 1957.[129]

Records of the parish in the custody of its recorder include a bundle of papers, dated 1777, relating to the succession of Henri Gerard. Some

123 / Winston De Ville and Jane G. Bulliard (trans. and eds.), *Marriage Contracts of the Attakapas Post, 1760–1803: Colonial Louisiana Marriage Contracts and the 1774 Census of Attakapas Post* (St. Martinville, La., 1966), 33–72; Mary Sanders, *Attakapas Records,* 26–41, 42–45, 47–50, 218–26; Nicholas R. Murray, *St. Martin Parish, Louisiana, 1760–1900. Computer-Indexed Marriage Records* (Hammond, La., 1982); Mrs. Druet W. Vidrine, "Recensement General des Attakapas, October 30, 1774," *Louisiana Genealogical Register,* XIII (March, 1966), 65–66.

124 / Calhoun, "County-Parish Government," 103.

125 / Nicholas R. Murray, *St. Mary Parish, Louisiana, 1739–1892. Computer-Indexed Marriage Records* (Hammond, La., 1981).

126 / Fortier (ed.), *Louisiana Sketches,* II, 413.

127 / Brasseaux, Conrad, and Robison, *Courthouses of Louisiana,* 158–59.

128 / Fortier (ed.), *Louisiana Sketches,* II, 625–26.

129 / Brasseaux, Conrad, and Robison, *Courthouses of Lousiana,* 177–78.

miscellaneous papers dating from 1800 are in the custody of the clerk of the court. Other records of the parish, 1793–1881, containing 113 items, are in the Howard-Tilton Memorial Library of Tulane University.[130] Microfilm of marriage records is in the Louisiana State Library.

West Feliciana Parish (St. Francisville). Feliciana Parish, created as one of the West Florida parishes in 1810, had its seat at St. Francisville until 1818, when it was moved to Jackson. Upon the division of the parish in 1824, that town was in East Feliciana, so the seat for West Feliciana was placed at St. Francisville.[131] Initially, rented quarters were used as the courthouse, but construction of a courthouse was started in 1829. That early structure was replaced in 1852 and again in 1903.[132]

West Feliciana Parish records date from 1787 and are described as being in good condition.[133] Conveyance records of real and personal property, dating from April 11, 1787, are filed alphabetically by name of vendor in 161 pigeonholes in the clerk's vault. There are also some acts of the trade or exchange of property from May 14, 1801; marriage licenses from 1791, entered in volumes alphabetically by the surname of the groom; and an alphabetical name index to the licenses. Plat books, arranged numerically by township number, date from 1799. Records of Feliciana and East Feliciana parishes, 1804–1823, in the Department of Archives and Manuscripts at Louisiana State University include fee books, docket books, court records, poll books, and registration books. An index of marriage records, arranged alphabetically by the name of the groom and showing the date of the marriage and the name of the bride, is in print.[134]

130 / Historical Records Survey, Louisiana [Inventory of Entries], in Beers Correspondence; Griffith, "Collections in the Howard-Tilton Library," 321.

131 / Louisiana, *Acts*, 1824, p. 26.

132 / Brasseaux, Conrad, and Robison, *Courthouses of Louisiana*, 182.

133 / Historical Records Survey, Louisiana, *Title-Line Inventory*, 1.

134 / Mrs. Stephen P. Dart, "West Feliciana Parish Marriage Index, 1791–1875," *Louisiana Genealogical Register*, XVI (June, September, 1969), 177–78, 242–45; XVII (June, 1970), 193–96; XVIII (March, December, 1971), 52–54, 314–16; Coutts and Whitley, "Inventory of Sources," 223; Nicholas R. Murray, *West Feliciana Parish, Louisiana, 1791–1875. Computer-Indexed Marriage Records* (Hammond, La., [1980?]).

7

Land Records

In order to promote settlement and to encourage the development of agriculture, the French government adopted a liberal policy in regard to land grants. The charter companies had the authority to make grants located along the Mississippi River and its tributaries, which served as the routes of travel. Early concessions were too large to be improved and cultivated by their owners; consequently, a royal order of October 12, 1716, directed that surplus lands were to be returned to the government and ceded to other inhabitants.[1] Accordingly, the Company of the West instructed the governor and the commissary in Louisiana to limit grants to two to four arpents frontage on the rivers and forty-six to sixty arpents in depth. Numerous concessions were made thereafter by the Company of the West and the Company of the Indies.[2] A 1731 census of landowners along the banks of the lower Mississippi River and another of owners in New Orleans are in print.[3] As representatives of the intendant of Louisiana, the commandants of the local posts approved the applications of settlers for land grants.

In the Spanish colonies, vacant lands were held to be the property of the crown. The title of the Indians to the land they actually occupied was respected. To promote the settlement and development of the colony, authority was given to colonial officials to make free grants of land.[4] Under

---

1 / Henry P. Dart (ed.), "The First Law Regulating Land Grants in French Colonial Louisiana [October 12, 1716]," *Louisiana Historical Quarterly*, XIV (April, 1931), 346–48.

2 / Heinrich, *Louisiane*, 113, 131, 159. A list of the names of the owners of these large tracts is in Gayarré, *History of Louisiana*, I, 241.

3 / Conrad (comp. and trans.), *First Families of Louisiana*, I, 49–56, 65–67.

4 / Haring, *Spanish Empire*, 257; C. Richard Arena, "Land Settlement Policies and Practices in Spanish Louisiana," in John F. McDermott (ed.), *The Spanish in the Mississippi Valley, 1762–1804* (Urbana, Ill., 1974), 56, 59.

his general authority Governor Alexandro O'Reilly issued on February 18, 1770, regulations regarding land grants.[5] These provided for granting tracts of specified river frontage and depths to newly arrived settlers, the grantees being required to construct levees and ditches, to repair roads and bridges, and to clear and fence the front part of their land within three years. The grants could not be sold until after three years and after the fulfillment of the prescribed conditions. A surveyor appointed by the governor was to fix the bounds of the grants, and these were to be recorded in a procès-verbal signed by the surveyor, the ordinary judge of the district, and two settlers of adjoining lands. Three copies of the procès-verbal were to be made; one was to be deposited in the office of the notary of the government and the *cabildo,* another delivered to the governor, and the third held by the proprietor, along with the titles of his grant. On September 9, 1797, Governor Manuel Gayoso de Lemos issued to the commandants instructions for making land grants to new settlers. The requirements covered residence, ownership of property, faithfulness in an occupation, and religion. Married applicants were to receive two hundred arpents of land and fifty more for each child. A new emigrant with property, willing to take an oath of fidelity, could obtain two hundred arpents for himself and his wife and twenty more for each slave, up to eight hundred arpents.[6]

A dispute between Governor Gayoso de Lemos and Intendant Juan Ventura Morales over the power to make grants of land was referred to Spain and resulted in the issuance of a royal order on October 22, 1798, transferring this power to the intendant. On July 17, 1799, Morales issued new regulations regarding grants of land.[7] Newly arrived settlers with written permission from the government to establish themselves on a chosen place could petition for a grant in an amount to be determined by their capacity and needs. The grantees were obliged to make within a year certain improvements in the way of levees, canals, highways, and bridges and within three years to clear and cultivate the front part of their grants. A procès-verbal showing the bounds of the grant was to be prepared by the surveyor general or a person designated by him and witnessed by the commandant or *syndic* of the district and two neighbors. The original procès-verbal and a certified copy were sent to the intendant in order that the title paper could be delivered. The original procès-verbal was then to be deposited in the office of the treasury official, and a record

5 / Holmes, *Gayoso,* 35.
6 / White (ed.), *New Collection of Laws,* II, 231–33.
7 / *Ibid.,* II, 234–45.

thereof was to be kept in the intendant's office with an alphabetical list. The surveyor was also to keep a record of the procès-verbal in a book and on the original copy of this was to be noted the folio of the book in which was recorded the figurative plat of the survey. The titles of concessions were also to be recorded in a numbered book in the office of the finances. Only persons in possession of real titles completed in accordance with the procedure described above would be regarded as legal owners of land. Those possessing land in virtue of formal titles given by the governors of the province were to be protected in their possessions, but others lacking title to lands they occupied were to be removed from them unless they could prove they had been occupying those lands for more than ten years, in which cases title could be obtained by paying a just recompense.

Land grants were made by the Spanish authorities in many localities and embraced a considerable quantity of land. Small grants were made to Acadians on both banks of the Mississippi and Amite rivers, on Bayou Lafourche, and in southwestern Louisiana.[8] Canary Islanders brought into the colony by the Spaniards were settled at Valenzuela and in the Opelousas district in southwestern Louisiana. In the 1780s Irish, German, and Americans were admitted into the colony provided they were Roman Catholics, but later the restriction as to religion was lifted.[9] A number of colonizing contracts were made for the settlement of French royalists and American Catholics. In 1785 Captain Juan Filhiol settled on a land grant at Fort Miró (Monroe) on the Ouachita River, where he was joined on another grant to the north given to Captain Guillaume de la Baume. Other large grants on the Ouachita were made in 1785 to the Marquis de Maison Rouge and the Baron de Bastrop, who were later joined by Colonel Abraham Morehouse.[10]

After the transfer of Natchez to the United States in 1798, Spanish inhabitants crossed over the Mississippi River and founded the new settlement of Concordia. In this area a large grant was made to Louis Bringier in consideration for services rendered to the Spanish government by his father Marius. Most of the grants made by the British in West Florida were never occupied or improved, so the Spanish were later able to make grants in the same areas. They continued to make grants in the

8 / Marchand, *Acadian Exiles*, 68.

9 / Caroline M. Burson, *The Stewardship of Don Esteban Miró, 1782–1792; a Study of Louisiana Based Largely on the Documents in New Orleans* (New Orleans, 1940), 24, 26.

10 / Jennie O. Mitchell and Robert D. Calhoun, "The Marquis de Maison Rouge, the Baron de Bastrop, and Colonel Abraham Morhouse, Three Ouachita Valley Soldiers of Fortune, the Maison Rouge and Bastrop Spanish Land Grants," *Louisiana Historical Quarterly*, XX (April, 1937), 289–462, contains numerous documents on these grants.

Florida parishes of Louisiana during the years 1803–1807, though the territory had been ceded to but not yet occupied by the United States.[11] By the time of the Louisiana Purchase, nearly all the land in the Sabine River territory had been granted by the Spanish. The total area embraced by private claims made prior to the transfer to the United States was estimated to cover not more than five million acres.[12]

The French and Spanish land grants, located on rivers and streams that were the means of transportation, extended back from narrow fronts on the rivers of about forty arpents or nearly eight thousand feet.[13] Grants were described and identified by natural features on the grounds, and the quantity of land in the grant was not known until a survey was made.[14] To remedy the problem of the lack of surveyors in the colony, the Company of the Indies sent out two brothers named Lassus to act as engineers in its name.[15] In 1737 François Saucier surveyed Bienville's land on the Mississippi River. During the period 1763–1765, Olivier de Vezin was serving as surveyor general of Louisiana.[16] Governor O'Reilly appointed surveyors in the different districts of Louisiana. Carlos Laveau Trudeau became surveyor general of Louisiana in 1780 and served throughout the remainder of the Spanish regime.[17] After the conquest of West Florida by the Spanish in 1779, such surveys as were done there were performed by deputies of the surveyor general of Louisiana. Concessions of land there often went unsurveyed or were poorly done by the local commandants or their subordinates.

Most of the land records held by the Spanish, which the United States undoubtedly had a right to under the treaty and which were important for the settlement of land claims, never came into the possession of federal officials. Commissioners William C. C. Claiborne and James

11 / Paul W. Gates, "Private Land Claims in the South," *Journal of Southern History*, XXII (May, 1956), 193.

12 / Harry L. Coles, Jr., "A History of the Administration of the Federal Land Policies and Land Tenure in Louisiana, 1803–1860" (Ph.D. thesis, Vanderbilt University, 1949), 68.

13 / James W. Taylor, "Louisiana Land Survey Systems," *Southwestern Social Science Quarterly*, XXXI (March, 1951), 276–78; Joy D. Eaton, "Early Louisiana Land Records," in *Eighteenth Annual Genealogical Institute Proceedings, 22 March 1975* (Baton Rouge, 1975), 32.

14 / Gayarré, *History of Louisiana*, I, 364.

15 / Surrey, *Calendar of Manuscripts*, 1480.

16 / Statement of Trudeau, New Orleans, March 17, 1808, in *The New American State Papers: Public Lands*, ed. Thomas C. Cochran, Irwin F. Greenbert, and Graham D. Taylor (Wilmington, Del., 1973), VI, 481.

17 / William Dunbar to the president, October 21, 1803, in Carter (ed.), *Territory of Orleans*, 85.

Wilkinson at the transfer of Louisiana in March, 1804, received from Intendant Morales, for the period after 1799, fifty-three sheets containing warrants of survey issued and plats of survey made during his administration.[18] Morales withheld the register of patents for titles issued after 1799 on the grounds that the work of separating the records ought to be done by the United States. Governor Claiborne applied to Trudeau and Morales for land papers but without success.[19]

Under an act of Congress approved March 2, 1805, John W. Gurley was shortly afterwards appointed register of the land office for the eastern part of the Territory of Orleans. Gurley reported to the secretary of the treasury on June 9 that the records of surveys from the year 1788 were in the hands of Trudeau. The land records received from the Spanish in 1804 were apparently transferred to Gurley, who turned them over to Ferdinand Ybanez, his deputy. During the fall of 1805, Ybanez was employed by Gurley and James Brown, United States attorney for the Territory of Orleans, in making an abstract of land grants from the records in Trudeau's possession.[20]

Upon receiving information from Brown that Morales intended to ship records of land surveys, grants, and concessions to Pensacola, Governor Claiborne applied to him for the records. Morales agreed to stop the removal of the records pending the return of the Marquis de Casa Calvo from the Louisiana frontier. This belated step on Claiborne's part was useless, however, for as Brown reported in his letter of December 11, important records relative to land claims and other property, which had been in the possession of Morales and his secretary, Carlos Ximenes, later notary of the Spanish government, had been sent to Pensacola the preceding summer.[21]

About this time the receipt of strict instructions from the president caused Claiborne to continue his efforts to secure the land records. Although he had long since been informed by Casa Calvo that the records in the possession of Andrés Lopez y Armestó, secretary of the Spanish government in New Orleans, did not relate to the domain and sover-

18 / James Brown to W. C. C. Claiborne, March 19, 1806, in Carter (ed.), *Territory of Orleans*, 613–14.
19 / Claiborne to the president, January 30, 1806, in Rowland (ed.), *Official Letter Books*, III, 255.
20 / John W. Gurley to Albert Gallatin, June 9, 1805, James Brown to Albert Gallatin, September 3, October 30, December 11, 1805, all in Carter (ed.), *Territory of Orleans*, 454–55, 496–98, 517–18, 545–48.
21 / Brown to Gallatin, December 11, 1805, in Carter (ed.), *Territory of Orleans*, 545–46.

eignty of Louisiana, Claiborne again demanded his records and succeeded in obtaining some notes of first concession.[22] Trudeau, upon the departure of Morales, resigned as surveyor general and refused to allow the land records relating to Louisiana in his possession, including original concessions and surveys of land, to be taken away, on the grounds that they were his personal property. Claiborne and Brown called upon Trudeau on February 1, 1806, to confer about the land records. The records' importance to the United States was pointed out to him, and he was warned their removal would not be permitted. Upon Trudeau's consenting to take the oath of allegiance to the United States, he was permitted to retain possession of the records.[23] That part of the records relating to lands in West Florida was taken by Vicente Sebastian Pintado, Trudeau's deputy, to Pensacola. In March, 1806, Claiborne received instructions from Secretary of State James Madison to take measures to recover the records carried away to Pensacola, in order to prevent inconvenience, forgery, and fraud in the settlement of the land claims. Claiborne consulted James Brown, who strongly recommended copying the registers that were in Morales' hands.

After Trudeau's death on October 5, 1816, his papers were purchased by the state of Louisiana. A Louisiana act of March 18, 1818, provided for the appointment of parish surveyors, of whom the one for Orleans parish was to have custody of the records taken over from Trudeau. That surveyor was to be ex-officio surveyor general of the state; the position was filled for many years by Louis Bringier. An additional purchase of Spanish land records resulted from the Louisiana act of February 29, 1848, which authorized the governor to obtain the records of Francois Gonsolin, the late Spanish surveyor for the district of Attakapas.[24] Some of Gonsolin's records, however, seem to have gone astray.

Small collections of land records are in other repositories in Louisiana and elsewhere. Land grants of French Louisiana, 1753–1769, containing 110 items, are in the Howard-Tilton Memorial Library of Tulane University, and in the same place are land surveys of Spanish Louisiana, 1785–1807, containing 50 items. The William L. Clements Library at the

22 / Claiborne to Madison, January 30, 1806, Claiborne to Marquis de Casa Calvo, February 6, 1806, Claiborne to Madison, January 30, 1806, all in Rowland, (ed.), *Official Letter Books*, III, 255, 260.

23 / Claiborne to Henry Dearborn, February 1, 1806, in Rowland (ed.), *Official Letter Books*, III, 257.

24 / Louisiana, Laws, Statutes, etc., *Acts of the Legislature*, 1818, pp. 158–64; Testimony of Louis Bringier, 1848, in Mitchell and Calhoun, "Marquis de Maison Rouge," 368; Louisiana, *Acts*, 1848, pp. 14–15.

University of Michigan acquired by purchase a collection of land records of Spanish Louisiana, including surveys, grants, petitions for land along the lower Mississippi River, 1787–1803, containing 103 items. In 1927 A. T. Whitbeck of Shreveport, Louisiana, presented to the Library of Congress about forty-eight manuscripts, comprised of correspondence of François Gonsolin, Carlos Trudeau, Louis LeBlanc, and others of the Attakapas district. Land surveys of West Feliciana dating from 1797 are in the Louisiana State Library. Records relating to Louisiana land grants, 1786–1821, and New Orleans street maps dating from 1765 are in the Louisiana State University Library.

In 1922 the Western Reserve Historical Society of Cleveland purchased from J. K. Smith of Grand Rapids, Michigan, a dealer in rare books and manuscripts, some Louisiana and Mississippi land records, 1768–1803, in two boxes and one package. These documents were described as surveys and legal documents, signed by Spanish officials, concerning lands on the banks of the Mississippi River from Natchez to New Orleans and some for Biloxi. In 1982 the Society deaccessioned these records and offered them for sale at a public auction to be held at the Swann Galleries in New York on November 4, 1982. After the state of Louisiana threatened to bring suit to recover the records as state property, four of the six lots were withdrawn. The Historic New Orleans Collection later purchased the two remaining lots. In November, 1984, that institution reached an agreement with the state of Louisiana by which it would complete the purchase of the survey records from the Western Reserve Historical Society, donate them to the state, but retain possession of them for a period of thirty years.[25] These surveyors' records, 1775–1827, include surveys of present-day Louisiana, Missouri, Alabama, and Arkansas by Carlos L. Trudeau, André LeSage, Josiah Nicholas, and Luke Collins. A microfilm copy of the collection is in the Louisiana State Archives. A new description of the records prepared by the Historic New Orleans Collection details them as Spanish colonial land grant papers, 1767–1803, in twenty-one folders, including petitions for land, land grants by the governors, land sales, and surveyors' certificates.

Vicente Sebastian Pintado, who had served as Trudeau's deputy since 1796, became surveyor general of West Florida in December, 1805, but did not take possession of the office at Pensacola until April 12, 1806. While holding that office and even after removing to Havana in 1817, Pin-

25 / Western Reserve Historical Society, *A Guide to the Manuscripts and Archives of the Western Reserve Historical Society*, comp. Kermit J. Pike (Cleveland, 1972), 58; Historic New Orleans Collection, *Newsletter*, III (Winter, 1985), 1–5.

tado continued to issue certificates of survey for lands in West Florida and for the sections of old Louisiana that had passed into American possession. James G. Forbes, while in Havana as an agent of the United States government for the transfer of West Forida to the United States and for the recovery of land records of Louisiana and West Florida, had several interviews with Pintado, who stated that he considered the land records to be his personal property and that if the United States government wanted them it would have to purchase them as it had those of Trudeau for Louisiana.[26] Pintado died in August, 1829, and possession of the land records passed to the control of his widow, Eulalia Valderas Pintado, who was made cognizant of their value by her husband's will.

The efforts of the United States government to settle land cases arising out of Spanish land grants in Louisiana and Florida resulted in the procurement of documents from the Spanish government. Pursuant to an instruction from the president, the secretary of state instructed Cornelius P. Van Ness, the United States minister in Spain, on May 14, 1830, to obtain pertinent documents. Accordingly, Van Ness communicated with the Spanish secretary of state but had no success until November 5, 1833, when he was furnished with copies of documents by that official. The fifteen documents received from Van Ness related to the government and land system of Louisiana and were published in English.[27] Van Ness later transmitted additional documents consisting of a list of the governors of Louisiana and copies of their commissions. On instructions from Washington, Van Ness attempted during 1833 and 1834 to obtain the assistance of the Spanish government in recovering the Pintado papers but was unsuccessful.[28]

Efforts by Señora Pintado to sell the Pintado papers to the United States government were also unsuccessful, though in May, 1833, she offered them, with an inventory, for fifteen thousand dollars. Roger B.

26 / Survey of Federal Archives, Louisiana, Pintado Papers, Transcripts of Land Claims and Miscellaneous Plats and Papers (New Orleans, 1940–41), I, x; James G. Forbes to John Q. Adams, June 25, 1821, in Clarence E. Carter (ed.), *The Territory of Florida, 1821–1824* (Washington, D.C., 1956), 94. Vol. XXII of Carter (ed.), *The Territorial Papers of the United States*, 26 vols.

27 / Martin Van Buren to Cornelius Van Ness, May 14, 1830, in Instructions to Ministers, General Records of the Department of State, RG 59, NA; Francisco de Zea Bermudez to Van Ness, November 5, 1833, in William R. Manning (ed.), *Diplomatic Correspondence of the United States: Inter-American Affairs, 1830–1860* (Washington, D.C., 1932–39), XI, 236–37; *Documents Relative to Louisiana and Florida, Received at the Department of State from the Secretary of State of Spain Through the Hon. C. P. Van Ness* ([Washington, 1833?]).

28 / Correspondence on this subject is in Manning (ed.), *Diplomatic Correspondence*, II, 259–61, 264–74.

Taney, the attorney general, not considering the papers sufficiently valuable, advised against the purchase but suggested obtaining copies. Señora Pintado thereupon sold the papers to some private citizens, including General John Wilson of Fayette, Missouri, who turned over a half-interest to Rezin P. Bowie, a planter of Iberville Parish, Louisiana, who soon disposed of half his interest to Colonel John R. White, also of Fayette, Missouri.[29] The object of these men was to obtain control of lands by using the Pintado papers.

In communications to the commissioner of the General Land Office of 1836–1838, Harry T. Williams, the surveyor general of Louisiana, attempted to interest the federal government in acquiring the Pintado papers. An act of Congress of March 3, 1839, appropriated twenty thousand dollars to purchase records relating to Spanish land grants that had formerly belonged to the Spanish surveyors in the territories of Orleans and Florida.[30]

Under instructions from the General Land Office, Williams arranged with the holders of the Pintado papers, including Señora Pintado, who still had some of them, for their conveyance to Washington, D.C., for examination. On March 5, 1840, Williams reported that an abstract of the papers had been prepared and that they contained 4,756 petitions in French, Spanish, and English; 4,756 orders of survey; 2,517 plats of tracts; and as many certificates of survey. On June 10, 1840, Williams reported his arrival in Washington, D.C., with the Pintado papers. On learning of the arrival, Levi Woodbury, the secretary of the treasury, instructed James Whitcomb, the commissioner of the General Land Office, to have some competent person or persons inspect and evaluate the papers. Although the committee of examiners considered that the papers would be useful to the government in adjudicating land claims, it did not recommend their purchase at the price asked.[31] The secretaries of the treasury and state accepted this advice, and the papers were taken back to Louisi-

29 / Survey of Federal Archives, Louisiana, Pintado Papers, I, xiv, 15–18; Roger B. Taney to the secretary of state, May 22, 1835, in Letters Sent Book, General Records of the Department of Justice, Record Group 60, National Archives; Survey of Federal Archives, Pintado Papers, I, xiv.

30 / 5 *Statutes* 347.

31 / James Whitcomb to Harry T. Williams, April 24, 1839, in Letters Sent Book, Private Land Claims, Book 5, Williams to Whitcomb, March 5, 1840, in Private Land Claims, Correspondence Relating to Pintado Papers, James Whitcomb, Samuel M. Roberts, John M. Moore, Joseph S. Wilson, and William T. Steiger to the secretaries of state and the treasury, July 23, 1840, in Letters Sent Book, Private Land Claims, Book 6, all three letters in Records of the Bureau of Land Management, RG 49, NA.

ana by Williams without, however, the abstract and schedule, which were kept since they had been prepared at the expense of the United States government.

The Pintado papers were eventually acquired by the Louisiana State University Library. After Rezin P. Bowie died in 1841, an inventory of the papers was prepared in February, 1842, for the probate court of New Orleans. The inventory prepared by William Christy was found by the Survey of Federal Archives in the New Orleans notarial records. It listed seventeen volumes, lettered but without dates, of petitions, grants, surveys, plats, field notes, sketches, and receipts for titles; four memorandum books also in Spanish; and eighteen bundles of old papers, consisting chiefly of letters in Spanish.[32]

In some manner that has not been ascertained, part of the surveyor's records of Spanish Louisiana and the Floridas were borrowed in 1872 from the U.S. surveyor general by the Hill Memorial Library of Louisiana State University and never returned. These survey records of private land grants with correspondence, 1765–1819, in ten volumes, consist of original and manuscript copies of surveys in Louisiana, Mississippi, Alabama, and Florida by Trudeau, Pintado, Ira C. Kneeland, William Dunbar, and others.[33]

In 1940 and 1941, the Survey of Federal Archives in Louisiana issued a translation and transcription of the Pintado papers at Louisiana State University, which was prepared by the Baton Rouge unit of the survey under the supervision of Marie L. Landry.[34] Book I contains a history of the papers by Stanley C. Arthur, the general supervisor of the survey, documentary exhibits consisting of copies of documents relating to the Pintado papers, and indexes to the papers. Books II–XI contain Spanish land grants, survey certificates, and copies of plats and maps for grants in Louisiana, Arkansas, Mississippi, Alabama, and West Florida for the years 1771–1818. Included are surveys and maps by Trudeau and Pintado in Louisiana and West Florida, and others by Christopher Bolling, Luke Collins, Jr., Hugh Coyle, William Dunbar, François Gonsolin, William Kneeland, and Thomas Power. An index to these volumes includes the names of individuals, bayous, places, rivers and other streams, districts, and settlements.[35] The Pintado papers are useful for local history, gene-

32 / Survey of Federal Archives, Louisiana, Pintado Papers, I, xxviii.
33 / Survey of Federal Archives, Louisiana, *Inventory of Federal Archives in the States, Series VIII, The Department of the Interior, No. 17, Louisiana* (New Orleans, 1941), 2.
34 / Survey of Federal Archives, Louisiana, Pintado Papers, II–XI.
35 / Sidney K. Eastwood, "The Pintado Papers," *New Orleans Genesis*, III (March 1964),

alogy, biography, and the administration of the Spanish land system. Sets of the translation of the Pintado papers are in the Louisiana State University Library, the Louisiana State Land Office, the Louisiana State Museum Library, and the National Archives Library.

A microfilm of the eleven volumes of the translated Pintado papers has been prepared on five reels by the Louisiana State Archives and Records Commission, which can supply copies. Copies of the microfilm are held by Louisiana State University, Tulane University, St. Martin Parish Library, the University of Southwestern Louisiana, the Mississippi Department of Archives and History, the P. K. Yonge Library of Florida History at Gainesville, Florida, and the University of West Florida at Pensacola.

In November, 1973, the Manuscript Division of the Library of Congress was offered by the Duluth, Minnesota, Public Library what were stated to be papers of David Burr, an American surveyor and a cousin of Aaron Burr, which had been given to the library by Mrs. Robert M. Adams, a local resident. After receiving the papers in January, 1974, and examining them, however, the Manuscript Division found that they were papers of Vicente S. Pintado, deputy surveyor general of Louisiana, 1796–1805, and surveyor general of West Florida, 1805–1817. The collection consists of 1,500 items for the years 1781–1842.[36] These include some of the papers that Pintado took with him from Louisiana to Pensacola in 1806 and other papers accumulated in that place. The collection also includes correspondence and land records of that part of Louisiana from the Mississippi River to the Pearl River and of the Gulf Coast of what is now Mississippi, Alabama, and West Florida. A chronological file of outgoing and incoming correspondence, 1785–1829, in four boxes, includes both official and personal correspondence and consists of communications from Spanish officials, Carlos L. Trudeau, William C. C. Claiborne, and Ira Kneeland, Pintado's deputy. Official land papers, 1781–1842, in two boxes, consist of chronologically arranged charts, transcripts, testimonies, wills, bills of sale, surveys, notebooks, land grants, petitions, deeds, and other papers. Maps and plats, 1793–1830, in twenty-one folders, are mostly hand-drawn maps of districts, areas, rivers, bays, plantations, and towns in Louisiana and West Florida. Some printed

---

137–47. A more complete index to the Pintado papers is in Baton Rouge Genealogical Society, "Index to Pintado Papers," *Louisiana Genealogical Register*, XV–XIX (September, 1968–June, 1972).

36 / *Library of Congress Quarterly Journal*, XXXII (July, 1975), 177–78.

maps are also in the collection. Microfilm of these Pintado papers, in six reels, is available on interlibrary loan from the Library of Congress, and copies of the microfilm can be purchased from its photoduplication service.

An effort to ascertain the provenance of the Pintado papers has elicited some information. According to the recollection of Robert M. Adams, Jr., a lawyer in San Francisco, the Pintado papers were part of the estate of his grandfather, Cuyler Adams, once a resident of Deerwood, Minnesota, whose ancestors included Burrs.[37]

Papers relating to land grants are in repositories in Louisiana and elsewhere. Records relating to Louisiana land grants, 1763–1785, are in the Kuntz Collection of Tulane University Library. Some Spanish Louisiana land papers, 1787–1803, containing 101 items that include petitions for land, land grants, and surveys, are in the William L. Clements Library, University of Michigan. The Felipe Bastrop papers, 1795–1819, a typescript in two volumes in the University of Texas Archives, relate in part to his colonizing activities in Louisiana. Louisiana land grants, 1787–1798, in one volume, and Carlos Trudeau surveys, 1797, are in the Library of Congress Manuscript Division. Collections of family papers, which are held by numerous repositories, usually contain land documents.

Boards of Land Commissioners

The Louisiana Purchase treaty of October 21, 1803, provided that the inhabitants of the ceded territory would be guaranteed the full enjoyment of their property. Accordingly, an act of Congress of March 2, 1805, provided that residents of the territory at the time of the signing of the treaty who had obtained from the Spanish or French governments registers of warrant or orders of survey for lands that were actually inhabited and cultivated were to be confirmed in their claims.[38] The Territory of Orleans was to be divided into two districts in each of which the president of the United States was to appoint a register. Two other persons to be appointed by the president in each district were to serve with the register as commissioners to ascertain the rights of persons claiming land under French or Spanish grants. They were to meet from December 1, 1805, to March 1, 1806, at the places designated by the president as the residence

37 / Robert M. Adams, Jr., to Henry P. Beers, November 11, 1983, in Beers Correspondence.
38 / 2 Statutes 323–29; Harry L. Coles, Jr., "The Confirmation of Foreign Land Titles in Louisiana," Louisiana Historical Quarterly, XXXVIII (October, 1955), 4–6.

of the register. The commissioners were to hear claims, examine witnesses and testimony, obtain public records and take transcripts from them, and decide all claims filed with the registers. A clerk was to be employed to keep minutes of proceedings and decisions. Transcripts of the decisions were to be made for transmittal to the surveyor general and the secretary of the treasury. The commissioners were also to make full reports of all claims filed with the registers, including the substance of the evidence presented and their own remarks, to the secretary of the treasury for presentation to Congress. The secretary of the treasury was also empowered to appoint agents to investigate claims that might be considered fraudulent. The commissioners were authorized to employ a translator to assist them in the transaction of business and in recording Spanish and French documents.

The board of commissioners for the eastern part of the Territory of Orleans was promptly organized. John W. Gurley was designated as register at New Orleans on March 30, 1805, and was informed that the district was to include the part of the territory that was east of the Mississippi River and the parishes on the west bank, including Lafourche.[39] During the summer of 1805, Benedict F. Van Pradelles and Joshua Lewis were appointed as commissioners to serve on the board with Gurley. James Brown, an attorney in New Orleans, was appointed agent for investigating land claims. One of Gurley's early tasks was to arrange for copying land records at New Orleans for the use of the commissioners of both districts in the territory. Gurley died in March, 1808, and was replaced by Van Pradelles; after the latter's death in December, 1808, he was replaced by Philip Grymes. Thomas B. Robertson had been appointed a commissioner in April, 1808.

The board of land commissioners for the eastern district was organized at New Orleans on December 1, 1805; they elected a clerk and received claim papers until the following March. But the filing of claims was exceedingly slow, and Congress was forced to adopt legislation in 1806 and 1807 to expedite the operations of the boards. The time for filing was extended to July 1, 1808, qualifications were liberalized, the registers were authorized to appoint deputies in the parishes, and the commissioners were empowered to hold hearings in the parishes to collect evidence. By June, 1811, 2,002 claims had been registered in the eastern district of Louisiana, and books containing transcripts of the decisions and reports of the board had been transmitted to Washington, D.C. The first report of

39 / Secretary of the treasury to John W. Gurley, March 30, 1805, in Carter (ed.), *Territory of Orleans*, 427.

the commissioners (Grymes, Lewis, and Robertson) on 444 claims was submitted to the House by the secretary of the treasury on January 8, 1812.[40] It contained lists of approved and rejected claims submitted by the deputy registers of the different parishes.[41] The lists contain information as to names of claimants, locations of claims, their extent, dates of survey, conveyances from original grantees, and data as to cultivation. The decisions of the commissioners were confirmed by an act of June 2, 1858. The entries in the commissioners' report of 1812 relating to Orleans Parish have been abstracted by two editors, Charles R. Maduell, Jr., and Agnes H. Anzalone, who consider the index in the *American State Papers, Public Lands*, which contains reports on land claims, to be of little value. Another publication by Maduell arranges the data by parishes as they existed in 1812 and gives for each parish the names of the claimants in alphabetical order.[42]

Some claimants did not file their claims in time for consideration by the first board of land commissioners, but later statutes of April 14, 1812, and February 27, 1813, permitted them to file and have their claims considered. A report of November 20, 1816, by Samuel H. Harper and Alfred Lorrain, the register and receiver, respectively, of the eastern district, embraced three general classes of claims, each divided into several kinds of claims. Each class of claims with its subdivisions contains descriptions of the claims, showing the name of each claimant and the location, dimensions, and nature of the claim. These claims were confirmed by an act of Congress of May 11, 1820.[43]

Another report by Samuel H. Harper on January 6, 1827, covers four classes of claims and gives information on the name of each claimant, the location and extent of the claim, surveys, and the recommendation of the

40 / Coles, "Confirmation of Land Titles," 6–8; Columbus Lawson to the secretary of the treasury, June 21, 1811, in Carter (ed.), *Territory of Orleans*, 938; *American State Papers, Public Lands*, II, 258–439.

41 / For a breakdown of the report, see Carter (ed.), *Territory of Orleans*, 937 n. 71.

42 / 11 *Statutes* 294; Charles R. Maduell, Jr., and Agnes H. Anzalone (eds.), "Abstracts of Land Grants in the County of Orleans Comprising the Present Parishes of Orleans, Jefferson, St. Bernard, and Plaquemines," *New Orleans Genesis*, XIV–XV (January, 1975–June, 1976); Charles R. Maduell, Jr., and Agnes H. Anzalone (eds.), "Abstracts of Land Grants in the County of German Coast (Now St. Charles and St. John the Baptist Parishes), Territory of Orleans," *New Orleans Genesis*, XV (June, 1976), 251–56, XVI (January, 1977), 24–30; Charles R. Maduell, Jr., *Federal Land Grants in the Territory of Orleans: The Delta Parishes . . . in 1812* (New Orleans, 1975).

43 / 2 *Statutes* 709, 807; *American State Papers, Public Lands*, III, 254–69; 3 *Statutes* 513–14.

register as to confirmation. An act of Congress of February 28, 1823, confirmed the claims in Harper's report.[44]

After the United States took over the region between the Mississippi and Perdido rivers, an act of Congress of April 14, 1812, created the state of Louisiana and annexed to it the territory east of the Pearl River. To settle the land claims in these newly acquired Florida parishes, a different method was employed. An act of Congress of April 25, 1812, set up two land offices, one east and one west of the Pearl River, each under a single commissioner who was to take evidence and report to Congress. For the district west of the Pearl River, a report by James O. Cosby was submitted to Congress on January 5, 1816, recommending 752 claims for confirmation and 260 for rejection. It contained registers of claims based on Spanish, French, and British grants that were recommended for confirmation and other registers of claims that were not recommended. Cosby also submitted a list of squatters on land east of the Pearl River and a supplementary list of two hundred names. An act of Congress of March 3, 1819, confirmed claims reported on favorably by the commissioners and those of squatters who had actually cultivated tracts before April 15, 1813.[45]

Another land office was set up by an act of March 3, 1819, at St. Helena Courthouse (now Montpelier, Louisiana), west of the Pearl River, at which persons who had not yet filed claims or who had additional evidence to file could do so until July 1, 1820. The reports of Charles S. Cosby and Fulwar Skipwith, the register and the receiver, respectively, were submitted in four installments during the years 1820–1822; they recommended 212 claims for approval and 57 for rejection and listed 936 settlers. The act of May 8, 1822, confirmed those claims, extended the powers of those officials in connection with the settlement of claims, and removed the office to Greensburg. Special acts allowed the filing of claims through 1827. The replacement of officials and other difficulties delayed another report on land claims in the St. Helena district until January 19, 1825.[46] The report by register Samuel J. Rannells and receiver William Kinchin contained five registers of claims, among them Spanish and British claims of which some were approved for confirmation and others not. On De-

---

44 / *American State Papers, Public Lands*, III, 578–99, printed also in *House Documents*, 18th Cong., 1st Sess., No. 103, pp. 11–63, Serial 97; 3 *Statutes* 727.

45 / 2 *Statutes* 708–709, 713–14; *American State Papers, Public Lands*, III, 39–76; 3 *Statutes* 528–29.

46 / 3 *Statutes* 528–29; *American State Papers, Public Lands*, III, 465–76, 505–508; 3 *Statutes* 707–708; *American State Papers, Public Lands*, IV, 438–62, 473–74; *House Documents*, 19th Cong., 1st Sess., No. 70, pp. 1–4, Serial 134.

cember 5, 1825, Rannells and Kinchin filed a supplementary report on 7 claims on which papers had been filed but which had not been reported by their predecessors. The approved claims were confirmed by Congress on May 4, 1826. Thomas G. Davidson and A. G. Penn, who were later the register and the receiver at St. Helena, submitted a favorable report on November 20, 1830, on 2 claims of John McDonogh, a New Orleans merchant. His claim to four tracts, under Spanish patents to David Williams, Guillermo Williams, William Estevan, and Domingo Assarette, was approved by an act of Congress of March 22, 1832.[47]

An act of Congress of February 6, 1835, provided that persons having claims that had been recognized as valid but not yet confirmed could present them within two years to the register and the receiver of the land office in which they were situated for confirmation. Accordingly, John Killian and Paris Childress submitted from Greensburg on June 27, 1837, a report on 21 numbered English and Spanish claims, showing the names of the present claimants, the names of original claimants, the locations, and the dates of cultivation and habitation, extending from 1786 to 1831. In transmitting the report of the secretary of the treasury on January 11, 1838, James Whitcomb, the commissioner of the General Land Office, recommended the confirmation of only four claims (numbers 10, 18, 19, and 20) for John Bird, Micajah Harris, Antonio and Stephen Ruchman, and L. Thompson. The Senate committee on private land claims concurred in its report to the Senate, and an áct of July 6, 1842, confirmed those claims.[48]

An act of July 4, 1832, allowed persons claiming land in the southeastern district of Louisiana until July 1, 1835, to present their claims to the register and the receiver at New Orleans. The report by Hilary B. Cenas and W. L. Robison was made to the secretary of the treasury on September 5, 1833, and was submitted by him to Congress on July 4, 1832. The reports are in four classes on 361 claims and present for each claim in paragraph form the name of the claimant, the location of the claim, the quantity of land, the names of neighboring owners, the nature of the claim, and the opinion of the register and the receiver as to its validity. The act of March 3, 1835, confirmed these claims with some exceptions and called for a full transcript of the title papers and the evidence relating to the numbers excepted. These documents were submitted by B. Z. Ca-

---

47 / House Documents, 19th Cong., 1st Sess., No. 56, pp. 1–4, Serial 134; 3 Statutes 159; House Documents, 21st Cong., 2nd Sess., No. 23, pp. 1–4, Serial 206; 5 Statutes 482.

48 / 4 Statutes 749–50; Senate Documents, 25th Cong., 2nd Sess., No. 97, pp. 1–38, Serial 315; 5 Statutes 492.

nonge and Maurice Cannon on December 1, 1835, and the claims were confirmed by an act of Congress on July 4, 1836.[49] Additional reports from the southeastern district made under the act of February 6, 1835, came from B. Z. Canonge and Richard M. Carter on December 14, 1836, and November 22, 1837. The 1836 report concerns thirteen claims and gives information on the claimants' names and the claims. The report of November 22, 1837, concerns forty-five claims that had been presented to them since their previous report. Some of these were recommended for confirmation because they were based on good titles, long possession, and continued cultivation. Because the evidence on some other claims was deemed to be feeble, these were left to the decision of Congress. A report of the Senate committee on private claims adopted the recommendation of the commissioner of the General Land Office and recommended on April 16, 1838, the confirmation of some claims and the rejection of others, giving the numbers of the claims. An act of Congress of July 6, 1842, confirmed those claims approved by the committee. That act also appropriated five hundred dollars for copying documents relating to the approved claims. Forwarded from New Orleans by register Peter Laidlaw and receiver Alg. Sidney Lewis, the transcripts were submitted to Congress, which ordered them to be printed.[50]

The act of March 2, 1805, for settling land claims in the Territory of Orleans stipulated that the western district was to include the settlements on the Red and Ouachita rivers within the parishes of Attakapas and Opelousas, with the office at Opelousas. John Thompson of Kentucky was appointed register there; the other members of the board of land commissioners for the district were a Mr. Trimble and Francis Vacher. Allan B. Magruder was designated as agent for investigating land claims suspected of being fraudulent but was dismissed in March, 1806. Other changes in personnel and in the laws governing the adjustment of land claims delayed the first report of the board until October 16, 1812.[51] The

49 / 4 *Statutes* 56–62; *American State Papers, Public Lands*, VI, 665–702, 903–11, also printed in *House Documents*, 23rd Cong., 1st Sess., No. 73, pp. 1–98, Serial 255; 4 *Statutes* 779–80; *American State Papers, Public Lands*, VIII, 343–80, also printed in *House Documents*, 24th Cong., 1st Sess., No. 55, pp. 4–80, Serial 287; 5 *Statutes* 126.

50 / *House Documents*, 24th Cong., 2nd Sess., No. 64, Serial 302; *Senate Documents*, 25th Cong., 2nd Sess., No. 197, pp. 1–49, Serial 316; *Senate Documents*, 25th Cong., 2nd Sess., No. 379, pp. 1–2, Serial 317; 5 *Statutes* 491–92; *House Documents*, 27th Cong., 3rd Sess., No. 1, pp. 1–189, Serial 419.

51 / 2 *Statutes* 324–29; Secretary of the treasury to John Thompson, March 30, 1805, secretary of the treasury to the President, June 26, 1805, both in Carter (ed.), *Territory of Orleans*, 428–30, 457; *American State Papers, Public Lands*, II, 258–439, 744–871, III, 77–269.

report by William Garrard, Levin Wailes, and Gideon Fitz provides information on several classes of claims in the parishes of Concordia, Ouachita, and Rapides, with tables of land claims showing the class of claims, the number, the register number, the names of claimants, the names of original proprietor or claimant, and the quantity of land. Included are the monthly returns of certificates issued by the commissioners, January 1, 1811–May 9, 1815, showing the date, the name of the person under whom the land was claimed, in whose favor it was issued, the basis of the claims, the location, and the quantity. Other reports by Garrard, Wailes, and Fitz, made on April 6, May 1, 11, and 14, 1815, concern land claims in Opelousas, Attakapas, Concordia, Ouachita, Natchitoches, and Rapides parishes. A further report by Garrard and Wailes on December 30, 1815, covers twelve classes of claims, with reports on individual claimants under each class. The claims included in that report were confirmed by an act of Congress of February 5, 1825. Reports with similar information were submitted in 1815 for the parishes of Natchitoches, Attakapas, Opelousas, and Concordia.[52]

Under the provisions of an act of March 3, 1811, the western part of Louisiana was divided into two districts. A land office was established in 1818 at Ouachita for the district north of the Red River, and Daniel J. Sutton was designated the register there. For the region south of the Red river (southwestern land district), the office was continued at Opelousas. A report of October 1, 1825, by Valentine King, the register there, presents data on ninety-six claims in paragraph form, giving the name of each claimant, the quantity of land claimed, its location, the nature of the documents filed, the opinion of the register as to the validity of the claim, and his recommendation as to confirmation. Acts of Congress of April 29, 1816, February 5, 1825, and March 31 and May 16, 1826, confirmed the claims reported upon by the officials at Opelousas. A report of May 15, 1840, from R. N. Kelley, the register at Opelousas, is arranged in numerical order from 1 to 179, and the report gives information about eight classes of claimants, the locations of their claims, and documents filed with the dates on which they were filed. The report also contains an abstract and an alphabetical list of Spanish and Rio Hondo claims. An act of confirmation was passed by Congress on July 6, 1841.[53]

---

52 / *American State Papers, Public Lands*, II, 804–71, III, 91–93, 119–50, 151–62, 77–119, 172–251; 4 *Statutes* 81; *American State Papers, Public Lands*, III, 77–150.

53 / 2 *Statutes* 662–63; *American State Papers, Public Lands*, IV, 490–518, also printed in *House Reports*, 19th Cong., 2nd Sess., No. 49, pp. 5–32, Serial 159, and in *House Documents*, 19th Cong., 1st Sess., No. 80, pp. 6–74, Serial 134; 3 *Statutes* 329; 4 *Statutes* 81, 152, 168; *House Documents*, 27th Cong., 2nd Sess., No. 33, pp. 20–75, 80–97, Serial 402; 5 *Statutes* 492.

An act of May 11, 1820, provided that persons claiming land west of the Mississippi River who had not submitted evidence could do so in the proper land office until December 31, 1820. In pursuance of that act, Daniel J. Sutton, the register of the district north of the Red River at Ouachita, submitted to the secretary of the treasury on January 1, 1821, a report listing four classes of claims in paragraph form, giving the name of each claimant and the quantity and location of the land. The claims in the first, second, and third classes—with certain exceptions in the first class, including those of the Baron de Bastrop—were confirmed by an act of February 28, 1823.[54] John M. A. Hamblin and R. Eastin, the register and the receiver at Ouachita, submitted on January 9, 1836, a report on claims by John Butler and John Sibley with the remark that the other claims were in such an imperfect state that no decisions could be made on them. They submitted documents relative to Butler's claim but stated that regarding Sibley's claim they had only oral testimony. Another report from the same officials, dated July 24, 1837, lists seventy-one numbered claims, with data regarding each and some original documents in both Spanish and English. Commissioner James Whitcomb of the General Land Office recommended on February 13, 1838, that only eight of the claims be recognized as quit claims against the claims of other persons; other numbered claims he did not recommend for confirmation. The claims recommended for confirmation by the register were confirmed by an act of Congress of July 6, 1842.[55] A one-volume land record book of the Ouachita district, 1808–1832, which was presented to the Historical Society of Pennsylvania in 1904, concerns the sale of the land of Abraham and Andrew Y. Morehouse.

After the acquisition of Louisiana in 1803, the western boundary of what became the state of Louisiana was in dispute with Spain until it was established at the Sabine River by the treaty of February 22, 1819. An act of Congress of March 3, 1823, provided that the register and the receiver of the district south of the Red River (Opelousas) were to receive and record evidence on land claims in the area between the Sabine River and the Rio Hondo, which constituted the neutral ground that had been in dispute. In accordance with that act, Valentine King and David L. Todd, the register and the receiver at Opelousas, submitted a report to the secretary of the treasury on November 1, 1824, giving the evidence that had been collected regarding individual claims. The report presents evidence on 280 claims in paragraph form, giving the names of the claimants, the

54 / 3 *Statutes* 573–74; *American State Papers, Public Lands*, III, 599–610; 3 *Statutes* 727.
55 / *House Documents*, 24th Cong., 1st Sess., No. 114, pp. 1–13, Serial 289; *Senate Documents*, 25th Cong., 2nd Sess., No. 196, pp. 1–290, Serial 316; 5 *Statutes* 492.

locations of the claims, testimony as to habitation and cultivation, and the opinions of the register and the receiver as to the validity of the claims. Congress, in an act of May 24, 1828, confirmed claims based on habitation and cultivation, except for 16 that were believed to be on land claimed by the Caddo Indians. On March 31, 1826, Congress confirmed 237 claims based on settlement and rejected 10 that were said to be based on Spanish grants.[56] Another report of May 15, 1840, by R. N. Kelley, the register at Opelousas, contains two alphabetical lists of the names of 179 claimants and shows the locations of their claims and the quantity of land claimed. An act of Congress of July 6, 1841, confirmed claims to land south of the Red River that had been reported on by Kelley.[57]

An act of Congress of August 3, 1854, revived earlier acts of 1823 and 1826 providing for the examination of titles to land in the neutral ground for a period of two years. A hearing was held at Natchitoches on August 6, 1855, by J. B. Cloutier and Thomas C. Hunt, the register and the receiver there, to consider 6 additional claims. Their report of August 6, 1855, gives the names of the 6 claimants and information regarding their claims, all of which were recommended for confirmation. The House committee on private land claims in a report of February 15, 1878, however, refused to confirm the claims because the proofs were inadequate, the claims had been filed late, and 4 of the claims had been abandoned.[58]

By 1836, when most of the boards of land commissioners in Louisiana had concluded their work, 8,857 private land claims in that state had been confirmed. Yet there remained other claims that had not been settled, and Congress in an act of June 22, 1860, provided that claimants in Louisiana, Missouri, and Florida could apply to commissioners for the confirmation of titles. Acts of March 2, 1867, and June 10, 1872, extended the act of 1860 for periods of three years. A report of February 28, 1870, by Charles Barnard and Henry L. Jones, the register and the receiver of the consolidated land office at New Orleans, recommended the confirmation of 6 claims embraced in Cosby's report of 1813.[59] Most of these claims, then in the name of Myra Clark Gaines, were rejected for lack of proper

56 / 4 Statutes 152; American State Papers, Public Lands, IV, 89–146, also printed in House Documents, 24th Cong., 1st Sess., No. 49, pp. 1–121, Serial 287; Act of March 31, 1826, 4 Statutes 152; 6 Statutes 382–83.
57 / House Documents, 27th Cong., 2nd Sess., No. 33, pp. 80–97, Serial 402; 5 Statutes 492.
58 / 10 Statutes 347; House Reports, 45th Cong., 2nd Sess., No. 222, pp. 1–3, Serial 1822.
59 / Senate Documents, 24th Cong., 1st Sess., No. 216, p. 11, Serial 281; 12 Statutes 85–88; 14 Statutes 544; 17 Statutes 378; House Executive Documents, 43rd Cong., 1st Sess., No. 60, pp. 1–91, Serial 1607.

documentation. Benjamin T. Ledbetter, the surveyor general of Louisiana, submitted to the General Land Office on October 18, 1886, a schedule of Louisiana private land claims on which 455 indemnity certificates for an aggregate of 317,736 acres had been issued. The report of the U.S. Public Land Commission of 1904 contains a table showing that the number of private land claims in Louisiana had reached 9,302 and that they embraced 4,347,891 acres.[60]

The *American State Papers, Public Lands,* in eight volumes that contain the reports of boards of land commissioners and of registers and receivers on land claims and other records of the U.S. Congress, is the most important collection of public documents on land claims. They contain important sources of information on land claimants, officials of Louisiana and of the United States, the administration of the land system, local history, and the geography and topography of Louisiana, as well as of Mississippi, Alabama, Missouri, and Arkansas. The individual volumes of that publication contain incomplete indexes. More useful is the consolidated index published in Philip W. McMullin's *Grassroots of America.* Extending chronologically beyond the compilation by McMullin is an extensive government publication that serves as an index to private claims.[61] The *American State Papers* and the congressional serials are available on microfilm from the Congressional Information Service, Inc., from which a price list can be obtained.[62] Sections of that publication can be purchased, but it is expensive and a special reader that enlarges the microfiche must also be obtained.

The data on land claimants published in the government publications cited above were based upon documents and testimony collected by the various boards of land commissioners. These printed materials are cited in detail because they are more readily available for research than are the records of the land offices and those of the Bureau of Land Management. Some of the materials in the congressional series were not printed in the *American State Papers.* Historical and genealogical societies

60 / *Senate Executive Documents,* 49th Cong., 2nd Sess., No. 67, pp. 1–6, Serial 2448; *Senate Documents,* 58th Cong., 3rd Sess., No.189, p. 140, Serial 4766.

61 / Philip W. McMullin (ed.), *Grassroots of America: A Computerized Index to the American State Papers, Land Grants and Claims (1789–1837), with Other Aids to Research (Government Documents Serial Set Number 2 Through 36)* (Salt Lake City, 1972); U.S. Congress, *Reports of the Committee on Private Land Claims of the . . . Congress, Senate Miscellaneous Documents,* 45th Cong., 3rd Sess., No. 81, Serial 1836; U.S. Congress, House of Representatives, *Digested Summary and Alphabetical List of Private Claims . . . Inclusive* [1851–71], *House Miscellaneous Documents,* 42nd Cong., 3rd Sess., No. 109, Serial 2036.

62 / The address of the CIS is 4530 East-West Highway, Suite 800 PL, Bethesda, MD 20814.

in the Mississippi Valley could collect these materials and publish them in indexed volumes that would be of great value for research. Some additional materials are in *The New American State Papers: Public Lands,* also in eight volumes, which was prepared from the original *American State Papers,* the congressional serials, and the records of Congress in the National Archives.

After the work of the boards of land commissioners had been concluded, there still remained a number of large Spanish land grants that had not been legitimized by the federal government. The claim of the Marquis de Maison Rouge on the Ouachita River for thirty square leagues in the parishes of Ouachita and Catahoula was approved by the board of land commissioners for the western land district on the grounds that it had been made under the proper circumstances. The grant of the Baron de Carondelet, also on the Ouachita, for twelve square leagues was not approved by the same board because it did not meet the conditions prescribed by the act of Congress of March 3, 1807.[63] A select committee of the House of Representatives decided that these claims should be handled judicially.

An act of Congress of June 17, 1844, gave jurisdiction over all land claims originating with French, Spanish, or British authorities to United States district courts. The act applied to Louisiana, Missouri, and Arkansas and to those parts of Mississippi and Alabama south of the 31st parallel between the Mississippi River and the Perdido River. In 1850 the Supreme Court rejected the Maison Rouge and Bastrop claims. Congress, however, in an act of January 27, 1851, gave preemptions and donations to certain purchasers and settlers on the grants. Another act of March 3, 1851, provided for the settlement of certain classes of private land claims within the Bastrop grant and for allowing preemption to certain actual settlers in the event of the adjudication of title in favor of the United States. A report of July 30, 1852, by Henry C. McEnery and John H. Dinkgrave, the register and the receiver at Monroe, divided the claims into two classes, the first containing thirty-nine claims based on bona fide purchases from Bastrop and the second containing twelve claims. Entries of head rights for individual claims are in paragraph form and give the names of claimants and data regarding their claims. The testimony was taken in the presence of those officials whose recommendations are included in the published report, which also includes voluminous docu-

63 / Coles, "Federal Land Policies in Louisiana," 145–50. Documents concerning these grants are in Mitchell and Calhoun, "Marquis de Maison Rouge," 289–462. Documents of 1794–97 concerning the Maison Rouge claim are in *House Documents,* 27th Cong., 2nd Sess., No. 151, Serial 403.

ments regarding the claims. In accordance with the recommendation of the Senate committee, the claims reported on were confirmed by an act of Congress of June 29, 1853.[64]

Among other large claims decided by the Supreme Court was that of Bernard D'Auterive to a tract of 450,000 acres, known as the Prairie de Vermilion, between the Mississippi River and the Atchafalaya River. The court rejected the claim.[65] The Houmas grant of 200,000 acres of valuable land, with a narrow frontage on the Mississippi River below Donaldsonville and extending back to the Amite River and Lake Maurepas, was in three subdivisions claimed by Donaldson & Scott, Daniel Clark, and William Conway.[66] In 1883 the Supreme Court held that the claim was valid only to the depth of eighty arpents from the Mississippi River and that the land beyond that point belonged to the public domain. The decision left many settlers in Ascension and Livingston parishes without titles.

Land Offices

While the adjudication of private land claims in the Orleans Territory was still going forward, Congress by act of March 3, 1811, provided for the establishment of land offices for the disposal of public lands. These were to be located at New Orleans for the eastern land district and at Opelousas for lands south of the Red River in the western land district; another was to be opened north of the Red River. The one for the last-named district was not located at Ouachita until 1818 because of a delay in surveying operations. For the districts east of New Orleans, the act of March 3, 1819, authorized land offices at St. Helena Courthouse and Jackson Courthouse (now Jackson). As a result of a further act of May 8, 1822, the St. Helena office was moved to Greensburg, which came to serve the whole territory east of the Mississippi and west of the Pearl rivers. The district offices were served by a register, whose duty it was to receive applications for land at public sales and to keep plats and enter upon them the lands sold, and a receiver of public monies, whose function it was to handle the funds received from purchasers, issue receipts, and remit funds to the Treasury. The act of 1819 also provided that the former commissioners of

64 / 5 Statutes 676; Coles, "Confirmation of Land Titles," 17; 9 Statutes 565, 597–98; Senate Executive Documents, 32nd Cong., 2nd Sess., No. 4, pp. 19–815, Serial 661; 4 Statutes 299–300.

65 / Coles, "Confirmation of Land Titles," 17.

66 / Louisiana State Land Office, Biennial Report of the Register, 1886, p. 7. Spanish documents regarding the grant and reports and correspondence of American officials are in Senate Documents, 28th Cong., 2nd Sess., No. 45, pp. 1–156, Serial 450.

land claims were to deposit their books, in which the claims and evidence regarding them had been recorded, with the registers of the different districts. An act of July 7, 1838, established a land office at Natchitoches for the northwestern land district.[67]

The business of the General Land Office was suspended in the southern states at the outbreak of the Civil War. Louis Palms, the register of the southeastern land district at New Orleans, kept custody of the records until they were taken over by the U.S. Army in February, 1863.[68] An inventory of the records prepared at that time and enclosed with General George Shepley's letter lists the records of the New Orleans office as follows:

> register of French and Spanish grants, orders of survey under the Spanish government, register of claims registered at New Orleans under the old Board of Commissioners, reports of the board, registers of claims under various acts, registers of certificates of purchase, registers of state selections, tract books, minutes of the board of land commissioners, list of patents, ledger, journal, sales book, register of locations, preemption declarations, maps and diagrams, preemption claims, warrants issued in favor of General Lafayette, surveyor general protests, caveats, decisions of the register and receiver, powers of attorney, list of locations, two cases of old papers and Spanish records.

Later that year the secretary of the interior informed the military governor of Louisiana that the secretary of the treasury had advised the acting collector of customs at New Orleans to receive and deposit the records in the custom house there. It appears, however, that except for eight bundles of charred papers, the records of the southeastern district were destroyed by fire in 1864. Late in 1864, steps were taken to restore the land offices in the South, and in 1866 the office in New Orleans was open for business, the former offices at Greensburg and Opelousas having been consolidated with it.[69] That same year the land offices at Monroe and

67 / 2 *Statutes* 662; 3*Statutes* 530; Malcolm J. Rohrbough, *The Land Office Business; the Settlement and Administration of American Public Lands, 1789–1837* (New York, 1968), 23, 25, 31; 5 *Statutes* 287.
68 / Brigadier General George F. Shepley to John P. Usher, March 2, 1863, filed with W. T. Otto, assistant secretary of the interior to J. M. Edmunds, March 18, 1863, in Letters Received, G 15155, Records of the Bureau of Land Management, 49, NA.
69 / J. P. Usher to G. F. Shepley, April 3, 1863, in Letter Book, Lands and Railroads Division, Records of the Office of the Secretary of the Interior, Record Group 48, National Archives; A. P. Dostie and Edward Hart to J. M. Edmunds, January 29, 1866, in Letters Received from Registers and Receivers, G 71276, Louis Palms to Walter R. Irwin, April 25, 1879, in Louisiana Miscellaneous Papers, Louisiana Private Land Claims, both in Records of the Bu-

Natchitoches were also reopened. The Monroe office was closed by an executive order effective January 1, 1879, the records being transferred to New Orleans. The New Orleans and Natchitoches offices were moved to Baton Rouge in 1911.[70] By presidential executive order of June 30, 1927, the records were transferred to the office of the Louisiana registrar of state lands in the old state capitol. This transfer was made in accordance with an act of May 28, 1926, which authorized the secretary of the interior to transfer to the state such records as were not needed by the United States.[71] In 1932 the records were moved with the office of the registrar of state lands to the new state capitol. In 1975 that office was in the state's Land and Natural Resources Building on Riverside Mall. The federal land records that documented the operations of United States land officials in Louisiana for over a century thus deposited in the state land office were examined by the Survey of Federal Archives of the Works Progress Administration in the 1930s, and an inventory was published. Summaries of the descriptions in that inventory with additional bibliography are presented here to facilitate the use of the records.

Records of the board of land commissioners of the eastern land district of the Territory of Orleans include a register of claims and decisions, 1811–1820, containing summaries of claims and decisions for the parishes of Acadia, Lafourche, Pointe Coupee, and part of Iberville, in one volume; a register's and receiver's report on three classes of claims west of the Pearl River, arranged alphabetically, 1816, in one volume; and a report of the register and receiver on four classes of claims filed under the act of May 11, 1820, also in one volume.

Records of the southeastern land district include reports of land commissioners, 1805–1837, in one volume; a record of confirmed claims, 1806–1810, in one volume, giving information on individual claims; correspondence with principal deputy surveyors south of the Tennessee River, 1805–1831, in ten bundles, three feet; and a one-volume file of township plats showing private claims, 1829–1834.

Records of the register's and receiver's office of the Greensburg land district include a one-volume index of abstracts of private land claims, 1813–1829; an exhibit of private land claims, 1769–1820, in one looseleaf book, containing an abstract of information on land grants from

reau of Land Management, RG 49, NA; Report of the Commissioner of the General Land Office, October 2, 1865, *House Executive Documents*, 39th Cong., 1st Sess., No. 1, p. 27, Serial 1248.

70 / Survey of Federal Archives, *Inventory of Archives in Louisiana*, 37. The descriptions of records that follow are from this inventory.

71 / 44 *Statutes* 672.

the French, British, and Spanish governments; abstracts on private land claims, 1813–1829, in four volumes, containing reports by James O. Cosby, Fulwar Skipwith, and Samuel J. Rannells, and William Kinchin; abstracts of orders of survey and certificates of survey; lists and memoranda related to land claims, 1813–1861, in one bundle, four inches; memos relating to private land claims, 1813–1900, in two volumes; patent certificates, 1819–1820 and 1829; and letters to deputy surveyors, 1818–1831, in two bundles, seven inches. For the St. Helena district there is a record of certificates of orders of survey, 1819–1837, in one volume, showing information on individual claimants.

Records of the western district include a one-volume index of abstracts of private claims, 1805–1858, arranged alphabetically; a minute book of the board of land commissioners, December 2, 1805–November 12, 1810, one volume, containing a chronological record of its proceedings; abstracts of private land claims, 1805, 1816, 1823, 1825–1826, 1828, 1842, and 1858, in one volume, containing abstracts of certificates issued by the commissioners under confirmatory acts of Congress for the parishes of Attakapas, Concordia, Natchitoches, Opelousas, Ouachita and Rapides; a record of evidence for complete titles, 1806–1808, in one volume, containing copies of grants, titles, and sales documents dating from 1769 for Spanish, French, and British grants; a record of evidence for complete titles, 1806–1808; commissioners' report book no. 7, 1806–1828, in one volume, containing a list of Spanish claims, claims in Concordia, Rapides, Opelousas, Ouachita, and Attakapas parishes; claims of the Baron de Bastrop, the Marquis de Maison Rouge, Abraham Morehouse, Joseph Gillard, Pierre Arceneau, sales by Indians, heirs of Maria St. Denis, and William Wikoff; the monthly return of certificates issued by commissioners, 1811–1814, in one volume, giving information on individual claims; minutes of proceedings of the board of land commissioners, January, 1811–May, 1815, in one volume; a general report of the land office at Opelousas, December 30, 1815, in one volume, giving information on individual claims; abstracts of preemptions and a register's report, September 8, 1826, one volume, containing Valentine King's report on individual claims; an original record book of Spanish claims by the register and the receiver of the Opelousas land office, 1834–1854, in one volume, containing information on individual claims; a record of preemption claims, 1838, also in one volume. At the time the foregoing records were examined by the Survey of Federal Archives, they were uniformly described as dirty, brittle, torn, and damaged by water and vermin.

Records of the district north of the Red River include three volumes of field notes of surveys and township plats, 1814–1834, containing surveys of township and section boundaries, and two bundles of early maps showing boundary lines of townships, 1821–1830. An exhibit of Rio Hondo claims, November 1, 1824, May 24, 1828, and November 19, 1860, in one volume, gives information on individual claims.

Records of the southwestern land district at Opelousas include one volume of abstracts of French and Spanish grants, with surveyors' certified statements, July 14, 1757–June 30, 1802, and February 4, 1806, containing abstracts of concessions and patented grants in the western district in registers kept by the French and Spanish governments; a one-volume record of decisions of the board of land commissioners of the district on Spanish claims, January–May, 1811, transmitted to the secretary of the treasury, showing the monthly return of certificates issued by the commissioners with information on claimants; letters from principal deputy surveyors to the surveyor general south of the Tennessee River at Washington, Mississippi, 1807–1821, in two bundles, one foot, one inch; plats and surveyors' certificates of 592 private claims, 1817–1835, in one volume; and township plats, 1832–1837, in large volumes showing acreage, including that in private claims. A small quantity of other records of the Opelousas land office, 1808–1849, comprising twenty items, includes letters of Levin Wailes, depositions regarding the boundaries of Rapides and neighboring parishes, and a list of the names of those who sold lands at the post of Opelousas during the years 1765–1805.

The Natchitoches district land office collection includes some records relating to private land claims. A volume of private claims, 1789–1875, contains a summary of old claims and claims considered by the board of land commissioners at Opelousas; Rio Hondo claims, 1823–1891, in seven bundles, one foot, eight inches, contain papers relating to claims between the Rio Hondo and the Sabine River; tract books, 1829–1892, in two volumes, contain data on individual claims; a record of patents delivered, 1833–1911, in four volumes, contains an alphabetical record. A published index to the tract books for the old Natchitoches district is a valuable tool for genealogists interested in locating their ancestors' lands in that district, which included Bossier, Caddo, Bienville, De Soto, Sabine, Natchitoches, and Vernon parishes and the western parts of Rapides, Winn, Grant, and Claiborne parishes.[72]

72 / Ennis M. Tipton, *Index to U.S. Tract Books, Northwestern Land District (Old Natchitoches District) in the Louisiana State Land Office, Baton Rouge, Louisiana* (Bossier City, La., 1981); see also Shelton B. McAnelly, "State Land Office Records, U.S. Tract Book Indexes: Greensburg District, Southwestern Land District, District North of the Red River, Southeastern Land District, Northwestern Land District," *Louisiana Genealogical Register*, XIX (March, 1972), 62–76.

Records of the Opelousas district land office include a list of French and Spanish patents, 1757–1802, in one volume, containing a record of twenty-four French and Spanish patents issued by various governors; records of the deputy register of the parish of Attakapas, 1796–1808, in one volume, containing copies of documents on land grants; letters and circulars received, 1805–1861, in thirty-seven bundles, ten feet, six inches; a one-volume list of surveys, 1807–1831; a record of old board claims and correspondence relating to claims, 1808–1815, in forty-five bundles, ten feet, two inches; board of commissioners certificates, June 17, 1811–November 17, 1813, containing A and B claims, numbers 851–2278, certified by the old board of commissioners, in one volume; a record of land claims under acts of Congress of March 10, 1812, and May 11, 1820, in one volume; claims, plats, sales, and conveyances, 1814–1862, in twenty bundles, five feet, six inches, including originals in French and Spanish; a copy of the report of the register and the receiver as commissioners of claims, December 20, 1815–February 5, 1825; plats and maps, 1818–1848, in half an inch; a one-volume final report of the register on land claims under the act of May 11, 1820, from July 1, 1820 to October 1, 1825; plat books, 1822–1927, in sixty-five volumes, ten feet; tract books, 1833–1901, in sixteen volumes, three feet, four inches; evidence taken before the register and the receiver as commissioners on claims, numbers 16–128, February 6, 1845–May 8, 1839, in one volume; an inventory of the archives of the southwestern land district, 1840–1841, and a schedule of maps, in two volumes; and one volume of correspondence with the General Land Office, 1840–1850. Records of the Opelousas land office, 1808–1849, comprising twenty items, including letters and papers of Levin Wailes, are in the Louisiana State University Department of Archives and Manuscripts.

The land records described in the preceding pages are available on microfilm in the Archives and Records Service of the Office of the Secretary of State of Louisiana and in the Louisiana State Land Office. Some microfilming was done in 1939 and 1940, but all of the records appear to have been microfilmed on nearly five hundred reels by the Gulf Oil Company, which began this task in 1959.[73] The microfilm includes the transcriptions and translations of land office records and of the Vicente S. Pintado papers prepared by the Survey of Federal Archives in Louisiana. An unpublished guide to the microfilm is available in the two repositories mentioned above. The land records are valuable for genealogical re-

---

73 / Letter from Charles C. Cain, archivist, Louisiana Archives and Records Service, to Henry P. Beers, November 30, 1983, in Beers Correspondence.

search, local history, and biography, supplying data supplementary to that in church registers.[74]

From 1939 to 1942, the Baton Rouge office of the Survey of Federal Archives prepared typed transcriptions and translations of the records relating to Spanish and British land grants that had been deposited in the state land office by the U.S. General Land Office. These include a volume of British grants, 1768–1779, Greensburg office, which contains copies of letters patent by Governor Peter Chester, sketches of grants, certificates of the attorney general, and certificates of survey.[75] British and Spanish grants considered by Charles S. Cosby and Fulwar Skipwith at Greensburg, 1819–1820, contain transcriptions and translations of grants, notices, and evidence, copies of surveys, certificates concerning the recording of the patents, statements of surveyors, orders of the governor of Louisiana, letters patent of the British governors of West Florida, and statements of the Spanish and British surveyor general and deputy surveyors, Carlos L. Trudeau and Elias Durnford.[76] These volumes contain useful indexes showing the names of grantees, claimants, and British, Spanish and American officials, and geographical features. Other volumes are available for Opelousas land claims. Copies of these transcriptions are in the Lousiana State University Library, and most of them are also in the National Archives Library.

A transcription of the Opelousas Land Claims, Book I, parts 1–2, from the U.S. land office archives in Baton Rouge, Louisiana, was made by the Survey of Federal Archives in Louisiana and published in New Orleans in 1939. This transcription is in the Louisiana State University Library, which also has another Survey of Federal Archives transcription concerning miscellaneous papers from the same Baton Rouge land office.[77]

74 / Ellen B. Moore, "Report from the State Land Office," *Louisiana Genealogical Register,* XVI (March, 1969), 1–4; Elizabeth S. Mills, "Land Titles: A Neglected Key to Solving Genealogical Problems: A Case Study at Natchitoches," *Louisiana Genealogical Register,* XXXI (Jan., 1984), 103–23.

75 / Survey of Federal Archives, Louisiana, Greensburg, U.S. Land Office Archives, Baton Rouge, Louisiana (Typescript; New Orleans, 1942). This book begins with p. 132 of the manuscript book; the rest is missing from the Land Office archives.

76 / Survey of Federal Archives, Louisiana, British and Spanish Grants, Notices and Evidences in Written Claims before Cosby and Skipwith, 1819–20, Book A, No. 3 (Parts 1–2). Greensburg Land Claims, U.S. Land Office Archives, Baton Rouge, Louisiana (Typescript; New Orleans, 1941).

77 / Survey of Federal Archives, Louisiana, Opelousas Land Claims, U.S. Land Office Archives, Baton Rouge, Louisiana, Book I, parts 1–2 ([New Orleans], 1939). This transcrip-

Surveyor General

The task of surveying the private land claims and the public land in the Territory of Orleans was placed by an act of Congress of March 2, 1805, under the supervision of the U.S. surveyor of lands south of the state of Tennessee. An act of April 21, 1806, authorized that official to appoint for each of the two districts principal deputy surveyors, who were to reside and keep an office in their districts. Accordingly, Isaac Briggs, who had been appointed surveyor general in 1805, designated Walker Gilbert for the eastern land district and Gideon Fitz for the western land district of the Territory of Orleans. These deputy surveyors were to execute or cause to be executed such surveys as might be authorized by law or as the land commissioners for the two districts might direct. Surveys of private land claims were to be done at the expense of the parties in cases where authenticated plats of the land as surveyed under the French, Spanish, or American governments had not been filed with the proper register or recorder or were not on file in the public records of the Territory of Orleans.[78] The surveyor general was to transmit general or particular plats of surveyed tracts to the register or the recorder and copies thereof to the secretary of the treasury and to retain other copies for his own office. The private land claims were plotted before the public lands were surveyed, and the names of the claimants were placed on the official township plats and entered into tract book records.

The survey of private land claims and public lands in Louisiana proceeded slowly and was constantly faced with a variety of difficulties. In 1806 and 1807, John Cook ran a base line on the 31st parallel of north latitude from the Mississippi River to the Sabine River, while Thomas Owings ran a meridian line from the Red River south to the Gulf of Mexico, and John Dinsmoor ran the meridian north. Because both lines were done inaccurately, the preparation of correct township maps was delayed. Subsequently, both lines had to be resurveyed. Because of the manner in which the French and Spanish land grants had been made—with narrow frontages on rivers—it was difficult to apply the rectangular system of surveys that had been prescribed for the region north of the Ohio River (the

---

tion is in the Louisiana State University Library along with another Survey of Federal Archives transcription entitled: Miscellaneous Letters, Papers, Protests, Evidences, Claims and Reports from the United States Land Office in Baton Rouge, Louisiana (Typescript; New Orleans, 1940).

78 / 2 *Statutes* 329, 393; Coles, "Federal Land Policies in Louisiana," 20; Act of March 3, 1807, 2 *Statutes* 441–42.

Northwest Territory) by the ordinance of 1785. Under this ordinance, townships six miles square were to be surveyed before public sale and were to be divided into thirty-six sections, each a square mile, containing 640 acres. To overcome the difficulties of applying the system in Louisiana, variations were permitted by law. During the period 1808–1812 the surveyors were largely engaged in surveying private land claims. After the War of 1812, surveys were completed in the southeastern and northern districts of Louisiana.[79] Under an act of Congress of March 3, 1819, a principal deputy surveyor was authorized for the land district west of the Pearl River. Silas Dinsmoor was given the appointment, and a number of deputy surveyors operated under his direction during the winter of 1819–1820.[80] Inefficient direction by the surveyor general slowed down surveys in the 1820s. The St. Helena meridian was surveyed in 1822, however, and townships east of the Mississippi were later surveyed from this line.

To eliminate the confusion that had developed in surveying operations in the region south of Tennessee because of the division of the work among three principal deputy surveyors, Congress, adopting the recommendations of the commissioner of the General Land Office, passed an act on March 3, 1831, providing for the appointment of a surveyor general for the state of Louisiana.[81] The office of the principal deputy surveyor for the district east of New Orleans was abolished, and the records, maps, etc., relating to lands in Louisiana were to be delivered to the surveyor general for that state. Horé B. Trist of Louisiana was appointed to the position on June 15, 1831. Late in the summer of that year, with the assistance of Samuel D. King, a special agent sent out from Washington, Trist worked at Washington, Mississippi, separating records relating to Louisiana.[82] He also arranged for taking over the records of the St. Helena district at Baton Rouge, the southwestern district at Opelousas, and the southeastern district at New Orleans.[83] The assembled records of the sur-

79 / C. Albert White, *A History of the Rectangular Survey System* (Washington, D.C., [1983]), 58, 11–14; Coles, "Federal Land Policies in Louisiana," 34–35.

80 / 3 *Statutes* 532; Coles "Federal Land Policies in Louisiana," 37–38.

81 / George Graham to the secretary of the treasury, December 15, 1825, in *House Documents*, 20th Cong., 1st Sess., No. 110, p. 21, Serial 171; Elijah Hayward to Powhatan Ellis, Public Land Committee, U.S. Senate, February 7, 1831, in *American State Papers, Public Lands*, VI, 267; 4*Statutes* 492–94.

82 / Miscellaneous Permanent Commissions, 1823–48, p. 212, Records of the Department of State, 59, NA; Horé B. Trist to Elijah Haywood, August 28, October 1, November 1, 1831, in Letters Received from Surveyors General, Records of the Bureau of Land Management, RG 49, NA; Report of the Commissioner of the General Land Office, November 30, 1830, *Senate Documents*, 21st Cong., 2nd Sess., No. 1, p. 61, Serial 203.

83 / Schedules of the records taken over are in a volume labelled "Abstracts of Papers

veyor general were deposited at Donaldsonville in an office located in a flammable wooden building. In December, 1843, the office was moved to Baton Rouge; in 1845, it was back again at Donaldsonville.

James Whitcomb, the commissioner of the General Land Office, submitted to the secretary of the treasury on March 26, 1838, proposals from the surveyors general of Louisiana, Alabama, Mississippi, and Arkansas for the construction of office buildings with fireproof vaults for the safekeeping of their records. In a report of July 5, 1838, the House committee on public lands recommended that Congress provide by law for the protection of the records of the surveying districts, which were the most complete ones on the public surveys, but nothing seems to have been done in response to this recommendation.[84]

The surveying of confirmed private land claims and public lands continued for many years under a succession of surveyors general. By 1841, that official was able to report that almost all of the original surveying had been completed but that some resurveying of private claims in the Greensburg district of eastern Louisiana was necessary in order to correct improperly located private claims. Surveying continued on a more limited scale in succeeding years, and by 1861 it was reported to be virtually completed. Throughout these years, as plats and field notes accumulated in the office of the surveyor general, copies were transmitted to the General Land Office. On February 19, 1880, G. H. Brewster, the surveyor general, sent to the General Land Office an abstract of located but unconfirmed private land claims giving information about individual claims.[85]

Soon after the secession of Louisiana from the Union, the surveyor general of Louisiana closed his office and informed the General Land Office of his intention to transfer its records to state authorities. During the war the records of the surveyor general were repossessed by the U.S. Army, moved to New Orleans, and placed in the fireproof section of the custom house there. Late in 1866, the General Land Office designated

Transferred to the Surveyor General for Louisiana under the Act of 3 Mar. 1831," Records of the Bureau of Land Management, RG 49, NA. When surveyors general were replaced by new appointees, inventories were often prepared. Such inventories are available in the records of the Bureau for 1873, 1881, and 1886.

84 / James Whitcomb to Levi Woodbury, March 26, 1838, in *House Documents*, 25th Cong., 2nd Sess., No. 23, pp. 1–2, Serial 322; *House Reports*, 25th Cong., 2nd Sess., No. 1042, pp. 1–3, Serial 336.

85 / Harry L. Coles, Jr., "Applicability of the Public Land System to Louisiana," *Mississippi Valley Historical Review*, XLVIII (June, 1956), 49–50; Report of the Commissioner of the General Land Office, November 30, 1861, in U.S. Department of the Interior, *Annual Report of the Secretary of the Interior*, 1861, p. 479; *Senate Executive Documents*, 46th Cong., 2nd Sess., No. 111, pp. 1–32, Serial 1885.

Henry C. De Ahua as a special agent to examine the records of the surveyor general and to report on their condition. In January, 1867, he reported finding nearly 4,000 maps of the five land districts of Louisiana and stated his intention to examine some dust-covered boxes containing loose maps in rolls as well as field notes and private land claim plats. The records were found to have suffered little destruction. In July, 1869, John Lynch, a newly designated surveyor general, arrived in New Orleans and applied himself to arranging and inventorying the records of the surveyor general then in the custody of the register of the consolidated land office. The office of the surveyor general remained at New Orleans until June 30, 1909, when it was transferred to Baton Rouge. It continued to function there until June 30, 1927, when the office was closed and its records were transferred to the custody of the register of state lands. This transfer was made under the act of May 26, 1926, which stipulated that when the public surveys in any state were so far advanced that it was no longer necessary to maintain the public survey office, its records could be turned over to the state, provided that it had made provision by law for their reception.[86]

The voluminous records of the surveyor general of Louisiana in the state land office consist of a variety of materials. Correspondence in a number of series includes correspondence with the commissioners of the General Land Office and other officials of that office, letters from deputy surveyors and others, letters from registers and receivers of land offices, correspondence with individuals and with the state land office, and circulars from the General Land Office. Survey records include deputy surveyors' field notes, survey plats of private land claims and other lands, tract books, maps, orders of survey, and certificates of location.[87] Records of a financial nature include abstracts of surveyors' accounts, ledgers, vouchers, surveying accounts, appropriation ledgers, and account books. Other records include inventories of records of the office, a list of patents of private claims, papers on private land claims, and annual reports of the surveyor general to the General Land Office.[88] Many of these materials

86 / Coles, "Public Land System," 51; A. P. Dostie and Edward Hart to J. M. Edwards, January 29, 1866, in Letters Received from Registers and Receivers, G 74631, Henry C. De Ahua to J. S. Wilson, January 7, 1867, in Letters Received, G 94067, John Lynch to J. S. Wilson, July 23, 1869, in Letters Received from Surveyors General, H 71174, all three letters in Records of the Bureau of Land Management, RG 49, NA; 44 *Statutes* 673.

87 / An alphabetical name index is available for tract books in McAnelly, "State Land Office Records."

88 / Detailed descriptions by series of the types of records listed are in the Survey of Federal Archives, Louisiana, *Inventory of Archives in Louisiana*, 1–23. See also Eaton, "Early Louisiana Land Records."

are duplicated in the other land records in the state land office and in the records of the Bureau of Land Management in Washington, D.C. The records are valuable not only for the administration of the surveying system in Louisiana but also for local history, biography, and the geography of the state. An index of the private land claims is available; the surveyors' field notes have been photostated, and some of the records have been microfilmed; microfilm of the surveyors' plats is in the St. Martin Parish Library.

Bureau of Land Management

At the time of the establishment of the federal government in 1789, the administration of public lands was placed under the jurisdiction of the secretary of the treasury. To relieve him of the details of that business, however, an act of Congress of April 25, 1812, established a General Land Office in the Department of the Treasury.[89] The increase in the business of that office necessitated a reorganization and enlargement of the staff, which was accomplished by an act of July 4, 1836.[90] It provided for a principal clerk for private land claims and a secretary, whose duty it was to certify and affix the seal of the office to all patents for public lands. In 1849 the General Land Office was placed in the newly established Department of the Interior; in 1946 it was consolidated with the Grazing Service of that department to form the Bureau of Land Management.

The adjudication, survey, and patenting of private land claims in Louisiana, Mississippi, Alabama, Florida, Missouri, and Arkansas resulted in the accumulation of consolidated files in the Bureau of Land Management. The most important file relating to private land claims is the land-entry papers or private land claim dockets, now in the Washington National Records Center of the National Archives. Filed alphabetically by state in strong jackets bearing identification data, these case files include notices and evidence of claims, petitions, certificates and plats of survey, affidavits, deeds, abstracts of title, testimony regarding claims, copies of federal court decisions, appeals, maps, 'plats, wills, marriage certificates, assignments, and related papers. For Louisiana, there are 5,323 dockets in ninety-four boxes, for Mississippi 544 dockets in seven boxes, for Alabama 593 dockets in twelve boxes, for Missouri 2,046 dockets in seven boxes, for Arkansas 227 dockets in three boxes, and for Flor-

---

89 / Rohrbough, *Land Office Business*, 49; 2 *Statutes* 716–18.
90 / Rohrbough, *Land Office Business*, 269–70; 5 *Statutes* 107–11.

ida 506 dockets in fifteen boxes.[91] These files contain not only the histories of claims but also data on local history of a more general nature. A variety of records that contain information concerning private land claims in Louisiana and other states of the Mississippi Valley are in the records of the Bureau of Land Management. Survey contracts, bonds, and related papers supply the names of deputy surveyors, the areas they surveyed, and the time and terms under which the surveys were done. The surveyors' field notes and plats, which were sent to the General Land Office by the various surveyors general, are useful in identifying private land grants. The township plats, which were prepared from the field notes, show the surveyed lines of a township six miles square. Since these are boundary records, they have been extensively used by surveyors, by courts engaged in settling property cases, by other state and local officials, and by individuals. They are available not only in the Bureau of Land Management in Washington, D.C., but also in state and county offices. The federal surveys of the French and Spanish land grants exhibit the progress of settlement before the United States acquired Louisiana. Tract books maintained by the bureau show the disposition of each tract of land, including a land description, the number of acres, the date of sale, the name of the purchaser or private claimant, the land office, the entry number, and the date of patents.[92] Sets of these that were kept in district land offices have found their way to state archives or historical societies. Original tract books that had been transcribed into other books for the General Land Office for Louisiana, Mississippi, Alabama, Missouri, Arkansas, and other states are in the National Archives. In the Bureau of Land Management, microfilm copies of the tract books are used for research. The tract books serve as an index to the case files that have been described above. Copies of the tract books for Louisiana are in the St. Martin Parish Library.

Other materials in the records of the Bureau of Land Management in the National Archives include a file of maps published by offices of surveyors general that show the progress of the land surveys. A file of

91 / U.S. National Archives, *Preliminary Inventory of the Land-Entry Papers of the General Land Office*, comp. Harry P. Yosphe and Philip P. Brower (Preliminary Inventories, no. 22) (Washington, D.C., 1949), 12; U.S. National Archives, *Guide to Genealogical Research in the National Archives* (Washington, D.C., 1982), 209, 217, 222.

92 / William D. Pattison, "Use of the U.S. Public Land Survey Plats and Notes as Descriptive Sources," *Professional Geographer*, n.s., VIII (January, 1956), 10–11; Robert W. Harrison, "Public Land Records of the Federal Government," *Mississippi Valley Historical Review*, XLI (September, 1954), 277–88; National Archives, *Guide to Genealogical Research*, 209, 215.

manuscript and annotated maps or the "old map file," 1790–1846, includes maps of the United States and of the public land states, land districts, boundaries, and private land claims. Most of the early maps show surveys by deputy surveyors and were prepared in offices of surveyors general or in the General Land Office.[93]

The process of confirming a land grant ended in a patent or an official certificate or deed that was issued by the General Land Office. These were kept in different series, corresponding to the land-entry papers that serve as an index to the record copies of patents. The patent books for states east of the Mississippi River and for the first tier of states west of that river are in the National Archives.

Some aids to research in the records of the Bureau of Land Management and of other government offices have been published. In 1960 the Louisiana Genealogical and Historical Society obtained, through a genealogist in Washington, D.C., a copy of a microfilm of an index to private land claims in Louisiana in the National Archives and published it in its periodical. Another aid to research in the vast materials of the federal government, published by Clifford N. Smith, calendars government correspondence and other archival materials for the period 1788–1810, when the United States land patent procedure was developed.[94] This work includes administrative correspondence of the U.S. Treasury Department, district land offices, surveyors general, boards of land commissioners, and the territorial governors.

Other records of the bureau include the reports of the numerous boards of land commissioners that functioned in different parts of Louisiana. The voluminous correspondence files of the bureau include letters sent to and received from registers, receivers, surveyors general, and individuals.[95] Early correspondence files of the Treasury Department are also pertinent.[96] Copies of the reports of the boards of land commis-

93 / U.S. National Archives, *List of Cartographic Records of the General Land Office (Record Group 49)*, comp. Laura E. Kelsay (Washington, D.C., 1964), 7.

94 / E. Russ Williams, Jr., "Index of Private Land Claims, State of Louisiana," *Louisiana Genealogical Register*, VII–XIV (June, 1960–December, 1967); Clifford N. Smith, *Federal Land Series: A Calendar of Archival Materials on the Land Patents Issued by the United States Government, with Subject, Tract, and Name Indexes*, Volume I, 1788–1810 (Chicago, 1972).

95 / U.S. National Archives, The General Land Office (Record Group 49), Administrative Records of the General Land Office, 1785–1955 (Typescript; Washington, D.C., 1973), 22–24.

96 / A list of the correspondence files of the Treasury Department relating to the administration of the public lands is in Clarence E. Carter (ed.), *The Territory of Mississippi, 1798–1817* (Washington, D.C., 1937–38), V, 210 n. 75. Vols. V–VI of Carter (ed.), *The Territorial Papers of the United States*, 26 vols.

sioners are in the records of the U.S. Congress and in the records of local land offices in Louisiana and the other states.[97] A researcher desiring to verify the spellings of names of private land claimants appearing in the published sources cited above, therefore, can do so in various collections of records. Some files of the Bureau of Land Management have been microfilmed by the National Archives. More extensive microfilming of the records of that bureau and those of other government agencies relating to Louisiana has been done by the Historic New Orleans Collection.

Copies of the reports of the boards of land commissioners that functioned in the different parts of Louisiana, Mississippi, Alabama, Missouri, and Arkansas that were sent to the Senate and the House of Representatives and the reports of the committees on private land claims of those bodies are in their records in the National Archives. These are filed by the name of the committee and thereunder chronologically. Many of these reports were published in the congressional serials and have been cited in the present work.

97 / U.S. National Archives, *Preliminary Inventory of the Records of the United States House of Representatives, 1789–1946 (Record Group 233)*, comp. Buford Rowland, Handy B. Fant, and Harold E. Hufford (Preliminary Inventories, no. 113) (Washington, D.C., 1959); U.S. National Archives, *Preliminary Inventory of the Records of the United States Senate (Record Group 46)*, comp. Harold E. Hufford and Watson G. Caudill (Preliminary Inventories, no. 23) (Washington, D.C., 1950).

8

ह**•**

Ecclesiastical Records

The earliest explorers and colonizers of Louisiana were served by French priests, who introduced the Catholic religion in the colony. La Salle, on his voyage down the Mississippi River in 1682, was accompanied by a Recollect, and at the end of that century when Iberville reached the coast of Louisiana, a Jesuit was on board his ship as the chaplain. After La Salle laid claim to Louisiana for the crown of France, the Seminary of Quebec in 1698 sent missionaries to serve among the Indians in the Mississippi Valley.[1] When white settlements were established in Louisiana, priests arrived to minister to their inhabitants; and when military posts were erected in the interior, chaplains were assigned to them.

The charter companies, under their agreements with the French government, were obligated to support the church, but they afforded only limited assistance. In 1722 the Company of the West divided Louisiana among several religious orders. A branch of the Franciscan order, the Capuchins from the Champagne province in France were assigned New Orleans and the portion of the colony west of the Mississippi River from the Wabash to Balize at the river's mouth. The Carmelites were given Mobile and the other posts east of the Mississippi, whereas the Jesuits were assigned the upper Mississippi Valley. The Capuchins served parishes as they were established at new settlements in Louisiana and were assigned as chaplains to military posts to serve their garrisons and to spread the gospel among the Indians. After the removal of the Carmelites from Louisiana, the Company of the Indies in 1726 reduced the area assigned to the Capuchins to the territory south of the Yazoo and Arkansas rivers. It placed the Indians in the mission field in the colony under the Jesuits,

1 / Charles E. O'Neill, *Church and State in French Colonial Louisiana; Policy and Politics to 1732* (New Haven, 1966), 15–17.

who were also allotted land in what is now the business district of New Orleans, where they established an experimental plantation. Following a dispute between the Capuchins and the Jesuits over ecclesiastical jurisdiction in Louisiana, the Jesuits were expelled from the province in 1763, and their land in New Orleans was confiscated and divided into lots. So at the end of the French regime in Louisiana, there were nine or ten Capuchins serving at parishes or Indian missions. The Capuchins had also established at New Orleans in 1725 the first school in Louisiana.[2]

The priests in Louisiana were joined in 1727 by a small group of Ursuline nuns. Under an agreement of September 13, 1726, between the Company of the Indies and Ursulines of Rouen, France, that provided for the care of the sick and the conduct of a school, a small group of Ursulines reached New Orleans in 1727. After being housed in a building rented for them by the company, the nuns moved in 1734 into a convent that had been built for them on Chartres Street by the government of the colony. Besides staffing a boarding school, a day school, and the royal hospital, the Ursulines also ran an orphanage. After the transfer of the colony to Spanish control, the Ursulines gave up the management of the hospital. The Ursuline Academy is still operated in a building completed on State Street in 1912.[3]

The archives of the Ursuline Academy date from the time of its authorization in 1726 and are still in its custody. The French materials include the royal order of 1726 authorizing the founding of the convent in Louisiana; a one-volume register of the reception of novices and their professions, together with obituary notices that contain valuable biographical data, March 4, 1726–1894; a record of deliberations of the community council, January 1, 1727–August 13, 1902, in one volume, containing a record of the decisions of the council, the results of triennial elections, and a description of the procession that occurred when the convent was occupied in 1734; the first register of the Congregation des Dames Enfants de Marie, May 28, 1730–August 15, 1744, in one volume, containing an account of the sodality and its rules, practices, members, and elections; and a journal of events, 1727–1853, also in one volume. A variety of other documents relate to the acquisition, leasing, and exchange of land and the rental of property in New Orleans, 1733–1813.[4]

---

2 / *Ibid.*, 130 and *passim*; Wilson, *Capuchin School*, 32.

3 / Heloise H. Cruzat, "The Ursulines of Louisiana," *Louisiana Historical Quarterly*, II (January, 1919), 5–23; Harnet T. Kane, *The Ursulines, Nuns of Adventure: The Story of the New Orleans Community* (New York, 1959), 89, 101, 177–80.

4 / Charles E. Nolan, *A Southern Catholic Heritage, Volume I, Colonial Period, 1704–1813* (New Orleans, 1976), 119–20, 127–33.

There are also blueprints, plans, and photographs. The records of the Ursuline nuns have not yet been microfilmed.

Records of the Ursuline Academy dating from the Spanish period include correspondence with ecclesiastical and civil authorities of Louisiana and Cuba, 1774–1813, containing twenty-two items; general accounts, October, 1789–October, 1812, in one volume, containing monthly summaries of receipts and expenditures; sacristy accounts, 1791–1922, containing information regarding items used in the chapel; documents relating to the treatment, purchase, and sale of slaves, October 26, 1776–March 17, 1803, containing three items; royal orders concerning the Ursuline Convent, foundlings and orphans, and religious institutions, 1789, 1793, 1802, also containing three items; and transcripts of documents in the Papeles de Cuba in the Archivo General de Indias, 1778–1803, having about thirty items, concerning the Ursulines.[5]

Some documents relating to the establishment of the Ursulines in New Orleans have been published. Documents concerning the creation of the order, the voyage to New Orleans, and the nuns' arrival there, 1726–1728, are in Henry C. Semple's history of the Ursulines.[6] The account of the voyage to New Orleans had been published earlier.[7] Translations of letters by one of the Ursuline sisters have also been published.[8]

Diocese of Quebec

The activities of the Catholic church in New France, the Great Lakes region, and Louisiana were under the jurisdiction of the vicar apostolic of New France after the arrival at Quebec of Bishop François de Montmorency de Laval in 1659 as this newly designated church official. In 1717, Bishop Jean Baptiste de St. Vallier designated the Reverend Dominic Varlet as vicar general over Louisiana except for the Jesuits, who continued under their own superior. In 1739, the Reverend Pierre Vitry, a

5 / Ibid., 115–27. See these pages for additional information regarding the records described above and other records of later date.

6 / Henry C. Semple (ed.), The Ursulines in New Orleans and Our Lady of Prompt Succor; a Record of Two Centuries, 1727–1925 (New York, 1925), 167–282.

7 / Marie Tranchepain de St. Augustin, Relation du voyage des premières Ursulines à la Nouvelle Orleans et de leur établissement en cette ville (New York, 1859). The relation was published in the Cramoisy series edited by John Gilmary Shea, who also published an English translation: "Account of the Voyage of the Ursulines to New Orleans in 1727," United States Catholic Historical Magazine, I (January, 1887), 28–41, and again by Marion Ware (trans.), "An Adventurous Voyage to French Colonial Louisiana: The Narrative of Mother Tranchepain, 1727," Louisiana History, I (Summer, 1960), 212–29.

8 / Myldred M. Costa (trans.), The Letters of Marie Madeleine Hachard, 1727–28 (New Orleans, 1974).

Jesuit, was named vicar general in an effort on the bishop's part to assert better control in Louisiana. The Reverend Dagobert de Longuory, superior of the Capuchin missions and pastor of St. Louis Church in New Orleans, was designated as vicar general in 1765. The transfer of sovereignty over that part of Louisiana west of the Mississippi River to Spain in 1763 and over Louisiana east of the Mississippi to the United States in 1783 eventually terminated the authority of the bishop of Quebec in the Mississippi Valley.[9]

The archives of the diocese of Quebec in the custody of the Seminary of Quebec date from 1659 and include a variety of documents relating to Canada and Louisiana. The correspondence is with Rome, religious orders and communities, parish priests, and missionaries.[10] Besides letters received, there are papal bulls and a register of letters sent. The Seminary of Quebec, which was founded by Bishop Laval, became his home and the repository of the records of the diocese. The records of the seminary are significant for the activities of the missionaries it sent to the Mississippi Valley. These records include correspondence, a journal of the superior of the seminary, contracts, and minutes of the council of the seminary. A calendar of the correspondence is in print.[11] An extensive collection of documents issued by the diocese, in which the first two volumes cover the years from 1659 to 1806, has been published. The collection is based on the holdings of the principal repositories in Canada, not just those of the bishopric. A later compilation contains correspondence with priests in the Illinois country, some of whom ministered in the area west of the Mississippi River that became Missouri. A compilation for later years from the same archives also contains correspondence with priests in the Illinois country.[12]

9 / Gilbert J. Garraghan, "The Ecclesiastical Rule of Old Quebec in Mid-America," *Catholic Historical Review*, XIX (April, 1933), 17–19; John D. G. Shea, *The History of the Catholic Church Within the Limits of the United States* (1886–92; rpr. New York, 1978), I, 555–56, 582–83; Garraghan, "Ecclesiastical Rule," 29–30; *New Catholic Encyclopedia* (New York, 1967), XII, 14–15.

10 / Lionel St. G. Lindsay, "The Archives of the Archbishopric of Quebec," *American Catholic Historical Society of Philadelphia Records*, XVIII (March, 1907), 10–11.

11 / Ivanhoë Caron, "Inventaire de la correspondance de Mgr. Louis-Philippe Mariaucheau d'Esgly, Évêque de Québec [1740–91]," *Rapport de l'archiviste de la province de Québec, 1930–31* (Québec, 1931), 185–98; Ivanhoë Caron, "Inventaire de la correspondance de Mgr. Jean-François Hubert, Évêque de Québec, et de Mgr. Charles-François Bailley de Messein, son coadjuteur," *Rapport de l'archiviste de la province de Québec, 1930–31* (Québec, 1931), 199–351; Ivanhoë Caron, "Inventaire de la correspondance de Mgr. Jean-Olivier Briand, Évêque de Québec, [1741 à 1794]," *Rapport de l'archiviste de la province de Québec, 1929–1930* (Québec, 1930), 47–136.

12 / Catholic Church, Archdiocese of Quebec, *Mandements, lettres pastorales et circulares des évêques de Québec*, ed. Henri Têtu and L'Abbé C.-O. Gagnon (Québec, 1887–88); Lionel St.

The archives of the diocese of Quebec also contain correspondence of Pierre de la Rue, the Abbé de l'Isle-Dieu, who was vicar general in France to look after the ecclesiastical affairs of New France and Louisiana. Appointed to that position by Bishop Pierre H. Dosquet of Quebec in 1734, he continued to serve until 1777. In performing his functions, he corresponded with the bishop and other church officials in Quebec and with officials of the Ministère de la Marine in Paris who were concerned with the administration of Quebec and Louisiana. Some of this correspondence has been published from the materials in the diocesan archives.[13]

Diocese of Cuba

Territorial agreements resulting from the Seven Years' War changed sovereignties in the Mississippi Valley. By the Treaty of Fontainebleau of 1762, France ceded to Spain the Isle of Orleans, in which New Orleans was situated, and all of Louisiana west of the Mississippi River. That part of Louisiana east of the Mississippi except the Isle of Orleans was ceded by France to England by the Treaty of Paris of 1763. The part of Louisiana ceded to Spain was placed in 1771 for ecclesiastical purposes under the authority of the bishop of Santiago de Cuba.[14] That official sent the Reverend Cyrilo Sieni de Barcelona to Louisiana as his vicar in 1772 with four other Capuchins. On March 6, 1785, Father Sieni was consecrated as auxiliary bishop for Louisiana, and he served in that capacity until his return to Spain in 1794.[15] In the fall of 1785, he made visitations to the churches in Louisiana. When the diocese of Havana was created in 1787, Louisiana and the Floridas were placed under its jurisdiction, and Bishop Sieni became the deputy of the bishop in New Orleans.

After the establishment of Spanish control at New Orleans in 1766, that part of Louisiana under Spanish sovereignty was placed under the ecclesiastical jurisdiction of the bishop of Santiago de Cuba. When Cuba was divided into eastern and western dioceses in 1787, Louisiana and the

G. Lindsay (ed.), "Letters from the Archdiocesan Archives at Quebec, 1768–1788," American Catholic Historical Society of Philadelphia Records, XX (December, 1909), 406–30; "Correspondence between the Sees of Quebec and Baltimore, 1788–1847," American Catholic Historical Society Records, XVIII (March–December, 1907), 154–90, 282–305, 435–67.

13 / Roger Baudier, The Catholic Church in Louisiana (New Orleans, 1939), 125, 133, 135, 140, 169, 174; Ivanhoë Caron, "Lettres et memóires de l'Abbé de l'Isle Dieu [1742–74]," Rapport de l'archiviste de la province de Québec, 1935–36 [1936–37, 1937–38] (Québec, 1936–38), 275–410, 331–459, 147–253.

14 / Documents Relative to Louisiana and Florida, 3, contains the text of the royal order addressed to Don Pedro Garcia, Mayoral, The Pardo, January 28, 1771.

15 / Baudier, Catholic Church in Louisiana, 196; New Catholic Encyclopedia, X, 384.

Floridas became part of the diocese of Havana.[16] Although the cathedral of the diocese of Santiago de Cuba was at Santiago de Cuba, the bishops had generally resided at Havana.

Only fragments of the archives of the diocese of Santiago de Cuba and the diocese of Havana have been preserved. Those at Santiago de Cuba include royal orders addressed to the dean and the chapter, 1622–1847, in three volumes and one bundle, containing little relating to Louisiana. The materials in the episcopal archives at Havana include royal orders, 1718–1845, in eighteen volumes, and correspondence, 1802–1831, in six bundles. A calendar of items in the Archivo Nacional de Cuba and in the archives of the diocese of Havana principally from the royal orders concerning Louisiana and West Florida, December 20, 1771–July 25, 1803, relate to Capuchin missionaries, payments to teachers, the proposed removal of the Ursuline nuns, missions and missionaries, an auxiliary bishop for Louisiana, Irish priests for West Florida, instructions regarding the marriages of Protestants, and a new church for New Orleans.[17]

Diocese of Louisiana and the Floridas

On the recommendation of the Spanish government, Pope Pius VI created the diocese of Louisiana and the Floridas on April 25, 1793, and in July, 1795, Bishop Luis de Peñalver y Cárdenas arrived in New Orleans from Cuba, where he had been a church official.[18] The newly completed St. Louis Church in that place was designated as his cathedral. The Spanish government hoped that the presence of a resident bishop would improve the status of the Catholic church in Louisiana. In extent the new diocese embraced the whole of the Mississippi Valley, being bounded on the east by the diocese of Baltimore and on the west by the diocese of Durango and Linares in New Spain.

The bishop's pastoral visits to the parishes of Louisiana beginning in 1795 are recorded in the parish registers. In that year he issued statutes for the governance of the clergy of the diocese until such time as a synod could be held to regulate the ecclesiastical affairs of the diocese.[19] Foreseeing that Spain would lose control of Louisiana, Bishop Peñalver requested a transfer, and in 1801 he became archbishop of Guatemala. On his departure he designated the Reverend Thomas Hassett as admin-

16 / *New Catholic Encyclopedia*, XII, 1073.
17 / Pérez, *Guide*, 24, 25–27, 100–104.
18 / Baudier, *Catholic Church in Louisiana*, 223.
19 / These have been printed in Spanish and English as "Statutes of the Diocese of Louisiana and the Floridas Issued by Rt. Rev. Luis Ignatius Peñalvery Cárdenas in 1795," *United States Catholic Historical Magazine*, I (October, 1887), 417–43.

istrator and the Reverend Patrick Walsh as assistant administrator of the diocese.

As a result of the efforts of James Edwards, librarian of the University of Notre Dame, to build up a national collection of Catholic archives at that institution, the archives of the diocese of Louisiana and the Floridas were transferred in the 1890s from the archdiocese of New Orleans to Notre Dame. After the Reverend Thomas McAvoy became archivist at Notre Dame in 1929, the New Orleans collection was reassembled from the historical and subject arrangements of the materials of the university collections, and a systematic calendaring of the items was started.[20] Between 1947 and 1970, photostatic copies of the documents were sent to the archdiocese of New Orleans. With the aid of a grant from the National Historical Publications and Records Commission, made in 1965, the microfilming of the records of the diocese of Louisiana and the Floridas was initiated and a guide prepared. The collection includes 809 items for the years 1576–1803, 40 items of which are for the years 1576–1783 and the rest for 1786–1803, on twelve rolls of microfilm. The first roll consists of the calendars of the collection, which had been prepared on three-by-five-inch cards in chronological order, and an alphabetical list of the names of the authors of the items in the collection, with dates, and of the names of persons and places under which materials in the collection were calendared. Brief descriptions of the materials on the eleven other rolls and the alphabetical list are in the published *Guide*. Copies of the microfilm of the records of the diocese of Louisiana and the Floridas are in the New Orleans Pubic Library, the Loyola University Library, the Louisiana State Museum, the Louisiana State Library, the Louisiana State University Library, St. Martin Parish Library, the University of Southwestern Louisiana, the Manuscript Division of the Library of Congress, the Archives Department of the diocese of Baton Rouge, the archives of the archdiocese of New Orleans, and the University of Missouri Western Historical Manuscripts Collection in Columbia, Missouri.

The records in the University of Notre Dame Library include the proceedings by which couples desiring to marry obtained dispensations because of family relationships in order that they might be married by church rites. As frequent intermarriages occurred among Acadian families, a file of dispensations developed. Other dispensations were sought for the waiving of bans. Data drawn from these files, which present

20 / Catholic Church, Diocese of Louisiana and the Floridas, *Guide to the Microfilm Edition of the Records of the Diocese of Louisiana and the Floridas, 1576–1803* (Notre Dame, Ind., 1967), 14; Nolan, *Southern Catholic Heritage*, I, 5.

useful genealogical information, have been published alphabetically by name and include the information usually found in marriage registers.[21] Some materials of the Spanish period are still in the custody of the chancery of the archdiocese of New Orleans. The collection includes correspondence of Bishop Cyrilo Sieni de Barcelona, October 25, 1781– October 15, 1785, in twenty-two items; royal decrees, orders, and declarations, July 21, 1779–September 12, 1785, in twelve items, including some printed documents; marriage dispensations and permissions to marry, October 12, 1778–October 7, 1785, containing around twenty items; miscellaneous documents, February 3, 1779–July 12, 1803, in about sixteen files; transcripts of documents from the archives of the Sacred Congregation of the Consistory in Rome concerning the creation of the diocese, April 3–25, 1793, containing six items. The chancery also has the Roger Baudier Collection, consisting of notes and other materials collected for his historical works on the Catholic church in Louisiana. Another item is a register of death and burial records of soldiers who died at the royal hospital in New Orleans, August 17, 1786–April 17, 1796, in one volume of which pages 1–21 are missing. The texts of some marriage dispensations that had not been transferred to the University of Notre Dame have been published from microfilm copies in the New Orleans Public Library.[22]

In the 1930s the Survey of Federal Archives prepared translations of materials in the Howard-Tilton Memorial Library of Tulane University. One small collection consists of documents by Father Patrick Walsh, Bishop Peñalver, and the bishop of Cuba. Translations of the letters of Antonio de Sedella, curé of St. Louis Parish, concern in part his differences with Father Walsh.[23]

Diocese of Baltimore

The Treaty of Paris of 1763 guaranteed religious freedom to the Catholics in the trans-Appalachian region. Because there was no responsible offi-

21 / Elizabeth B. Gianelloni, "Genealogical Data from the Records of the Diocese of Louisiana and the Floridas," *Louisiana Genealogical Register,* XVIII (September, December, 1971), 201–10, 302–309, XIX (March, 1972), 1–18.

22 / Nolan, *Southern Catholic Heritage,* I, 5–11; Shirley C. Bourquard, *Marriage Dispensations in the Diocese of Louisiana and the Floridas, 1786–1803* (New Orleans, 1980).

23 / Survey of Federal Archives, Louisiana, Translations of Documents in Spanish and French Relating to Padre Antonio de Sedella and His Ecclesiastical Differences with Vicar-General Patrick Walsh of the St. Louis Cathedral, 1791–1807 (Typescript; New Orleans, 1937–38); Survey of Federal Archives, Louisiana, The Letters of Padre Antonio de Sedella, Curé of the San Luis Cathedral, New Orleans [1785–1816] (Typescript; New Orleans, 1940).

cial of the Catholic church in the English colonies on the seaboard, the bishop of Quebec continued his administration there. After the establishment of American independence in 1783, however, a movement developed for the organization of the Catholic Church in the new nation. In 1784 the prefect of the Congregation of the Propaganda Fide in Rome designated the Reverend John Carroll as prefect apostolic in the United States.[24] Carroll was a native of Maryland who had been educated in France and ordained a Jesuit there; after returning to the United States in 1774, he had become active in Catholic affairs and was named pastor of St. John's Church at Rock Creek, Maryland. Bishop Jean François Hubert of Quebec transferred to Father Carroll the administration of ecclesiastical affairs south of the Great Lakes. In 1789, Carroll was elected the first bishop of Baltimore, with a diocese covering the entire area of the United States. Besides keeping in contact with the bishop of Quebec, he also corresponded with Bishop Peñalver. Designated as archbishop of Baltimore in 1808, he continued in the position until his death in 1815.

After the United States acquired New Orleans and the trans-Mississippi region in accordance with the Louisiana Purchase treaty of 1803, new arrangements were made for ecclesiastical rule at New Orleans. On September 1, 1805, Pope Pius VII placed the vacant diocese of Louisiana under Bishop Carroll of Baltimore, and at the end of the next year he designated the Reverend John Olivier, who was then serving as pastor at Cahokia, as his vicar general at New Orleans. Louis William DuBourg, a Sulpician, was named in 1812 as administrator at New Orleans and on September 24, 1815, was consecrated as bishop of Louisiana in Rome.[25] Because of a controversy with the pastor and the church wardens of St. Louis Cathedral in New Orleans, he took up residence in St. Louis, Missouri, on reaching the United States in 1818 but moved in 1823 to New Orleans. When the diocese of Louisiana was divided into the dioceses of New Orleans and St. Louis in 1826, Bishop DuBourg became bishop of the former.

The principal repository of John Carroll manuscripts is the Archives of the Archdiocese of Baltimore (formerly called the Baltimore Cathedral Archives), which are housed in a fireproof vault in the chancery office of the archdiocese of Baltimore.[26] The collection includes a file of incoming and outgoing letters, 1750–1815, four boxes, arranged alphabetically;

24 / New Catholic Encyclopedia, XII, 15; Thomas T. McAvoy, A History of the Catholic Church in the United States (Notre Dame, Ind., 1969), 45–46.

25 / Fortier (ed.), Louisiana Sketches, I, 179; McAvoy, History of the Catholic Church, 87.

26 / John T. Ellis, "A Guide to the Baltimore Cathedral Archives," Catholic Historical Review, XXXII (October, 1946), 341–45.

letters received, 1786–1815, ten boxes, arranged alphabetically by the names of the correspondents; letters sent, 1786–1815, two boxes, arranged alphabetically; letters sent book, August 20, 1799–August 10, 1815, in one volume. An index on three-by-five-inch cards is arranged chronologically. Transcripts of Carroll's correspondence obtained by John D. G. Shea, historian of the Catholic church in the United States, from the Vatican and elsewhere are in the Georgetown University Archives. Photostatic copies of Carroll's letters and reports obtained from foreign archives are in the Dominican House of Studies at the Catholic University of America.

In 1952 the American Catholic Historical Association appointed a committee under the chairmanship of the Reverend John T. Ellis to collect reproductions of John Carroll's writings for a published compilation. Those on the committee were Henry J. Browne, archivist of the Catholic University of America, and the Reverend Charles H. Metzger, S. J., and Annabelle M. Melville, both historians of Carroll's period.[27] The committee collected reproductions from numerous repositories in the United States, Canada, and England, which were then arranged in a chronological file and card-indexed. In 1969, funding was provided for publication, an editor appointed, an office set up at the Catholic University of America, and the collecting of Carroll's writings renewed. The publication that resulted contains only letters sent by Carroll, from 1755 (mostly from 1772) to November 23, 1815.[28] But letters received by him were also collected in order to have them available for use in the editing process, and the copies of these letters are available in the Department of Archives and Manuscripts of the Catholic University of America. Letters sent by Carroll to Bishop Luis Peñalver y Cárdenas, Bishop William DuBourg, Pierre Clément de Laussat, American officials, and Vatican officials relating to Louisiana both before and after its acquisition by the United States are in the Carroll papers. A compilation of documents from the archives of the Congregation of the Propaganda Fide in Rome relating to Carroll's appointment as bishop of Baltimore has been published.[29] Several compilations of letters received by Carroll have also been published.[30]

27 / Henry J. Browne, "Report of the Committee on the John Carroll Papers," *Catholic Historical Review*, XXXIX (April, 1953), 40–43.

28 / Thomas O. Hanley (ed.), *The John Carroll Papers* (Notre Dame, Ind., 1976). See vol. I, pp. xxxv–xxxvi, for a list of repositories supplying Carroll items.

29 / E. I. DeVitt (ed.), "Propaganda Documents: Appointment of the First Bishop of Baltimore [1783–89]," *American Catholic Historical Society Records*, XXI (December, 1910), 185–236.

30 / Published under the editorship of E. I. DeVitt in the *American Catholic Historical*

Diocese of Baton Rouge

On July 20, 1961, part of the archdiocese of New Orleans was set up as the diocese of Baton Rouge. In 1962 Bishop Robert E. Tracy established a department of archives and history in the chancery headquarters. Located at first in St. Joseph's School, the department was moved in 1967 to the newly completed Catholic Life Center. An air-conditioned vault in that building became the repository of the older records of the diocese. The records of parishes dated prior to 1870 are described in a guide prepared by Elizabeth J. Doyle. The department's collection of parish records for the colonial period includes St. Joseph Church at Baton Rouge, Ascension Church at Donaldsonville, Assumption Church at Plattenville, St. Francis Church of Pointe Coupee at New Roads, St. Gabriel Church at St. Gabriel, and St. James Church at St. James.[31] Volunteer workers, including Elizabeth B. Gianelloni, Albert J. Robichaux, Jr., George A. Bodin, Catherine B. Futch, Mrs. Edwin A. Broders, and Marguerite Webb, began preparing indexes on cards that were filed alphabetically by name in boxes; their individual contributions are listed under the names of the different churches. Some of these have been published in the *New Orleans Genesis* and the *Louisiana Genealogical Register*. Abstracts of the records of the church at Pointe Coupee and the Acadian church of St. Charles-aux-Mines, prepared under the direction of Nora Lee Pollard, who had been appointed diocesan archivist in 1977, were published in 1978.[32] A third volume prepared under the supervision of Mrs. Pollard contains 6,682 baptismal records, 1,285 marriage entries, and 2,144 burial entries compiled from forty-six registers deposited in the archives of the diocese. The parishes reported on include Ascension at Donaldsonville, Assumption at Plattenville, St. Francis at Pointe Coupee, St. Gabriel at St. Gabriel, St. James at St. James, and St. Joseph at Baton Rouge. Entries are arranged alphabetically by last name.[33] Searches are made in the records and certified copies are provided for a fee. The early records were kept in French and Spanish and are being translated and indexed by a staff of volun-

---

Society Records, XVIII–XX (March, 1907–December, 1909), 389–96, these letters contain little on Louisiana.

31 / Catholic Church, Diocese of Baton Rouge, *A Guide to Archival Material Held by the Catholic Diocese of Baton Rouge*, comp. Elizabeth J. Doyle (Baton Rouge, 1964); Elizabeth B. Gianelloni, "Tour of Department Archives of the Catholic Diocese of Baton Rouge," in *Genealogical Institute, 14th, Proceedings, 17 April 1971* (Baton Rouge, 1972), 21.

32 / Catholic Church, Diocese of Baton Rouge, *Diocese of Baton Rouge Catholic Church Records, Volume I, 1707–1769* (Baton Rouge, 1978).

33 / Catholic Church, Diocese of Baton Rouge, *Diocese of Baton Rouge Catholic Church Records, Volume III, 1804–1819* (Baton Rouge, 1982).

teers. Another compilation arranged alphabetically by name contains ab-stracts of data from the records of other churches in the custody of the diocese of Baton Rouge, including Ascension (Donaldsonville), St. Landry (Opelousas), St. Francis of Assisi (Pointe Coupee), St. Martin of Tours (St. Martinville), St. James (St. James), and St. Gabriel (St. Gabriel). This compilation by the Reverend Donald J. Hébert also contains data from civil records in courthouses, thus permitting a comparison and facilitat-ing the location of pertinent records. A similar compilation by Father Hébert concerns Lafourche and Terrebonne parishes.[34]

Acadians

A settlement made early in the seventeenth century by the French on the east coast of Canada became known as Acadia. The scene of warfare be-tween the French and the British during the succeeding century, it was finally ceded by the Treaty of Utrecht of 1713 to the British, who renamed it Nova Scotia. At the outbreak of the Seven Years' War, believing that the Acadians might side with the French, the British transported them to En-glish and French ports, ports in the English colonies on the Atlantic sea-board, and islands in the Caribbean. During the war some Acadians were transported from European and English colonial ports to Louisiana and after the Treaty of Paris of 1763 made their way back to Canada.[35]

When the Acadians were expelled from Nova Scotia by the British in the 1750s, they carried off with them records of the church of St. Charles-aux-Mines at Grand Pré. These documents were eventually deposited in the rectory of St. Gabriel Church at St. Gabriel, Louisiana, where a Mis-sissippi River flood destroyed some of them in 1893. Three surviving vol-umes, now in the diocese of Baton Rouge archives, contain entries for baptisms, marriages, and funerals, August 14, 1707–November 10, 1748, with 2,244 entries supplying much information on families at St. Charles-aux-Mines, many of whom settled in Louisiana.[36] Transcripts of the records of St. Charles-aux-Mines and of St. Jean-Baptiste at Port Royal are in the Public Archives of Canada.

Much information regarding Acadians who settled in Louisiana has appeared in a variety of publications. In the 1960s George A. Bodin began tracing his own ancestors and in the process collected material regarding collateral lines. His compilation presents alphabetically by name informa-

---

34 / Donald J. Hébert, *Southwest Louisiana Records;* Donald J. Hébert, *South Louisiana Records.*

35 / Arthur G. Doughty, *The Acadian Exiles: A Chronicle of the Land of Evangeline* (To-ronto, 1916), 155–59.

36 / Donald J. Hébert, *Acadians in Exile* (Cecelia, La., 1980).

tion derived from the records of St. Charles-aux-Mines and some twenty-five other churches.[37] For the records of St. Charles-aux-Mines, a more complete listing is the alphabetical abstract published by the diocese of Baton Rouge.[38] Another compilation contains lists obtained from the Public Archives of Canada of Acadians who were transported to English colonies whence some made their way to Louisiana, where they settled among other French-speaking settlers.[39] The Public Archives of Canada has a card index to published materials relating to the Acadians.

Descendants of Acadians in Louisiana will find useful for their genealogical research various compilations in English of baptismal, marriage, and funeral data derived from church records of the maritime provinces of eastern Canada, including Nova Scotia and Prince Edward Island, whence the Acadians had been expelled in 1755. Winston De Ville's compilation, arranged by church parishes or geographical areas, shows details of family relationships. His work was continued by Milton and Norma Rieder, who abstracted the church records of Beaubassin and Port Royal. Personal data derived from Acadians who were held on Belle-Isle-en-Mer, an island in the Bay of Biscay off the coast of Brittany, has been published.[40]

The most complete description of archival sources relating to Acadians has been prepared by the Centre d'Études Acadiennes at the Université de Moncton, Moncton, New Brunswick, Canada. It presents information about archival and manuscript sources in Canada, France, England, the United States, and Spain.[41] An English translation of the general inventory on pages 673–710 in the Centre's publication has been brought out by Father Hébert.[42] A collection of documents concerning the

37 / George A. Bodin, *Selected Acadian and Louisiana Church Records* (St. Martinville, La., 1968, 1970).

38 / Diocese of Baton Rouge, *Catholic Church Records,* I, 1–135. Abstracts of the records of St. Charles-aux-Mines had appeared earlier: Mrs. Edwin A. Broders, Catherine Futch, and Marguerite W. Webb, "Acadian Records from the Parish of St. Charles-aux-Mines, Grandpré, St. Gabriel Church," *New Orleans Genesis,* IX–XIV (September, 1970– January, 1975).

39 / Janet Jehn, *Acadian Exiles in the Colonies* (Covington, Ky., 1972–82).

40 / Winston De Ville (comp. and trans.), *Acadian Church Records, 1679–1757* (Mobile, Ala., 1964); Milton P. Rieder, Jr., and Norma G. Rieder (trans. and eds.), *Beaubassin, 1712–1748* and *Port Royal, 1702–1721* (Metairie, La., 1976–77), vols. II and III of Rieder and Rieder (eds.), *Acadian Church Records;* Mathé Allain (trans.), "Records of Belle-Isle-en-Mer," *Attakapas Gazette,* XVI (Winter, 1981), 165–71; XVII (Summer–Winter, 1982), 76–83, 123–31, 183–92.

41 / Moncton, Université de, Centre d'Études Acadiennes, *Inventaire general des sources documentaires sur les Acadiens* (Moncton, 1975–77), I, 1–382. Volumes II–III contain exensive bibliographies of secondary materials on the Acadians.

42 / Donald J. Hébert, *Acadians in Exile,* 671–710.

expulsion of the Acadians, 1729–1769, has been published.[43] Papers relating to Nova Scotia and the Acadians are in the British Museum.[44]

Parish Registers

Microfilm of the registers of the Catholic churches of Louisiana for the colonial period and later years is in the archives departments of the dioceses of Louisiana. The Department of Archives of the diocese of Baton Rouge by 1972 had microfilm of the records of all the Catholic churches in the twelve civil parishes in the diocese and permitted their use for research. This practice saves the original records from the inevitable wear resulting from repeated handling for research. A survey conducted by Charles Nolan in the 1970s revealed that the participating dioceses had microfilmed all or part of their oldest church records, many of which were in need of repair and restoration.[45] The chancery of the archdiocese of New Orleans has copies of church registers; however, they are not available for research by individuals or for microfilming, but research is done by staff members. The chancery has begun a long-range program of computerizing the names in the registers with the aim of publishing those names.

Other repositories in Louisiana have microfilm of the registers of Catholic churches. The St. Martin Parish Library at St. Martinville has microfilm of the handwritten transcripts of the records of St. Francis Church of Natchitoches, St. Landry Church of Opelousas, St. Gabriel Church of St. Gabriel, and St. Martin of Tours Church of St. Martinville, obtained early in the 1900s by the Public Archives of Canada. The New Orleans Public Library has the same microfilm. The Louisiana State Archives and Records Service at Baton Rouge has microfilm of the registers of St. Martin of Tours and of St. Francis in Natchitoches and of those church registers in the custody of the archives department of the diocese of Baton Rouge. The Public Archives of Canada have microfilm of the early records of the churches at Natchitoches, Opelousas, St. Charles, St. Gabriel, and St. Martinville.[46]

43 / Placide Gaudet, *Acadian Genealogy and Notes*, in Canada, Public Archives, *Report Concerning Canadian Archives for the Year 1905* (Ottawa, 1906), II, Appendix A, Part III. See also Beers, *French in North America*, 250–52.

44 / Oscar W. Winzerling, *Acadian Odyssey* (Baton Rouge, 1955), 209.

45 / Gianelloni, "Tour of Department Archives," 18–19; Charles E. Nolan, "The Bicentennial Archival Project of the Catholic Province of New Orleans," *Genealogical Institute, 19th, Proceedings, 20 March 1976* (Baton Rouge, 1976), 33–34.

46 / "St. Martin Parish Library Microfilm Collection as of March, 1973," *Genealogical*

The growth of the Catholic church in Louisiana has resulted in the expansion of the church's organization. The diocese of Louisiana, established in 1815, was divided in 1826 into the dioceses of New Orleans and St. Louis. On July 19, 1850, the archdiocese of New Orleans was established. The diocese of Natchitoches was created on July 29, 1853, from the northern part of the diocese of New Orleans. It was changed in 1910 to the diocese of Alexandria and in 1977 to the diocese of Alexandria-Shreveport. On January 11, 1918, southwestern Louisiana was detached from the archdiocese of New Orleans and set up as the diocese of Lafayette. Another part of the archdiocese of New Orleans became the diocese of Baton Rouge on August 15, 1961.[47] Archivists are usually included on diocesan chancery staffs.

By the canon law of the Catholic church, priests have always been required to keep registers of baptisms, marriages, burials, and confirmations. The parochial registers are considered to be confidential and are not open to genealogical research, though priests furnish registers for the use of the families whose relatives appear therein. In France the government required recordings by the priests, thus constituting them recorders for the state. Even before the issuance of a decree by the Louisiana Superior Council in 1723 requiring the maintenance of registers, the priests had initiated the practice.[48]

The parochial registers were kept in much the same manner in Louisiana by both the French and Spanish priests, and entries were made in French, Spanish, and sometimes Latin. The baptismal registers show the date of birth and baptism, the name of the infant, the names of its parents, grandparents, and sponsors, and the signature of the priest. The entries might also show the place of birth, as it was not always the place where the baptism occurred, and the places of origin of the parents or grandparents.

The church registers are useful for more than personal and family data. They contain information about the spread of settlement, farming and other occupations, slavery, including the locality or tribes in Africa from which the slaves came, and the arrival of Acadians. Remarks appear infrequently as to significant happenings of the colony. The registers also furnish information on the history of the churches, their pastors, their

---

Institute, 16th, Proceedings, 31 March 1973 (Baton Rouge, 1974), 40–43; Canada, Public Archives, Union List of Manuscripts, 720–21.

47 / New Catholic Encyclopedia, I, 303, VIII, 317, X, 383.

48 / Cora C. Curry, Records of the Roman Catholic Church in the United States as a Source for Authentic Genealogical and Historical Material (Washington, D.C., 1935), 1–2; Winston De Ville, Gulf Coast Colonials: A Compendium of French Families in Early Eighteenth Century Louisiana (Baltimore, 1968), 11; O'Neill, Church and State in French Colonial Louisiana, 237–38.

buildings, and their parishioners. The marriage registers contain the names, ages, and places of birth of the groom and the bride, the names of the parents, sometimes the signatures of relatives of the groom and the bride, and the signature of the priest. Burial registers give the name, age, the place of birth, the date of burial, and sometimes the names of the parents, the religion, the occupation, and the nationality of the deceased. The registers contain entries concerning slaves and other persons of mixed blood, but these are often less useful because the names are incomplete. Many priests traveled by horseback or canoe to neighboring settlements, where they performed sacerdotal functions and recorded them in the church registers that accompanied them on their travels.

In 1975 the archdiocesan bicentennial commission of the archdiocese of New Orleans proposed the preparation of an inventory of the church records of the province of New Orleans, which included Louisiana, Alabama, and Mississippi. Charles E. Nolan, a tutor at the Gables Academy in New Orleans, was engaged to direct the project. He visited each depository and gathered information in order to prepare descriptions by series in the original languages for baptismal, marriage, and funeral registers and other series. The guide that Nolan produced is the principal source of information for the descriptions of church records that follow, but it contains no information about the many publications incorporating data from these records. Another guide to church records is arranged alphabetically by civil parishes and alphabetically thereunder by the names of places and gives the opening dates of church registers by years only.[49]

Parish Churches

Baton Rouge, St. Joseph Church. Originally called Our Lady of Sorrows, the church has been known as St. Joseph since 1822. After Governor Bernardo de Gálvez captured Baton Rouge in 1779, it and West Florida remained under Spanish control until 1810. An Irish priest from Spain was assigned to Baton Rouge in 1793. The Baton Rouge church served the two outposts of Manchac and New Feliciana.

The records of St. Joseph Church are preserved in the Baton Rouge chancery. The earliest registers begin in the Spanish period and extend into the American period. A register of baptisms contains baptisms of whites from October 24, 1793, to June 2, 1806, and baptisms of Negroes from April 11, 1800, to January 10, 1818. These baptisms were performed at Baton Rouge, Manchac, New Feliciana, Bayou Sara, and neighboring areas; they are recorded on 368 pages of loose sheets. Another register of

49 / Nolan, "Bicentennial Archival Project," 30–36; Nolan, *Southern Catholic Heritage;* Donald J. Hébert, *A Guide to Church Records in Louisiana, 1720–1975* (Eunice, La., 1975).

baptisms, June 2, 1806–May 6, 1821, is in a bound volume, and a further record of baptisms and marriages, 1807–1835, is on loose sheets. A register of marriages, January 15, 1793–April 30, 1821, in a bound volume and some loose items, includes marriages performed at Baton Rouge, Manchac, and New Feliciana. Other entries for marriages performed from 1800 to 1810 and some to 1840 at the places mentioned above and also at Rapides, the Plains, Bayou Tunica, Thompson's Creek, and Pointe Coupee are on loose sheets. A register of interments, September 12, 1793–December 16, 1815, in one volume, completes the list of early records.[50]

Several publications present some information derived from the records of St. Joseph Church. A brief list of baptisms contains only the last names of the infants, though the registers themselves contain the usual valuable genealogical information on the parents and grandparents and their places of origin. Another publication gives the names of deceased persons and the page numbers of the register on which the names appear.[51] Some "miscellaneous" records of the church in the Baton Rouge chancery comprise numbered items with entries relating to marriages. Item 83 contains an alphabetical list of the names of persons married at Natchez, New Feliciana, and Baton Rouge, September 1, 1794–June 10, 1805. Item 84C gives the names of nine Protestants married at Bayou Sara, New Feliciana, and Natchez in 1798 and 1799. Item 85 contains the names of seven men married in 1800 at Baton Rouge, New Feliciana, Red River, or Rapides. Item 86 gives the names of parties married during the years 1801–1808 at Baton Rouge, Manchac, Bayou Sara, and Feliciana. Item 87 contains the names of twenty-two persons, both Protestant and Catholic, married in 1805 at Baton Rouge, Bayou Sara, Tunica, and New Feliciana. Item 88 contains the names of parties in nineteen marriages performed in 1806 at Baton Rouge, Amite River, Thompson's Creek, Bayou Sara, and New Feliciana and of five infants who were baptized. The participants in other marriages performed at Baton Rouge, Bayou Sara, and Thompson's Creek in 1807 and 1808 are given in item 89. Nine other marriages performed in 1809 at Bayou Sara and Baton Rouge are entered in item 90. Ten marriages that were solemnized in 1810 at Bayou Sara, New Feliciana, Thompson's Creek and Pointe Coupee appear in item 91.[52]

50 / Nolan, *Southern Catholic Heritage*, 98–100.

51 / Elizabeth B. Gianelloni, "Earliest Baptismal Records (1793–1806) of St. Joseph Cathedral, Baton Rouge," *Louisiana Genealogical Register*, XVIII March, 1971), 89–93; Mrs. Edwin A. Broders, "Funerals from Sept. 12, 1793, to Dec. 17, 1815, Our Lady of Sorrows Church, Baton Rouge, La.," *Louisiana Genealogical Register*, XI (June, 1964), 21–24.

52 / Alphabetical lists of the names of the parties to the marriages and of the names of the infants baptized are in Elizabeth B. Gianelloni, "'Miscellaneous' Records of St. Joseph

Destrehan, St. Charles Borromeo Church. In 1723 St. John the Baptist Church was built at Lucy on the west bank of the Mississippi for the Germans living there. The settlers had moved to the east bank of the Mississippi by 1740, and a new church, named St. Charles Borromeo, was built at Destrehan. After the burning of that church and most of its records in 1877, a new church was built and became popularly known as the "Little Red Church," serving as a landmark for shipping on the Mississippi River. The only remaining record, a register of baptisms, marriages, and funerals, January 6, 1739–March 30, 1755, in one volume, is in the New Orleans chancery. A copy of this record and a card index to its contents are in the Louisiana State Museum Library. Alphabetical lists of the names of persons in the surviving volume have been published. That for marriages shows the names of the parties, the parents, and the witnesses and the dates of the ceremonies.[53]

Donaldsonville, Ascension Church. A Capuchin priest established a church at the junction of the Mississippi River and Bayou Lafourche in August, 1772.[54] The records of the parish deposited in the Baton Rouge chancery include a register of baptisms, marriages, and deaths from 1772, in one volume; baptisms, August 30, 1772–October 24, 1784; marriages, August 24, 1772–February 27, 1786; and funerals, August 31, 1772–February 2, 1789. A register of baptisms of whites, November 24, 1785–January 30, 1823, in 484 pages of loose sheets; a register of baptisms, marriages, and burials of Negroes, August 27, 1786–October 7, 1827, in 308 sheets; a register of marriages of whites, April 18, 1786–October 5, 1829, in 376 sheets; and a one-volume register of funerals, November 25, 1786–November 6, 1841.

The records of the parish have been used to prepare a compilation regarding the Acadian families who settled there. The compilation is arranged in dictionary form by the name of the head of the family, with dates of marriage and death and the names of children. An abstract of the earliest register, 1772–1789, arranged alphabetically by name, has been published.[55]

Cathedral, Baton Rouge," *Louisiana Genealogical Register,* XVI (June–December, 1969), 121–25, 283–87, 329–30.

53 / Nolan, *Southern Catholic Heritage,* 47; Alice D. Forsyth, "Marriages, Baptisms, and Deaths of the Little Red Church [1739–55]," *New Orleans Genesis,* I (January–September, 1962).

54 / Marchand, *Ascension Parish,* 26.

55 / Marchand, Jr., *Old Settlers in Family Groups;* Elizabeth B. Gianelloni, "Earliest Records of Ascension Church, Donaldsonville," *New Orleans Genesis,* IX (January, 1970), 11–22.

Edgard, St. John the Baptish Church. A church was built on the west bank of the Mississippi in 1772 on land that had been set aside by Governor O'Reilly. A Capuchin, the Reverend Bernard de Limpach, became pastor and initiated the registers. Despite the destruction of the church by flood in 1819 and by fire in 1918, the records have survived and were rebound in the 1960s. The register of baptisms, August 9, 1772–December 31, 1817, in three volumes, includes in the one for 1792–1796 a record of the baptisms of Negroes, mulattoes, and some Indians, February 14, 1796–July 21, 1818. In the register of marriages, November 24, 1772–September 29, 1818, in two volumes, the second volume contains financial records for 1776–1800 on pages 1–38 and 131–46; an inventory of church property, July 27, 1779, and March 5, 1786, on pages 199–204; and funeral accounts on pages 295–96. The one-volume register of funerals covers 1772–1815.[56]

Galveztown, St. Bernard Church. To observe the British in West Florida, in 1779 Governor Gálvez established a settlement on the Amite River below its junction with Bayou Manchac. Named after the governor, it became the home of English and American refugees and Canary Islanders. St. Bernard Church, built around 1780, was served intermittently by a pastor; at other times it shared one with St. Gabriel Church, with which it was joined in 1809.[57]

The records of St. Bernard are in the Baton Rouge chancery and are both separate and mingled with those of St. Gabriel. The collection includes a register of baptisms of whites and Negroes, from around 1780 to April 14, 1787, and from July 6, 1791, to August 21, 1807, in one volume; a register of baptisms, marriages, and funerals, January 25, 1781–October 16, 1785, with records of both St. Bernard and St. Gabriel; a register of

56 / Nolan, *Southern Catholic Heritage*, 79; Jack Belsom, "St. John the Baptist Parish Church, Edgard, Louisiana," *New Orleans Genesis*, IX (March, 1970), 110–11; Irna A. Centanni, "Index to First Book of Baptisms of St. John the Baptist Parish, Edgard, Louisiana, August 1772 to December 1791," *New Orleans Genesis*, IX (March, 1970), 114–31; Irna A. Centanni, "St. John the Baptist Church, Edgard, Louisiana, Second Book of Baptisms, January 1792 to February 1796," *New Orleans Genesis*, XI (January, September, 1972), 46–49, 378–83; Irna A. Centanni, "St. John the Baptist Church, Edgard, Louisiana, Third Book of Baptisms, March 12, 1796–April 8, 1817," *New Orleans Genesis*, XII (January, March, 1973), 57–62, 170–75; Irna A. Centanni, "Index to the First Book of Marriages, St. John the Baptist Parish, Edgard, Louisiana, November 14, 1772, to August 18, 1807," *New Orleans Genesis*, IX (September, 1970), 321–38; Mrs. Lionel J. Zeringue, "St. John the Baptist Church, Edgard, Louisiana, Index of Funerals, Book 1, September 6, 1772, to December 21, 1815," *New Orleans Genesis*, IX (September, 1970), 321–38.

57 / V. M. Scramuzza, "Galveztown: A Spanish Settlement of Colonial Louisiana," *Louisiana Historical Quarterly*, XIII (October, 1930), 598.

persons of color, 1782–1843 (no entries for 1798–1802 and 1806–1827), in one volume; a register of baptisms, marriages, and funerals, and marriage investigations, 1783–1803, contained in one loose-leaf binder, deposited in the St. Louis Cathedral archives in New Orleans; a one-volume register of baptisms of St. Gabriel and St. Bernard, October 30, 1785–March 18, 1821; register of baptisms at St. Gabriel and St. Bernard, including baptisms at St. Gabriel, 1787–1791, baptisms at St. Bernard from 1787 to February 24, 1791, St. Bernard marriages, May 27, 1787–October 19, 1789, St. Bernard funerals, September 10, 1787–April 7, 1791, in one volume; a register of marriages of whites, October 27, 1785–May 10, 1859, also in one volume.[58]

Mansura, St. Paul's Church. After a visit by Bishop Peñalver to the area in 1796 when Father Antonio de Sedella opened a baptismal register, an Irish priest was appointed there. During the frequent intervals when no priest was attached to the parish, it was served by priests from Opelousas, St. Martinville, Natchitoches, and Pointe Coupee. The old Avoyelles church was eventually replaced by one in Mansura, to which the records were taken.

The records include a one-volume register of baptisms of whites, October 31, 1796–November 19, 1807, a one-volume register of Indians and Negroes, October 31, 1796–August 22, 1841, and a register of funerals, 1803–1804.[59] The records are indexed in Bodin's *Acadian and Louisiana Church Records.*

Morganza, St. Ann's Church. In the eighteenth century, the area around Morganza was served by the priest from the St. Francis mission at Pointe Coupee. This arrangement continued through the nineteenth century, though the establishment of new churches at New Roads and Chenal reduced the area attached to Pointe Coupee. A new church built at Morganza in 1915 was named St. Ann's. A register of marriages of St. Ann's, 1786–1812, is in the Department of Archives of the diocese of Baton Rouge.[60]

Natchitoches, St. Francis Church. Although a military post was established at Natchitoches in 1714, no priest arrived until about 1728, and none was stationed there regularly for many years. The name of the earli-

58 / *Ibid.*, 600, 604.
59 / Nolan, *Southern Catholic Heritage*, 102–103.
60 / Mrs. Arthur F. Ortiz, "St. Ann's Church Records, Morganza, Louisiana," *New Orleans Genesis*, VII (January, 1968), 68–74.

est church was St. Francis of Assisi, but its name was changed in 1853 to St. Mary and in 1856 to Immaculate Conception. The records were originally kept in small booklets; they have since been bound into large volumes and are difficult to follow. In the registers of baptisms, marriages, and funerals, 1729–1822, in four volumes, the last register, for 1801–1822, contains entries for Negroes and Indians. A one-volume register of baptisms, June 17, 1776–November 1, 1796, includes entries for Negroes. A register entitled "baptisms of whites and Indians, 1796–1801," contains baptisms of Indians and whites, 1796–1801, funerals of whites, 1796–1801, baptisms of Negroes, 1795–1801, funerals of Negroes, 1796–1801, and marriages of whites and negroes, 1786–1801. A one-volume register of funerals, July, 1793–November, 1796, contains funerals of whites, July 23, 1793–September 27, 1796, and of Negroes, July 5, 1793–November 3, 1796. One small booklet contains a record of expenditures for funerals and anniversary masses, April 30, 1783–April, 1786. An inventory and description of the church and presbytery and their contents, May 9, 1738, is a copy made in 1903.[61] Spanish Franciscans from the mission San Miguel at Los Adaes, Texas, while on visits to Natchitoches, performed religious rituals there that they recorded in the registers of the mission.

After negotiations on behalf of the Public Archives of Canada with the bishop of Alexandria and the pastor of the Church of the Immaculate Conception, the old registers for 1729–1795 were taken to New Orleans in 1962 and microfilmed.[62] Microfilm of the registers of this parish is also in the Colonial Records Collection of the University of Southwestern Louisiana and in the St. Martin Parish Library.

Several publications containing data regarding individuals obtained from the records of St. Francis Church have appeared. A compilation on baptisms contains the names of the infants baptized, their parents and godparents, and sometimes the places of residence of the parents. Broader in coverage is an indexed translation based on baptismal, marriage, and funeral records of 1734–1764.[63] Extremely useful for genealogi-

61 / Nolan, Southern Catholic Heritage, 54–56.
62 / Blaise C. D'Antoni, "The Church Records of North Louisiana," Louisiana History, XV (Winter, 1974), 62–63.
63 / Catherine B. Futch (comp. and trans.), "Baptisms Recorded at the Church of St. Francis of Assisi—Now the Church of the Immaculate Conception, Natchitoches, Louisiana, 1734–1743," New Orleans Genesis, VIII (June, 1969), 243–52; Blaise C. D'Antoni (comp. and trans.), The Natchitoches Registers, 1734–1764, Volume One, Being a Compilation of Baptismal, Marriage and Funeral Records of the Poste Saint Jean Baptiste de Natchitoches for the Years 1734–1764 (New Orleans, 1970).

cal and historical research is a large compilation of Elizabeth S. Mills containing edited translations of the original register entries.[64] She found the baptismal and marriage records nearly complete and the burial records far less complete for the colonial period. Through the use of the registers, the spread of families into other parts of northern Louisiana and the growth of the dominance of the English element can be traced, for recordings concerning them can be found in the registers of St. Francis Church.

New Orleans, St. Louis Cathedral. After several other buildings had been used as temporary quarters, a church was completed in New Orleans in 1727 and named St. Louis after the king of France. It continued in use until 1788, when the building and some of the records were destroyed by fire. A new church was constructed during the years 1789–1794 by means of a gift from Andrés Almonester y Rojàs, a wealthy member of the *cabildo.* After the establishment of the diocese of Louisiana and the Floridas in 1793, the new church was designated as the bishop's cathedral. The present cathedral, constructed in 1850 on the site of the old Spanish structure, was restored in 1976.[65]

The St. Louis Cathedral archives are in the archives of the archdiocese of New Orleans and are housed in the building adjacent to the cathedral. For several decades the archives have been in the charge of archivists who have prepared finding aids and translations to facilitate the use of the records for genealogical research.

The earliest record of baptisms in New Orleans, January–December, 1728, was kept by the civil authorities, and a copy obtained from the État Civil series in the French archives is in the Louisiana State Museum and photocopies are in the St. Louis Cathedral archives.[66] The original registers of baptisms from which were prepared the numerous published compilations that are cited here are in the archives of the archdiocese of New Orleans. The registers of baptisms of St. Louis Cathedral, January 1, 1731–December 27, 1733, January 1, 1744–March 30, 1759, and June 21, 1767–April 26, 1806, contained in nine volumes, show the names of each infant, the parents, the grandparents, the sponsors, and the priest, and

64 / Elizabeth S. Mills (trans. and ed.), *Natchitoches, 1729–1803; Abstracts of the Catholic Church Registers of the French and Spanish Post of St. Jean Baptiste des Natchitoches in Louisiana* (New Orleans, 1977); see also Elizabeth S. Mills, "Selected Extracts from the Registers of the Parish of St. François des Natchitoches," *Louisiana Genealogical Register,* XXIII (June, 1976), 151–61, which contains information relating to baptisms.

65 / John S. Kendall, *History of New Orleans* (Chicago, 1922), II, 705.

66 / Winston De Ville, "List of Children Baptized in the Parish of New Orleans in 1728," *Louisiana Genealogical Register,* X (June, 1963), 32.

the date and place of birth. Other registers include those of baptisms of Negroes, May 5, 1798–September 11, 1804, in two volumes, and registers of baptisms of Negroes and mulattoes, January 1, 1777–April 29, 1798, in four volumes. Two books of baptisms and marriages include baptisms from January 1, 1759, to April 27, 1762, and January 1, 1763, to September 18, 1766.[67] Much of the data in these registers is available in compilations published in *New Orleans Genesis*, which it would be worthwhile to republish in one indexed volume.[68]

A number of registers of marriages are also extant. The earliest, for July 1, 1720, to December 4, 1730, is a copy made by Father Antonio de Sedella. It includes marriages at Biloxi, Yazoo, Fort Louis, and Natchez and contains eleven marriages of Negroes and three acts of adjuration of heresy. A compilation by Winston De Ville contains his notes on a Spanish priest's transcripts of earlier records written by the French missionary priests who served in the church. De Ville's book presents data derived from the first book of marriages and the first book of baptisms alphabetically by name. The St. Louis marriage registers of 1720–1736 show the names of places where German colonists were born—Alsace, Baden, Würtemberg, Saxony, Bavaria, and Lorraine—and contains entries regarding colonists who moved to other parts of the Mississippi Valley.

67 / Nolan, *Southern Catholic Heritage*, 36–38.

68 / Alice D. Forsyth and Hewitt L. Forsyth, "Extrait des registres pour les baptêmes de l'église paroissialle de la Nouvelle Orleans de l'année 1729–30," *New Orleans Genesis*, VI (March, 1967), 103–105; Mrs. Fred O. James, "Baptismal Register of St. Louis Cathedral, 1731–1753," *New Orleans Genesis*, V (September, 1966), 297–304; Mrs. Fred O. James, "Baptismal and Marriage Register—No. 1, Jan. 1, 1731–Dec. 27, 1733, St. Louis Cathedral—New Orleans," *New Orleans Genesis*, V (September, 1966), 297–302, VI (June, 1967), 206–207; Mrs. Fred O. James, "St. Louis Cathedral Baptismal Register—Book III, March 3, 1753, to March 30, 1759," *New Orleans Genesis*, VI (June, September, 1967), 206–207, VII (January, March, 1968), 35–37; Mrs. Fred O. James, "St. Louis Cathedral Baptismal Book IV, Jan. 1, 1759, to Apr. 27, 1762," *New Orleans Genesis*, VII (January, 1968), 37–43; Alice D. Forsyth, "Baptismal Book, V–VI, 1763–1771, St. Louis Cathedral Archives," *Louisiana Genealogical Register*, XXII (June, 1975), 173–79; Mrs. Fred O. James, "St. Louis Cathedral, New Orleans, Louisiana, Baptismal Book VI—June 20, 1767, to December 31, 1771," *New Orleans Genesis*, VII (January–June, 1968), 43, 122–27, 215–19; Mrs. Fred O. James, "St. Louis Cathedral Baptismal Register, Vol. VII, Jan. 3, 1772–Dec. 30, 1776," *New Orleans Genesis*, VII (June, September, 1968), 219–20, 323–28, VIII (January, 1969), 5–9; Mrs. Fred O. James and Albert Robichaux, Jr., "St. Louis Cathedral Baptismal Book I, Jan. 9, 1777, to May 11, 1786," *New Orleans Genesis*, VIII (March, June, 1969), 122–29, 215–21; Irna A. Centanni, "St. Louis Cathedral Baptismal Book 2, May 12, 1786, to June 5, 1796," *New Orleans Genesis*, VIII (June, September, 1969), 221, 317–23, IX (January, March, 1970), 27–33, 142–46; Charles L. Mackie, "St. Louis Cathedral Baptismal Register 3—1796–1802," *New Orleans Genesis*, X (January, March, 1971), 22–31, 128–35; Paul H. F. Bernard, "St. Louis Cathedral Baptismal Register 4—1802–1806," *New Orleans Genesis*, X (June, September, 1971), 220–27, 364–68.

Other registers of marriages are for January 15, 1759–November 15, 1763, January 8, 1763–September 18, 1766 [these two are in the books of baptisms and marriages referred to above], January 17, 1764–January 22, 1774 (including entries for Pointe Coupee), and February 6, 1777–June 9, 1806. These registers contain extensive genealogical information, and the names appearing in the various registers have been published. In order to preserve the last register of marriages for the Spanish period (May 1, 1784–June 9, 1806) from further damage while it is used for research, the information in it has been excerpted and published under the editorship of Alice D. Forsyth, who became the full-time archivist of the cathedral archives in 1966.[69]

To fill a gap in the burial records of St. Louis Cathedral, photocopies of earlier registers of funerals were obtained from the Archives Nationales in Paris. These cover January 1, 1724–February 11, 1728, and January 12, 1730–August 17, 1734, including those of 1721–1723 in Biloxi.[70] Other records include a three-volume register of funerals, January 4, 1772–June, 1790, October 3, 1784–September 8, 1793, and September 13, 1793–December 24, 1803; and a two-volume register of funerals of freedmen and slaves, September 8, 1790–January 16, 1806.[71]

A number of publications present data derived from the registers of funerals and facilitate their use. Extracts from the early registers give alphabetically the names of the persons interred and the page numbers of the registers in which the information is found. The same information is available in another publication for the years 1772–1793. Two compilations by Alice Forsyth for the same years contain much fuller data, including the name of the deceased, age, place of birth, date of burial,

---

69 / Hewitt L. Forsyth and Alice D. Forsyth, "Saint Louis Basilica Marriage Records, July 1st 1720 to December 4th 1730," *New Orleans Genesis*, V (June, 1966), 190–211; Winston De Ville, *The New Orleans French, 1720–1733; a Collection of Marriage Records Relating to the First Colonists of Louisiana Province* (Baltimore, 1973); Alice D. Forsyth, "St. Louis Cathedral Archives, Marriages Entered in Baptismal Register IV—May 1, 1759, to November 15, 1762," *New Orleans Genesis*, VI (June, 1967), 226–30; Hewitt L. Forsyth and Alice D. Forsyth, "Marriage Register of St. Louis Basilica Archives, January 17, 1764, to January 22, 1774, Register B," *New Orleans Genesis*, V (September, 1966), 305–309; "St. Louis Cathedral Marriage Book B, 1764–1774," *Louisiana Genealogical Register*, XXII (June, 1975), 180–82; Hewitt L. Forsyth and Alice D. Forsyth, "Marriage Register of St. Louis Basilica—Volume 1, February 6, 1777–April 13, 1784," *New Orleans Genesis*, V (September, 1966), 309–12; Alice D. Forsyth (ed.), *Louisiana Marriages, Volume I, A Collection of Marriage Records from the St. Louis Cathedral in New Orleans During the Spanish Regime and the Early American Period, 1784–1806* (New Orleans, 1977).

70 / Irma A. Centanni, "Extracts from the Register of Burials in New Orleans, 1724–1726, 1729–30, 1734," *New Orleans Genesis*, VI (January–June, 1967), 27–28, 105–106, 220–21.

71 / Lucille M. B. Fortier, "Funeral Records—[St. Louis Cathedral] 1772–1793," *New Orleans Genesis*, V (June, September, 1966), 211–14, 313–17, VI (January, 1967), 24–26.

names of parents, place of residence, religion, occupation, and nationality.[72] Such comprehensive coverage makes it unnecessary to consult the original record. Another compilation for the period 1803–1807, however, gives only the names of the deceased and the page number.[73]

Some other records are also available in the archives of St. Louis Cathedral. The first book of confirmations of the diocese, 1789 to June 27, 1841, contains a record of confirmations for 1789–1801 and a list of confirmations for 1813–1841. For the Spanish period there are more than four thousand entries. Besides the names of the children confirmed by the bishop, the book contains the names of parents and godparents. The bishop traveled extensively throughout the diocese, and besides entries for residents of St. John the Baptist, St. Charles, Avoyelles, Pointe Coupee, Baton Rouge, and other parishes in Louisiana, there are others for residents of Pass Christian, Natchez, Mobile, Pensacola, Fort Barrancas, and Deer Island near Biloxi. The entries are for whites, mulattoes, and others of mixed white and Negro ancestry. After being stored for years in a vault and inaccessible for research because of its poor condition, the volume was translated in the 1960s by Hewitt L. Forsyth and Alice D. Forsyth and Marlene Zeringue. About 90 percent of the volume could be pieced together and translated. An index to the confirmations gives the dates and the places of residence of the individuals confirmed.[74] A record of the accounts and deliberations of the church wardens, from 1747 to February 20, 1804, in two volumes, provides information regarding the parish and the church building. A collection of miscellaneous documents, 1781–1797, concerns the church, some of its prominent members, and the diocese.[75] Entries concerning the early settlers on the German Coast, which later became the parishes of St. Charles, St. John, and St. Martin, are in the St. Louis registers.

Opelousas, St. Landry Church. The settlers around the French military post at Opelousas were served by priests from Pointe Coupee and At-

72 / Alice D. Forsyth, "St. Louis Cathedral Funeral Register, 1772–1790—Excerpts," *Louisiana Genealogical Register,* XXII (September, 1975), 207–12; Alice D. Forsyth, "St. Louis Cathedral Funeral Register, 1793–1803," *Louisiana Genealogical Register,* XXII (June, 1975), 126–31.

73 / Hewitt L. Forsyth, "Funeral Records—St. Louis Cathedral—1803–1807," *New Orleans Genesis,* VI (September, 1967), 328–29, VII (January, March, 1968), 52–57, 140–45.

74 / St. Louis Cathedral, New Orleans, *Confirmaciónes—Libro primero de confirmaciónes de esta parroquis de Sn. Luis de la Nueva Orleans* (New Orleans, 1967); Jack Belsom, "Index to Confirmaciónes," *New Orleans Genesis,* X (January, 1971), 96–98.

75 / Nolan, *Southern Catholic Heritage,* 43–46.

takapas before the parish was begun around 1770. In 1787 Dr. Joseph de Arazona translated into English the records he found on loose sheets of paper and entered them into registers. The records include a register of baptisms, marriages, and funerals, May 19, 1776–October 29, 1786, in one booklet; a register of baptisms, May 19, 1776–July 29, 1813, in two volumes; a register of baptisms, marriages, and funerals of persons of color and Negroes, April 22, 1787–November 1, 1812, in one volume; a register of marriages, April 23, 1787–October 19, 1830, in two volumes; and a register of funerals, April, 1787–December 22, 1819, in one volume.[76]

Several publications contain information derived from the St. Landry Church records that is of assistance to researchers. The names of persons in the marriage registers with page numbers to those records are in a compilation by Father Donald Hébert, who is also the compiler of another work that abstracts information from the baptismal, marriage, and funeral records. Less extensive is another compilation by Gladys De Villier. Information from the registers on baptisms, 1776–1785, marriages, 1780–1806, and burials, 1780–1806, is available in another publication.[77] Microfilm of the registers is in the Public Archives of Canada and the University of Southwestern Louisiana.

Plattenville, Assumption Church. A Spanish Capuchin established a church on Bayou Lafourche in 1793, seven miles below the military post at Valenzuela. The records of Assumption Church have survived intact and are preserved in the Baton Rouge chancery. They include a two-volume register of baptisms, April 24, 1793–August 5, 1803, and November 21, 1803–August 10, 1815; a register of baptisms of Negroes and mulattoes, September 29, 1793–December 25, 1841, in one volume and loose sheets; a register of marriages of whites, April 22, 1793–April 14, 1817, in one volume; a register of funerals of whites, May 2, 1793–January 23, 1838, in one volume; a one-volume register of funerals of Negroes and mulattoes, November 17, 1796–January 24, 1877; records of deliberations of the church wardens, January 11, 1794–April 8, 1925, in one volume, with a gap from 1796 to 1811; and financial accounts, April 9, 1798–August 11, 1817, part of

76 / *Ibid.*, 69–71.
77 / Donald J. Hébert (trans.), "St. Landry Catholic Church—Opelousas, Louisiana, Marriages, Volume I, 1787–1830," *New Orleans Genesis*, XII–XIV (September, 1973–September, 1975); Gladys De Villier, *The Opelousas Post: A Compendium of Church Records Relating to the First Families of Southwest Louisiana, 1776–1806* (New Orleans, 1972); Jeanne Grégorie, "Les Acadiennes dans un seconde patrie: La Louisiane," *Revue d'histoire de l'Amérique française*, XV (March, 1962), 572–93, XVI (June, September, December, 1962), 105–16, 254–66, 428–35.

one volume. The records of Assumption Church have been indexed by George Bodin.[78]

Pointe Coupee, St. Francis of Assisi Church. The first priest assigned to Pointe Coupee in 1728 was a French Capuchin, but a church was not erected there until 1738. Encroachment by the Mississippi River forced removal of the church to a site outside of New Roads in 1760 and in 1895 and to New Roads itself in 1963.

The records of St. Francis now in the Baton Rouge chancery include a register of baptisms, marriages, and funerals, August 7, 1727–October 29, 1785, in four volumes. The first volume contains entries for Attakapas, Opelousas, and Arkansas. Other baptisms, marriages, and funerals, August 1, 1769–July 11, 1784, are on loose sheets. There are also four other registers: a register of baptisms, January 5, 1786–October 2, 1814, in one volume, a register of baptisms and funerals of Negroes and slaves, January 8, 1786–May 17, 1839, in one volume; a register of marriages, May 20, 1786–June 15, 1841; and a register of funerals, October 29, 1785–August 4, 1841, in one volume.[79]

A compilation of genealogical interest based upon the records of St. Francis Church presents data in alphabetical order by family name and chronologically thereunder. Besides the principals, the entries include the names of parents, their places of birth, their ages, and the names of witnesses; there are also entries for Indians and slaves. The data in the records of St. Francis are available in an alphabetical abstract for the years up to the end of 1769. Alphabetical name indexes of marriages are also in print.[80]

St. Bernard, St. Bernard Church. The settlers on the Mississippi River below New Orleans, including the French, the Spanish, Canary Islanders, and Acadians, were ministered to by clergy from St. Louis Church in New Orleans. In 1785 a priest was designated for the church that was built there, which was named St. Bernard. When it ceased being an independent church in 1916, it became a mission of Our Lady of Lourdes

78 / Nolan, *Southern Catholic Heritage*, 93–95; Bodin, *Selected Church Records.*
79 / Nolan, *Southern Catholic Heritage*, 50–52.
80 / Winston De Ville (ed.), *First Settlers of Pointe Coupee: A Study, Based on Early Louisiana Church Records, 1737–1750* (New Orleans, 1974); Diocese of Baton Rouge, *Catholic Church Records*, I, 136–244; Mrs. Arthur F. Ortiz and Hazel B. Bell, "Pointe Coupee Marriages—1728–1785," *Louisiana Genealogical Register*, XXIII (December,1976), 339–50; Morrison (comp.), *Index—Early Marriages.*

Church in Violet. The records were moved to Our Lady of Lourdes and remained there when St. Bernard again became independent in 1968. Only part of the records of St. Bernard survive. The first book of baptisms, for 1787–1801, and the first book of marriages, for 1787–1821, have been lost. The register of baptisms of Negroes, February 15, 1787–May 10, 1857, in one volume, is at St. Louis Cathedral in New Orleans. The other records still at Violet, Louisiana, include the second book of baptisms of whites, January 1, 1801–May 3, 1851, in one volume; the first book of funerals of whites, June 6, 1787–September 9, 1878, in one volume, from which pages 19–92, for March 20, 1791, to September 10, 1813, are missing; and the first book of funerals of Negroes and persons of color, October 25, 1787–May 5, 1887, also in one volume.[81]

Some indexes to the records of St. Bernard Church have been published. These include an index to the register of baptisms, arranged by years, and a record of interments for 1787–1791.[82] Microfilm of the register of baptisms, marriages, and burials of St. Bernard is in the Tulane University Library.

St. Gabriel, St. Gabriel Church. In 1772 a church that had been built by Acadians on the Iberville Coast below Baton Rouge was removed to St. Gabriel. After being visited by Spanish priests for several years, the church was assigned as pastor a French Capuchin, who was followed by some Spanish priests.

Records of St. Gabriel in the Baton Rouge chancery include a register of baptisms, marriages, and funerals, April 22, 1773–May 5, 1780, in loose sheets; a register of baptisms, marriages, and funerals, January 25, 1781–October 16, 1785, including records of St. Bernard of Manchac, in one volume; a register of baptisms of persons of color, 1782–1843, in one volume and loose sheets; a register of baptisms of whites, October 30, 1785–March 18, 1821, including entries for St. Bernard in Galveztown, in one volume; a register of baptisms, marriages, and funerals, December 4, 1785–August 3, 1865, in one volume; a register of baptisms of St. Gabriel and St. Bernard at Galveztown (1787–1791), June 7, 1787–May 21, 1859, in one volume; an index of baptisms, 1773–1831, in one volume; a register of

---

81 / Nolan, *Southern Catholic Heritage,* 91–92.
82 / Alice D. Forsyth, "Baptismal Register [St. Bernard Church at] Our Lady of Lourdes Church—Violet, La., 1801–1851," *New Orleans Genesis,* V (March–September, 1966), 164–68, 238–40, 352–55, VI (March, 1967), 121; Lucille M. B. Fortier, "Our Lady of Lourdes Catholic Church, Violet, La.—Interment Records [1787–91]," *New Orleans Genesis,* IV (March, 1966), 319–20.

marriages of whites, October 27, 1785–May 10, 1859; an index of marriages, 1773–1831, in one volume; and a register of funerals of whites, October 4, 1785–March 26, 1856, in two volumes. In the New Orleans chancery are accounts of church wardens from around 1787 to 1831, in loose
sheets. A miscellaneous collection of records at St. Louis Cathedral includes marriages and marriage investigations dating from October 19,
1788, to April 19, 1826.[83] Microfilm of the St. Gabriel Church records is in
the St. Martin Parish Library and in the Center for Louisiana History of
the University of Southwestern Louisiana.

An abstract of the information in the records of St. Gabriel Church
arranged in an alphabetical compilation has been published. This gives
the names of the individuals baptized, married, or buried, the names of
sponsors at baptisms, the names of parents, sponsors, and grooms and
brides, and witnesses, and the dates. A chronological abstract of the
records relating to marriages at St. Louis Cathedral has been published.[84]
A transcription made in 1906 of the register of marriages, 1773–1859, in a
single volume containing 788 pages, is in the Public Archives of Canada.

St. James, St. James Church. A resident priest was designated in 1770 for
the area on the west bank of the Mississippi, midway between New Orleans and Baton Rouge. The majority of the inhabitants by that time were
Acadians.

The records of St. James in the Baton Rouge chancery include both
loose sheets and bound volumes. Baptisms, marriages, and funerals,
1767–1804, on loose sheets include baptisms, June 4, 1770–May 1, 1783;
marriages, May 21, 1770–September 3, 1781; funerals, February 8, 1773–
May 2, 1783; funerals of Negroes, October 21, 1796–April 4, 1804; and
copies of two earlier baptisms, 1767 and 1769. The volumes include a register of baptisms, February 2, 1786–February 9, 1828; a register of marriages of whites, December 27, 1786–August 12, 1861; and a register of
funerals, April 5, 1794–July 2, 1857.[85]

Using the faded and worn pages of the registers, Elizabeth B.
Gianelloni, archivist of the diocese of Baton Rouge, has compiled a publication on baptisms for 1757–1783, showing the names of infants and
their parents, another on burials for 1773–1783, and a third on marriages
of 1770–1781, showing the names of grooms and brides, the year, and the

83 / Nolan, *Southern Catholic Heritage,* 65–68.
84 / Alice D. Forsyth, "Saint Gabriel of Iberville—Iberville Parish, Louisiana," *Louisiana Genealogical Register,* XXII (June, 1974), 137–43.
85 / Nolan, *Southern Catholic Heritage,* 73–74.

page numbers of the register. An alphabetical name index to the marriages of 1785–1861 has been published, as has another list of marriages for 1796. A record of burials for 1796, showing names and dates of interment from January 8 to December 25 of that year, is also in print. A list of the persons confirmed at St. James by the bishop in 1796 shows the names of the individuals and of their parents and godparents.[86]

St. Martinville, St. Martin of Tours Church. Attakapas Post, near which Acadians, Canary Islanders, and Frenchmen settled, was visited by priests from Opelousas, Pointe Coupee, and Ascension for fifteen years before a priest was assigned to it in 1781.[87] Several names that did not endure were applied to the church before it became known as St. Martin in 1792.

The earliest record of St. Martin is a certified copy on loose sheets of baptisms and marriages, June 5, 1756–May 4, 1773, made from the registers at Pointe Coupee. That record and others were used by the Reverend Michael Barrière in 1796 to compile a register of baptisms, marriages, and funerals, June 5, 1756–September 21, 1794. Some of the entries made by Father Barrière were found in registers in Opelousas, Lafourche, Pointe Coupee, Natchitoches, and New Orleans. A register of baptisms of free Negroes and slaves contains baptisms, May 11, 1765–January 11, 1766, February 10–May 21, 1782, and May 27, 1787–August 15, 1802, and funerals, May 17–November 24, 1765, and May 17, 1787–January 27, 1818, with a gap from 1791 to 1794. Other records include a register of baptisms, marriages, and funerals, 1773–1779, and January 27, 1782–May 16, 1787, in three volumes; a register of marriages and baptisms of Spaniards, including marriages from May 21, 1787–July 27, 1802, and baptisms, May 20, 1787–September 3, 1797, with baptismal entries from surrounding areas;

86 / Elizabeth B. Gianelloni, "St. James Parish Church Records: Baptisms, 1757–1783," *New Orleans Genesis*, VII (January, 1968), 7–13; Elizabeth B. Gianelloni, "St. James Parish Church Records: Burials, 1773–1783," *New Orleans Genesis*, VII (January, 1968), 14–15; Elizabeth B. Gianelloni, "St. James Parish Church Records: Marriages, 1770–1781," *New Orleans Genesis*, VII (January, 1968), 1–6; Albert J. Robichaux, "Marriage Records, 1785–1861, St. James Church, St. James, Louisiana," *New Orleans Genesis*, X (September, 1971), 310–29, XI (January, 1972), 50–59; Catherine B. Futch (comp. and trans.), "Marriages Performed at the Church of Santiago de Cabanoce, Known Now as St. James Catholic Church, St. James Parish, Louisiana, for the Year 1796," *New Orleans Genesis*, VIII (January, 1969), 47; Catherine B. Futch (comp. and trans.), "Burials from Santiago de Cabanoce Church, Now Known as St. James Catholic Church, St. James Parish, Louisiana, for the Year 1796," *New Orleans Genesis*, VIII (January, 1969), 48–49; "List of Persons Confirmed at Cabahanoce, by the First Bishop of Louisiana and the Floridas (Cabahanoce, Parish of St. Jacques de Cabahanoce) May 11, 1800," *New Orleans Genesis*, IV (June, 1965), 191–92.

87 / Griffin, *Attakapas Country*, 28, 76, 214–15.

and a register of baptisms of whites, October 1, 1787–July 14, 1816, in two volumes.[88]

Alphabetical name indexes for the marriages, 1756–1816, have been compiled by Father Donald Hébert. A chronological record of premarital investigations compiled by Father Barrière, January 11, 1796–June 24, 1804, gives the names of the prospective grooms and brides, the names of their parents, the places from which they emigrated, their religion, and any previous marriages. The church registers were also used in preparing a list of Attakapas area families.[89]

88 / Nolan, *Southern Catholic Heritage*, 57–62.

89 / Donald J. Hébert (trans.), "St. Martin of Tours Church, St. Martinville, La., Index of Marriages [1756–1816]," *New Orleans Genesis*, X (September, 1971), 330–34, XI (January, March, 1972), 33–39, 114–29, XIII (January, September, 1974), 59–64, 385–90, XIV (January, March, 1975), 13–18, 202–206; Donald J. Hébert (trans.), "St. Martin of Tours Church—St. Martinville, Louisiana, Information Produced on the Single State of Persons Marrying by Fr. Michel Bernard Barrière," *New Orleans Genesis*, XI (June, 1972), 277–83; Jacqueline O. Vidrine, "Attakapas Area Families (Non-Acadians)," *Louisiana Genealogical Register*, XXI (March, 1974), 57–63.

II

The Records of Mississippi

9

❧

History and Government

In 1699 a French exploring expedition led by Pierre Le Moyne, Sieur d'Iberville, selected a site for a settlement on Biloxi Bay where Fort Maurepas was built. For a number of years, nearby Ship Island was used as the harbor for the exploration and settlement of the coast. In 1719 the capital was moved back to old Biloxi from Mobile, and in 1721 it moved west of the entrance of the bay to Fort Louis at new Biloxi, which became a permanent settlement. Biloxi and Mobile were temporarily the sites of the capital of colonial Louisiana, but that was permanently moved in 1723 to New Orleans.[1]

Some of the other posts established by the French to control the Indians and counter the advance of the English developed into permanent settlements. Fort Rosalie (Natchez) was built in 1716 on bluffs above the Mississippi by Jean Baptiste Le Moyne, Sieur de Bienville. Farther north, Fort Pierre was built in 1715 near the mouth of the Yazoo River, and in 1718 Fort St. Claude was built on an elevated point ten miles above the mouth of that river. During a campaign against the Chickasaw Indians in 1739, Bienville built Fort Assumption at Chickasaw Bluffs (Memphis).[2]

When Spain entered the American Revolution as an ally of France in June, 1779, the opportunity arose for it to recover West Florida. In the summer of that year, Governor Bernardo de Gálvez of Louisiana advanced up the Mississippi River with a large body of troops and forced the surrender of Manchac, Baton Rouge, and Fort Panmure. He canonaded Fort Charlotte at Mobile and received its surrender on March 14, 1780. He then waged a successful campaign with forces from Louisiana

1 / Rowland, *History of Mississippi*, I, 205–16.
2 / *Ibid., passim.*

and Cuba against Pensacola, which surrendered on May 9, 1781. After this conquest Gálvez was designated as governor of West Florida, as well as of Louisiana, and he was given the rank of lieutenant general and the title of count. The Treaty of Paris of September 3, 1783, concluding the Revolutionary War, provided for the return of the Floridas to Spain.[3]

Natchez District Records

West Florida after the Spanish conquest of 1779–1781 was attached for governmental purposes to Spanish Louisiana.[4] A governor functioned at Pensacola, but he was subordinate to the governor of Louisiana. The territory, which had formerly been French and British, was divided into the Government of Baton Rouge and the Mobile District. The local commandants at Natchez, Baton Rouge, and Mobile exercised both military and civil authority, each performing the functions of legislator, judge, notary, custodian of deeds and records, mayor, and chief of police.[5] The intendant of Louisiana also had jurisdiction in West Florida.

After the British surrender at Natchez on October 5, 1779, following their capitulation at Baton Rouge, Carlos de Grande Pré, who had participated in the campaign against West Florida, was designated as commandant at Natchez.[6] The growth in the population of the district because of the immigration of many Americans made it necessary for the district to have a separate government. Manuel Gayoso de Lemos, a lieutenant colonel newly arrived from Spain, assumed the position of governor at Natchez in June, 1789.[7] The governmental structure at Natchez included a secretary who assisted the governor with paperwork, a post adjutant, a royal inspector, a storekeeper, and constables. The royal hospital treated civilians as well as those in the military service.

To thwart the designs of American land speculators, Gayoso de Lemos arranged in 1791 for the construction of Fort Nogales (Vicksburg) on high bluffs above the Mississippi River at the mouth of the Yazoo River. After a treaty with the Indians at Fort Nogales in 1790, farther east the Spanish built Fort Confederation in 1794 on the Tombigbee River near

3 / John A. Caruso, The Southern Frontier (Indianapolis, [1963]), 253–57.
4 / Caughey, Gálvez, 214.
5 / Dunbar Rowland, Mississippi: Comprising Sketches of Counties, Towns, Events, Institutions, and Persons, Arranged in Cyclopedia Form (Atlanta, 1907), II, 312.
6 / Caughey, Gálvez, 158–59, 214.
7 / Holmes, Gayoso, 33.

old Fort Tombecbé in what became Alabama and Fort San Fernando in 1795 at Chickasaw Bluffs, which became Memphis.[8]

Land grants were made by the French in the region east of the Mississippi River and continued to be made by Spain after its acquisition of West Florida. Warrants of survey were issued to the surveyor general of Louisiana, and it was his deputies who performed the surveys in West Florida during the Spanish period.[9] In most cases the prescribed procedures in regard to paper work were not completed, and the titles were largely incomplete.[10]

The first acquisition of territory from Spain by the United States resulted from the Treaty of San Lorenzo of October 27, 1795, by which the United States obtained the territory north of the 31st parallel—territory that had been in dispute since 1783. The boundary between the United States and the Spanish Floridas was to run due east along the 31st parallel from the Mississippi to the Apalachicola, down the middle of that river to its junction with the Flint, east from that point to the head of the St. Mary's River, and down the middle of that stream to the Atlantic Ocean. The treaty also provided that the Spanish garrisons north of the boundary were to be removed within six months after its ratification.[11]

Following the ratification of the treaty in 1796, orders were sent from Spain to Governor Carondelet of Louisiana directing him to execute its provisions. He issued instructions for the evacuation of the Spanish garrisons and the dismantling of the forts. In March, 1797, Forts San Fernando and Confederation were abandoned and razed. But before the evacuation of the other posts was accomplished, their commandant received orders from the governor to delay action; he had received new orders from Spain directing him to retain the posts until Spain reached an agreement with the United States concerning conflicting provisions of its treaties with Great Britain, Spain, and France. The Spaniards proved unequal to the task of ruling the turbulent Americans at Natchez, however, and that place and Fort Nogales came into the possession of the United States in March, 1798. After the running of the boundary line showed Fort St. Stephens (San Estevan de Tombecbé) to be north of the line, the fort was transferred to American possession in May, 1799.[12] Captain Isaac

8 / Whitaker, *Spanish-American Frontier*, 168–69, 178.

9 / William Dunbar to the president, October 21, 1803, in Carter (ed.), *Territory of Orleans*, 85.

10 / W. C. C. Claiborne to the president, January 20, 1803, in Rowland (ed.), *Official Letter Books*, I, 264.

11 / David Miller (ed.), *Treaties*, II, 319–20.

12 / Whitaker, *The Mississippi Question*, 52–56, 66.

Guion of the U.S. Army, who had taken command of the troops at Natchez on December 6, 1797, remained as military and civil governor of the district. His civil duties were taken over on August 6, 1798, by Governor Winthrop Sargent, newly appointed executive of the Territory of Mississippi, constituted by act of Congress of April 7, 1798.

Upon the withdrawal of the Spanish from Fort Panmure at Natchez, the records were left in charge of John Girault, who had become their custodian in 1794. Governor Sargent delayed taking action in regard to the Spanish records, because of the illness of his secretary, John Steele, who reached Natchez during the fall of 1798, and because of his many engagements. In a letter to Steele on March 22, 1799, however, the governor stated that he wanted the public records of the district taken over from Girault.[13] No immediate action occurred, for on June 6, 1799, Girault addressed a letter to Steele asking to be relieved of the records.[14] Apparently received by Steele at this time, the documents were found to be the complete records for the period 1781–1798, embracing fourteen thousand pages of administrative, legal, property, land, and miscellaneous papers.

Provision soon had to be made for the care of these important records. At the beginning of 1800, Steele appointed an old settler, Peter Walker, as his assistant to copy and translate the Spanish records upon which calls were being made for legal purposes. Steele's term of office expired on May 6, 1802, but as no successor was immediately appointed, he retained and serviced the records until their delivery to the new secretary, Cato West, on June 9, 1803. The last item on a list of the records prepared at the time of the transfer was "2. Barrells of Books papers. & Styled Spanish Records____."[15] On July 30, 1805, Robert Williams, soon after becoming governor, secured custody of the records from West. Under a territorial act of March 4, 1803, authorizing the translation, indexing, and binding of the Spanish records, Governor Williams appointed David Harper as keeper and translator of the records. Most, if not all, of the records were translated and indexed and with the originals were placed in the archives of Adams County, of which Natchez is the county seat, first with the clerk of the probate court, then with the clerk of the chancery court.[16]

13 / Dunbar Rowland (ed.), *The Mississippi Territorial Archives, 1798–1803. Executive Journals of Governor Winthrop Sargent and Governor William Charles Cole Claiborne* (Nashville, 1905), I, 117.

14 / Mississippi Department of Archives and History, *Annual Report*, 1904–1905, pp. 14–15.

15 / Carter (ed.), *Territory of Mississippi*, V, 255.

16 / Mississippi Department of Archives and History, *Annual Report*, 1904–1905, p. 15, *Annual Report*, 1953–55, p. 22.

Toward the close of its first century under American dominion, Mississippi developed an interest in its history. The Mississippi Historical Society, permanently organized in 1890, became an active agent in fostering legislation pertaining to archives.[17] The Mississippi Historical Commission was created by the legislature in 1901, and in 1902 its report to the legislature on the sources of the history of the state was published.[18] A further act of February 22, 1902, established the Mississippi Department of Archives and History, of which Dunbar Rowland became director.

When Rowland investigated the archives in the old state capitol under his jurisdiction, he found none for the period before the American occupation. But on a trip to Natchez in May, 1903, he located fifty well-bound volumes of Spanish records with translations in the office of the chancery clerk of Adams County.[19] Two years later he effected the transfer of the original Spanish records from Natchez to his own custody in the state capitol at Jackson.[20] Here this valuable collection was classified and improved physically for the use of historical students. A description of the forty volumes of the Natchez district records, 1781–1798, held by the chancery court was published by Rowland himself. The collection included royal orders from the crown; proclamations and orders from the governor general and the district commandant; records of civil and criminal lawsuits; petitions for the redress of grievances; bills of sale of personal property, including slaves; wills; inventories of estates; reports and statements of executors and administrators; land records, including grants, patents, deeds, plats, and certificates of survey; laws and regulations issued by the governors general and the district commandants; and correspondence between the officials and the people. An abstract of the records indexed by personal names has been published. The variety of documentation is useful for personal, economic, social, and legal history of the district. These records and the Harper translations were microfilmed in the 1950s by the Microfilm Company of Louisiana, New Orleans, under the sponsorship of the National Society of Colonial Dames in the State of Mississippi. The Mississippi Department of Archives and

17 / Charles S. Sydnor, "Historical Activities in Mississippi in the Nineteenth Century," *Journal of Southern History*, III (May, 1937), 139–60.
18 / Franklin L. Riley, "The Department of Archives and History of the State of Mississippi," American Historical Association, *Annual Report*, 1903, vol. I, p. 476; Mississippi Historical Commission, "An Account of the Manuscripts, Papers, and Documents Pertaining to Mississippi in the Public Repositories Within the State of Mississippi," *Mississippi Historical Society Publications*, V (1902).
19 / Mississippi Department of Archives and History, *Annual Report*, 1903–1905, p. 13.
20 / *Ibid.*, 1904–1905, p. 16.

History has the twenty-four reels of microfilm and can supply copies.²¹ A copy is in the John C. Pace Library of the University of West Florida in Pensacola and at other places.

In the Manuscripts Division of the Library of Congress is a miscellaneous group of manuscripts in French and Spanish of the Natchez district acquired by purchase in 1919. The five hundred pieces in the collection cover the years from 1781 to 1820. Natchez district land papers, 1738–1803, in two boxes and one package, are held in the Western Reserve Historical Society in Cleveland, Ohio. This collection includes surveys and legal documents, signed by Spanish governors and United States officials, relating to land grants on the banks of the Mississippi River from Natchez to New Orleans.²²

21 / Rowland, *Mississippi Sketches*, I, xii; May Wilson McBee (ed.), *The Natchez Court Records, 1767–1805: Abstracts of Early Records* (1953; rpr. Baltimore, 1979); Mississippi, Department of Archives and History, *Guide to Official Records in the Mississippi Department of Archives and History*, comp. Thomas W. Henderson and Ronald E. Tomlin (Jackson, [1975]), 16.

22 / Western Reserve Historical Society, *Guide to Manuscripts and Archives*; *National Union Catalog of Manuscripts*, 1975, entry 1428.

10

ૐ

Archival Reproductions, Documentary Publications, and Manuscripts

Official interest in the history of the state developed slowly in Mississippi. The Mississippi Historical Society, founded in 1890, was not very effective until Franklin L. Riley, formerly president of Hillman College, was appointed a history professor at the University of Mississippi in 1897. He became secretary-treasurer of the society and initiated its publications series in 1898, serving as its editor until 1914. With members of the society, he succeeded in persuading the state legislature to authorize in March, 1900, the formation of the Mississippi Historical Commission to undertake a search for and examination of sources for the history of the state. The culmination of these activities was the establishment by legislative act of February 22, 1902, of the Mississippi Department of Archives and History. The Department was to be housed in the state capitol and was to be responsible for the care and custody of the state archives and for the collecting and editing of official records and other materials on the history of the state. In March, 1902, the board of trustees selected Dunbar Rowland, who had practiced law in Memphis and Coffeeville, to be the director of the department and the secretary of the commission.[1]

After classifying a small collection of state archives that came into the custody of the department, Rowland turned his attention to the procurement of reproductions from European archives relating to the history of Mississippi. On a visit to Paris in the summer of 1906, he arranged with

1 / Conrad W. Case, "Franklin L. Riley and the Historical Renaissance in Mississippi, 1897–1914," *Journal of Mississippi History*, XXXII (August, 1970), 195–227; Robert R. Simpson, "The Origin of the Mississippi Department of Archives and History," *Journal of Mississippi History*, XXXV (February, 1973), 1–14.

Victor Tantet, the director of the Archives des Colonies, for the transcription of documents relating to Mississippi. Tantet supplied a calendar of pertinent documents, which the department published.[2] After Tantet's death by suicide in June, 1907, Rowland arranged with the Carnegie Institution of Washington, which was initiating an investigation of European archives, for the transcription of materials on Mississippi. Waldo G. Leland, the agent of the institution in Paris, supervised from 1907 to 1912 the copying and binding of transcripts.[3] These were later microfilmed by Bell and Howell of Wooster, Ohio, on sixty-nine reels. Translations of selected documents were eventually edited and published.[4] A fourth volume of edited documents prepared for publication, mislabeled and misfiled, was not found until nearly fifty years later. Subsequently a well-qualified editor was found to complete the series. The addition of new, largely unpublished documents resulted in the publication of two more volumes on the French dominion.[5] The series is useful for research into the relations with the Natchez, the Choctaw and the Chickasaw Indians, Indian trade, economic and religious life, and Bienville's career in Louisiana during the years 1704–1743. As a participant in the Louisiana Colonial Records Project initiated by the University of Southwestern Louisiana in 1967, the department received sixty-nine reels of microfilm of the G13A series, Correspondance Générale, Louisiane, Archives des Colonies, containing the correspondence received by the French government from its officials in Louisiana. The department also has microfilm of records of the Ministère de la Marine from the port of Brest, one of the principal French ports having communications with Louisiana.[6]

In procuring transcripts relating to Mississippi from Spanish archives, Rowland had the assistance of William R. Shepherd, another agent of the Carnegie Institution, who was sent to Spain to gather descriptive data regarding material in its archives relating to the United States. Information furnished by Shepherd enabled Rowland to publish data relative to materials in the Archivo General de Indias at Seville, the Archivo Histórico Nacional in Madrid, and the Archivo General de

2 / Mississippi Department of Archives and History, *Annual Report*, 1905–1906, pp. 59–132.

3 / Beers, *French in North America*, 165–88.

4 / Mississippi Department of Archives and History, *Guide*, 16; Dunbar Rowland and Albert G. Sanders (trans. and eds.), *Mississippi Provincial Archives, [1701–1743], French Dominion* (Jackson, Miss., 1927–32).

5 / Dunbar Rowland and Albert G. Sanders (trans. and eds.), *Mississippi Provincial Archives, French Dominion, Volume IV, 1729–1748, Volume V, 1749–1763*, rev. and ed. Patricia K. Galloway (Baton Rouge, 1984).

6 / Mississippi Department of Archives and History, *Guide*, 16.

Simancas. Descriptions of *legajos* in the Papeles de Cuba, from which copies were made, are in print.[7] Transcripts from the Archivo General de Indias on the Spanish dominion in Mississippi, 1759–1820, in nine volumes, were transmitted from Spain in 1909. The transcripts were later microfilmed by the Micro Photo Division of Bell and Howell on seven reels; on the first reel was the list of materials that had been supplied by Shepherd. Copies of the microfilm are also in the libraries of the University of Southern Mississippi at Hattiesburg, the University of West Florida at Pensacola, Florida State University at Tallahassee, and other places.[8] Typescripts of correspondence of Bernardo de Gálvez, 1779–1781, in one volume, are in the Mississippi Department of Archives and History. Some of the transcripts have been translated, but no printed series has been published. In 1951 the Alabama Department of Archives and History secured microfilm copies of the transcripts from the French, Spanish, and British archives that had been obtained by the Mississippi Department of Archives and History. The latter department has copies of the microfilm obtained by Jack D. L. Holmes, formerly of the University of Alabama at Birmingham, on Spanish Alabama, 1780–1813, in twenty-nine reels, and microfilm of the correspondence of Bernardo de Gálvez, 1779–1781, in one reel.

Other documents concerning Mississippi have also been published. The treaty of October 27, 1795, with Spain provided for the appointment of surveyors by both the United States and Spain to run and mark the boundary along the 31st parallel and to prepare plats and keep journals of their proceedings. Andrew Ellicott, who had participated in the survey of the Mason-and-Dixon line and had surveyed the boundary of the District of Columbia, was designated as commissioner of the United States. Captain Stephen Minor, the Spanish commandant at Natchez, and William Dunbar, a Scottish mathematician and astronomer living on a plantation south of Natchez, were appointed by Spain. Dunbar's report and correspondence are in the Papeles Procedentes de la Isla de Cuba, in the Archivo General de Indias. Other papers of Dunbar, 1776–1810, in seven volumes and thirty-four items, are in the Mississippi Department of Archives and History.[9] Letters and papers of Dunbar, March, 1766–October 5, 1810, in print include letters to Governor Sargent and Manuel Gayoso de Lemos.

7 / Mississippi Department of Archives and History, *Annual Report*, 1905–1906, pp. 49–55; Hill, *Descriptive Catalogue*, xxvi, 474–79.

8 / Coker, "Research in the Spanish Borderlands," 54.

9 / Hill, *Descriptive Catalogue*, 151, 153; Jack D. L. Holmes (ed.), "William Dunbar's Correspondence on the Southern Boundary of Mississippi, 1798," *Journal of Mississippi History*, XXVII (May, 1965), 187–90.

Dunbar's report has been published; the reprint includes a few letters concerning the survey.[10] Other correspondence of Dunbar from 1798 on the boundary is also in print.[11] Ellicott's journal of 1798–1800 was deposited in the archives of the Department of State but was subsequently destroyed by fire, along with the building in which it had been deposited. The journal and some correspondence of 1797 and 1798 had already been published. A few letters to the secretary of state and extracts from Ellicott's journal and letters to his wife, 1796–1800, are also in print. A printed copy of the journal, his report, and correspondence, 1796–1802, in three volumes, concerning the work and progress of the commission and its expenses are in the National Archives.[12] Correspondence of Captain Isaac Guion, U.S. Army, who occupied Natchez late in 1797 with Spanish and American officers, is in print.[13]

A few censuses and other lists contain the names of early Mississippians. A December, 1699, census of officers and others comprising the garrison of Fort Maurepas on Biloxi Bay shows their names and occupations. In the same publication are a May 25, 1700, census of Biloxi, a 1704 list of marriageable girls, a 1722 list of military and civilian personnel at Biloxi, and a November 28, 1729, list of persons massacred at Natchez. An alphabetical list of names is based on colonial and later censuses dating from 1788.[14] A 1792 census of the inhabitants of the Natchez district contains the names of people at different settlements.[15] Another 1792 list con-

10 / William Dunbar, "Report of Sir William Dunbar to the Spanish Government at the Conclusion of His Services in Locating and Surveying the Thirty-First Degree of Latitude," ed. Franklin L. Riley, *Mississippi Historical Society Publications*, III (1900), 185–205; reprinted in Mrs. Dunbar Rowland, *Life, Letters and Papers of William Dunbar . . .* (Jackson, Miss., 1930), 78–99.

11 / Carter (ed.), *Territory of Mississippi*, V, 3–8, 126–27, 131–34.

12 / Josiah Meigs to Andrew Ellicott, March 1, 1816, in Carter (ed.), *Territory of Mississippi*, VI, 661 and n. 82; Andrew Ellicott, *The Journal of Andrew Ellicott, Late Commissioner . . . for Determining the Boundary Between the United States and the Possessions of His Catholic Majesty in America* (Philadelphia, 1803), 38–116, 167–72; Catharine Van Cortlandt Mathews, *Andrew Ellicott, His Life and Letters* (New York, [1908]), 126–94; U.S. National Archives, *Preliminary Inventory of Records Relating to International Boundaries* (Record Group 76), comp. Daniel T. Goggin (Preliminary Inventories, no. 170) (Washington, D.C., 1968), 69.

13 / Isaac Guion, "Military Journal of Captain Isaac Guion, 1797– 1799," Mississippi Department of Archives and History, *Annual Report*, 1907–1908, pp. 25–113.

14 / Maduell (comp. and trans.), *Census Tables for French Louisiana*, 1–8, 32–33, 104–16; Ronald V. Jackson, Altha Polson, and Shirley P. Zachrison, *Early American Series, Early Mississippi Census, Volume 1, 1788– 1819* (Bountiful, Utah, 1980).

15 / Dunbar Rowland, "Mississippi's Colonial Population and Land Grants," *Mississippi Historical Society Publications, Centenary Series, Volume I* (Jackson, Miss., 1916), 405–28; also in Rowland, *History of Mississippi*, I, 326–34.

tains the names of heads of families only and shows them to be mostly of English, Scottish, and Irish origin. Lists are also available of the persons who took the oath of allegiance in 1798 and 1799 at the time of the annexation to the United States. An oath of allegiance by residents of the Natchez district to the United States, subscribed to in 1798, shows the names of people in different settlements. Also in print are lists of persons who died at Fort Biloxi. A list of the order of the first families of Mississippi, with a compilation of genealogical data on the members, is also in print.[16]

Papers of Spanish and American officials, military officers, and others held by repositories in Mississippi and elsewhere supply important additional documentation on affairs in the region. The principal repository of materials on Mississippi's colonial and territorial periods is the Mississippi Department of Archives and History, which on its founding in 1902 took over custody of the state's official records. These include the papers of the first two governors, who had dealings with Spanish officials, among them the correspondence and papers of Winthrop Sargent, 1798–1801, in one box. Other papers of Sargent, who had served previously as secretary of the Territory Northwest of the Ohio, are held by the Historical Society of Pennsylvania, for 1754–1809, containing one hundred items, the Massachusetts Historical Society, for 1772–1948, containing two thousand items, and the Ohio Historical Society, Columbus, for 1778–1865, twenty-one boxes. With a grant obtained from the National Historical Publications and Records Commission, the Massachusetts Historical Society sponsored the microfilming of the Sargent papers in its custody and those in the Ohio Historical Society on seven reels and published a guide to the microfilm.[17] William C. C. Claiborne, a member of Congress from Tennessee, was appointed on May 25, 1801, to succeed Sargent as governor of the Mississippi Territory; he served in that capacity until his designation as a commissioner to receive the transfer of Louisiana, and from October, 1804, he served as governor of the Territory of Orleans. Materi-

16 / Norman E. Gillis, *Early Inhabitants of the Natchez District* ([Baton Rouge, 1963]), 13–26; Mrs. Boyd C. Edwards and Bickham Christian, "Lists of Persons Taking the Oaths of Allegiance in the Natchez District, 1798–99," *National Genealogical Society Quarterly*, XLII (September, 1954), 108–16; Elizabeth S. Mills, "Deaths at Biloxi, 1699–1700," *Louisiana Genealogical Register*, XXII (June, 1974), 130; Irna A. Centanni, "Louisiana, État Civil 1720–1724. Registre de ceux qui sont morts au vieux Fort Biloxi pendant l'administration de M. Damion depuis le huit août 1720," *New Orleans Genesis*, VI (September, 1967), 388–90; Charles O. Johnson (ed.), *The Order of the First Families of Mississippi, 1699–1817* (Ann Arbor, Mich., 1981).

17 / Massachusetts Historical Society Library, *Guide to the Microfilm Edition of the Winthrop Sargent Papers*, ed. Frederick S. Allis, Jr., and Roy Bartholomee (Boston, 1965).

als on Claiborne's career include correspondence and papers of Claiborne as governor, 1801–1810, in one box, and the executive journals and letter-books of Governors Sargent and Claiborne, 1798–1817, in fifteen volumes. Other Claiborne papers are held by the University of Mississippi at Oxford and include communications of Captain Isaac Guion. The executive journals of Sargent and Claiborne and Claiborne's letter books are in print and are cited above.[18] An account book of William Dunbar, 1776–1793, is in the University of North Carolina Library, Southern Historical Collection. Letters of Governor Gayoso de Lemos to his wife are in the Mississippi Department of Archives and History, as are letters of Captain Isaac Guion, who participated in the American occupation of the boundary area following the Treaty of San Lorenzo.

Collections in other repositories also contain materials relating to Mississippi. Stephen Minor, a native of Pennsylvania, joined the Spanish army at New Orleans during the revolution, participated in the campaign against Pensacola, and in 1781 was appointed adjutant of Fort Panmure at Natchez. He continued in the service of Spain at that place, serving as acting governor from July 24, 1797, to March 31, 1798. When Dunbar became ill, Gayoso de Lemos named Minor to replace him as boundary commissioner, and from September 1, 1798, until the end of December, 1800, he participated in the surveying operations. After the departure of the Spanish, he remained at Natchez as a planter and Spanish agent.[19] Minor family papers in the Louisiana State University Department of Archives and Manuscripts include correspondence, deeds, and plantation records. Other Minor family papers, dating from 1764, are in the Howard-Tilton Memorial Library of Tulane University.

The Andrew Ellicott papers, 1777–1829, consisting of 925 items, available on two reels of microfilm in the Library of Congress, Manuscript Division, contain correspondence, maps, charts, and reports on astronomical observations concerning his work on the survey of the southern boundary. That repository also has the Mary L. Webb Land Grant Collection, containing some early land grants of Mississippi, and letters concerning claims to Yazoo land grants, 1790–1815, in 46 items. Ephraim Kirby was commissioned as one of the land commissioners of the United States in Washington County, Territory of Mississippi, to assist in the adjustment of land claims during 1803 and 1804. He left papers dated chiefly 1780–1804, now held by Duke University Library. José Vidal was secre-

18 / Rowland (ed.), *Mississippi Territorial Archives;* Rowland (ed.), *Official Letter Books.*
19 / Jack D. L. Holmes, "Stephen Minor: Natchez Pioneer," *Journal of Mississippi History,* XLII (February, 1980), 18–25.

tary to Manuel Gayoso de Lemos at Natchez from 1787 to 1797 and later commandant of the Spanish post of Concordia, Spanish Louisiana, and consul at Natchez after the Spanish evacuation. The Vidal papers, dating from 1764, in the Louisiana State University Department of Archives and Manuscripts, include documents in Spanish relating to land grants, transfers, and surveys of the late 1790s. Papers of Isaac Briggs in the Briggs-Stabler Papers held by the Maryland Historical Society include materials on the survey of the Mississippi and Louisiana territories.

11

❧

Records of Local Jurisdictions

After the Revolutionary War, the southern states of Georgia, South Carolina, and North Carolina claimed the Mississippi River as their western boundary. In 1783, Georgia extended its legislative jurisdiction to include the Natchez district along the Mississippi River, and in 1785 it created Bourbon County to take in that region. Congress, however, asserted the title of the federal government to the trans-Appalachian territory. South Carolina relinquished its claim in 1787, and North Carolina in 1790.[1]

An act of Congress of April 7, 1798, provided for settling the claims of Georgia to western lands and established the government of the Territory of Mississippi. As created by section three of that act, the Territory of Mississippi was designated as the tract of country bounded on the west by the Mississippi River, on the north by a line drawn due east from the mouth of the Yazoo River to the Chattahoochee River and on the south by the 31st parallel of north latitude. That part of the Louisiana Purchase obtained by the treaty of April 30, 1803, with France was annexed by act of Congress of February 24, 1804, to the Territory of Mississippi. Following the cession by Georgia of its claim to western lands in 1802, an act of Congress of March 27, 1804, added the tract of country north of the Mississippi Territory, south of the state of Tennessee, and bounded on the east by the state of Georgia, to that territory. After the admission of Louisiana as a state in 1812, the tract of country east of the Pearl River, west of the Perdido River, and south of the 31st degree of north latitude was annexed by an act of Congress on May 14, 1812, to the Territory of Mississippi. An enabling act of March 1, 1817, provided for the admission of the western

1 / Franklin K. Van Zandt, *Boundaries of the United States and of the Several States* (Washington, D.C., 1976), 47, 50, 100.

196

part of the territory as a state; the eastern part was established as the Territory of Alabama by an act adopted two days later.[2]

The subdivision of the Spanish Natchez District into Mississippi counties began with the territorial legislature's act of April 2, 1799, which created Adams and Pickering counties. Within a few years, parts of those counties were formed into Wilkinson, Claiborne, Amite, Franklin, and Warren counties.[3] Natchez became the seat of Adams County, and the Spanish records of Natchez, whose history is given above, were left intact there in the custody of the chancery court. They were placed at some time in a fireproof room in the courthouse. In January, 1802, the name of Pickering County was changed to Jefferson, and part of it became Claiborne County. The counties of Claiborne, Jefferson, Adams, and Wilkinson were located along the Mississippi River. Deeds relating to the ownership of land in Adams County dating from 1780 are in the Mississippi Department of Archives and History.[4]

After the creation of Mississippi Territory in 1798, Governor Winthrop Sargent arrived at Natchez on August 6 and set about organizing the government. General James Wilkinson arrived with a body of soldiers in the next month, and Fort Adams was constructed on the Mississippi River near the boundary during 1798 and 1799. After the establishment of the seat of government at Washington in 1802, Fort Dearborn was constructed nearby for defense against the Choctaws. Subordinate officials were appointd and a legislature established. Much of the interior of the territory was occupied by Choctaw and Chickasaw Indians. Cessions of land by the Choctaws in 1805, 1816, and 1820 and by the Chickasaws in 1816 permitted settlement of the land and its organization into counties. An act adopted by the Mississippi General Assembly in January, 1821, resulted in the removal of the capital to Jackson near the geographical center of the state.[5]

Under the Louisiana treaty of 1803, the United States claimed that French Louisiana extended east to the Perdido River not far west of Pensacola Bay, which would have given it Mobile; but Spain maintained that the boundary was the old western boundary of West Florida, which gave the United States only New Orleans east of the Mississippi. Although the United States did nothing, in the meantime its citizens moved into the disputed area in larger numbers than ever, and in 1810 they set up the West

2 / Rowland, *History of Mississippi*, I, 339–40, 355, 390, 403, 453, 482.
3 / *Ibid.*, I, 340–43, 355, 363, 528.
4 / Mississippi Department of Archives and History, *Guide*, 56.
5 / Rowland, *History of Mississippi*, I, 374, 384, 386, 528.

Florida Republic. As a result, the Americans occupied Baton Rouge and West Florida as far east as the Pearl River in December, 1810; this area was annexed to the Territory of Orleans. The remainder of West Florida claimed by the United States, the district between the Pearl and the Perdido River, was added to the Mississippi Territory by an act of Congress of May 14, 1812, but occupation was not actually effected until the army entered Mobile in April, 1813.[6] Thus Spanish possession on the gulf coast of Florida was reduced to the limits existing between their holdings and the French settlements prior to the Seven Years' War.

An Orleans Territory ordinance of December 7, 1810, set up that part of the territory south of the Mississippi Territory, east of the Mississippi River, and extending to the Perdido as Feliciana County. Another territorial ordinance of April 25, 1811, establishing parish boundaries in that county, set up Biloxi Parish between the Pearl River and the river running into Biloxi Bay and Pascagoula Parish eastward from that river to the limits of the county.[7] In January, 1811, Governor Claiborne sent Dr. William Flood to organize the government of the two parishes, and a number of persons were appointed as justices of the peace. After the admission of Louisiana as a state with reduced territory, this part of what had been the Territory of Orleans—east of the Pearl River, west of the Perdido River, and south of the 31st parallel—was added to the Territory of Mississippi.[8] On May 14, 1812, the newly annexed Mobile district was organized into the counties of Hancock and Harrison.[9]

6 / Ibid., I, 410–11, 448, 451.
7 / Historical Records Survey, Louisiana, County-Parish Boundaries, 23, 26.
8 / Act of May 14, 1812, 2 Statutes, 734.
9 / Rowland, History of Mississippi, I, 452, 674, 729.

12

Land Records

An act of Congress of March 3, 1803, stipulated requirements for land claims: persons or their legal representatives who had been residents of the Mississippi Territory on October 27, 1795, and who had before that date obtained from either the British government of West Florida or from the Spanish government warrants or orders of survey for lands within that territory—lands that were actually inhabited and cultivated by them—were to be confirmed in their claims. Two land offices were to be established, one in the county of Adams for the lands west of the Pearl River and one in the county of Washington for lands east of the Pearl River. Registers and receivers were to be appointed for these offices, and persons claiming land were to present to the registers before the end of March, 1804, every grant, order of survey, deed, conveyance, or other written evidence of their claims for recording in books to be kept for that purpose. The register and two other persons to be appointed by the president were to serve as commissioners to ascertain the rights of persons claiming land. The commissioners were to meet on December 1, 1803, and were to appoint a clerk who would keep minutes of the proceedings and record evidence of the commissioners' decisions. Claimants whose applications were approved were to be given a certificate of confirmation of which record would be kept in the land office.[1]

The board of land commissioners for the district west of the Pearl River met at Washington, in the Mississippi Territory, where the register's office was located. The appointment of register was given to Edward

1 / 2 *Statutes* 229–35; Robert V. Haynes, "The Disposal of Lands in the Mississippi Territory," *Journal of Mississippi History*, XXIV (October, 1962), 233–35.

Turner, but he was replaced in 1805 by Thomas H. Williams.[2] Thomas Rodney of Delaware and Robert Williams of North Carolina were designated as commissioners. The board was authorized to employ a clerk and a translator and interpreter. These officials met at Washington from December 1, 1804, to June, 1807, to receive and consider evidence on land claims. While engaged in considering claims, the commissioners had published in the June 3, 10, and 17, 1806, issues of the *Mississippi Messenger* at Natchez a list of Spanish claims.[3] The commissioners' report was completed on July 3, 1807, and transmitted to the secretary of the treasury, by whom it was submitted to the House of Representatives on January 2, 1809.

The published report contains abstracts of different kinds of claims. Abstract A is a list of 51 claims of nonresidents held under British grants legally and fully executed and duly recorded during 1769–1779. This report shows the register number, the name of the present claimant, the name of the original grantee or claimant, the quantity of land, its location, and the date of patent for each claim. Abstract B contains 19 Spanish claims that were disallowed by the board on suspicion of being antedated and containing information similar to that in Abstract A. Abstract C contains claims of minors founded on warrants of survey, etc., and disallowed by the board. Abstract D is a report of 149 claims founded on British or Spanish warrants of survey that were disallowed by the board under the act of March 31, 1808. Abstract E shows the register number, the claimant's name, the date of title, the name of the original claimant, the location, the quantity, the original of the title, and the date of title, with remarks as to the nature of the evidence produced. Also in print are four registers (A–D) containing abstracts of certificates issued to claimants by the board at Washington and entered at the register's office there; these provide information about the names of 1,458 individual claimants and their claims. Persons whose claims had been confirmed by the registers of the land offices east and west of the Pearl River and to whom certificates of confirmation had been issued had their claims confirmed by an act of June 30, 1812, and when their claims had been approved by the General Land Office, they were to be issued patents.[4]

An act of March 31, 1808, supplemental to that of March 31, 1803, provided that certain settlers on the Mobile River in the Mississippi Territory

2 / Detailed instructions with forms were sent to Turner by the secretary of the treasury on July 27, 1805; see Carter (ed.), *Territory of Mississippi*, V, 226–35.

3 / This list is reprinted in Mrs. W. O. Harrell, "A List of Claims on Spanish Patents in Mississippi, 1796," *Journal of Mississippi History*, VIII (July, 1946), 148–51.

4 / *American State Papers, Public Lands*, I, 598–908, esp. 859–907; 2 *Statutes* 765–66.

east of the Pearl River who resided near the boundary line run in accordance with the treaty of October 27, 1795, and whose claims had not been decided on were to have until October 1, 1808, to file notice of their claims with the register, who, along with the receiver, was to decide the claims and to grant certificates.[5]

An act of Congress of March 3, 1819, for adjusting claims to lands and establishing land offices in the districts east of New Orleans authorized the officers appointed to those offices to examine land claims and to issue certificates for confirmed claims. Willoughby Barton was appointed register at Jackson Courthouse in March, 1819, to consider claims east of the Pearl River and was instructed to keep registers of the different kinds of claims that were approved.[6] To aid him in his investigation, he was provided with the report that had been prepared by William Crawford, formerly a land commissioner in Alabama. William Barnett, who was appointed receiver at Jackson Courthouse, was associated with Barton. Their report of August 17, 1820, on claims east of the Pearl River in southern Mississippi and southern Alabama was printed.[7] The report contains seven registers of different kinds of claims, with a total of 236 claimants, and shows the names of the original claimants, along with the origins of the claims, the quantities and locations of the land, when and by whom surveyed, and the dates of cultivation and habitation.

An act of Congress of May 24, 1828, gave claimants to land in the Jackson Courthouse district until January 1, 1829, to present their titles to the land commissioners in that district. A report by William Howze and G. B. Cameron, the register and the receiver of the district of Jackson Courthouse, dated January 15, 1829, contains brief registers of claims to lands within the limits of that district lying below the 31st parallel of north latitude (formerly Louisiana) founded on complete grants obtained from either the French, British, or Spanish governments that were valid according to the laws, usages, and customs of those governments.[8] Reports numbered one to four contain 14 claims founded on written evidence and give the names of the claimants, their allegiance, the date, the quantity of land claimed, the locations, by whom issued, dates of survey, by whom, and the dates of inhabitation and cultivation. Reports five and

5 / 2 Statutes 480.

6 / 3 Statutes 528–32; Josiah Meigs to Willoughby Barton, March 22, 27, 1819, in Clarence E. Carter (ed.), The Territory of Alabama, 1817–1819 (Washington D.C., 1952), 586–88, 593, vol. XVIII of Carter (ed.), The Territorial Papers of the United States, 26 vols.

7 / American State Papers, Public Lands, III, 444–55, printed also in Senate Documents, 16th Cong., 2nd Sess., No. 3, Serial 42.

8 / 4 Statutes 299; Senate Documents, 20th Cong., 2nd Sess., No. 85, pp. 1–5, Serial 182.

six are lists of actual settlers prior to April 15, 1813, and show the names of the present and original claimants, the dates of original settlement, the dates of present settlement, and the locations, showing a total of 32 claimants in report five and 37 in report six. These claims were confirmed by an act of May 28, 1830. The total number of private land claimants in Mississippi was 1,154, and the quantity of land they covered amounted to 773,087 acres.[9]

The first land offices in the Territory of Mississippi were authorized by an act of March 3, 1803, which provided for the establishment of offices in Adams and Washington counties.[10] The office for the district west of the Pearl River in Adams County was set up at Washington, which became the first territorial capital, and the office for the district east of the Pearl River was placed at St. Stephens on the Tombigbee River in Washington County. In accordance with the act of Congress of February 25, 1811, the land office for the sale of lands ceded by the Cherokee and Chickasaw Indians was moved from Nashville to Huntsville in Madison County, Mississippi Territory.[11] A land office for Jackson Courthouse (later Augusta) for the adjustment of land titles and the disposal of public lands was authorized by an act of March 3, 1819. That part of the district east of the Pearl River lying within the state of Mississippi was formed by an act of May 6, 1822, into the district of Jackson County, effective on October 30. The land office for this district was placed at Jackson, which had become the territorial capital in 1820. To serve the people in the northern part of the state, a land office was set up at Columbus by an act of March 2, 1833.[12]

In 1869, four years after the United States government resumed control of the land offices in Mississippi, those offices were consolidated, along with their records, in the office at Jackson. A brief description of the records, presented in general terms rather than by land office and series, was prepared by the Mississippi Historical Commission.[13] The collection included written evidence of foreign land claims; land patents; more than 150 volumes of old records, including ledgers, journals, correspondence volumes, receivers' accounts, abstracts of warrants, and orders of survey issued by the Spanish government for the district of Natchez; records of the proceedings of the boards of land commissioners; files of rejected applications for land grants; and letters from the commissioner of the General Land Office. Systematically arranged collections of township plats

9 / 4 *Statutes* 408–409; U.S. Public Lands Commission, *Report*, 1905, p. 140.
10 / 2 *Statutes* 230.
11 / Carter (ed.), *Territory of Mississippi*, VI, 203.
12 / 3 *Statutes* 530, 680–81; 4 *Statutes* 662.
13 / Mississippi Historical Commission, "Manuscripts in Public Repositories," 148–580.

and tract books and other records numbered more than 300 volumes. When the land office at Jackson was closed in 1925, the records in its custody were transferred to the General Land Office in Washington, D.C., and had not been returned to Mississippi by the late 1930s because the state legislature refused to make funds available for the cost of shipping them.[14]

An act of Congress of March 3, 1803, provided for the appointment of a surveyor of lands south of the state of Tennessee who would employ deputy surveyors to survey lands, plats of which were to be sent to the registers of land offices and to the secretary of the treasury. The appointment was given to Isaac Briggs of Pennsylvania, who after a long voyage down the Mississippi River reached Washington, Mississippi Territory, in August, 1803. In December, 1803, Briggs reported that two deputies were engaged in running the meridian line south from Washington to intersect the boundary line that had been run by Andrew Ellicott. Little was accomplished during the years 1805 and 1806, however, for it was difficult to engage surveyors: the wages offered were low, and the board of land commissioners was slow in issuing orders of survey. In March, 1805, Briggs engaged Gideon Fitz and John Dinsmoor to run surveys in Washington County (later Alabama) north from a stone monument on Ellicott's boundary line 206 miles east of the Mississippi River. This line became the St. Stephens meridian, while the international boundary was the baseline. Briggs also hired Charles DeFrance and George Davis in April, 1805, to survey west of the Pearl River, and two other deputies were sent to the district east of the river.[15] He later reported that those surveys would be completed by January 1, 1807. Briggs left the territory late in 1806 and was succeeded in March, 1807, by Seth Pease, a New Englander who had surveyed in the Western Reserve in Ohio. The delay in surveying confirmed private land claims prevented their incorporation into the general plat, but sales of public lands began in the territory in August, 1809.

After the resignation of Pease in July, 1810, the survey continued in the region south of the Tennessee River under a succession of principal or deputy surveyors. Thomas Freeman reached Washington in the Territory of Mississippi on July 31, 1810, and served until his death in November, 1821.[16] By September, 1811, a plat of old Washington County with the greater part of the preemption and other private claims marked on it had

14 / Survey of Federal Archives, Mississippi, *Inventory of Federal Archives in the States, Series VIII, The Department of the Interior, No. 23, Mississippi* (New Orleans, 1941), 1.

15 / 2 *Statutes* 233; White, *Rectangular Survey System,* 47, 55, 56; Isaac Briggs to the secretary of the treasury, April 11, 1805, in Carter (ed.), *Territory of Mississippi,* V, 398–99.

16 / Rohrbough, *Land Office Business,* 44. See White, *Rectangular Survey System,* 211, for the names of the surveyors general in Mississippi with their dates of appointment.

been completed, and a year later the remaining land east of the Pearl River had been surveyed.[17] By July, 1814, plats for the remaining part of the district west of the Pearl River were well advanced. By the end of September, 1815, 7,500,000 acres east and west of the Pearl River and the 345,000 acres of Madison County had been surveyed.

In the spring of 1816, Freeman appointed Charles DeFrance and William Brown as district surveyors to correct improper surveys that had been made of claims approved by land commissioners.[18] Surveys in the district west of the Chattahoochee River during 1816 and 1817 were delayed by unfriendly Indians, illness among the surveyors and laborers, and scarcity of provisions. Surveying and mapping sometimes proceeded slowly. It was not until February, 1817, that Freeman was able to send to the General Land Office a general and connected map with township maps of the country between the Tombigbee and Chickasawhay rivers that had been surveyed under the direction of Briggs.

To facilitate surveying operations, Congress adopted recommendations made by the commissioner of the General Land Office and passed an act of March 3, 1831, authorizing separate surveyors general for Louisiana, Mississippi, and Alabama and the division of existing records among them. In accordance with an act of March 2, 1833, Gideon Fitz, then the surveyor general of Mississippi, removed his office in July from Washington to Jackson, which had become the seat of the state government.[19]

In his annual report, submitted on November 30, 1848, the commissioner of the General Land Office reported that 30,174,080 acres of land in Mississippi had been surveyed and the plats returned to that office and to the district land offices.[20] He added that numerous retracings and resurveys had been made to locate private claims and supply lost field notes and to correct erroneous surveys. On October 31, 1849, the surveyor general of Mississippi transferred the records of his office to the secretary of state of Mississippi in accordance with the act of Congress of June 12, 1840.[21] In 1892 the records were placed in the custody of the state land

17 / George S. Gaines to the secretary of the treasury, September 11, 1811, J. I. Moore to Edward Tiffin, August 24, 1812, both in Carter (ed.), *Territory of Mississippi*, VI, 220, 318.

18 / Josiah Meigs to Thomas Freeman, April 8, 1816, in Carter (ed.), *Territory of Mississippi*, VI, 676.

19 / George Graham to Richard Rush, January 24, 1828, *House Documents*, 20th Cong., 1st Sess., No. 110, pp. 5–8, Serial 171; 4 *Statutes* 492–94, 662.

20 / Report of the Commissioner of the General Land Office, November 30, 1848, *Senate Executive Documents*, 30th Cong., 2nd Sess., in *New American State Papers, Public Lands*, II, 240.

21 / White, *Rectangular Survey System*, 112, 211; 5 *Stat.* 485–85. This act authorized such transfers when the surveys within a state were completed.

office, created by the state legislature to take over land records that had been held by several offices.

A varied collection of records of the surveyor general of Mississippi, 1803–1849, was still in the state land office in Jackson when the records were examined by the Survey of Federal Archives in the 1930s. A correspondence copy book, 1803–1813, contains copies of correspondence of surveyors general in Mississippi and Louisiana with the secretary of the treasury and others. A correspondence copy book, 1828–1839, in one volume, contains correspondence of the surveyor general in Jackson with the commissioner of the General Land Office on a variety of subjects; and another correspondence copy book, 1831–1843, also in one volume, contains correspondence from the General Land Office concerning resurveys, the settlement of claims, and the expenditure of funds. Field notes and records of surveyors from 1805 to 1876 in ten volumes cover districts east of the Pearl River, other sections of the state, especially the southern and southwestern parts, districts south of the Tennessee River, and those east and west of the Pearl River. One file of field notes for 1809–1837 contains copies of a Spanish map of January 21, 1788, showing land grants to individuals and a grant made by the Spanish government to John Burnett, Jr., on July 8, 1810. A small file of certificates of survey issued by the board of land commissioners for the district west of the Pearl River, March 13, 1810, concerns claims in Natchez. Book A, a record of claims east of the Pearl River, 1820–1848, contains a record of original grants. Book B, a record of claims east of the Pearl River, 1827–1831, contains a record of claims west of the meridian line and in the city of Mobile. A map of the boundary between Tennessee and Mississippi, 1837, shows townships and ranges. Other survey records relate to the Choctaw and Chickasaw land cessions.[22]

Other records of the surveyor general in the Mississippi Department of Archives and History include: board of land commissioners, west of the Pearl River, journal extracts, 1803–1807, in one volume; bonds, oaths, contracts of deputy surveyors, chain carriers, clerks, etc., 1803–1841; claim files, from about 1803 to 1835; correspondence, 1803–1840; land applications and payment registers, 1808–1818; receipts, from about 1803 to 1835; salary accounts, from about 1803 to 1845; surveys, no date. In the same repository are records of the U.S. land office for the district west of the Pearl River, 1817–1852, and microfilm of the Mississippi land records, 1792–1853, in seventy-eight reels. A volume described as a land book of

22 / Survey of Federal Archives, Mississippi, *Inventory of Federal Archives in the States, Series VIII, The Department of the Interior, No. 23, Mississippi*, 1–9.

Mississippi Territory surveyors, from 1817 to December 1, 1820, containing descriptions of townships, ranges, and sections in the Mississippi Territory and some in Alabama, was found by the Survey of Federal Archives in the new post office at Montgomery.[23]

Records of the Bureau of Land Management containing materials relating to private land claims in Mississippi and other states and territories are described in the part of this book on Louisiana. A list of records relating to claims in Mississippi, including series begun in the Treasury Department before the General Land Office was created, is in print. Another list of reports of boards of land commissioners, reports of registers and receivers, and related papers is also in print.[24] Maps, field notes, and correspondence relating to the survey of the boundary line along the 31st degree of latitude by Andrew Ellicott and William Dunbar and resurveys by Wells, Whitner, and John Coffee are also in the records of the Bureau of Land Management. A record of written evidence of land claims in the Natchez district, 1767–1805, in seven volumes, lettered A–G, contains files relating to 2,098 claims, of which 361 were missing in 1952. Summaries of the information in this record are in print.[25]

Records of the old Private Land Claim Division in the records of the Bureau of Land Management (Record Group 49) in the National Archives include the following: reports on British and Spanish claims in the area west of the Pearl River, including some Yazoo claims, 1795–1808, in volume 158; a report of the board of land commissioners on private land claims in the area east of the Pearl River, Mississippi, 1798–1828, in volume 143A; a register of claims presented in the area west of the Pearl River, 1803–1806, in one volume; proceedings of the board of land commissioners in the area west of the Pearl River, 1803–1807, in volumes 146–50; an index to confirmation certificates in the area west of the Pearl River, Mississippi, 1803–1814, in volume 151; an index to claims in the area west of the Pearl River, 1803–1814, in one volume; written evidence on private grants in the area west of the Pearl River, 1803–1818, in eight volumes; journals of the board of land commissioners in the area west of the Pearl River, 1803–1818, in five volumes; a register of claims in the area west of the Pearl River, 1803–1818, in volume 6; a report of proceedings of the board of land commissioners for the area east of the Pearl River, 1804–1805, in volumes 152–53; a journal of decisions and certificates issued

23 / Mississippi Department of Archives and History, *Guide*, 4; Survey of Federal Archives, Alabama, *Inventory of Federal Archives in the States, Series VIII, The Department of the Interior, No. 2, Alabama* (Birmingham, Ala., 1941), 10.

24 / Carter (ed.), *Territory of Mississippi*, V, 210 n. 75, 231–32 n. 16.

25 / McBee (ed.), *Natchez Court Records*, 354–510.

in the area west of the Pearl River, Washington, Mississippi, 1805–1806, in volume 145; record copies of land certificates in the area west of the Pearl River, 1805–1807, in four volumes; abstracts of certificates in the area west of the Pearl River, Washington, Mississippi, 1804–1807, in volume 144; a report of the register of the area east of the Pearl River on private land claims based on British and Spanish warrants, 1805–1815, in volume 159; a record of evidence filed with the board of land commissioners for the area east of the Pearl River, 1813–1814, in volumes 202–204; reports from Jackson Courthouse on private land claims east of the Pearl River, 1813–1820, in volume 162; a record of petitions on private land claims filed at Jackson Courthouse, 1819–1829, in volume 154; and an abstract of private land claims in Mississippi, 1848, in volume 229.[26]

26 / U.S. National Archives, The General Land Office (Record Group 49), Administrative Records of the General Land Office, 1785–1955 (Typescript; Washington, D.C., 1973).

13

ॐ

Ecclesiastical Records

When the Sieur d'Iberville established a post on the Mississippi coast at old Biloxi, the Reverend Bordenave of the Society of Foreign Missions became its chaplain. The Reverend Paul du Ru, who had also come with Iberville, and his successors labored among the Indians along the Gulf Coast.[1] A copy of a register of burials of Fort Biloxi, August 8, 1720–September 4, 1722, obtained by Professor Alcée Fortier from the Archives de la Marine in Paris, is in the Tulane University Library.[2] A register of marriages, July 1, 1720–December 4, 1730, containing 227 pages and an index and showing marriages at Biloxi, Yazoo, Fort Louis, and Natchez, is in the St. Louis Cathedral archives at New Orleans. A register of deaths at Fort Biloxi, 1720–1723, giving names and dates of death, prepared for the bishop of Quebec, has been published from a transcript in the Library of Congress.[3]

In the 1780s, English-speaking settlers moved into West Forida, Alabama, and Mississippi from the seaboard colonies, where the new United States government had established control. In 1785 Governor Estevan Miró of Louisiana recommended that a parish be established at Natchez and provided with an Irish priest from a Spanish seminary. On land at Natchez purchased by the governor from Stephen Minor, the Church of the Savior (San Salvador) was built during the years 1790–1792. The earliest priest there was the Reverend William Savage. His successor, the Rev-

1 / Richard O. Gerow, *Catholicity in Mississippi* (Natchez, Miss., 1939), 7–14.
2 / Celestin M. Chambon, *In and Around the Old St. Louis Cathedral of New Orleans* (New Orleans, 1908), 94.
3 / Nolan, *Southern Catholic Heritage*, 39; Winston De Ville, "Register of Deaths at Old Fort Biloxi, Mississippi, 1720–1723," *National Genealogical Society Quarterly*, LV (March, 1967), 45–48.

erend Francis Lennan, moved to New Feliciana in 1798 after the United States assumed control north of the 31st parallel; he continued to serve Natchez as well.[4]

Some early records of San Salvador Church have survived. In the chancery of the diocese of Jackson, St. Mary Cathedral, Jackson, Mississippi, is the first book of baptisms, January 19, 1789–June 25, 1806, in one volume and loose sheets; the first book of baptisms of pardos and Negroes, May 15, 1796–August 6, 1804; and a register of funerals of pardos and Negroes, May 23, 1796–February 20, 1798.[5] In the diocese of Baton Rouge archives are the following records: the first book of marriages, September 1, 1788–May 9, 1798, in thirty pages; another record of marriages, September 1, 1794–June 10, 1805, miscellaneous records item 83, that includes marriages of Catholics and Protestants and persons of mixed blood; a register of marriages performed at Bayou Sara, New Feliciana, and Natchez, 1798–1799, miscellaneous records item 84C, covering nine marriages of Protestants; a register of marriages, June 10, 1801–May 7, 1810; a register of funerals, October 15, 1788–March 14, 1798, in booklet form. Translations of marriages performed at Natchez, September, 1783, to January 9, 1803, are in print.[6] The records in the custody of the diocese of Jackson were indexed between 1925 and 1942 to facilitate their use.

During the Spanish period, other Catholic churches were established in West Florida. On land at Cole's Creek (Villa Gayoso) bought by Governor Miró, a church was built in 1791 and 1792 and was served by the Reverend Gregory White after 1792. In the same year Father Francis Lennan was appointed to the new post established at Fort Nogales (Vicksburg) and also ministered at the settlement of New Feliciana (St. Francisville).[7]

4 / Gilbert C. Din, "The Irish Mission to West Florida," *Louisiana History*, XII (Fall, 1971), 315–31.

5 / Nolan, *Southern Catholic Heritage*, 30–31.

6 / Gianelloni, "'Miscellaneous Records," 121–25, 283–87, 329–30; Catherine B. Futch and Mrs. Edwin A. Broders, "Marriages of Early Natchez Settlers Primarily Protestant Performed at Natchez, Mississippi, by Father Francis Lennan of the Order of Franciscan Irish Capuchins," *New Orleans Genesis*, VI (January, June, 1967), 84–87, 222–25.

7 / Din, "Irish Mission," 320–27; Jack D. L. Holmes, "Father Francis Lennan and His Activities in Spanish Louisiana and West Florida," *Louisiana Studies*, V (Winter, 1966), 263.

III

The Records of Alabama

14

ð

History and Government

After a much earlier temporary occupation of Mobile Bay by the Spanish during the years 1559–1561, Pierre Le Moyne, the Sieur d'Iberville, led a French expedition to explore Mobile Bay and the coast to the west and established Fort Maurepas on Biloxi Bay in 1699. He left there in January, 1702, and set up Fort Louis on the Mobile River, but because of flooding he moved in 1711 to the mouth of the river, where Fort Dauphin was erected. Fort Condé was built at Mobile by Jean Baptiste Le Moyne, the Sieur de Bienville, in 1711 as a replacement for Fort Louis. The seat of the colony was moved to new Biloxi in 1720 when Fort Dauphin was cut off by a sand bar. Mobile became the head of the Mobile district in 1721 when Louisiana was divided into nine governmental districts.[1]

No serious attempt was made by the French to settle the interior of Alabama. They established forts to promote relations and trade with the Indians and to prevent penetration by the English from Carolina. Fort Toulouse was erected in 1717 near the junction of the Coosa and Tallapoosa rivers, but it was abandoned in 1763. During his campaign against the Chickasaws, Bienville built Fort Tombecbé on the Tombigbee River in 1736. It was occupied by the French until 1768.

The commandant at Mobile was the governmental factotum in control of both military and civil affairs. He commanded the soldiers, appointed the *alcaldes* who served as inferior judges, and functioned himself as the superior judge, notary, and custodian of deeds and records. In his judicial capacity he had jurisdiction over almost every kind of dispute, such as contracts, attachments, and damages; his normal judicial practice was to keep a record of the original papers, testimony and

---

1 / Albert B. Moore, *History of Alabama* (University, Ala., 1934), 35–43.

decrees, and later proceedings. Both civil and criminal matters were handled, and appeals could be made to the governor in New Orleans. The commandant was assisted in the record keeping by a succession of notaries. There were also other officials: a royal commissary, a commissary of the marine, an armorer, a land surveyor, royal quartermaster, custom house guards, and a surgeon of the hospital.[2]

A war that broke out between England and Spain at the beginning of 1762 resulted in the English capture of Cuba, Martinique, and other islands in the West Indies. This conflict became part of the larger Seven Years' War, in which England was pitted against France in North America and Europe. Under the Treaty of Paris of February 10, 1763, Spain ceded Louisiana east of the Mississippi and East and West Florida to England in exchange for Havana and Manila. A detachment of British troops under Major Robert Farmar took possession of Mobile on October 20, 1763. Fort Condé was repaired and renamed Fort Charlotte after the young queen of England. Fort Tombecbé was occupied by the British, but they did not garrison Fort Toulouse. Under the British the region west of the Apalachicola River became West Florida, with its capital at Pensacola.[3]

During the Spanish campaign against West Florida in 1780, Bernardo de Gálvez captured Fort Charlotte on March 14 and occupied Mobile. It was governed thereafter as a part of Louisiana under a succession of commandants whose functions were similar to those of the earlier French commandants. Notaries continued to assist the commandants. After the conclusion of the Revolutionary War, Spain remained in control of West Florida, and the United States gained possession of the region to the north.[4] In 1790 the Spanish built Fort San Estevan (St. Stephens) on the Tombigbee River north of Mobile. In 1794 Fort Confederation was constructed sixty miles farther north, where Fort Tombigbee had formerly stood.

Mobile District Records

What is now Alabama was part of Louisiana during the French and Spanish regimes, and land grants were made there in accordance with the prevailing regulations and practices. After 1810, land grants were made in Mobile and on the east side of the river and the bay of Mobile by the governors of Louisiana. The French did not colonize the interior, leaving it

2 / Hamilton, *Colonial Mobile, passim*.
3 / Moore, *History of Alabama*, 46–47.
4 / Caruso, *Southern Frontier*, 253–55, 315.

instead in the possession of the Indians. The governor general of Spanish Louisiana made direct grants in Alabama or had surveyor general Carlos L. Trudeau or the commandant at Mobile place applicants in possession. Grants for grazing and farming were made on the Mobile River and in the neighborhood of St. Stephens and below on the Tombigbee River. Vicente Sebastian Pintado, who had been deputy under Trudeau, succeeded him as surveyor general of West Florida in December, 1805; Joseph P. Collins was the deputy surveyor at Mobile.[5]

The outbreak of the War of 1812 afforded the United States an opportunity to complete its possession of the rest of West Florida between the Pearl and Perdido rivers. Congress, by the act of May 14, 1812, annexed this region to the Territory of Mississippi. To prevent its use by the British as a base of operations, Congress on February 12, 1813, authorized the president to take over the territory as far as the Perdido. Accordingly, General James Wilkinson effected a peaceful occupation of Mobile on April 15, Captain Cayetano Perez yielding Fort Charlotte without a struggle. The agreement of April 13, 1813, between those two officials providing for the occupation contained no stipulation regarding the local archives.[6] The tract of country added to the Mississippi Territory by the act of Congress of May 14, 1812, was organized into Mobile County by a proclamation of Governor David Holmes of that territory on August 1, 1812. Cessions of lands obtained from the Cherokees, the Choctaws, and the Chickasaws were occupied by settlers from Virginia, the Carolinas, Georgia, Tennessee, and Kentucky. This influx of population resulted in the creation by the act of Congress of March 3, 1817, of the Territory of Alabama from that part of Mississippi north of the 31st degree of north latitude between the Perdido River and the western boundary of Georgia. William W. Bibb of Georgia was appointed governor on September 25, 1817, and the territorial legislature met at St. Stephens on January 19, 1818. An act for the admission of Alabama as a state was adopted on March 2, 1819.[7]

Under the direction of Governor David Holmes of the Mississippi Territory, steps were taken to establish the local government and to secure the archives. While the governor was in Mobile in the latter part of April, 1813, he received from the Spanish some bundles of records, comprising three hundred papers of original grants of land for the years 1763–1810.[8] Harry Toulmin, judge of the eastern or Tombigbee district of

5 / Hamilton, *Colonial Mobile*, 139–42, 263–68, 420–31.
6 / 2 *Statutes* 734; Hamilton, *Colonial Mobile*, 360–61.
7 / Carter (ed.), *Territory of Mississippi*, VI, 305–306; 3 *Statutes* 371–73, 489.
8 / Harry Toulmin to James Monroe, June 23, 1813, in Carter (ed.), *Territory of Mississippi*, VI, 377–79.

the Territory of Mississippi since 1804, had accompanied the governor to Mobile and, remaining there as the governor's representative, succeeded in recovering additional records. Through an army officer supplied by Colonel John Bowyer, who was commanding a work on the Perdido River, Toulmin applied to Governor Mateo Gonzalez Manriques at Pensacola for other land records that it had been learned had been carried there.[9] Upon receiving the governor's reply, dated June 3, in which was enclosed a letter to Lieutenant Juan Estevez, a Spanish artillery officer still in Mobile, that instructed him to deliver the documents, Toulmin delivered the letter to the lieutenant. They went to a house, where Toulmin had in the meantime located more records, and the lieutenant began separating them. When Toulmin objected to this procedure and placed a seal on the trunk, the lieutenant washed his hands of the matter. Toulmin then took possession of the records. Upon examination, he found them to contain bills of sale, private contracts, letters of emancipation, wills, estates, procès-verbaux in civil and criminal cases for the years 1786–1813, except 1812, and to be three times as great in bulk as the records that had been delivered to Holmes.[10] He placed them under oath with Zenon Orso, notary public at Mobile, in whose hands he had also deposited the records received by Holmes that in the interval had been in the office of a Mr. Acre, the land commissioner's clerk. Toulmin reported that some of the papers he had recovered related to lands above the old boundary line, but he recommended that they should remain in Mobile. His examination also revealed that there were no records or plats of government property at Mobile. He learned from Governor Manriques that these records had been entrusted to the care of Captain Cayetano Perez, who was a fugitive from arrest, and consequently the documents could not be produced.[11]

The translation of the land papers among the records obtained from the Spanish was provided for by an act of January 9, 1833, passed by the Alabama legislature. Copies of the translation were to be placed in the office of the clerk of the county court of Mobile—then the depository of the Spanish records—in the U.S. land office at St. Stephens, and in the office of the secretary of state. Not until March 3, 1840, however, did Governor Arthur L. Bagby issue a commission to Joseph E. Caro for the performance of the work. He completed the task in 1841 and was paid thirty-five hundred dollars. The translation comprised two volumes, one of

9 / Harry Toulmin to Don Mateo Gonzalez Manriques, May 24, 1813, in Carter (ed.), *Territory of Mississippi*, VI, 368–69.

10 / Toulmin to Monroe, June 23, 1813, in Carter (ed.), *Territory of Mississippi*, VI, 377–79.

11 / Deposition of Samuel H. Garrow, June 4, 1814, in Carter (ed.), *Territory of Mississippi*, VI, 438–39.

which contained Spanish grants and other land transactions from 1763 to 1803, and the other, land records from November 12, 1715, to January 18, 1812. Copies of these volumes are among the colonial records in the Mobile County probate court, where they have been for many years. Pursuant to the act, other copies were placed in the office of the secretary of state. The set which went to the St. Stephens' land office was in the Montgomery land office in 1900.[12] The copy of the second volume, which was received at the St. Stephens' land office on July 29, 1841, is now in the General Land Office, Washington, D.C. The Survey of Federal Archives found another copy of that volume in the Alabama Department of Archives and History. An abstract of the translated Mobile records for 1781–1795 shows the names of the grantees and the locations and dates of the grants.[13] Peter J. Hamilton presents considerable information derived from the land records in his *Colonial Mobile*.

No map of Mobile was received with the records of that place. On a visit to Mobile in 1818, Thomas Freeman, surveyor of the United States south of the state of Tennessee, was unable to obtain either the original plan of that town or a copy of it. He was furnished with a copy of a plan that had been borrowed from the War Department. In 1819 he received one from Silas Dinsmoor, who had received it from General Eleazer W. Ripley, the U.S. Army commander at New Orleans. This map had been drawn by Shelypeaux, a French surveyor, on October 20, 1760, and certified by Carlos L. Trudeau, the Spanish surveyor, on May 4, 1780.[14]

When the Spanish commandants of Mobile, Fort Confederation, and Fort St. Stephens evacuated those places during the Spanish withdrawal in 1813, they carried off the administrative records that had been accumulated there. The records included correspondence with the governor and other officials of Louisiana, civil and criminal proceedings, censuses, lists of inhabitants, warehouse accounts, records of brands, and other papers. Indexes of the documents of Mobile and Forts Confederation and St. Stephens, 1800, are available.[15]

In Mobile, judicial power was exercised by the commandant and the *alcalde* in both civil and criminal cases. No record was kept of the proceedings conducted by the *alcalde*. The commandant handled more se-

12 / Alabama, *Acts*, 1833, p. 25; Alabama History Commission, *Report of the Alabama History Commission . . . 1900*, ed. Thomas M. Owen (Montgomery, Ala., 1901), 98.
13 / Mrs. John H. Mallon, Jr., "Mobile Translated Records, 1781–1795," *Deep South Genealogical Quarterly*, V (February, 1968), 144–59.
14 / Silas Dinsmoor to Thomas Freeman, October 5, 1819, in Carter (ed.), *Territory of Alabama*, 709. The map is reproduced in Hamilton, *Colonial Mobile*, 134–35.
15 / Hill, *Descriptive Catalogue*, 104.

rious cases, including contracts, attachments for debts, and damages. A petition was followed by the commandant's order, which was followed by a notice from the notary. The testimony at the trial was recorded and, together with the decrees and later proceedings, was preserved in the archives. The same court heard both civil and criminal cases; appeals could be taken to the tribunal at New Orleans and thence to Cuba and to Spain.[16]

The executive and judicial proceedings of the Mobile district, 1759–1813, in twenty-five bundles lettered A through Z, containing 1105 items, and a bundle lettered A², 1811–1818, were long held by the office of the probate judge at Mobile. Powers of attorney comprised 154 items. When Hamilton used these records for his *Colonial Mobile*, they were kept in black cypress boxes. After an extensive search in the 1960s Winston De Ville could find only empty boxes and concluded that the records had been destroyed, perhaps inadvertently, or stolen.[17]

16 / Hamilton, *Colonial Mobile*, 280–90.

17 / Thomas M. Owen, "Alabama Archives," *American Historical Association Annual Report*, 1904 (Washington, D.C., 1905), 528–29; De Ville, "Manuscript Sources in Louisiana," 223.

15

❧

Archival Reproductions, Documentary Publications, and Manuscripts

Under an act of the General Assembly of Alabama of December 10, 1898, the Alabama History Commission was formed from members of the Alabama Historical Society to undertake an investigation of the sources for the history of the state. The commission's report contains brief descriptions of materials in United States and European repositories. When the Alabama Department of Archives and History was created in 1900, one of its tasks was the procurement and publication of documents on the French, Spanish, and English dominions. But Thomas M. Owen, a lawyer and president of the Alabama History Commission who was appointed director of the department, was never able to accomplish the assignment.[1]

Peter J. Hamilton, a lawyer in Mobile who had prepared a description of materials in foreign archives relating to Alabama for the *Report* of the Alabama History Commission in 1900, obtained materials from French archives for use in preparing his *Colonial Mobile*. Illustrations and maps published in that work were supplied to him by the French Ministère de la Marine. In 1909, through Leon Bogaert, an archivist about whom he was informed by Secretary Henry Vignaud of the American legation in Paris, he obtained copies of correspondence of early officials of Louisiana for the years 1709–1712. He was then revising his work on colonial Mobile and kept the transcripts in his private library. Most of his collection was destroyed by fire. He obtained copies of other materials from the Louisiana Historical Society and the Howard-Tilton Memorial Library of Tulane.

1 / Alabama History Commission, *Report, 1900*, pp. 7–8; Mitchell B. Garrett, "The Preservation of Alabama History," *North Carolina Historical Review*, V (January, 1928), 19.

Since 1959, Jack D. L. Holmes, formerly of the University of Alabama at Birmingham, has been engaged in building up his own collection of documentary reproductions and other materials relating to colonial Louisiana. His earliest activities in Spanish archives occurred during 1961 and 1962 while he was on a Fulbright fellowship, followed by other visits during 1964 and 1966. The 1966 work was supported by grants from the American Association for State and Local History, the American Philosophical Society, and the University of Alabama. At that time he acquired reproductions relating to Spanish Alabama and the Mobile district, 1780–1813, in twenty reels, containing twenty thousand pages. Under the terms of his grants-in-aid, he furnished the institutions at both Tuscaloosa and Birmingham with copies of the microfilm and also supplied copies at cost to Auburn University, the University of Southern Mississippi, the Mississippi Department of Archives and History, Tulane University, the University of Florida, and Florida State University. In 1968 with another grant-in-aid from the University of Alabama at Birmingham, he obtained documentary reproductions on Spanish Pensacola. On further visits to Spain in 1974, 1975, and 1978, assisted by grants from the University of Alabama at Birmingham, and Jack McIlhenny of the Louisiana Tabasco Company, he secured microfilm on the American Revolution and other subjects. The Holmes collection consists of eighty-five reels of microfilm and six 4-drawer filing cases of xerox and typescript copies of documents. Since 1979 he has devoted his time to his own historical projects.[2]

Documentary publications relating primarily to other parts of colonial Louisiana contain some materials concerning Alabama. Descriptions of these publications are presented in the parts of this work on Louisiana and Mississippi. Abstracts of communications from Governor Pierre de Rigaud de Vaudreuil to the commandant at Mobile and to other posts in Alabama and his speeches to the Indians, July 5, 1743–July 30, 1747, have been published. A volume containing extensive excerpts from British and Spanish documents concerning the successful defense of Mobile by José de Espeleta and his management of the affairs of that place during 1780 and 1781 is in print.[3]

Other, briefer, publications concerning Alabama are useful chiefly for genealogical research. A 1706 census of Fort Louis at Mobile gives the names of heads of families, the numbers of children, and the numbers of

2 / Jack D. L. Holmes to Henry P. Beers, April 5, 1985, with list of his publications, in Beers Correspondence.

3 / Barron (ed.), *Vaudreuil Papers*, 2, 287–426; Francisco Rojos de Borja Medina, *José de Ezpeleta, Governador de la Mobile, 1780–1781* (Seville, 1980).

animals. Another census of Fort Louis and of neighboring villages, June 25, 1721, shows the names of men (and their occupations), women, children, French servants, Negro slaves, Indian slaves, horned cattle, and horses. The same information is in another census of March, 1725. These censuses are also printed in another compilation, which contains a census of the habitants of Mobile of January 1, 1726.[4] In print also is a list of French inhabitants of Mobile who took the oath of allegiance to Great Britain, October 2, 1764. A list of the names of Anglo-Saxon inhabitants of Alabama who assembled at Mobile on January 15, 1787, to take the oath of allegiance to Spain is also in print.[5] A list of inhabitants of Fort St. Stephens in 1797 gives the names of males, their ages, and their nationalities. Juan de la Villebeuvre, commandant of Fort St. Stephens, compiled a census of the settlers in the district that consists of an alphabetical list of the names of males, largely English.[6] Citations to other censuses and lists of the Spanish period are in print.[7]

Available finding aids yield little information about manuscripts concerning colonial Alabama. The Panton, Leslie and Company traded out of Florida with the Indians north of the border. A large collection of records of the firm in the Mobile Public Library includes correspondence of Spanish officials of Louisiana. The Peter J. Hamilton Collection, 1564–1888, in the Alabama Department of Archives and History contains materials collected by him for his *Colonial Mobile*.

4 / "1706 Census at Fort Louis de la Louisiane (Mobile)," *Deep South Genealogical Quarterly,* I (August, 1963), 30; "Census of the Habitants of Fort Louis de la Mobile and the Surrounding Villages, June 28, 1721," *Deep South Genealogical Quarterly,* I (March, 1964), 136–39; "Census of the Inhabitants of Dauphine Island, Mobile, and Pascagoula taken by Monsieur Perry, March, 1725," *Deep South Genealogical Quarterly,* I (December, 1963), 86; Maduell (comp. and trans.), *Census Tables for French Louisiana,* 9–10, 11–14, 23–27, 48, 62–64.

5 / Ruth Warren, "List of Inhabitants of Mobile [1764]," *Deep South Genealogical Quarterly,* III (May, 1966), 629–30; Sidney L. Villeré, "List of French Inhabitants of Mobile in West Florida, Who Took the Oath of Allegiance and Fidelity to His Britannic Majesty King George III, October 2, 1764," *New Orleans Genesis,* VI (March, 1967), 117–18; Winston De Ville, "Some Non-French Inhabitants of Alabama, 1787," *Louisiana Genealogical Register,* XXI (March, 1974), 42–44.

6 / Winston De Ville, "Fort St. Stephens in 1797," *Deep South Genealogical Quarterly,* V (February, 1968), 159–60; Jack D. L. Holmes (comp.), "1797 Alabama Census According to Spanish Records," *Alabama Genealogical Quarterly,* VIII (September, 1966), 123–24.

7 / See the footnotes in Jack D. L. Holmes, "Alabama's Forgotten Settlers: Notes on the Spanish Mobile District, 1780–1813," *Alabama Historical Quarterly,* XXXIII (Summer, 1971), 87–97, and Hill, *Descriptive Catalogue,* index, 513, 545.

16

Land Records

The adjustment of land claims in Alabama began while that area was part of the Territory of Mississippi. An act of Congress of March 3, 1803, for regulating grants of land south of the Tennessee River provided that the register of the land office of Washington County and two other persons to be appointed by the president were to serve as commissioners to ascertain the titles of land claimants. After hearing claimants testify as to their claims and considering documentary evidence, the commissioners were to issue certificates of confirmation. Ephraim Kirby of Connecticut and Robert C. Nicholas of Kentucky were appointed as commissioners in July, 1803, and reached Fort Stoddert in January, 1804.[1] At that military post on the Mobile River above the junction of the Tombigbee and the Alabama, the commissioners, along with register Joseph Chambers, began their sessions on February 2, 1804, in quarters provided by the commander of the garrison.

The board of commissioners completed its sessions in July and then prepared a report for submission to Congress. The journal of the commissioners east of the Pearl River, including proofs relative to claims, has been published. Filed with the board was a total of 269 claims, of which 192 were located west of the Tombigbee River and 77 east of that river.[2] The report contains an abstract of 17 British grants of nonresidents, fully executed and recorded according to the land act of 1803 but not confirmed to the holders under the articles of agreement and session, each showing the name of the original grantee, the name of the present claimant, the

1 / 2 *Statutes* 230; Alan V. Briceland, "The Mississippi Territorial Land Board East of the Pearl River, 1804," *Alabama Review*, XXXII (January, 1979), 43–44, 46; David Lightner, "Private Land Claims in Alabama," *Alabama Review*, XX (July, 1967), 192–93.

2 / *American State Papers, Public Lands*, I, 645–858; Briceland, "Mississippi Land Board," 58–66.

date of the grant, the number of acres, their location, any conditions annexed to the grant, and evidence showing the fulfillment of the conditions. An abstract of claims east of the Pearl River founded on British or Spanish warrants or orders of survey and not confirmed by former laws regulating grants of land in the Mississippi Territory filed with the register during the period February 2–June 11, 1804, shows similar information concerning the grantees or claimants. Published also are the commissioners' certificates showing the numbers and dates of the patents, the places where they were recorded, the names of the original and the present grantees, the quantity and location of the lands, and the dates and derivations of titles. These include: Register A, certificates granted on British and Spanish patents; Register B, certificates on which patents may issue without any payment of purchase money; Register C, certificates on which patents may issue without any payment of purchase money, but not until judicial decision shall have been obtained about conflicting British claims; Register D, preemption certificates; Register E, preemption certificates on which patents may not issue until a judicial decision shall have been obtained against the conflicting British claims; Register F, British patents on which no certificates have been issued; and Register N [G], claims presented, December, 1805.[3]

The act of March 3, 1803, referred to above did not provide for the adjustment of land claims east of the Tombigbee River. The board of commissioners allowed claims to be filed without requiring the same completeness in the submission of documents.[4] In April, 1805, however, the board began considering claims located east of the Tombigbee and Mobile rivers. An act of March 2, 1805, however, stipulated that persons having claims to land lying east of the Tombigbee and Alabama rivers had until May 1, 1805, to file them.[5]

The act of April 25, 1812, provided for a board to consider the claims lying east of the Pearl River. William Crawford of North Carolina was appointed land commissioner in June, 1812, and was engaged until October 20, 1814, in collecting evidence on land claims.[6] His report was completed by his clerk in June, 1815, conveyed to Washington, D.C., by Crawford himself, and presented to the House of Representatives by Josiah Meigs, the commissioner of the General Land Office, on January 2, 1816.[7] The

3 / *American State Papers, Public Lands*, I, 603–608, 626–27, 628–44.
4 / Ephraim Kirby and Joseph Chambers to the secretary of the treasury, August 3, 1804, in Carter (ed.), *Territory of Mississippi*, V, 329.
5 / Briceland, "Mississippi Land Board," 66; 2 *Statutes* 323.
6 / 2 *Statutes* 713–16; Carter (ed.), *Territory of Mississippi*, VI, 426 n. 82; Petition to Congress by William Crawford, November 1, 1815, in Carter (ed.), *Territory of Mississippi*, VI, 565.
7 / The report is printed in *American State Papers, Public Lands*, III, 7–38.

224 / The Records of Alabama

report contains eleven registers of different kinds of land grants from the French, British, and Spanish governments, with a total of 505 grants. A twelfth list contains the names of 174 actual settlers who had no claims. The report included a list with more than 150 claims that were not recommended for confirmation. Besides the names of the present claimants, the registers show the names of the original claimants, the nature of the claims and from what authority they derived, the dates, the quantities of land, the names of the officials by whom they were issued, the dates of surveys and the names of the surveyors, and the dates of cultivation and habitation. Of the claims for lots in Mobile, 88 were recommended for confirmation. Translations of French and Spanish documents dated from 1710 to 1813 concerning 5 claims of Nicholas Baudin, Joseph Chastang, and Harry Toulmin are included in the report.[8]

The report of August 17, 1820, by Willoughby Barton, the register at Jackson Courthouse, and William Barnett, the receiver at that place, on land claims east of the Pearl River in southern Mississippi and southern Alabama has also been published. The report approved some claims and disallowed others. An act of May 8, 1822, confirmed all claims to lots in the town of Mobile based on complete grants derived from either the French, British, or Spanish authorities; also all claims to lots in the town founded on orders of survey, requêtes, permissions to settle, or other written evidence bearing a date prior to December 20, 1803; also all claims to lots founded on private conveyance; and all other claims to lots that appeared to have been built upon or improved and occupied on or before April 15, 1813.[9]

An act of Congress of March 3, 1827, authorized claimants to land, town lots, or out-lots in that part of the former land district of Jackson Courthouse embraced in the state of Alabama whose claims had been presented to the commissioners appointed to examine titles and claims to lands in that district or to the register and receiver at Jackson Courthouse acting as commissioners under the act of March 3, 1819. These claimants were allowed until September 1, 1827, to present their claims to the register and receiver at St. Stephens. The commissioners were to hold sessions at Mobile and such other places as were necessary and were to appoint a clerk capable of acting as translator. A report of February 29, 1828, by John B. Hazard and John H. Owen, the register and the receiver, has been published. The report lists ten abstracts, containing 110 claims, and four special reports. The abstract shows the number of the claim, the

8 / Ibid., III, 20–33.
9 / Ibid., III, 444–50, printed also in *Senate Documents*, 16th Cong., 2nd Sess., No. 3, pp. 1–11, Serial 42; 3 *Statutes* 699–700.

name of the claimant, the name of the original claimant, the origin of the claim, the date, the quantity of land, its location, and the dates of habitation and cultivation. The special reports concern the claims of Thomas Price to land in Mobile, of Nicholas Baudin to an island in the Fowl River called "Grosse Point," of legal representatives of Joseph Chastang and Baptiste Laurendine to a tract called St. Luis, located between Three-Mile Creek, the Mobile River, and Bogue, and of the Church of the Immaculate Conception to land in Mobile on Dauphin Street. An act of Congress of March 2, 1829, confirmed the 2 claims in abstract A, number 1, and the 24 claims in abstracts D, number 1, and E, number 1, for twenty-four lots in Mobile.[10] This act also provided for the issuance of certificates of confirmation and patents.

In succeeding years, Hazard and Owen collected evidence on additional land claims and prepared reports for submission to the General Land Office. A report by Hazard and Owen of February 26, 1831, presents abstracts of claims of Samuel Acre and the heirs of Cornelius McCurtin, which show the origin of the claims, their locations, the quantity of land, the names of the original owners, the quantity allowed, and the dates of possession, with a recommendation for confirmation.[11] Another report of May 3, 1832, presents abstracts regarding 3 claims that show similar information. A report of February 16, 1834, contains information regarding the claim of Andria Demetry. The claim of John Baptiste Budreux to a tract called Bellefontaine near the mouth of the Pascagoula River was the subject of the report of March 24, 1834.[12] Reports five and six, completed on May 23, 1834, present data on 14 additional claims.[13] A special report by Hazard and Owen of July 3, 1834, concerns a claim by the heirs of Miguel Eslava to land in the city of Mobile. A seventh report, dated September 16, 1845, concerns a claim originally owned by William Fisher. An eighth report, from James Magoffin and Theodore J. Wilkinson, the land officers at St. Stephens, dated February 28, 1839, concerns a lot in Mobile, the original claimant of which was Hugo Krebs.[14]

10 / 4 *Statutes* 239–40; *American State Papers, Public Lands,* V, 493–508, published also in *Senate Documents,* 20th Cong., 1st Sess., No. 159, pp. 1–19, Serial 166, and in *House Documents,* 20th Cong., 1st Sess., No. 285, pp. 1–19, Serial 175; 4 *Statutes* 358.

11 / *American State Papers, Public Lands,* VI, 430–31, printed also in *House Documents,* 22nd Cong., 1st Sess., No. 197, pp. 1–4, Serial 220.

12 / *American State Papers, Public Lands,* VI, 490, 958, VII, 164.

13 / *Ibid.,* VII, 172–73, printed also in *Senate Documents,* 23rd Cong., 1st Sess., No. 434, pp. 1–3, Serial 243, and in *House Documents,* 23rd Cong., 1st Sess., No. 496, pp. 1–6, Serial 259.

14 / *American State Papers, Public Lands,* VII, 330–31; *Senate Documents,* 25th Cong., 3rd Sess., No. 278, pp. 1–3, Serial 342.

Congress passed personal relief laws between 1818 and 1858 that confirmed the claims of at least thirty individuals to a total of 20,000 acres of Alabama land. As late as 1884, other land claims in Alabama remained unadjudicated. By 1904 a total of 448 private claims covering 251,602 acres of land had been confirmed in Alabama.[15] These private claims embraced some of the most valuable land in the state, located along the Mobile or the Tombigbee rivers or other waterways. In succeeding years Hazard and Owen collected evidence on additional land claims and prepared reports for submission to the General Land Office.

The records of the boards of land commissioners of Alabama were presumably turned over to the local U.S. land office. The Survey of Federal Archives inventory of the records of the land offices in Alabama describes only one volume that can be recognized as a board record. The volume is labeled "Mississippi Territory, Board of Commissioners, East of Pearl River to the Register of the Land office for the land of the United States lying east of Pearl River" and covers from August 7, 1805, to September 4, 1857.[16]

Land offices were established in Alabama while it was still part of the Territory of Mississippi, and they continued to be set up thereafter to handle the growth of the land office business. An act of Congress of March 3, 1803, authorized a land district east of the Pearl River in Washington County and resulted in the opening of a land office at St. Stephens in 1810. The Huntsville land district in the northern part of the territory was authorized in 1807; an office opened there in July, 1810, and transferred in 1832 to Montgomery. Sales of land located in Alabama were held at Milledgeville, Georgia, until the removal of the land office at that place to Cahaba in 1818. The office was moved from Cahaba to Greenville in 1856. An act of May 6, 1822, provided that the part of the district of Jackson County lying within the state of Alabama was to be part of the district east of the Pearl River in Alabama and that a transfer of books, records, surveys, etc., was to be made. Section three of the act of March 3, 1827, required the officers of the land office at Augusta, Mississippi, "to separate, so far as practicable, from the titles to land in Mississippi, all such papers or claims, or evidence of claims, for any tract of land or town lot, lying in the State of Alabama, and certify the same generally to the Register of the Land Office at St. Stephen's, in the State of Alabama."[17]

15 / U.S. Public Lands Commission, *Report*, 1904, p. 140.

16 / Survey of Federal Archives, Alabama, *Inventory of Federal Archives in the States, Series VIII, The Department of the Interior*, No. 2, *Alabama*, 10.

17 / 2 *Statutes* 230; Evelyn Bush, "United States Land Offices in Alabama, 1803–1879," *Alabama Historical Quarterly*, XVII (Fall, 1955), 147; 3 *Statutes* 680–81; 4 *Statutes* 239.

After the Civil War, the United States resumed the control of the land business in Alabama with the appointment of a register and a receiver at Montgomery.[18] The St. Stephens office was moved to Mobile in 1867, but in 1879 the office at that place was consolidated with the one at Montgomery, which had become the repository of the records of other Alabama land offices before and after the war. In response to the executive order of March 12, 1927, the land office at Montgomery, located since 1883 in the U.S. Post Office Building, was closed at the end of June, 1927. At that time, some of the records were sent to the General Land Office in Washington, D.C., and others were turned over to the University of Alabama Library and to the Alabama Department of Archives and History. An act of May 28, 1926, had authorized the secretary of the interior to transfer the records of land offices that were abolished to the custody of the states in which they were located.[19]

The Special Collections Department of the University of Alabama Library has twenty-nine volumes of U.S. public land office records relating largely to the administration of the lands by that office. Volume thirteen, however, is described as containing land grants from England, France, and Spain to grantees in Mobile, West Florida, and the Mississippi Territory, as well as marriage contracts, wills, and plats of land grants, descriptions of islands, etc., April 5, 1738–1813.[20]

The U.S. land office records in Alabama that were transferred in 1927 from the land office at Montgomery to the custody of the state were examined in the 1930s by the Survey of Federal Archives. At that time they were in three different buildings in Montgomery, but in 1940 they were transferred to the newly completed World War Memorial Building on Washington Avenue, which had been constructed for the exclusive use of the Alabama Department of Archives and History. The records of the General Land Office dating from 1800 to 1927 in the custody of that agency were originated by land commissioners, land surveyors, and registers and receivers of land offices. Records of the board of land commissioners, appointed under the act of March 3, 1803, for the district east of the Pearl River, August 7, 1805–September 4, 1857, in four volumes, concern the adjustment of private land claims in that district. The inventory

18 / U.S. General Land Office, *Annual Report*, October 3, 1865, *House Executive Documents*, 29th Cong., 1st Sess., No. 1, p. 27, Serial 1248.

19 / Survey of Federal Archives, Alabama, *Inventory of Federal Archives in the States, Series VIII, The Department of the Interior*, No. 2, *Alabama*, 9; 44 *Statutes* 672.

20 / List of U.S. Public Land Office Records in the Special Collections Department of the University of Alabama Library, April 24, 1984 (copy supplied to Henry P. Beers by the library).

published by the Survey of Federal Archives, disregarding archival provenance, does not describe the records of the early Alabama land offices by
individual office and series. Most of the entries relate to several offices
and several record series. The entries include field notes, plat books, tract
books, patent records, registers, journals, correspondence, receipts, account books, and ledgers.[21]

The Alabama Department of Archives and History has a list of U.S.
General Land Office records in its custody, including materials in each
land office relating to private land claims.[22] Records for the St. Stephens
land office include: Spanish land grants, 1788–1798, in book 001, indexed,
microfilmed; surveyor John Coffee's field notes, 1817–1819, in book 002; a
register of transfers of private land claims, 1818, in book 004; patents,
1814–1854, in book 005; private claims, receipts, dated December 1, 1824–
February 12, 1825, in book 010, containing six pages; private land claims,
1827–1847, indexed (book 011); field notes, 1823–1849, in book 031; and
field notes on the land district east of New Orleans and east of Pearl River
(now Washington County and the top of Mobile County), around 1803–
1811, in book 068. The voluminous records of the Huntsville land office
include: tract book, 1821–1856, townships 1–14, ranges 9W–17W, in book
161; tract book, from township 2, range 7, to township 4, range 7, 1830–
1837, in book 166; tract book, 1842–1885, in book 170; rejected private land
claims, 1888–1896, in book 202; tract book for Huntsville and Lebanon
land offices, 1830–1869, in book 226; and survey field notes, township 35,
range 3E (now in Jackson and Madison counties) in book 246. For the
Tuscaloosa office, there are tract books dating from 1820, in books 435–38;
for the Sparta and Elba offices, there are tract books, 1822–1857, in books
507, 511. For the Sparta office, there are field notes, 1840–1848, in book
509, and survey field notes, township 4, range 22E (now in Coffee County),
1823, in book 527. For the Montgomery (Tallapoosa) office tract books,
1832–1846, in books 601, 602, 607, 609, 610, and 642, and field notes,
1832–1834, in book 603. The department also has microfilm of county
tract books in thirty-seven reels. An abstract of tract books of the Huntsville office in nine volumes was turned over by the National Archives to
the Atlanta Federal Records Center in 1984.

21 / Reproductions from the tract book of Madison County, Alabama, which was
settled early in the 1800s are printed in Margaret M. Cowart, *Old Land Records of Madison
County, Alabama* (Huntsville, Ala., 1979).

22 / Untitled xerographic copy supplied to Henry P. Beers in October, 1984, has been
listed in the bibliography as: List of U.S. General Land Office Records in the Department of
Archives and History, State of Alabama (Montgomery, n.d.). This list will be turned over by
the author to the National Archives.

Indexes have been published for some of the records in the Alabama Department of Archives and History. An index to Spanish land grants shows the name of each grantee, his occupation, the name of the official making the grant, the date of the grant, its location, and the grantee's place of residence. Many of the grants were in Mobile and Biloxi and on the Tombigbee and Pascagoula rivers. Data about land claimants whose claims were disapproved and who were also the purchasers of public lands can be found in records kept by receivers of public monies. A chronological record of the names of purchasers at the Sparta land office, 1822–1860, shows the names of purchasers, their places of residence, the numbers of the townships and ranges, and the dates of purchase. Another publication concerns purchasers at the Cahaba land office beginning in 1817.[23]

Surveying began in Alabama when it was part of the Mississippi Territory, under the direction of the surveyor south of the Tennessee River. In 1815, Thomas Freeman had surveys and resurveys made east of the Pearl River in the neighborhood of the Tombigbee River.[24] In April, 1816, he was in St. Stephens to arrange with surveyors for surveying west of the Chattahoochee River. An act of Congress of March 3, 1817, authorized the appointment of a surveyor of lands of the United States in the Mississippi Territory lying north of a line to be drawn from the Mississippi River through Fort Williams to the western boundary of the state of Georgia. John Coffee was appointed to the new position on March 6, 1817, and was instructed to begin surveying in the area between the Tennessee River and the southern boundary of the state of Tennessee.[25]

After the creation of the Alabama Territory on March 3, 1817, both Freeman and Coffee were directing surveys in that territory, the former from St. Stephens and the latter from Huntsville. This anomalous situation was corrected by an act of April 20, 1818, which extended Coffee's authority over the whole of the Territory of Alabama. Both Freeman and Coffee transmitted field notes, survey plats, and maps to the General Land Office and to registers' offices. In accordance with the act of April 20, 1818, Freeman was instructed on May 8, 1818, to transmit to the surveyor

23 / Marilyn D. Hahn, *Old St. Stephen's Land Office Records & American State Papers, Public Lands*, Vol. I, *1768–1888* (Easley, S.C., 1983); Marilyn D. Hahn, *Old Sparta & Elba Land Office Records & Military Warrants, 1822–1860* (Easley, S.C., 1983), 1–22; Marilyn D. Hahn, *Old Cahaba Land Office Records & Military Warrants, 1817–1853* (Mobile, Ala., 1981).

24 / Thomas Freeman to Josiah Meigs, May 15, 1816, in Carter (ed.), *Territory of Mississippi*, VI, 685.

25 / 3 *Statutes* 375–76; Gorton T. Chappell, "John Coffee: Surveyor and Land Agent," *Alabama Review*, XIV (July–October, 1961), 192, 247; Josiah Meigs to John Coffee, March 17, 18, 1817, in Carter (ed.), *Territory of Mississippi*, VI, 778–81.

general of Alabama all the maps, surveying contracts, field notes, and other papers relating to the Alabama Territory. These materials were apparently received by Coffee. The difficulties of adjusting and of surveying private land claims in Alabama delayed land sales there.[26] Despite Coffee's enlarged authority, Freeman continued to be concerned with the completion of surveys in the Alabama Territory and sent materials concerning them to both the General Land Office and Coffee. Illness forced Coffee to move north to Nashville in the spring of 1819, but surveyors whom he had engaged continued to work. Back in Huntsville by August, Coffee reported in November on the appointment of Christopher C. Stone and Charles M. Lawson as deputy surveyors to survey in the St. Stephens district.

Another anomaly in the administration of the survey in Alabama permitted land south of the 31st parallel in Alabama to be surveyed by one of the principal deputy surveyors for Louisiana. This problem was corrected by an act of February 28, 1824, which directed that the surveying of public and private lands in that area be done under the direction of the surveyor for Alabama.[27] The act also provided that the deputy surveyor of the district east of New Orleans and east of the Pearl River was to return plats of all private claims within the state of Alabama to the surveyor for that state.

An act of Congress of March 3, 1831, effecting a reorganization of the surveying system in the South, provided that Louisiana, Mississippi, and Alabama were to be under separate surveyors general and that records held by one of them relating to another state were to be transferred. John Coffee, who had moved his office from Huntsville to Florence in 1823, died in July, 1833, and was succeeded by James H. Weakley, formerly the principal clerk in the office. By the end of November, 1848, a total of 32,462,080 acres of land had been surveyed or were in the process of being surveyed, and plats had been returned to the General Land Office and the district land offices.[28] About the end of October, 1849, the surveyor general's office was closed. After several months, during which Weakley had the records compared, indexed, and arranged, they were boxed and delivered in June, 1850, to the Office of the Secretary of State of Alabama in Montgomery.

Records of the U.S. surveyor general for Alabama in the Alabama Department of Archives and History include: letter books, December 15,

26 / 3 *Statutes* 466–67; Lightner, "Private Land Claims in Alabama," 204.
27 / 4 *Statutes* 6.
28 / 4 *Statutes* 493; Report of the Commissioner of the General Land Office, November 30, 1848, *Senate Executive Documents*, 30th Cong., 2nd Sess., No. 2, pp. 240–41, Serial 530.

1827–July 3, 1833, August 3, 1839–August 1, 1848, in two volumes, with the volumes for 1833 to 1839 missing; field notes of surveys in seventy-five volumes; descriptive notes of old Washington County surveys in two volumes; tract books arranged by counties, in sixty-six volumes; field notes by deputy surveyor Silas Dinsmoor, begun March 19, 1821, in one volume; plat books of districts, in nineteen volumes; miscellaneous field notes of Creek, Cherokee, Choctaw, and Chickasaw lands, in fifty-four volumes; and retraced surveys, 1842–1844, in thirteen volumes.[29] Field notes and survey plats had been destroyed when the office of the surveyor general in Florence burned in December, 1827. These were replaced by copies of transcripts that had been sent to the General Land Office. A volume described as the land book of Mississippi Territory surveyors, from 1817 to December 1, 1820, found by the Survey of Federal Archives in the new post office in Montgomery, contains descriptions of townships, ranges, and sections. Papers of John Coffee, 1796–1887, containing fifteen hundred items, in the Alabama Department of Archives and History, and other Coffee papers dating from 1770 in the Tennessee Historical Society include materials relating to his surveying and land activities.

Besides the materials in the records of the Bureau of Land Management in the National Archives relating to all of the public land states, described here at the end of the chapter on Louisiana land records, there are other materials concerning Alabama specifically. These include a docket of private land claims east of the Pearl River, 1804–1818, in volume 155; a docket of the board of land commissioners at St. Stephens, Alabama, 1848, in volume 174; a report of land commissioners on claims in Alabama, 1828, in volume 176; Louisiana and Alabama notices of private land claims under Spanish and French grants, October, 1712, in volume 208; reports of commissioners on claims, 1819 and 1820, and registers of certificates to land in Alabama, 1815, 1822, 1823, and 1830, all in volume 209; a record of old private land claims, 1776–1803, in volume 211; and translated court and other British, French, and Spanish land claims in Alabama, 1715–1812, in volume 212. The bureau's holdings also include materials on the survey of the line of demarcation between the United States and Spanish Florida in 1799 and 1800 and the survey of the Alabama-Mississippi boundary in 1820. An index to the private land claim dockets relating to Alabama is in print.[30]

29 / Alabama History Commission, *Report, 1900,* pp. 98–99.

30 / Fern Ainsworth, *Private Land Claims: Alabama, Arkansas, Florida* (Natchitoches, La., 1978).

17

ॐ

Ecclesiastical Records

From the beginning the Catholic church was involved in the settlement of Alabama. A Jesuit priest accompanied Iberville in 1698, and in 1703 others arrived to serve as chaplain to the garrison and missionaries to the Indians. A parish was set up at Mobile in 1703 by the bishop of Quebec, who sent priests from the Society of Foreign Missions of Paris and Quebec. Missions were established among the Indians and maintained until the time of the British occupation. A mission erected at Dauphin Island ten miles above Mobile served the Apalachee Indians, and others were maintained at the more distant forts Toulouse and Tombigbee. Jesuit missionaries served at Fort Toulouse and among the more distant Choctaws and Chickasaws in western Alabama. Those missions were terminated following the expulsion of the Jesuits. Priests of the Recollect order took over the churches at Mobile and Dauphin Island in 1722 and then the Indian missions, and they continued to serve throughout the remainder of the French period.[1] The priests at Mobile sometimes brought the sacraments to the inhabitants of Dauphin Island, Pascagoula, and Fort Tombigbee. A new church completed at Mobile in 1741 was named Notre Dame de la Mobile.

After the British occupation of Alabama, the Reverend Ferdinand, a Capuchin, continued to serve as pastor at Mobile until 1769, but except for short visits during the 1770s to administer the sacraments, the Capuchins forsook Mobile. After the Spanish occupied Mobile in 1779, Governor Bernardo de Gálvez required officials to attend services in the Church of the Immaculate Conception there. A new church was completed in 1793, and Spanish priests and some Irishmen educated at Span-

1 / Michael Kenny, *Catholic Culture in Alabama: Centenary Stories of Spring Hill College* (New York, 1931), 11–25.

232

ish seminaries continued to serve. During the Spanish period, Mobile was part of the diocese of Cuba and later the diocese of Louisiana and Florida, but the northern part of the province was under the bishop of Baltimore. In 1825, Alabama and Florida were set up as a vicariate apostolic. Alabama and West Florida were constituted the diocese of Mobile in 1829.[2]

The registers of Notre Dame de Fort Condé de la Mobile, 1704–1764, are in the chancery office of the archdiocese of Mobile. The baptismal registers date from September 6, 1704, and show the name and birth date of the infant or person baptized, the parents' names, the maiden name of the mother, the father's occupation, the priest's name, and the signatures of parents, sponsors, and witnesses. Entries for Indian slaves show their tribal affiliations. The earliest registration of marriages, May 1, 1724–February 8, 1726, is in the register of baptisms for 1704–1778, pages 50–61, and shows the names of the groom and the bride and the date of the ceremony. A list of the names of the parties to the marriages, the date, and the page numbers in the record is in print.[3] A record of marriages is continued in another book for 1726–1812. The registers were kept during the English period from 1764 to 1780 but are less complete. Many of the principal citizens were English and there were Episcopal ministers to serve them, but their records have disappeared.[4]

On taking control at Mobile in 1780, the Spanish changed the name of the parish to Purissima Concepción, which was later Anglicized to Immaculate Conception. The Spanish continued the different registers but in a less careful manner. In 1793 a separate register was begun for Negroes, who by that time included freedmen as well as slaves. Like those kept by the French priests, the registers contain the names of people, their occupations, and sometimes their signatures. There is a register of baptisms of the offspring of Americans living on the Tombigbee River and its environs, June 6, 1780–July 4, 1807. Marriage records sometimes include statements of permission from the commandant at Mobile or from the parents of couples from Mobile, Tombigbee, Tensaw, Pascagoula, and other places.[5] The registers contain documents on breach of promise

2 / *New Catholic Encyclopedia*, IX, 987.
3 / Jacqueline O. Vidrine, "Marriages Entered in Baptismal Book 1, Archives of the Archdiocese of Mobile-Birmingham Chancery Office—Mobile, Alabama," *New Orleans Genesis*, IX (March, 1970), 198.
4 / Alabama History Commission, *Report, 1900*, pp. 130–31; Jay Higginbotham, *Old Mobile: Fort Louis de la Louisiane, 1702–1711* ([Mobile, Ala.], 1977), 557.
5 / Jack D. L. Holmes, "Genealogical and Historical Sources for Spanish Alabama, 1780–1813," *Deep South Genealogical Quarterly*, V (February, 1968), 131.

234 / The Records of Alabama

suits, copies of royal and church regulations concerning the marriages of Protestants and other matters, adjurations by Protestants rejecting their faith and accepting the Roman Catholic faith, and a record of confirmations by the bishop of Louisiana in 1791. The registers are of great value for information concerning the French, Spanish, English, American, and German settlers in Mobile and its vicinity.

Copies of the registers of the Parish of the Immaculate Conception are in various repositories. A microfilm copy of the handwritten copy that was made about 1900 for the Public Archives of Canada is in the New Orleans Public Library and the St. Martin Parish Library. Other microfilm copies are in the University of Southwestern Louisiana, and in the Public Archives of Canada. Using typed transcripts of the registers in the Alabama Department of Archives and History that were prepared by the Work Projects Administration, Winston De Ville prepared an alphabetical list of the names of colonists in the Mobile area, showing their names, occupations, names of wives, names and dates of birth of children, dates of burial, names of Indian slaves, sometimes the places of birth, and the dates of marriage. Most were soldiers and natives of France and Switzerland.[6] A transcription in English of the marriage record has been published.[7] This publication also contains a list of landholders in West Florida, 1766–1770, drawn from Elias Durnford's map of 1772.[8]

6 / De Ville, *Gulf Coast Colonials*, 17–64.

7 / Jacqueline O. Vidrine, *Love's Legacy. The Mobile Marriages Recorded in French, Transcribed, with Annotated Abstracts in English, 1724–1786* (Lafayette, La., 1985).

8 / *Ibid.*, 396–401.

IV

The Records of Missouri

18

History and Government

Under both the French and the Spanish, Upper Louisiana formed part of the province of Louisiana. Because settlement progressed slowly in this remote region, at the time of the transfer to the Spanish there were only two settlements—Ste. Geneviève and St. Louis. In the fall of 1765, Louis St. Ange de Bellerive surrendered Fort de Chartres on the east bank of the Mississippi River to a British officer and crossed the river to St. Louis. In 1767, Captain Francisco Riu, on orders from Governor Antonio de Ulloa of Louisiana, built Fort Carlos at the mouth of the Missouri River. He was replaced there in March, 1769, by Lieutenant Pedro Piernas. On the instructions of General Alexandro O'Reilly, who took possession at New Orleans in August, 1769, for the Spanish, Lieutenant Piernas took over from St. Ange at St. Louis on May 20, 1770.[1]

In March, 1770, Governor O'Reilly established the office of lieutenant governor of Upper Louisiana, including St. Louis, Ste. Geneviève, and the district of Illinois. Possessed of executive, judicial, and military authority, the lieutenant governor was the superior of the post commandants, conducted relations with the Indians, issued trade permits, and made land grants. New Madrid on the Mississippi River in southeastern Missouri was subordinate to the governor at New Orleans until 1799, when it was placed under the authority of St. Louis.[2]

Under the Spanish, new settlements were made at St. Charles, Cape Girardeau, and New Madrid; these, together with Ste. Geneviève and St. Louis, became administrative districts. The commandants of these dis-

---

1 / Louis Houck, *A History of Missouri, from the Earliest Explorations and Settlements Until the Admission of the State into the Union* (Chicago, 1908, II, 42–43, 49, 194.

2 / *Ibid.*, I, 298, 347, II, 195–99.

tricts exercised civil and military duties. Small detachments of the stationary regiment of Louisiana served at St. Louis and Ste. Geneviève, and militia augmented the military forces. *Syndics* appointed by the commandants tried matters coming within their jurisdiction; arbitration was also used to settle minor disputes. Notaries and recorders assisted in record keeping. The local records were in charge of the commandants.[3]

After taking possession at New Orleans in November, 1803, the American commissioners pressed Pierre Clément de Laussat, the French commissioner, for an order to effect the transfer of St. Louis and the other posts in Upper Louisiana. Laussat obtained a letter from the Marquis de Casa Calvo and Manuel de Salcedo, the Spanish commissioners, dated December 30, 1803, for the transfer of Louisiana, authorizing Carlos DeHault DeLassus, commandant at St. Louis, to make the transfer. He enclosed it in a letter of his own to DeLassus, in which he commissioned Captain Amos Stoddard, U.S. Army commander at Kaskaskia, as his agent.[4] According to the instructions of the Spanish commissioners, inventories were to be prepared of the archives and receipts were to be required for those given up. On January 24, 1804, these orders and others they themselves prepared were dispatched by General James Wilkinson and William C. C. Claiborne to Stoddard, who was to act as military and civil governor after assuming authority for the United States.[5] Captain Stoddard forwarded the orders he had received for DeLassus on February 18, and on February 25 he arrived at St. Louis with a small command. On March 9, 1804, he took possession for France and on the following day for the United States.[6]

The records of St. Louis and those of other posts in Upper Louisiana were transferred to American custody soon after the transfer of authority to the United States. On the day that he turned over St. Louis to Stoddard, DeLassus issued a circular to the commandants of the posts, informing them of the change of government and instructing them in regard to the archives. The commandants were soon called upon to surrender their posts and the public archives. At. St. Louis, Stoddard rented a house for the security of the records and the transaction of business, also employing Marie Pierre Leduc, the former secretary of DeLassus. With instructions to take with him correspondence not relating to land, DeLassus left St. Louis with its administrative records by boat on Novem-

3 / *Ibid.*, I, 343–48, 359–60, 379, II, 197–99, 203.
4 / *Ibid.*, II, 356–57.
5 / Wilkinson to the secretary of war, January 23, 1804, in Carter (ed.), *Territory of Orleans*, 168–71.
6 / Houck, *History of Missouri*, II, 358.

ber 16, 1804. As he descended the Mississippi, he picked up records at Ste. Geneviève, Cape Girardeau, and New Madrid, arriving at New Orleans on January 18, 1805.[7] He delivered the correspondence and other papers of the archives of St. Louis and its dependencies, together with an inventory of May 24, 1805, of the whole, to Casa Calvo.[8] These records were shipped with those of the governors of Louisiana to Pensacola, and eventually they became part of the Papeles de Cuba in the Archivo General de Indias at Seville.

7 / *Ibid.*, II, 363–69.
8 / Hill, *Descriptive Catalogue*, xxxviii.

19

?➔

Archival Reproductions, Documentary
Publications, and Manuscripts

The first historian to obtain extensive reproductions from Spanish archives relating to Missouri was Louis Houck, a lawyer and railroad builder
who was a resident of Cape Girardeau. After selling his interest in the
railroad in 1902, he was able to devote himself to writing a history of Missouri during the Spanish and territorial periods. In order to accomplish
this task, he needed transcripts of documents from Spanish archives. On
his request, James A. Robertson, a specialist in Romance languages who
had worked in the Spanish archives, arranged for the procurement of
transcripts from the Archivo General de Indias at Seville. José González
Verger, the assistant chief of the archive, supervised the copying from the
Papeles de Cuba, *legajos* 2357 to 2368. Translations of the documents were
made by and under the supervision of Robertson. Houck eventually gave
the transcripts to the Missouri Historical Society.[1] Typed copies of some
of the transcripts were prepared for the Wisconsin State Historical Society, which had earlier procured copies from the French Archives des
Colonies. Houck's transcripts have been superseded by the more reliable
photographic reproductions available in Louisiana repositories and in the
Manuscript Division of the Library of Congress.

Early in the nineteenth century the Missouri Historical Society at St.
Louis obtained transcripts from the Papeles de Cuba prepared for it by
the officials of the Archivo General de Indias. This small collection of five
hundred pages includes ministerial instructions, correspondence, memorials, reports of exploring and military expeditions, and materials on the

---

1 / William T. Doherty, Jr., *Louis Houck: Missouri Historian and Entrepreneur* (Columbia,
Mo., [1960]), 98–112.

intrigues of American and Spanish officials in the Mississippi Valley.[2] The Society also has photographic copies of dispatches of the Spanish governors of Louisiana, 1768–1791, obtained from the Carnegie Institution of Washington, D.C. Microreproductions from French and Spanish archives are also in the Western Historical Manuscripts Collection at the University of Missouri.

In 1909, Louis Houck, historian of Missouri, published at his own expense a two-volume compilation of documents. This publication contains the English texts for documents dated from 1767 to 1803, presented in chronological order. The variety of documents gives information on affairs in Upper Louisiana, including administration and defense, Indian trade and affairs, the fur trade, militia, exploration, American military activities, settlement, products, mining, and ecclesiastical affairs. Inventories of records of different dates for the various settlements show the development of the archives. Censuses of settlements and rosters of militia companies supply data on individuals.[3]

In 1946 the St. Louis Historical Documents Foundation was organized to publish manuscripts relating to the colonial history of St. Louis. Some St. Louis historians became its officers: Charles E. Peterson, president, John F. McDermott, secretary, and the Reverend John F. Bannon, S. J., treasurer. Joseph Desloge, a St. Louis capitalist, subsidized the foundation's publications.[4] Abraham P. Nasatir, a professor at San Diego State Teachers College, using the reproductions he had obtained in earlier years from French and Spanish archives, other reproductions in the Library of Congress and the Missouri Historical Society, and original documents in the last-named repository, prepared an extensive collection of English translations of documents relating to the exploration and topography of the Missouri Valley, the Indian policy of the Spanish government, trade rivalry, Indian relations, relations with the clergy, and other subjects.[5]

Few other documents concerning Upper Louisiana have been published. Pursuant to an instruction from Governor O'Reilly, an oath of allegiance to Spain was taken on November 19, 1769, by the inhabitants on the upper Mississippi. The text of the oath and the signatures or marks of the inhabitants are in print. Censuses taken in 1791 of the inhabitants of St. Louis, Ste. Geneviève, and Carondelet show for each settlement the

---

2 / Houck, *History of Missouri*, I, viii.

3 / Louis Houck (ed.), *The Spanish Regime in Missouri* (Chicago, 1909).

4 / *Missouri Historical Society Bulletin*, III (October, 1946–July, 1947), 77–78.

5 / Abraham P. Nasatir (trans. and ed.), *Before Lewis and Clark: Documents Illustrating the History of Missouri, 1785–1804* (St. Louis, 1952).

names of the inhabitants and the number of white men and women. Each list is followed by compiled supplementary data on each man, including the names of his parents, his father's place of residence, the name of his wife, the time and place of his death, and the place of his burial.[6]

Since the admission of Missouri as a state in 1820, the Office of the Secretary of State has been the custodian of the legislative and executive records of the state. These were kept in unsatisfactory conditions in the capitol, where extensive losses were suffered from fires.[7] A state records act of 1965 established a records management and archives survey in the Office of the Secretary of State. Aside from land records that were transferred from federal land offices, from the recorder of land titles at St. Louis, and from the surveyor general, the secretary of state has no records pertaining to the eighteenth century.[8] No microreproductions have been obtained from French and Spanish archival repositories in Europe, and no documentary publications have been prepared.

The official records of French and Spanish Missouri can be supplemented by extensive collections of manuscripts in repositories in that state and elsewhere. The most important collector of manuscripts is the Missouri Historical Society. Founded in 1866, the society developed slowly with the support of a small number of loyal members. It acquired its own building in 1886 and in 1913 occupied the Jefferson Memorial Building, which had been constructed for its use at the site of the main entrance to the grounds of the World's Fair of 1904.[9] The society's collections have been acquired largely since that time. Because neither the society nor most other repositories in Missouri have published guides to their collections, data has to be gleaned from a variety of sources.

The New Madrid archives of the Missouri Historical Society include letters from the Baron Francisco Hector de Carondelet and his successors to Thomas Portell and Carlos DeHault DeLassus, commandants at New Madrid, May 14, 1792–July 15, 1798, to Henri Peyroux, October 19, 1798–November 24, 1801, and to Jean Lavallée, February 1, 20, 1804. Letters and private papers of the Reverend Pierre Gibault, 1761–1804, comprising thirty-four items, are another holding in the New Madrid archives, placed

6 / Henry P. Dart (ed.), "The Oath of Allegiance to Spain," *Louisiana Historical Quarterly*, IV (April, 1921), 205–15; Alice D. Forsyth, "The Spanish Regime in Missouri—(Part I—Saint Geneviéve) (Part II—Saint Louis) Upper Louisiana," *New Orleans Genesis*, XIV (March, June, September, 1975), 116–22, 267–71, 357–64.

7 / Posner, *American State Archives*, 164–65.

8 / Missouri, Office of the Secretary of State, *A Guide to the Missouri State Archives, 1975* (Jefferson City, 1975), 7–11.

9 / George R.Brooks, "The First Century of the Missouri Historical Society," *Missouri Historical Society Bulletin*, XXII (April, 1966), 274–301.

in the hands of the commandant there at the time of Gibault's death.[10] Jean Gabriel Cerré, a trader at Kaskaskia from 1704 on, sent hunters to the Missouri River and continued in the fur trade after his removal in 1780 to St. Louis, where he also became a *syndic*. Papers of Cerré are in the holdings of the Missouri Historical Society.

Another fur trading company based in St. Louis was that of the Chouteaus, including Auguste Chouteau, who founded the company in 1764 with Pierre Laclède de Liguest, a Frenchman who moved up from New Orleans, Pierre Chouteau, Pierre Chouteau, Jr., and René Chouteau. The extensive collection of Chouteau business and family papers dating from 1752 in the Missouri Historical Society Collections includes correspondence, diaries, bills, accounts, inventories, contracts of engagements, bills of lading, ledgers, and other business papers.[11] The Chouteaus traded not only with Indians west and northwest of Missouri but also with merchants in Canada and Louisiana. Auguste Chouteau became a considerable landowner and engaged in stock raising. He was a slave owner and a militia officer. The papers of Jacques Clamorgan, a St. Louis merchant who was elected director of the Missouri Company, which promoted trade with the Indians on the Missouri River, are in the Missouri Historical Society Collections and the Bancroft Library of the University of California. Carlos DeHault DeLassus, a native of Lille, France, entered the Spanish military service and was sent to Louisiana, where he served as commandant at New Madrid from 1796 to 1799 and as lieutenant governor at St. Louis from 1799 to 1804. An extensive collection of his and family papers date from 1758. Some papers of Manuel Gayoso de Lemos are held by the society.[12] Documents from the society's collections were used by Nasatir in his compilation on the Missouri River.

The society's holdings include other trader's papers. Charles Gratiot, a native of Switzerland, moved to Cahokia in 1777 and thence in 1780 to St. Louis, where he engaged in the fur trade and filled positions in the town government. His papers include an account book, 1777–1784, and letter books, 1769–1797, which have been edited as a doctoral dissertation.[13] Pierre Laclède de Liguest, a native of the south of France, was educated at the military academy at Toulouse, came to New Orleans in 1755,

10 / Historical Records Survey, Missouri, *Early Missouri Archives (New Madrid, 1791–1804, Vol. II* (St. Louis, 1942), 20–26.

11 / Mary B. Cunningham and Jeanne C. Blythe, *The Founding Family of St. Louis* (St. Louis, 1977), 3; *National Union Catalog of Manuscripts,* 1964, entry 313.

12 / Holmes, *Gayoso,* 289; *National Union Catalog of Manuscripts,* 1964, entry 334.

13 / Warren L. Barnhart, "The Letterbooks of Charles Gratiot, Fur Trader: The Nomadic Years, 1769–1797" (Ph.D. dissertation, St. Louis University, 1972).

and formed a partnership there with Gilberto Antonio de St. Maxent to engage in trade with the Indians of the Missouri country, later moving to St. Louis.[14] A small collection of Laclède papers date from 1769. Other Laclède papers are in the Chateau Bedous in the south of France. Manuel Lisa, a native of New Orleans, became a merchant there as a young man but soon moved his business to St. Louis. A small collection of his papers for the years 1772–1820 is particularly useful for his early years in St. Louis.[15] Some papers of Kenneth MacKenzie, an associate of the Chouteaus, also concern his land holdings. Pierre Menard, another associate of the Chouteaus, took the oath of allegiance to the Spanish government at New Madrid in 1795. His papers, dating from 1796 to 1826, also include some papers of his agent, Jean Adrien Langlois. The papers of Benito Vasquez, fur trader and captain of militia at St. Louis, also concern the family's land holdings. Besides the papers of individual fur traders, the Missouri Historical Society has an extensive collection of other materials on the fur trade, including agreements and correspondence between traders, explorers, frontier guides, and businessmen.[16]

A variety of other materials are also held by the Missouri Historical Society. The Vallé family papers, dating from 1742, include items concerning François Vallé, a Canadian who became commandant at Ste. Geneviève in 1762 and engaged in iron mining.[17] A collection of Missouri governors' papers includes some papers of Spanish lieutenant governors. Papers on Indians contain items on the Spanish period, as do collections on the militia and slavery. Papers of Captain Amos Stoddard, 1762–1813, containing sixty items, include his correspondence of 1803 and 1804 with Laussat, the French commissioner, and DeLassus, the lieutenant governor at St. Louis, on the transfer of that and other posts to the United States.[18] Documents relating to the transfer, November 7, 1803–September 30, 1804, are in print.[19] John B. C. Lucas, who was appointed judge and land commissioner in the territory in 1805, is represented by a collection dating from 1754. Wilson Price Hunt papers, 1758–1949, containing two hundred items, relate to land in St. Louis and its vicinity. Land papers, dating from 1766, include land grants, petitions, and surveys.

14 / Cunningham and Blythe, *Founding Family*, 3.
15 / Richard E. Oglesby, *Manuel Lisa and the Opening of the Fur Trade* (Norman, Okla., 1963), 221.
16 / *National Union Catalog of Manuscripts*, 1976, entry 237, 1965, entry 690.
17 / *Ibid.*, 1976, entry 236.
18 / *Ibid.*, 1973, entry 166.
19 / "Transfer of Upper Louisiana, Papers of Captain Amos Stoddard," Missouri Historical Society *Glimpses of the Past*, II (May–September, 1935), 76–122.

Other repositories in Missouri and elsewhere also have collections of papers. Moses Austin, a Connecticut Yankee who had had some experience in lead mining on the New River in Virginia, moved to the Ste. Geneviève district of Missouri in 1797, obtained a land grant from Governor Carondelet, and started mining lead at Mine à Breton. From his own smelter he shipped shot and sheet lead to New Orleans and Cuba. His papers in the University of Texas Library include correspondence and other documents of the years 1797–1805 with DeLassus and Antoine Soulard.[20] The materials relating to Auguste Chouteau in the St. Louis Mercantile Library are his journal of 1762 and 1763 relating to the founding of St. Louis and papers of 1787–1819, comprising forty-two items, including correspondence with Louisiana officials. An extensive collection of the papers of Pierre Menard in the Illinois State Historical Library in Springfield, Illinois, dates from 1780 and contains letters of other Missouri traders.[21] Other Menard papers, 1748–1800, comprising one hundred items, are held by the Chicago Historical Society. The Charles F. Gunther Collection, also held by the Chicago Historical Society, contains letters of some Spanish officials and traders of Missouri, including DeLassus, Francisco Cruzat, Pierre Laclède, Thomas Portell, and Pedro Piernas.

Correspondence of George Morgan relating to the colony he founded at New Madrid, 1788–1790, is in the Illinois Historical Survey Collections of the University of Illinois and in the Library of Congress, Manuscript Division.[22] Copies of this correspondence were obtained by Louis Houck and published.[23]

The State Historical Society of Missouri was organized in 1898 and has been housed in the University of Missouri Library at Columbia. It did not have a manuscripts department until the 1930s, and the guide to manuscript depositories published by the Historical Records Survey in 1940 listed no materials on the colonial period.

20 / Eugene C. Barker (ed.), *The Austin Papers*, American Historical Association, *Annual Report*, [1919] (Washington, 1924), II, pts. 1 and 2.
21 / *National Union Catalog of Manuscripts*, 1962, entry 40.
22 / *Ibid.*, 1978, entry 1744.
23 / Houck, *Spanish Regime in Missouri*, I, 275–99.

20

❧

Records of Local Jurisdictions

An act of Congress of March 26, 1804, set up the Louisiana Purchase into the Orleans Territory and established the part north of the 33rd degree of latitude as the Louisiana District, making it subordinate to the governor of the Indiana Territory. Captain Amos Stoddard continued in charge of civil affairs at St. Louis, and Major James Bruff arrived to take over the military command on July 1, 1804. The commandants of the districts and other Spanish officials were continued in office. Governor William Henry Harrison of the Indiana Territory issued a proclamation on October 1, 1804, dividing the Louisiana District into the five districts of St. Charles, St. Louis, Ste. Geneviève, Cape Girardeau, and New Madrid and describing their boundaries. These districts continued in existence after the creation of the Territory of Louisiana by the act of March 3, 1805.[1] On October 1, 1812, the newly established Missouri Territory was divided by Governor Benjamin Howard into five counties to which were given the names of the previous districts. During the territorial period these large counties were reduced in size by the creation of new counties from them.[2]

Ste. Geneviève District.   Ste. Geneviève was founded about 1725 by Frenchmen who moved across the Mississippi River from Kaskaskia. It was named for the French saint who is the patroness of Paris. The village was gradually eaten away by the river, and by the 1790s it had been completely removed to a site three miles farther north. The district was settled

1 / 2 *Statutes* 287–89; Clarence E. Carter (ed.), *The Territory of Louisiana-Missouri, 1803–1821* (Washington, D.C., 1943–51), XIII, 51–52, vols. XIII–XV of Carter (ed.), *The Territorial Papers of the United States*, 26 vols.; 3 *Statutes* 331–32.

2 / Floyd C. Shoemaker, *Missouri and Missourians: Land of Contrasts and People of Achievements* (Chicago, 1943), I, 225–28.

by Frenchmen from Canada, other Frenchmen who moved across the Mississippi River after the Revolutionary War, and by Englishmen from Maryland, Virginia, and Pennsylvania. The Spanish established a fort with a small garrison. In 1804 the village had fifty houses and a population of about 250. The bounds of the district were Apple Creek on the south, the Meramec River on the north, the Mississippi on the east, and to the west as far as the Louisiana Territory extended. Parts of the county of Ste. Geneviève created in 1812 were later formed into Washington, Iron, Madison, Perry, and St. Francis counties.[3]

On bluffs near Ste. Geneviève, some French royalist refugees from Gallipolis on the Ohio River established New Bourbon in 1793. Approving this enterprise, Governor Carondelet appointed as its commandant Pierre DeHault DeLassus de Luziere, who remained in the position until the transfer to the United States in 1804. An inventory of the documents of the post was prepared on March 16, 1804.[4] Not able to compete with nearby Ste. Geneviève, New Bourbon gradually disappeared.

At the time of the transfer of Ste. Geneviève to the United States in March, 1804, an inventory of the records that passed to the custody of the local authorities was prepared.[5] These records were deposited with the Missouri Historical Society in three groups, the first coming in 1916. They contained around three thousand documents for the period 1761–1854. These records have been translated, transcribed by typewriter, microfilmed, and indexed by the society and the National Youth Administration.[6] Renewed interest in the archives of Ste. Geneviève resulted from the formation in 1967 of the Foundation for the Restoration of Ste. Geneviève. To promote that undertaking, the Ste. Geneviève archives have been returned to the county. Microfilm of these archives is in the library of the State Historical Society (through which arrangements can be made for copies), the University of Missouri Library, the Missouri State Archives, and the library of Southeast Missouri State University at Cape Girardeau. St. Louis University has translations, transcriptions, and microfilm.

The archives of Ste. Geneviève, 1723–1803, consist of a variety of documents listed by types in an inventory, along with the names of the parties concerned and the dates. The collection includes marriage contracts, marriage certificates, concessions of land granted by the commandants,

3 / Lucille Basler, *The District of Ste. Geneviève, 1725–1980* (Greenfield, Mo., 1980), 1, 5–6.
4 / Houck, *History of Missouri*, I, 363–65; Hill, *Descriptive Catalogue*, xxxvii.
5 / Hill, *Descriptive Catalogue*, xxxvii.
6 / Robert E. Parkin, *Parkin's Guide to Tracing Your Family Tree in Missouri* (St. Louis, 1979), 8.

and deeds and indentures for land and buildings; land transactions, including renunciations and relinquishments, exchanges of property, mortgages, surveys and plans, public sales of real estate, and mines; Louisiana transfer papers; bills of sale for personalty, etc.; notices of sales; oaths of allegiance; powers of attorney, appointments, agreements, contracts, etc.; engagé bonds, notes and obligations, miscellaneous receipts, statements of accounts, and receipts; litigations; bills of sale for slaves, slave emancipations; exchanges and mortgages, inquests, and ordinances; gifts, letters, inquests, estate papers, including inventories, sales, and emancipations of minors; and wills. Alphabetical lists of the names of persons in the different types of documents and the dates are in the Historical Records Survey inventory. Bound manuscripts include a record of a court of inquiry, 1766–1767; a register of hearings, Robinet, notary, 1766–1769; papers of Jean Baptiste Vallé, delivered to Olivier, 1766–1803. Other listings include miscellaneous, marriages, mortgages, and sales, 1799–1800.[7]

St. Louis District. In the spring of 1764 the Louisiana Fur Company set up a trading post on the high bluffs on the west bank of the Mississippi River below the mouth of the Missouri. That company had been formed by Pierre Laclède de Liguest and Gilberto Antonio de St. Maxent after they obtained from Governor Kerlérec the monopoly of trade with the Indians on the Missouri River. Laclède, the leader of the company's employees, named the settlement St. Louis in honor of King Louis IX.[8] In 1765 after the British assumed control in Illinois, Louis St. Ange de Bellerive, the commandant at Fort de Chartres, Joseph Lefebvre, the attorney, and Joseph Labuxiere, the notary, removed to St. Louis. The names of early inhabitants of St. Louis can be ascertained from the signatures of an oath of allegiance to Spain subscribed to on November 19, 1769.[9] An inventory of the archives of St. Louis for the period from April, 1766, to May 2, 1770, when the Spanish assumed sovereignty included 194 documents.[10] An inventory dated March 10, 1804, was also prepared of the documents that were transferred to the United States.[11] Dated from 1766

7 / Historical Records Survey, Missouri, *Early Missouri Archives, [Volume I, Ste. Geneviève, St. Charles]* (St. Louis, 1941), 1–75.

8 / Houck, *History of Missouri*, II, 7–8.

9 / Henry P. Dart (ed.), "The Oath of Allegiance to Spain," *Louisiana Historical Quarterly*, IV (April, 1921), 205–15.

10 / Frederick L. Billon, *Annals of St. Louis in Its Early Days Under the French and Spanish Dominations, 1764–1804* (St. Louis, 1886), 94–95. Inventories of May 19, 1775, November 27, 1787, and 1799 are printed in Louis Houck (ed.), *Spanish Regime in Missouri*, I, 126–30, 258–64, II, 261–67; those of November 27, 1787, July 20, 1792, and December 26, 1799, are listed in Hill, *Descriptive Catalogue*, xxxv, xxxvii.

11 / Hill, *Descriptive Catalogue*, xxxv, xxxvii.

to 1804, they comprised 2,985 documents. When the United States took possession, the St. Louis district included all the territory between the Missouri and Meramec rivers, extending indefinitely to the west.

Under an ordinance adopted by the St. Louis City Council on July 16, 1912, the colonial archives of St. Louis were deposited with the Missouri Historical Society in St. Louis. For the period from 1766 to 1804, the collection included more than 3,000 documents, including deeds, marriage contracts, wills, inventories, mortgage books, compacts, powers of attorney, sales of property, and miscellaneous documents. The society arranged the records in folders in steel filing cases. The collection documents the personal and business transactions of the early residents of St. Louis and the early history and exploration of the area. An index to the marriage contracts, 1764–1804, is in print.[12] Arranged alphabetically by the name of the groom, it also shows the names of the bride and the parents, prior and current places of residence, the property settlement, and other personal information.

Transcriptions, translations, and microfilm of the early records of St. Louis are in various repositories. Transcriptions and translations prepared by Edward Barry in the 1850s are in the recorder's office in St. Louis. Some copies of documents dating from 1764 in the St. Louis archives, including the diary of Carlos DeHault DeLassus, 1764–1842, and typewritten copies of translations of St. Louis archives from 1767, prepared by Ysabel C. Sandoval and Joseph Wheless in 1907–1918, are in the Washington University Library.[13] A miscellaneous collection of papers of the lieutenant governors and commandants of Upper Louisiana dating from 1725 is in the repository of the Missouri Historical Society.

Other settlements in the St. Louis district included Florissant, St. André, and Carondelet. Florissant, called San Fernando de Florissant by the Spanish, was settled in the 1780s fourteen miles northwest of St. Louis and in the late 1790s had a population made up of Creoles, Canadians, and Americans, all engaged in agriculture. Documents on Florissant dating from 1790 and consisting in part of typewritten transcripts are deposited with the Missouri Historical Society, which also has microfilm.[14] Other transcripts concerning Florissant are at St. Louis University. St. André (San André del Misury), a new collection of settlers near the mouth of the Missouri River, was placed on October 1, 1798, under the

12 / *Missouri Historical Society Collections*, IV (1912), 121; Historical Records Survey, Missouri, *Guide to Depositories of Manuscript Collections in the United States: Missouri* (St. Louis, 1940), 10; *National Union Catalog of Manuscripts*, 1973, entry 160; St. Louis Genealogical Society, *StLGS Index of St. Louis Marriages, 1804–1876* (St. Louis, [1973]), iii–iv.
13 / *National Union Catalog of Manuscripts*, 1977, entry 1296.
14 / *Ibid.*, 1965, entry 1495.

command of James Mackay, a former trader on the Missouri River. Carondelet was adopted as the name of the settlement that developed on the Mississippi below St. Louis after Clément Delor de Treget was given a grant of land near the mouth of the Rivière des Pères. Pedro de Treget succeeded his father as commandant of the village, which was eventually absorbed by St. Louis.[15]

St. Charles District. The district of St. Charles was located between the left bank of the Missouri River and the right bank of the Mississippi. Besides the village of St. Charles, founded in 1780 on the left bank of the Missouri about twenty-six miles above its mouth, there was the settlement of Portage des Sioux, founded in 1799 on the Mississippi by Creoles and Canadians. By the time of the American acquisition, most of the inhabitants were immigrants from the United States.[16] Howard County, formed in 1816, took over part of St. Charles.

The early records of St. Charles County were deposited with the Missouri Historical Society in November, 1909, by order of the county court. The notarial archives of the St. Charles district, 1790–1804 (some of later date, up to 1832), include property deeds, marriage contracts, land concessions, mortgages, litigation papers, sales and emancipations of slaves, agreements and contracts, public sales and inventories, receipts, wills, estate papers, documents relating to lead and iron mines, and miscellaneous papers.[17] The names of the parties involved and the dates of the transactions are given in the inventory. Transcriptions and translations of the St. Charles archives, 1790–1806, are in the Missouri Historical Society Collections. Use of these materials is facilitated through an index.

Cape Girardeau District. In 1793, Louis Lorimier, an Indian trader and partisan, by permission of Governor Francisco de Carondelet settled with some Delaware and Shawnee Indians on a rock ledge on the Mississippi, 150 miles south of St. Louis. Lorimier served as the commandant, but no fort was built there. American families soon began settling in the district, and by 1804 the majority of the population was American in origin. Barthélemi Cousin served as secretary and interpreter for Lorimier and was also a deputy surveyor. Named after a French officer, the Sieur de Girardot, the district was bounded on the north by Apple Creek and on the south by Typwappity Bottoms.[18]

15 / Houck, *History of Missouri*, II, 245, 249, 363, 64, 233, 363.
16 / *Ibid.*, II, 79.
17 / Historical Records Survey, Missouri, *Early Missouri Archives*, I, 76–87.
18 / Houck, *History of Missouri*, II, 167–88.

The Historical Records Survey found records of Cape Girardeau in the vault in the county clerk's office. These included last wills and testaments, 1801–1805, in one volume of twenty pages, and a probate court record, 1801–1805, also in one volume of twenty pages. Other early records were reported to be in various county offices. At that time, unbound official papers formed part of the holdings of the Cape Girardeau County Historical Society.[19] Microfilm of the Cape Girardeau archives is in the Missouri Historical Society repository.

New Madrid District. In 1788, George Morgan, who had been a trader for Baynton & Wharton in the Illinois country and later a United States Indian agent during the Revolutionary War, was given a large concession west of the Mississippi River by Diego Gardoqui, the Spanish ambassador in the United States. The grant extended nearly three hundred miles from Cinque Hommes (now St. Como in Perry County, Missouri) south to the mouth of the St. Francis River in Arkansas. Leaving a farm in New Jersey on which he had been living, Morgan recruited a party of settlers and led them in 1789 to a point on a bend in the Mississippi River in southeastern Missouri; there he founded a village, which he named New Madrid. Governor Esteban Miró of Louisiana did not approve the concession but allowed the settlement to proceed and sent Lieutenant Pierre Foucher to erect a post there. Morgan soon lost interest and returned to the East via New Orleans. Some of the settlers left, but a steady stream of Americans began arriving.[20] W. C. C. Claiborne, when descending the Mississippi in the fall of 1801, found that though the fort had been destroyed by fire, a few soldiers were still there.

The post of New Madrid was surrendered by Juan Lavallée, the commandant, to Captain Daniel Bissell, Captain Stoddard's agent, on March 18, 1804. A March 20, 1804, inventory of the records that were transferred is in print and lists a total of 1,358 pieces for the period 1791–1804.[21] Through the efforts of Louis Houck, formerly a lawyer of Cape Girardeau and a historian of Missouri, the New Madrid County court adopted an order in February, 1908, transferring the early archives of the county to

19 / Historical Records Survey, Missouri, *Early Missouri Archives*, I, 88, 93.

20 / Houck, *History of Missouri*, II, 108–28; Max Savelle, *George Morgan, Colony Builder* (New York, 1932), 203–22; *National Union Catalog of Manuscripts*, 1966, entry 1920; Philip M. Hamer (ed.), *A Guide to Archives and Manuscripts in the United States* (New Haven, 1961).

21 / *National Union Catalog of Manuscripts*, 1962, entry 1978, 1978, entry 1744, published as "Narrative of the Founding of St. Louis," in John McDermott (ed.), *Early Histories of the Founding of St. Louis* (St. Louis, 1952), 45–59, and published as "Chouteau's Journal of the Founding of St. Louis," in French and English in *Missouri Historical Society Collections*, III (1911), 349–66.

the Missouri Historical Society in St. Louis. The records had already been arranged and bound by Houck. The Historical Records Survey found that the eleven volumes in the collection contained 1,432 instruments, some consisting of many parts. The survey published an alphabetical list of the types of documents in the collection, showing the inclusive dates and the number of pieces for each type. These types included acknowledgments of debts, agreements, baptisms, burial and death certificates, contracts, contracts of lease, donations, estates, exchanges of property, letters and private papers of Carondelet, DeLassus, Gayoso de Lemos, and Trudeau, letters and accounts of Father Pierre Gibault, letters and private papers of Joseph Lamoureux, litigation papers, marriage contracts, mortgages and sureties, petitions, powers of attorney, promissory notes, public sales, receipts, sales, slave sales, slave emancipations, warranty deeds and deeds of sale, and wills. The number of pieces in each category of document is shown in another list prepared by the Historical Records Survey.[22]

Papers of George Morgan, 1775–1822, containing forty-three items, in the Library of Congress, Manuscript Division, were received at different times from members of the Morgan family. The collection includes official and personal correspondence and relates in part to the settlement he promoted on the west bank of the Mississippi that became New Madrid.

22 / Houck (ed.), *Spanish Regime in Missouri*, I, 274–99.

21

ใ๊

Land Records

Under the authority bestowed on them by the governor of Louisiana, the French commandants in Upper Louisiana made grants of land in the royal domain. These grants were made at Ste. Geneviève and at St. Louis and vicinity.[1] Between 1766 and 1770, St. Ange de Bellerive granted eighty-one lots in St. Louis, each one arpent in front and forty arpents in depth, adjacent to the common fields that were cultivated by the settlers. The commandant lacked the authority to grant titles; he merely made assignments to the occupants. When Lieutenant Governor Pedro Piernas assumed authority for the Spanish in Missouri in 1770, he confirmed the grants that had been made by the French. With the authority of subdelegates, the commandants at St. Louis and New Madrid could make grants, and the governor general of Louisiana made some directly.[2]

The Spanish made free concessions of land in Missouri, charging only for surveys, the wages of chainmen and axmen, and plats. Concessions were supposed to be confirmed by the governor general, or later by the intendant of Louisiana, but because of the expense involved, few settlers obtained complete titles. Some grants were made verbally without any written instruments. The abundance of land and the practice of being able to hold, sell, or bequeath it without complete titles promoted carelessness regarding titles.[3]

The villagers of Upper Louisiana were provided with common fields for cultivation, in which they were assigned narrow strips with small frontages and great depths. The villages were also assigned commons

---

1 / Shoemaker, *Missouri and Missourians*, I, 194–95.

2 / Houck, *History of Missouri*, II, 217.

3 / E. M. Violette, "Spanish Land Claims in Missouri," *Washington University Studies*, VIII (Humanistic Series, no. 2) (April, 1921), 171–75.

that were used for grazing and the procurement of firewood. Large grants of land made by the governor general included seven thousand arpents at Cape Girardeau to Louis Lorimier, the Indian agent, ten thousand arpents in that district to Jacques St. Vrain, and concessions for lead mining to Moses Austin and Christopher Hay. James Mackay was rewarded for his 1795 voyage of discovery up the Missouri River with a grant at St. André. Auguste Chouteau, prominent trader, received a large grant on the Missouri for a country residence and another north of St. Louis for a farm. Large acquisitions of land by speculators between the date of the treaty of acquisition by the United States in 1803 and its occupation in 1804 caused later difficulties in connection with the adjustment of titles.[4]

During the early years of the Spanish tenure, surveys of land were neither regularly nor carefully made. From 1770 to 1772, Martin M. Duralde surveyed lots in St. Louis, and in 1780 Auguste Chouteau prepared a map of that town on which are shown the names of landowners.[5] A map of St. Louis prepared by René Paul in 1823 for the city shows the names of landowners.[6] The commandants of each district selected surveyors to survey lands. In February, 1795, however, Governor Carondelet appointed as surveyor general of Upper Louisiana Antoine Soulard, who settled at St. Louis.[7] Deputies who performed surveys included Joseph Story at New Madrid, Barthélemi Cousin at Cape Girardeau, James Rankin and James Richardson at St. Louis, James Mackay at St. André, and Thomas Maddin at Ste. Geneviève. Silas Bent, the first principal American surveyor in Missouri, reported that the surveys in Upper Louisiana had been executed in a most careless manner.[8]

Use of the Livres Terriens during many years in the office of the recorder of land titles at St. Louis so frayed them that the recorder recommended they be copied. This recommendation was approved on November 16, 1853, and by the following July the copy had been completed.[9]

4 / Houck, History of Missouri, II, 216–17, 226–27, 233; John F. McDermott, "Auguste Chouteau, First Citizen of Upper Louisiana," in John F. McDermott (ed.), Frenchmen and French Ways in the Mississippi Valley (Urbana, Ill., 1969), 6; Lamont K. Richardson, "Private Land Claims in Missouri," Missouri Historical Review, L (January, 1956), 135–37.

5 / Houck, History of Missouri, II, 24, 50, 205.

6 / "St. Louis Real Estate in Review," Missouri Historical Society Glimpses of the Past, IV (October–December, 1937), 122. When this article was published, a copy of Paul's map was in the street commissioner's office in St. Louis.

7 / Amos Stoddard, Sketches, Historical and Descriptive, of Louisiana (1812; rpr. New York, 1973), 249.

8 / Silas Bent to Jared Mansfield, December 21, 1806, in Carter (ed.), Territory of Louisiana-Missouri, XIV, 52.

9 / Adolphe A. Renard to Justin Butterfield, May 12, September 15, November 4, 1851,

After being certified as an exact and faithful copy of the original Livres Terriens, the single-volume transcript became part of the archives of the recorder's office. This volume was sent to the General Land Office in Washington, D.C., in 1866 and still exists.[10]

For certain localities the papers recorded in the Livres Terriens were abstracted in record books prepared by order of Captain Stoddard. On the day of the transfer, he issued a proclamation directing the recording of all grants in the proper offices by May 15 and the filing of original petitions and orders of survey in the offices of the district commandants.[11] Attested copies were to be furnished the claimants filing the original papers. This measure assured a record of the grants and provided a safe depository for the original papers. Five books containing records of grants of land in New Bourbon, Ste. Geneviève, Portage des Sioux, St. Charles, St. André, and New Madrid resulted from this order. For many years these books were in the office of the recorder of land titles at St. Louis.[12]

In addition to the original French and Spanish land records, there are some record books of land titles labelled A, B, C, D, and E, which pertain to the colonial period of Missouri. The act of March 2, 1805, directed the recorder of land titles to record all evidence presented to him of claims to land in the District of Louisiana that had been granted by the French or Spanish governors or settled and cultivated without grants before December 20, 1803. Accordingly, James L. Donaldson began the record in September, 1805, which was continued until 1829.[13]

Other records of the Spanish period are in the custody of the Missouri secretary of state in Jefferson City. These include the following: a register of land surveyed in New Madrid by Joseph Story, 1794–1800, in one volume; a *registre d'arpentage*, Soulard's surveys, 1798–1806, in two volumes, containing plats of survey prepared from field notes for the districts of St. André, Ste. Geneviève, St. Louis, New Bourbon, St. Charles,

---

August 2, 1853, in Miscellaneous Private Land Claims Correspondence, Records of the Bureau of Land Management, RG 49, NA; John Wilson to Adolphe A. Renard, October 15, 1852, November 16, 1853, July 7, 1854, in Letter Book, Private Claims, Nos. 28–30, Records of the Bureau of Land Management, RG 49, NA.

10 / This volume bears the title "Record of Six Livres Terriens with Index" and contains a note to the effect that it was received at the General Land Office with a letter of June 25, 1866, from Frederick Mosberger, recorder of land titles at St. Louis.

11 / Houck, *History of Missouri*, II, 374.

12 / These books are listed in manuscript inventories of the records of that office of June 11, 1830, and May 15, 1845, which are in the Records of the Bureau of Land Management, RG 49, NA.

13 / Adolphe Renard to Justin Butterfield, November 4, 1851, in Miscellaneous Private Land Claims Correspondence, Records of the Bureau of Land Management, RG 49, NA.

New Madrid, and the left bank of the Missouri River.[14] An abstract for St. André from this register has been published and shows for areas larger than three hundred arpents the date and area of each survey, the dates of the orders of survey, and the date on which certified copies were given, 1797–1804.[15] Some of the Spanish certificates of survey, 1794–1803, are accompanied by indentures, wills, and other documents.

Other materials relating to Spanish land grants in Missouri are in manuscript repositories. A collection of Spanish land grants, territorial and state land records, and maps, 1766–1885, containing one thousand items, is in the Missouri Historical Society Collections at St. Louis. A Soulard map of 1795 is in the Newberry Library at Chicago. Documents relating to Soulard's appointments are in the Archivo Nacional de Cuba. Antoine Soulard papers and maps, 1766–1875, comprising one hundred items, also held by the Missouri Historical Society, relate chiefly to his activities as surveyor general. Other land papers dating from 1766 and an extensive collection of maps are in the possession of the State Historical Society of Missouri at Columbia.

The act of Congress of March 2, 1805, required land claimants with grants obtained from the French or Spanish governments in Upper Louisiana before October 1, 1800, to present to the recorder of land titles at St. Louis notices of their claims in writing, together with pertinent documents, which were all to be recorded in books kept for that purpose. The act provided for the appointment of the recorder and of two other persons who, together with the recorder, were to act as a board of land commissioners to consider the land claims. The president appointed James L. Donaldson, the attorney general of the territory, as recorder and John B. C. Lucas, judge of the territorial court, and Clement B. Penrose, a Pennsylvania politician, as commissioners.[16] The act of Congress that established the territories of Louisiana and Orleans nullified all grants of land made in the ceded territories between the Treaty of San Ildefonso of October 1, 1800, and the cession of the territory at New Orleans on December 20, 1803. William C. Carr was designated as the agent to investigate land claims, Charles Gratiot as the clerk, and Philip M. Leduc as the translator.

14 / Survey of Federal Archives, Missouri, *Inventory of Federal Archives in the States, Series VIII, The Department of the Interior, No. 24, Missouri* (St. Louis, 1938), 3; Missouri, Office of the Secretary of State, *A Guide to the Missouri State Archives, 1975* (Jefferson City, 1975), 10.

15 / *American State Papers, Public Lands,* V, 848–65, and *House Documents,* 24th Cong., 1st Sess., No. 270, pp. 149–68, Serial 292.

16 / 2 *Statutes* 323; Richardson, "Private Land Claims in Missouri," 271–72; Shoemaker, *Missouri and Missourians,* I, 199.

The board of land commissioners began hearings at St. Louis on December 1, 1805, to receive evidence presented by claimants and witnesses. These were prolonged by new legislation that liberalized the provisions of the original acts. The act of April 21, 1806, required inhabitation and cultivation for a period of only ten years prior to December 20, 1803, and allowed one or more of the commissioners to conduct sittings at places other than St. Louis.[17] The act of March 3, 1807, lengthened the time for filing claims to July 1, 1808, and stipulated that the commissioners were to deliver to the surveyor general copies of their decisions and to give copies of certificates of patents to the claimants and to the register or recorder of the local land office.[18]

In 1806 one or more of the commissioners also conducted sessions in accordance with the act of 1806 at New Madrid, Ste. Geneviève, and Cape Girardeau. In October, 1806, Donaldson left the territory and was replaced in April, 1807, by Frederick Bates, who had been a land commissioner in the Michigan Territory. In succeeding years the board made circuits of the settlements in the territory to receive and hear evidence concerning claims. When the work of the board was completed in January, 1812, its report was carried to Washington, D.C., by Clement B. Penrose and delivered to the secretary of the treasury on March 20, 1812.[19]

On December 1, 1812, the report was submitted to the House of Representatives by the commissioner of the General Land Office.[20] The report showed that the board had considered 3,340 claims and had confirmed 1,340.[21] Of the claims confirmed, 712 were based on legal concessions, 80 others on orders of survey, 425 on settlement rights, and 123 for having been held in possession for ten years. Most claims were small, for 250 acres or less; only 5 were for more than 500 acres. A list of 101 certificates issued by the commissioners in December, 1808, shows for each certificate the date, the name of the claimant, in whose favor it was issued, the nature of the claims, the name of the water course, the number of acres, the number of arpents, and the district. The reports on individual claims are presented in paragraph form and show the claimant's name, the location of his claim, testimony as to habitation and cultivation, and the deci-

17 / 2 *Statutes* 391–94.
18 / 2 *Statutes* 440–42. A note respecting other legislation on land claims in Missouri Territory is in Carter (ed.), *Territory of Louisiana-Missouri*, 106 n. 32.
19 / Clement B. Penrose to Albert Gallatin, March 20, 1712, in *American State Papers, Public Lands*, II, 447–51. An appropriation of $500 was made by an act of June 12, 1812 (4 *Statutes* 443), to compensate Penrose for conveying the two large volumes to Washington.
20 / *American State Papers, Public Lands*, II, 463–729.
21 / Shoemaker, *Missouri and Missourians*, I, 200.

sion of the commissioners. Certificates of confirmation for 235 claims in the territory (including Arkansas) give the order, the warrant of survey, the claimant's name, the quantity of land, and its location.[22] Data from the commissioners' report of 1812 with indexes of names are in publications issued in 1983.[23] Papers of John B. C. Lucas, one of the early land commissioners, are deposited with the Missouri Historical Society.

An act of Congress of June 13, 1812, confirmed claims to town and village lots and out-lots, common field lots, and commons in, adjoining, and belonging to the several towns or villages of Portage des Sioux, St. Charles, St. Louis, St. Ferdinand, Village à Robert, Carondelet, Ste. Geneviève, New Madrid, New Bourbon, Little Prairie, and Arkansas that had been inhabited prior to December 20, 1803. After the dissolution of the board of land commissioners, the function of ascertaining land titles passed to Frederick Bates, the recorder of land titles. The June 13, 1812, act that confirmed claims to land inhabited prior to December 20, 1803, gave him the same powers in respect to claims filed before December 1, 1812, and in regard to claims that had been filed with the commissioners but had not been decided by them. He was to report to Congress on both types of claims. An act of March 3, 1813, extended to January 1, 1814, the time for filing written evidence or other testimony concerning claims of which notice had already been filed. An act of April 12, 1814, confirmed to residents in the territory those grants actually located or surveyed before March 10, 1814.[24]

Bates made a report to the General Land Office on November 1, 1815, on 312 claims of William Russell, who had taken the claims over from the original owners. A list that accompanied the report shows the names of the original claimants, the locations of the claims, and other data.[25] Only 23 of these claims were confirmed.

The report by Bates on the Missouri Territory land claims was completed on February 2, 1816, and carried by him to Washington, D.C. It contains a report on claims entered under the acts referred to above. It shows by whom the concession was made, the date of survey, the claimant's name, the quantity of land claimed, its location, when ownership started, and the opinion of the recorder on the amount confirmed. A list of certificates shows the certificate number, the quantity of land, the sur-

22 / American State Papers, Public Lands, II, 689–91, 463–688, III, 327–31.
23 / Carolyn Ericson and Frances Ingmire, First Settlers of the Missouri Territory, Volume I, Grants from American State Papers, Class VIII, Public Lands, and First Settlers of the Missouri Territory Containing Grants in the Present States of Missouri, Arkansas, and Oklahoma, Volume II (Nacogdoches, Tex., 1983).
24 / 2 Statutes 748–50, 751–52, 812–14; 3 Statutes 121.
25 / American State Papers, Public Lands, III, 365–70.

vey, the claimant's name, the location, and the opinion of the recorder.[26] Out of a total of 2,555 claims submitted, Bates confirmed 1,746, rejected 801, and gave conditional confirmation to 8.[27] An act of Congress of April 29, 1816, confirmed claims—village claims, grants of the late board of commissioners, and grants and confirmations under the several acts of Congress—reported on favorably by Bates in his reports of November 1, 1815, and February 2, 1816. An act of March 3, 1819, extended the provisions of the act of April 12, 1814, to Howard County.[28] Frederick Bates papers, 1800–1864, comprising 835 items and letter books of 1807–1812, are in the Missouri Historical Society Collections.

In succeeding years, claimants of rejected, illegal, and unauthorized grants, many acquired from early settlers by speculators, pressured Congress through their representatives and by means of memorials to create a new board of land commissioners. An act of July 9, 1832, provided that the recorder of land titles and two commissioners to be appointed by the president were to examine files in the recorder's office that had been founded upon incomplete grants, concessions, warrants, or orders of survey issued by French or Spanish authorities prior to March 10, 1804. A supplementary act of March 2, 1833, extended the provisions of the earlier act to include donations of land held by virtue of settlement and cultivation.[29]

The first report of land commissioners Albert G. Harrison and Lewis F. Linn and recorder Frederick R. Conway was submitted to the General Land Office on November 27, 1833.[30] It contains data on 142 numbered claims, including documents, and tabulations of descriptive information on grants, including the names of claimants and the locations of the claims. There are also minutes of the proceedings of the board—containing statements of claimants and of witnesses and testimony as to the genuineness of signatures—and the opinions of the board as to confirmation. In 1834, Linn left the commission to become a U.S. senator, and Harrison left to become a congressman. They were replaced by James S. Mayfield and James H. Relfe. On December 5, 1834, the commissioners made a report on claims they considered to be entitled to confirmation.[31] This

26 / *Ibid.*, III, 314–65.

27 / Shoemaker, *Missouri and Missourians*, I, 200.

28 / 3 *Statutes* 329, 517.

29 / 4 *Statutes* 565–67, 661–62.

30 / *American State Papers, Public Lands*, VI, 715–901, printed also in *House Documents*, 23rd Cong., 1st Sess., No. 79, Serial 255 and in *House Documents*, 24th Cong., 1st Sess., No. 59, pp. 1–365, Serial 288.

31 / *American State Papers, Public Lands*, VII, 773–907, printed also in *House Documents*, 24th Cong., 1st Sess., No. 59, pp. 366–587, Serial 288, and in *House Documents*, 23rd Cong., 2nd Sess., No. 197, Serial 275.

report was also arranged by claim numbers, from 143 to 255, and it presented evidence from the records of the board, similar to that described above, and copies of Spanish documents. The board's report of September 30, 1835, by James H. Relfe, Falkland H. Martin and Frederick R. Conway, presented similar information on claims 256 to 345, with recommendations in favor of confirmation.[32] A reprint of this document has an index of names, which makes it more useful for research.[33]

For a second class of claims, numbers 1–152, adversely reported on, there are also contemporary documents and minutes of the board of land commissioners.[34] Descriptive information is published about each claim, along with the names of the claimants and the locations of the claims. A collection of opinions and reports respecting land claims in Missouri that were submitted by the board of land commissioners on June 3, 1836, is also in print.[35]

The decisions of the Missouri land commissioners under the acts of 1832 and 1833 that were laid before Congress by the General Land Office were approved with named exceptions by an act of Congress of July 4, 1836.[36] In addition, the act reserved the right of adverse claimants to try the validity of their claims in court. Some of the excepted claims were later approved by special acts of Congress.

In later years efforts were made to secure congressional approval of other disputed land claims in Missouri. A report of the Senate committee on public lands of July 19, 1850, concerns five classes of claims, containing a total of twenty-six claims that were not recommended for confirmation.[37] Congress did not confirm a large number of claims reported on favorably by the commissioners under the act of March 2, 1805, and supplementary acts. An act of Congress of February 10, 1814, confirmed the claims of Daniel Boone to one thousand arpents under a concession made to him by the Spanish government in 1798.[38] These and other claims became the subject of additional Congressional documents. A report of the House committee on private land claims of January 18, 1819, on the claims of James Mackay included a bill for his relief; an act for that purpose was

32 / American State Papers, Public Lands, VIII, 20–243, printed also in Senate Documents, 24th Cong., 1st Sess., No. 16, Serial 280.

33 / Missouri Land Claims (New Orleans, 1976).

34 / American State Papers, Public Lands, VIII, 112–234, printed also in Senate Documents, 24th Cong., 1st Sess., No. 16, pp. 403–409, Serial 280.

35 / American State Papters, Public Lands, VIII, 789–871, printed also in House Documents, 24th Cong., 1st Sess., No. 270, Serial 292.

36 / 5 Statutes 126.

37 / Senate Reports, 31st Cong., 1st Sess., No. 168, pp. 1–4, Serial 565.

38 / 6 Statutes 127–28.

adopted on April 20, 1818.[39] The same committee reported on February 15, 1826, on a petition with supporting documents of François Vallé and others to Mine La Motte. Again, the committee reported on February 27, 1832, on the claims of thirty-one inhabitants of Old Mines. A further report concerns the claims of inhabitants of St. Louis County. An act of Congress of May 24, 1826, confirmed a claim of François Vallé, Jean Baptiste Vallé, Jean Baptiste Pratte, and others to Mine La Motte.[40]

A report of the House committee on private land claims of March 12, 1858, reported a bill for the confirmation of some of the excepted claims. An act of June 2, 1858, approved the location of private land claims that had been reported on by the recorder and the two commissioners under the acts of July 9, 1832, and March 2, 1833, and entered in the transcript of the decision transmitted to the General Land Office. This act listed the names of the claimants and the numbers of the claims, as follows:

1st class

33	Manuel de Liza	292	Andrew Chevalier
34	Francis Lacombe	293	Joseph Silvain
44	John Coontz and Hempstead	298	John P. Cabanis
57	Matthew Saucier	301	William Hartley
67	Charles Tayon	307	William Morrison
74	Sons of Joseph M. Pepin	308	Solomon Bellew
87	Louis Lorimier	309	Paschal Detchemendez
89	Bartholomew Cousin	310	Baptiste Amure
95	Manuel Gonzales Mora	323	Alexander Maurice
104	Seneca Rawlins	334	John Baptiste Vallee
106	William L. Long	338	Israel Dodge
133	Joachim Liza		

2d class

6 Regis Loisel

A House report of March 19, 1860, recommended for confirmation the claims of Israel Dodge, Walter Fenwick, and Mackay Wherry, which had been approved by the board of 1833 but rejected by Congress.[41]

Persons claiming land obtained by grants and other instruments dated prior to the cession to the United States were authorized by an act of June 22, 1860, to make application for the confirmation of their claims.

39 / *American State Papers, Public Lands,* III, 407–409; 3 *Statutes* 213.

40 / *House Reports,* 19th Cong., 1st Sess., No. 75, Serial 141; *House Documents,* 22nd Cong., 1st Sess., No. 274, pp. 1–2, Serial 221; *House Reports,* 34th Cong., 2nd Sess., No. 268, Serial 914; 6 *Statutes* 386–87.

41 / *House Reports,* 35th Cong., 1st Sess., No. 463, pp. 1–5, Serial 968; 11 *Statutes* 294; *House Reports,* 36th Cong., 1st Sess., No. 113, pp. 1–2, Serial 1067.

Notices in writing, together with evidence in support of their claims, were to be filed with the recorder of land titles for the state of Missouri, who was appointed a commissioner to hear and decide the claims. Subsequent acts kept this legislation in effect into the 1870s. After hearing evidence in cases presented to him, the recorder decided favorably in respect to large claims presented by Jacques Clamorgan, Peter Provenchére, François Vallé, Jr., Jean Baptiste Vallé, and François Vallé. The commissioner of the General Land Office approved the first two claims, but disallowed the recorder's decisions in favor of the last two claims on the grounds that the papers filed were inadequate. The House committee on private land claims, however, thought that all four claims should be approved and reported their approval in a bill on January 28, 1876.[42] The total number of private land claims in Missouri was 3,748, covering an area of 1,130,051 acres.[43]

An act of Congress of May 26, 1824, provided that persons claiming land in Missouri under French and Spanish grants could present petitions for the review of their claims to the district court of the United States for Missouri. By 1828, decisions had been handed down by the court in only three cases. Judicial review was revived by acts of May 24, 1828, and June 17, 1844.[44] Records of the district court relating to land claims proceedings, 1824–1849, are in the Federal Records Center in Kansas City.

During the Spanish period there was little settlement in the northern part of Upper Louisiana in what became Iowa. In 1788, Julien Dubuque, a Canadian, was given permission by the Fox Indians to work lead mines in the vicinity of what became Dubuque, and in 1796 he was given a concession there by Governor Francisco de Carondelet. Because of debts he owed to Auguste Chouteau, in 1804 he sold part of the Spanish Mines to that St. Louis merchant. In September, 1806, the board of land commissioners at St. Louis approved the claim, but the secretary of the treasury disapproved and a Supreme Court decision of 1854 was unfavorable. Later, the United States government acquired the land by purchase from the Indians.[45] Basil Giard, a companion of Dubuque, obtained in 1800 a

42 / 12 Statutes 85–88; House Reports, 44th Cong., 1st Sess., No. 24, pp. 1–3, Serial 1708.
43 / U.S. Public Lands Commission, Report, 1904, p. 140.
44 / 4 Statutes 52–56; Shoemaker, Missouri and Missourians, I, 261; 4 Statutes 298; 5 Statutes 676.
45 / Edgar R. Harlan, A Narrative History of the People of Iowa (Chicago, 1931), I, 15–16. Documents relating to the origin of the Dubuque claim and the memorial of Pierre Chouteau, Jr., and others for the confirmation of the claim and the report of the Senate Committee are in Senate Documents, 29th Cong., 1st Sess., No. 256, Serial 474.

concession in the district of St. Charles on the west bank of the Missis-sippi River across from Prairie du Chien at what became the town of Mar-quette in Clayton County. Documents relating to this tract, including Giard's petition, Lieutenant Governor DeLassus' concession, a plat of the grant for 5,780 acres, and extracts from the minutes of the board of land commissioners at St. Louis, are in print. That board finally approved the claim in 1814, and after a survey was made in 1838, a patent was issued in 1844.[46] Copies of documents relative to the grant are in the district court records at Dubuque. Louis Honoré Tesson was given a concession of about 6,000 acres at the head of the Des Moines rapids at what became Montrose in Lee County. The grant was finally validated by a Supreme Court decision of 1852.

Land surveys began in Iowa in 1836, under the direction of the sur-veyor general at Cincinnati; two years later when a surveyor general for Iowa was appointed, he opened his own office at Dubuque. Surveying operations ceased in Iowa in 1862, and in 1868 the survey records were transferred to the custody of the state of Iowa.[47]

In 1981 the land office in the Office of the Secretary of State of Iowa transferred to the state archives of Iowa land records dating from 1800 to 1890 comprising 34½ cubic feet. The collection includes correspondence, reports, abstracts, field notes, plats, maps, and other materials relating to land sales and surveys. Contained in these records are the original field notes and plat of Basil Giard's claim. Other records transferred to the state archives in the same year included original survey plats, 1835–1860, in ten volumes, and copies of plats, 1835–1860, in twelve volumes.[48]

The opening of land offices in the Missouri Territory was postponed by the delay in the adjudication of private land claims. Those claims had to be located on the township maps before the bounds of the public land could be ascertained and their sale proclaimed. Land offices were opened at St. Louis in 1815 and at Jackson in Cape Girardeau County and Franklin in Howard County in 1818. The first land sale occurred at St. Louis in 1818.[49]

According to the act of Congress of July 31, 1876, abolishing the of-fice of recorder of land titles of the state of Missouri from and after Sep-

46 / Edgar R. Harlan, "Claim of Basil Giard," *Annals of Iowa*, 3d ser., XVI (April, 1929), 622–27; P. L. Scanlan and Marian Scanlan, "Basil Giard and His Land Claim in Iowa," *Iowa Journal of History*, XXX (April, 1932), 224–30.

47 / Thomas Donaldson, *The Public Domain, Its History, with Statistics* (Washington, D.C., 1884), 195, also in *House Miscellaneous Documents*, 47th Cong., 2nd Sess., No. 45, Se-rial 2158.

48 / *Annals of Iowa*, 3d ser., XLV (Winter, 1981), 576–77, XLVI (Summer, 1981), 64.

49 / David D. March, *History of Missouri* (New York, 1967), I, 240, 245, 247, 242.

tember 30, 1876, such of the records of that office as were not required by the United States were to be transferred to the state of Missouri. All of the records of the office were shipped to the General Land Office in Washington, D.C., for examination. An inventory was prepared of those to be transferred to the state authorities at Jefferson City.[50] Actual delivery of the records at Jefferson City was made on September 27, 1879, when Lee Harrison, special agent of the General Land Office, procured a receipt on the back of the inventory from James E. McHenry, the register of lands.

This inventory of over two hundred pages contains detailed information about the records. It gives a list of the volume records; an alphabetical index to title papers, deeds, conveyances, receipts, petitions, notices, plats of surveys, certificates, etc., to be found in the record books; a list of papers not recorded; and lists of bundles of letters, affidavits, decisions of the board of land commissioners, surveys, plats, orders of survey, and correspondence. The General Land Office retained at this time the original Livres Terriens and the five volumes of records of grants of land resulting from the order of Captain Stoddard. Upon the abolition of the office of register of lands in 1891, the land records were transferred to the Office of the Secretary of State of Missouri, where they were in the custody of the land clerk. In 1908 the records were kept in a basement room that was poorly lighted and without fire protection.[51] When examined by the Survey of Federal Archives in the 1930s, the records were kept in a vault on the first floor of the state capitol in Jefferson City.

The records transferred by the recorder of land titles in Missouri to the state of Missouri in 1879 included those of the boards of land commissioners that had functioned in Missouri. Minutes of the board of land commissioners, December, 1805–September, 1835, in seven volumes, contain a chronological record of meetings of the board and supply information about claims that were presented and evidence regarding them and about the appointment of officers to the board. An index to the minutes of the board of land commissioners, 1805–1812, in one volume, covers the first four volumes of the minutes. Other records include original certificates of land claims and grants, 1805–1876, $4\frac{1}{2}$ inches by $7\frac{1}{2}$ inches, folded papers and ten boxes, and an index volume; correspondence of the commissioners with the Treasury Department, 1805–1843, in

50 / 19 Statutes 121; Inventory of records and papers received at the General Land Office from the late office of the recorder of land titles at St. Louis, Missouri, which are to be transferred to the State authorities of Missouri at Jefferson City, vols. 51, Records of the Bureau of Land Management, RG 49, NA.

51 / Jonas Viles, "Report on the Archives of the State of Missouri," American Historical Association, Annual Report, 1908 (Washington, D.C., 1909), 346.

one volume; Louisiana land commissioners' certificates, December, 1808–January, 1812, in seven volumes and an index volume, covering certificates, numbers 1–1342, issued to land claimants in the Territory of Missouri; a register of commissioners' certificates, February, 1809–January, 1812, in one volume; an index of land commissioners' certificates, February, 1809–1812, in one volume; a register of opinions given by the commissioners, 1809–1812, in one volume, concerning lands in the districts of St. Louis, New Madrid, Cape Girardeau, St. Charles, and Ste. Geneviève; confirmations by the board and the recorder Frederick Bates, 1817–1852, also in one volume, concerning confirmations in Ste. Geneviève and St. Charles counties; separate decisions by the board of land commissioners, 1837, in one bundle, 4 inches, containing evidence of claims that came before the board mostly recommended for confirmation.[52]

Records of the recorder of land titles are also in the custody of the secretary of state at Jefferson City. Record books of land titles, September, 1805–1829, in five volumes arranged chronologically and an index volume, contain a variety of copies of Spanish papers documenting the claims and American documents concerning the confirmation and survey of the claims. An index to records of land titles, 1805–1829, in three volumes, contains an incomplete name index of claimants. Recorder Bates's minutes, July 17–November 26, 1807, and July 1, 1812–June, 1818, in one volume, contain a chronological record of Bates's actions as commissioner to adjust land claims under the act of June 12, 1812, and later acts concerning the settlement of claims. Recorder Bates's decisions, 1815, in one volume and an index volume, contain a record of his opinions on claims entered under the act of June 12, 1812, for lots in the towns of Ste. Geneviève, Portage des Sioux, New Madrid, St. Charles, St. Louis, and Little Prairie. The one-volume index to recorder Bates's decisions for 1815 contains an alphabetical name index to claimants. The decisions entered in the foregoing volumes were the basis for his report to the General Land Office.

Minutes of recorder Theodore Hunt and other records, 1824–1872, in seven volumes, contain a record of testimony taken before Hunt under the act of Congress of May 26, 1824, concerning village lots, out-lots, and common field lots in and around St. Louis, Carondelet, St. Ferdinand, Prairie des Noyes, Mine à Breton, New Madrid, and Little Prairie. Other records include a separate record of private land claims in the vicinity of

---

52 / Survey of Federal Archives, Missouri, *Inventory of Federal Archives in the States, Series VIII, The Department of the Interior, No. 24, Missouri* (St. Louis, 1938), 4–6, 9; Viles, "Report on the Archives of Missouri," 345–49.

St. Louis; a volume containing a list of proofs by Hunt; and patent certificates issued by Hunt, 1824–1830, and by other recorders, 1830–1872, in seven volumes. Hunt's minutes, 1824–1830, in one volume, contain a name index, and there is also an index in a separate volume. A one-volume book of confirmation certificates, 1834–1874, contains copies of 162 confirmation certificates issued by the recorder on claims to town and village lots, out-lots, and common field lots confirmed by an act of June 13, 1812, entered chronologically.[53]

A description of records of the Bureau of Land Management relating to the adjudication, survey, and patenting of private land claims has been presented in the part of this book that concerns Louisiana, where the titles of published works facilitating research in those records and of published compilations based upon the records are also given. A published list of the principal series of records of the General Land Office in the National Archives is in print.[54]

The earliest arrangements for land surveying in the District of Louisiana were temporary in character. James Wilkinson, the governor in the region, kept Antoine L. Soulard, who had been the Spanish surveyor general, in charge of surveying. This arrangement was continued by Governor William Henry Harrison of the Indiana Territory, to which the District of Louisiana was made subordinate by the act of March 26, 1804. The situation in the district was regularized by the act of February 28, 1806, which extended the authority of the surveyor general of the United States over the public lands of the United States in the Territory of Louisiana and authorized him to appoint deputy surveyors. The selection by Jared Mansfield, the surveyor general at Cincinnati, of Silas Bent, an experienced surveyor of Ohio, was approved by the secretary of the treasury. Bent reached St. Louis in September, 1806, and served until he was designated as a judge in February, 1813. Surveying was impeded in the Missouri Territory because of the slowness of the land commissioners in adjusting claims, the distance from St. Louis of tracts to be surveyed, and the scarcity of surveyors, but Bent was able to send some plats to Washington in January, 1812. The act of June 13, 1812, directed the principal deputy surveyor to survey land claims that had been confirmed by the board of land commissioners into townships six miles square, according to the system that had been adopted for the Northwest Territory and the Orleans Territory.[55] General and connected plats were to be prepared and

53 / Survey of Federal Archives, Missouri, *Inventory of Federal Archives in the States, Series VIII, The Department of the Interior,* No. 24, Missouri, 3–5, 7, 10.

54 / Carter (ed.), *Territory of Louisiana-Missouri,* XIII, 158–60 n. 10.

55 / 2 *Statutes* 287–89, 352–53; Albert Gallatin to Jared Mansfield, July 3, 1806, Silas

sent to the surveyor general, who was to transmit copies to the recorder of land titles and to the General Land Office.

From 1813 to 1824, during William Rector's long tenure as principal surveyor at St. Louis, extensive surveys were executed in Missouri and Arkansas. Pursuant to the act of June 13, 1812, he started the survey of the out boundary lines of the several towns and villages where claims were confirmed by that act. In 1815 he engaged Joseph C. Brown to survey the base line due west from the confluence of the Mississippi and St. Francis rivers, and Prospect Robbins to survey the standard meridian due north from the junction of the Arkansas and Mississippi rivers.[56] Rector reported on January 15, 1816, that the survey of the base line from the St. Francis to the Arkansas River measured 84½ miles and that the fifth principal meridian from the mouth of the Arkansas River to the Missouri River measured 317 miles.[57] To promote economy and accuracy, the practice was adopted early in 1816 of surveying private claims and public lands at the same time.[58] Data necessary for surveying the private claims were furnished by the recorder of land titles. The provision by the act of April 29, 1816, for a surveyor of public lands in the territories of Illinois and Missouri made Rector independent of the surveyor general, who at that time was located at Chillicothe, Ohio, 566 miles distant.[59] In effect, he became the surveyor general of the Illinois and Missouri territories, the latter still including Arkansas.

In succeeding years extensive surveys were executed by deputy surveyors hired by Rector. In 1816, surveys were made of lands on both sides of the Missouri River, and in 1817 of lands located between the Mississippi River and the fifth principal meridian and west of that meridian. In January, 1819, the task of surveying the exterior boundary lines of townships north of the base line and east of the fifth principal meridian was assigned to surveyor Nathaniel Cook. Later surveys were performed in Cape Girardeau County; by 1822, millions of acres had been surveyed in St. Louis, Howard, and Cape Girardeau counties.[60] A list of the names of the owners of land in the city of St. Louis whose holdings were surveyed

Bent to the secretary of the treasury, January 28, 1812, both in Carter (ed.), *Territory of Louisiana-Missouri*, XIII, 536, XIV, 514–15; 2 *Statutes* 750–51.

56 / 2 *Statutes* 748; White, *Rectangular Survey System*, 61, 67.

57 / Rector to Edwin Tiffin, January 15, 1816, in Carter (ed.), *Territory of Louisiana-Missouri*, XV, 103–104.

58 / Josiah Meigs to Edward Tiffin, March 6, 1816, in Carter (ed.), *Territory of Louisiana-Missouri*, XV, 124.

59 / 3 *Statutes* 325–26.

60 / *American State Papers, Public Lands*, III, 533.

in 1823 by René Paul has been published. In 1824, Rector was removed for nepotism, involving the hiring of several brothers as surveyors and sub-contractors; he was replaced temporarily by William Clark. In May, 1825, William McRee, a former colonel in the army's Corps of Engineers, assumed the regular appointment as surveyor general in St. Louis. McRee's inattention to his duties produced a serious backlog in the work of the office and caused his dismissal by President Andrew Jackson on March 15, 1832.[61]

During the next thirty years, surveys of private land claims in Missouri continued under a succession of surveyors general.[62] They hired deputy surveyors under contract and had plats prepared from the surveyors' field notes for the use of the local land offices and for dispatch, together with copies of the contracts, field notes, and plats, to the General Land Office. Surveys of claims in towns and villages went on throughout these years and gave employment to a number of surveyors, including Joseph C. Brown and William H. Cozzens. A statement showing progress made in surveying private claims confirmed by the act of July 4, 1836, was published in the report of the surveyor general for 1851. Another compilation concerning surveys in St. Charles County is also in print. Reproductions of fifteen plat books of Clay County for townships 50–54, with an alphabetical list of the claimants' names and an overall index of names, are in print.[63]

As principal deputy surveyor at St. Louis, William Rector was responsible for making survey contracts and directing the execution of those contracts. Prior to 1816, when he became surveyor general of Illinois and Missouri, Rector sent copies of survey contracts, field notes, plats, and descriptions of subdivisions to the surveyor general at Cincinnati and later at Chillicothe, where they were copied for dispatch to Washington, D.C. This practice ceased in 1816, and the act of April 29, 1816, directed that survey records pertaining to lands within the territories of Missouri and Illinois were to be delivered to Rector by the surveyor general northwest of the Ohio. Thereafter, copies of survey records were forwarded from St. Louis to the General Land Office. In succeeding years

---

61 / "St. Louis Real Estate in Review," Missouri Historical Society, *Glimpses of the Past*, IV (October–December, 1937), 117–77; Rohrbough, *Land Office Business*, 168, 186–90, 260.

62 / A list of the names of the surveyors general is in White, *Rectangular Survey System*, 212.

63 / *House Executive Documents*, 32nd Cong., 1st Sess., No. 52, pp. 17–19, Serial 640; Robert E. Parkin, "Index of U.S. Government Surveys of Land Grants in St. Charles County," *St. Louis Genealogical Society Quarterly*, VII (December, 1974), 77; Katherine G. Bushman (comp.), *Index of the First Plat Book of Clay County, Missouri, 1819–1875* ([Staunton, Va.?, 1967]).

as surveyors general were replaced by new appointees, inventories of the records that were transferred were prepared and copies were sent to the General Land Office. On November 9, 1863, the office of the surveyor general at St. Louis was closed and its records inventoried and transferred by William Cuddy to Thomas Nelson, the recorder of land titles.[64] The recorder was instructed to allow access to the records only to honorable and trustworthy persons and to allow no papers to be removed from his control.

In 1866, Joseph S. Wilson, an agent of the General Land Office, examined the surveying archives in the recorder's office at St. Louis and flagged the greater portion of them for retention in Missouri. Certain other maps of a general character and others of mixed character, relating to private land claims and other land interests not yet finally disposed of by official action in Washington, D.C., were to be retained by the United States. Wilson reported that he found the records to be in admirable condition, systematically arranged and housed in the post office building, which was a fireproof structure. In 1874 the surveyor general's records were transferred from St. Louis to the office of the register of state lands at Jefferson City.[65]

When the Survey of Federal Archives of the Works Progress Administration began operating in Missouri in 1936, it located the records of the surveyor general of Missouri in a vault in the state land department of the Office of the Secretary of State in the state capitol at Jefferson City. A file entitled "Spanish claims and United States public land surveys, Missouri, 1790–1857," arranged numerically by survey number, 3½ inches by 8 inches, folded documents, 7 feet, contains survey records of towns, villages, common fields, and school lands with plats, papers relating to the boundary survey of St. Louis, contracts with surveyors, an inventory of field notes, a list of claims, petitions, depositions, summonses, caveats, protests, permissions to settle, orders of survey, and confirmations of claims; Bent's surveys, 1807–1811, in one volume, indexed, containing surveys of land in St. Louis and vicinity with a list of town lots and a list of lots confirmed by the board of land commissioners; an exhibit of private land claims in Missouri, 1808–1867, in one volume, arranged numerically by claim number and alphabetically, containing a list of confirmed

64 / 3 *Statutes* 326; William Cuddy to J. M. Edmunds, November 9, 1863, in Letters Received from Surveyors General of Illinois and Missouri, G26467, Records of the Bureau of Land Management, RG 49, NA.

65 / *House Executive Documents*, 39th Cong., 2nd Sess., No. 2, pp. 400–401, Serial 1284; White, *Rectangular Survey System*, 212.

private land claims; information relative to surveys in the Grand Prairie, 1811–1855, in one volume, containing a chronological record of instructions to deputy surveyors and data regarding land claims derived largely from the original Livres Terriens; record books, 1812–1876, in ten volumes, containing plats of surveys and descriptions of boundary lines of confirmed land claims, including surveys of towns, 1818–1851, in ten volumes; an index to records of private land surveys, 1812–1876, in two volumes, including one volume that contains a numerical index to 3,344 surveys and another volume that contains an alphabetical index of claimants' names; field notes of Missouri private surveys, 1816–1855, in variously sized volumes, 10 feet, with an index volume, relating mostly to southeastern Missouri; a one-volume index to public and private surveys in Missouri, 1815–1862; general correspondence, 1824–1863, in four volumes, indexed, containing correspondence between the General Land Office and other parties and the surveyor general at St. Louis relating to plats and surveys; a one-volume register of certificates of relocation, 1837–1860, containing a chronological list of new locations for which certificates were issued because of interference with claims in the report of the board of land commissioners confirmed by an act of Congress of July 4, 1836; surveys of Joseph C. Brown, 1838–1862, in six volumes, containing plats and descriptions of surveys in districts and villages and common fields mostly in St. Louis, Jefferson, St. Charles, and Cape Girardeau counties, plus a volume containing a list of original claimants with the numbers of the commissioners' certificates; a one-volume inventory of archives of the surveyor general's office, 1845.[66]

Records of land surveyors in Missouri in the custody of the Missouri secretary of state include a register of land surveyed by Joseph Story, 1794–1800, in one volume; a registre d'arpentage of Soulard's surveys, 1798–1806, in two volumes, containing plats and descriptions of the boundaries of claims in the various districts of Missouri; Bent's surveys of land claims in St. Louis and vicinity with plats, 1807–1811, in one volume, indexed; an exhibit of confirmed private land claims in Missouri, 1808–1867, in one volume, with an index volume; information relative to surveys in the Grand Prairie, chronologically arranged, 1811–1855, in one volume; a record book of surveys, 1812–1876, in ten volumes, with plats and descriptions of boundary lines; an index to records of private land surveys, 1812–1876, in two volumes; field notes of Arkansas surveys, December, 1815–January, 1816, in one volume; an index to public and private sur-

66 / Survey of Federal Archives, Missouri, *Inventory of Federal Archives in the States, Series VIII, The Department of the Interior, No. 24, Missouri,* 2–11.

veys, 1815–1862, in one volume; correspondence relating to plats and surveys, 1824–1863, in four volumes; surveys of village holdings, lots, and common fields by Joseph C. Brown, 1838–1862, in six volumes.[67]

Records of the Bureau of Land Management in the National Archives containing materials relating to private land claims and surveys in Missouri are described in the section of this volume on Louisiana. A list of the document series relating to the survey and sale of public land in the Missouri Territory is in print, as are the texts of surveying contracts between William Rector and Joseph C. Brown, October 9, 1815, and Rector and Nicholas Rightor, February 20, 1820, and lists of surveying contracts made by Rector during the periods October to December, 1815, 1819, 1820, and February to April, 1821.[68] Rector's general instructions to deputy surveyors are also printed.[69]

67 / Ibid., 3, 5–9, 11.

68 / Carter (ed.), Territory of Louisiana-Missouri, XIV, 799 n. 94, XV, 89–91, 587–89, 91–92, 494–95, 589 n. 6, 696–98 n. 70.

69 / White, Rectangular Survey System, 301–12.

22

⁊ꝱ

Ecclesiastical Records

Jesuit missionaries accompanied the early French explorers to the upper Mississippi region and the Great Lakes area and in 1674 established the first mission among the Kaskaskia Indians in the Illinois country. Priests of the Seminary of Foreign Missions of Quebec established a mission among the Cahokia Indians in 1699 and later served the church of St. Anne at Fort de Chartres, which maintained the chapel of St. Joseph at Prairie du Rocher.[1]

The earliest settlers at Ste. Geneviève had to cross the Mississippi to Kaskaskia for religious ministrations. In 1759 the Reverend Philibert F. Watrin, S.J., moved across the river to become the first pastor at Ste. Geneviève. He was succeeded by the reverends Sébastian L. Meurin, Pierre Gibault, Francis Hilaire, and after a hiatus from 1778 to 1796 James Maxwell, an Irishman. A large wooden church that had been built had to be moved in 1794 to the new town site. The church of St. Joachim at Ste. Geneviève had as its dependencies the Salines and Old Mines.[2]

The registers of the Ste. Geneviève church were kept on loose sheets from 1759 until 1865, when they were bound in separate sets of baptisms, marriages, and burials, four volumes in each set. Copies of the marriage and death records, 1760–1781, are in the Western Historical Manuscripts Collection, the Clarence W. Alvord Papers, in the University of Missouri Library.[3] Other typewritten copies made by Ida M. Schaaf in the early 1940s are held by the Missouri Historical Society, which also has micro-

1 / Henry P. Beers, *The French & British in the Old Northwest: A Bibliographical Guide to Archive and Manuscript Sources* (Detroit, 1964), 53–56.

2 / Basler, *District of Ste. Geneviève*, 284–86.

3 / Ida M. Schaaf, "Sainte Geneviève, Missouri, Catholic Records," *National Genealogical Society Publications*, 5 (1935), 7; *National Union Catalog of Manuscripts*, 1968, entry 1320.

film of the register for 1759–1885. Transcripts are also in the holdings of the National Genealogical Society in Arlington, Virginia.

The first Catholic priest to say mass and administer sacraments in Missouri was the Reverend Sébastian L. Meurin, a former Jesuit, who crossed the Mississippi from Kaskaskia in the 1760s. The Reverend Pierre Gibault, who joined Father Meurin at Kaskaskia in 1760, also performed services in Missouri. The palisaded church built in 1770 at St. Louis on a lot designated by the commandant was replaced by a log cabin in 1776. The Reverend Bernard Limpach, a Capuchin, became the first resident pastor in 1776 and continued in his post until 1789.[4] The Reverend Pierre Joseph Didier, a Benedictine friar, served there from 1794 to 1799. Some Spanish priests served at St. Louis and other posts in Missouri, but after the transfer of sovereignty to the United States, they departed.[5]

In order to share a priest with a new church that had been started at St. Charles, the people of Florissant began building their own church. The local commandant provided a site for the church, and the people completed the building of St. Ferdinand Church in 1790. The first baptismal register was opened there by Father Didier, the curé at St. Charles, who continued to serve St. Ferdinand after moving to St. Louis in 1793. The earliest entry in the burial register was on November 19, 1790. A marriage register was also kept. Copies of the records of the church at Florissant are in the Missouri Historical Society.[6] Handwritten transcripts of the baptismal and marriage records of St. Ferdinand made by Oscar Collet are at St. Louis University.

After the establishment of New Madrid, Father Pierre Gibault moved across the Mississippi from Cahokia and became the pastor of St. Isidore Church there and its dependencies at Arkansas Post and Little Prairie. He took an oath of allegiance to the Spanish government on July 23, 1793, and received an annual stipend of six hundred dollars from the royal treasury.[7] Permission was obtained in 1799 to construct a church, a parochial house, and a bakehouse, of which descriptions and inventories were prepared at the time of the cession to the United States in March, 1804.[8]

Papers of Father Pierre Gibault, 1783–1801, including miscellaneous letters, marriage licenses, and miscellaneous accounts, cover the period

4 / *New Catholic Encyclopedia*, VI, 464, IX, 763, XII, 907.

5 / Gilbert J. Garraghan, *Saint Ferdinand de Florissant: The Story of an Ancient Parish* (Chicago, 1923), 94–96.

6 / *Ibid.*, 81, 84; *National Union Catalog of Manuscripts*, 1965, entry 1405.

7 / John Rothensteiner, "Historical Sketch of Catholic New Madrid," *St. Louis Catholic Historical Review*, IV (July, 1922), 119–20.

8 / Houck (ed.), *Spanish Regime in Missouri*, II, 339–40.

when he served at New Madrid. The registers of births, marriages, and burials that must have been kept in accordance with the general practice have not been located.

Copies of the registers of the old parishes have been made, and indexing was started in the early 1900s. St. Louis University has indexes or transcriptions of the records of the churches of St. Louis, St. Charles, Florissant, Portage des Sioux, Ste. Geneviève, and Old Mines.[9] Microfilm of the registers of all the churches in the archdiocese of St. Louis, made around 1955, is in the chancery of the archdiocese. The parishes have the original registers and microfilm, which is generally made available to researchers.[10] No church was built at Cape Girardeau during the Spanish period.

The earliest recordings concerning the residents of the oldest settlements in Missouri are in the registers of the churches in the still older villages of the Illinois country on the eastern side of the Mississippi. Before churches were established in Missouri, the registers of the churches at Kaskaskia, Cahokia, Prairie du Rocher, Fort de Chartres, and Vincennes continued to receive entries regarding Missourians. Information concerning those registers is in print, and copies of the registers are in the repository of the Missouri Historical Society, St. Louis.[11]

Ecclesiastical jurisdiction over the Illinois country and Louisiana was exercised by the bishop of Quebec and continued to be in the hands of that official after the transfer of Canada and Louisiana to the British by the Treaty of Paris of 1763. Bishop Joseph Olivier Briand appointed Father Sébastian Meurin as vicar general in the Illinois country and made Father Pierre Gibault his assistant.[12] The Treaty of Paris of 1783 transferred to the United States sovereignty over the part of Louisiana that was east of the Mississippi and terminated the authority of the bishop of Quebec there because the region west of the Mississippi was transferred to Spain.

9 / Historical Records Survey, Missouri, *Guide to Depositories of Manuscript Collections in the United States: Missouri*, 11.

10 / Parkin, *Guide*, 8–9.

11 / Beers, *French & British in the Old Northwest*, 55–56.

12 / Some of their correspondence has been published: "Correspondence between Abbé Gibault and Bishop Briand, 1768–1788," *American Catholic Historical Society of Philadelphia Records*, XX (December, 1909), 406–30; Fintan G. Walker (ed.), "Some Correspondence of an Eighteenth Century Bishop with His Missionaries, 1767–1778," *Catholic Historical Review*, XXVII (July, 1941), 186–200; Lionel St. George Lindsay (ed.), "Letters from the Archdiocesan Archives at Quebec, 1768–1788," *American Catholic Historical Society of Philadelphia Records*, XX (December, 1909), 406–30. Some description of the archives of the Bishop of Quebec is in the chapter on Louisiana.

V

The Records of Arkansas

23

ॐ

History and Government, and Records
of Local Jurisdictions

In March, 1682, Robert Cavelier, Sieur de La Salle, and Henri de Tonti
with a small party of Frenchmen reached the mouth of the Arkansas
River and took formal possession of the country in the name of the king
of France. Four years later, Tonti established at the mouth of the river a
post that became a way station for parties traveling on the Mississippi
River between New Orleans and the Illinois country. After John Law
failed to establish a settlement there in 1720, the colonists withdrew to the
lower Mississippi River. A small garrison was set up at Arkansas Post,
which became the base of hunters, trappers, and traders. In 1722 the area
became one of the nine districts into which Louisiana was divided for
governmental purposes. The post was moved upstream by the French
and later by the Spanish, who took control in 1768 after the cession of
Louisiana to Spain.[1] During the Spanish regime Fort Miró was established in 1783 by Juan Filhiol at Écore a Fabre (now Camden, Arkansas).
Later, Campo de la Esperanza (now Hopefield, Arkansas) was established on the Arkansas bank of the Mississippi, opposite Fort San Fernando de las Barrancas. In 1794 Governor Francisco Hector de Carondelet
of Louisiana granted to the Chouteaus a trade monopoly with the Osages.

Arkansas Post was taken over by Captain James B. Manny, U.S.
Army, from a Spanish officer on March 23, 1804, both officers signing at
that time an inventory of the post's archives.[2] The Arkansas district, in-

---

1 / David Y. Thomas, *Arkansas and Its People: A History, 1541–1930* (New York, 1930), I,
19–23; Gilbert C. Din, "The Spanish Fort on the Arkansas, 1763–1803," *Arkansas Historical
Quarterly*, XLII (Autumn, 1983), 270–83.
2 / Hill, *Descriptive Catalogue*, xxxvii.

cluding what became Oklahoma, remained part of the Louisiana Territory in 1805 and later, with the change in the name of the territory in 1812, part of the Missouri Territory. Arkansas continued as part of the New Madrid district of that territory until 1808, when it became a separate district.[3] In December, 1813, Arkansas County was created, with the seat at Arkansas Post. An act of March 2, 1819, to be effective on July 4, 1819, created the Arkansas Territory, which included the Indian country on the west. Subsequent acts of 1824 and 1828 reduced the extent of the territory on the west by making what became Oklahoma part of the Indian country.[4] Arkansas was admitted as a state on June 15, 1836.

Records of local jurisdictions begin at the time of the transfer of Arkansas Post and Campo de la Esperanza in March, 1804, when inventories of the records and the royal property at those places were prepared.[5] The records of Arkansas Post covered personal and business transactions that took place before the commandant, who acted as notary. A small quantity of records relating to that post, 1751–1755, is in the custody of the Missouri Historical Society. The Arkansas History Commission has microfilm of a typed translation of records relating to Arkansas Post, 1720–1787, in two reels, privately collected.[6]

Several of the early Arkansas counties have records relating to private land grants, including deeds and survey records. The plat books of Crittenden County show land holdings at Campo de la Esperanza. In December, 1938, when searching for Spanish records in the Arkansas County records at De Witt, the Historical Records Survey found only a few marriage records of 1797 in a probate court record of 1814.

Agencies to collect and preserve historical sources developed slowly in Arkansas. Through the efforts of John H. Reynolds, the Arkansas Historical Association was organized at the University of Arkansas in 1903 and began assembling newspapers, other printed materials, and manuscripts. An act of the Arkansas legislature of April 27, 1905, provided for the creation of the Arkansas History Commission, consisting of five members to be appointed by the president of the association to ascertain the extent and condition of materials on Arkansas history and to report on the status of historical work in the state. A report prepared by Professor

3 / Dallas T. Herndon, *Annals of Arkansas, 1947: A Narrative Historical Edition* (Hopkinsville, Ky., [1947]), I, 67.

4 / 3 *Statutes* 493–96; Van Zandt, *Boundaries of the United States*, 118–19.

5 / Houck (ed.), *Spanish Regime in Missouri*, II, 336–42.

6 / Richard W. Hale, Jr. (ed.), *Guide to Photocopied Historical Materials in the United States and Canada* (Ithaca, N.Y., 1961), 9318.

Reynolds and others recommended the establishment of a repository in the state house and of a department to take care of the archives of the state. An act of May 31, 1909, authorized a permanent commission of seven members appointed by the governor. Since 1951 the Arkansas History Commission has been housed in the west wing of the old state capitol, to which a three-story archives annex was added in the 1950s and 1960s.[7] For materials on the colonial years of Arkansas, however, researchers must depend on repositories outside the state, such as the Missouri Historical Society and the Manuscript Division of the Library of Congress.[8]

7 / Posner, *American State Archives*, 49–52.
8 / Historical Records Survey, Missouri, *Guide to Depositories of Manuscript Collections in the United States: Missouri*, 10.

24

ॐ

Land Records

Most of the land grants in Arkansas originated during the Spanish period. In 1682 La Salle granted to Henri de Tonti a tract on the Arkansas River that was never occupied. In 1718 a large grant was made on that river to John Law for a colony that was never settled. Late in the Spanish period, Frenchmen and Americans settled on the rivers in eastern and southern Arkansas, but a census taken in 1799 showed only 368 inhabitants. After the cession of Louisiana to the United States, the land transfers accelerated as they did in other parts of the acquisition. Spanish officials were careless about land documents, a practice that made it difficult for American officials who became concerned with the adjudication of land claims.[1] Because Antoine L. Soulard, the Spanish surveyor in Missouri, employed no deputies in the Arkansas region, land claims went unrecorded there.[2]

For many years, a number of large land grants made by the Spanish in Arkansas were the subject of litigation. Carlos de Villemont, the commandant at Arkansas Post from 1790 to 1803, was granted in 1795 a large tract on the western bank of the Mississippi River at Chico Point. The land was not occupied until 1823, when the village of Villemont was established on the bank of the Mississippi. Villemont's heirs brought suit in 1847 to obtain a valid title but were unsuccessful because of the length of time that had elapsed before the occupation of the grant.[3] The claim of land speculator William Bell to land at Hot Springs that was supposed to

1 / Herndon, *Annals of Arkansas*, I, 53–54.
2 / John B. C. Lucas to Albert Gallatin, January 4, 1806, in Carter (ed.), *Territory of Louisiana-Missouri*, XIII, 381.
3 / Herndon, *Annals of Arkansas*, I, 62. Documents concerning this grant are in *Senate Documents*, 24th Cong., 2nd Sess., No. 89, pp. 1–14, Serial 298.

have been granted to Juan Filhiol, the commandant of the district of Ouachita, by Governor Estevan Miró of Louisiana was proven by the testimony of James McLaughlin, a resident of the area, to be based on false documentation.[4] The claim of Elisha Gabriel and William Winter to 1,275 acres on the Arkansas River was invalidated in 1832 when it was found that the claim was based on false certificates without an original grant being presented.[5] In 1797 Governor Carondelet granted to the Baron de Bastrop a tract eighty miles above the mouth of the Ouachita River on what became known as the Bayou Bartholomew.[6] After the United States took possession of Louisiana, Bastrop transferred two-thirds of the grant to Abraham Morehouse, who, after litigation, was awarded a small part of the grant. The titles of a few persons who bought land from Bastrop were confirmed, but most of his grant was restored to the public domain.

Inasmuch as the Arkansas district was part of the Louisiana Territory (1804–1812) and then of the Missouri Territory (1812–1819), land claims there were considered by the board of land commissioners that was set up at St. Louis in 1805. During the summer of 1808, Frederick Bates, the recorder at St. Louis, traveled to Arkansas Post to receive testimony on claims, and during his absence other testimony was received at St. Louis.[7] The remoteness of the Arkansas settlers from St. Louis and the fact that the initial law relating to the settlement of land claims had not been promulgated there caused a delay in the filing of claims in St. Louis.[8] The act of June 13, 1812, gave to the recorder of land titles at St. Louis the task of continuing to adjust land titles in the Missouri Territory, including Arkansas. The land claimants in the Arkansas district were allowed by an act of August 2, 1813, until July 1, 1814, to deliver notices in writing and written evidence of their claims to the recorder at St. Louis. The report of the land commissioners in the Missouri Territory on December 1, 1812, contained reports on land claims in the New Madrid district of Arkansas.[9] The report by the recorder at St. Louis, February 2, 1816, also covered claims in Arkansas, giving lists of confirmed claims with information about individual claims.[10]

4 / Herndon, *Annals of Arkansas*, I, 56.

5 / Gates, "Private Land Claims in the South," 185–89.

6 / Herndon, *Annals of Arkansas*, I, 63.

7 / Frederick Bates to Albert Gallatin, July 22, 1808, in Thomas M. Marshall (ed.), *The Life and Papers of Frederick Bates* (St. Louis, 1926), II, 7–11, 47–48.

8 / Petition to Congress by Inhabitants of Arkansas District, [March 11, 1812], in Carter (ed.), *Territory of Louisiana-Missouri*, XIV, 526–29.

9 / 2 *Statutes* 751–52; 3 *Statutes* 86–87; *American State Papers, Public Lands*, II, 704–28.

10 / *American State Papers, Public Lands*, III, 314–31, 355–57, and 357–61 on rejected claims.

The board of commissioners at St. Louis, consisting of recorder Frederick R. Conway and commissioners James H. Relfe and Falkland H. Martin, submitted a report to the Senate on September 30, 1835, on land claims in the Arkansas Territory.[11] The report recommended for confirmation the claims of the following ten claimants: John Baptiste Dardenne, John Hynam, —— Couissat, John Dortillier, Joseph Duchassin, James Moore, Michael Aquetin, —— Graver, Baptiste Socier, and Jacques Vincent. On the claims for James McKim, the evidence was not considered sufficient. Evidence for the claims from the minutes of the board includes the number of the claim, the name of the original claimant, the number of arpents, the nature and date of the claim, by whom it was granted, by whom it was surveyed, and its location. There were 248 private land claims in Arkansas for a total of 110,090 acres. A list of the French and Spanish land grants in Arkansas is in print.[12]

An act of Congress of February 17, 1818, authorizing the president to establish additional land offices in the Missouri Territory, provided for the opening of land offices in the counties of Arkansas and Lawrence. A further act of March 17, 1820, authorized the president to appoint a receiver of public monies and a register of the land office for the district of Lawrence County. Accordingly, registers and receivers were appointed in 1820 for the offices at Little Rock on the Arkansas River and Batesville on the White River in Lawrence County. The Arkansas land district (Little Rock) was enlarged by an act of April 5, 1826, which added the area south of the base line that had been run west from the junction of the Mississippi and St. Francis rivers.[13] By the same act, the area north of the base line and west of the Lawrence land district was added to the Lawrence land district.

By 1832 the surveys of the public lands in Arkansas had advanced to the point where additional land offices were necessary. Elijah Hayward, the commissioner of the General Land Office, submitted to the acting secretary of the treasury on March 24, 1832, a plan for four land districts in the Arkansas Territory, including the Red River district with the office at Washington, the Fayetteville district in the northwestern part of the territory with the office at Fayetteville, the Arkansas district in the southeastern part of the territory with the office at Little Rock, and the White River district with the office at Batesville.[14] An act of Congress of June 25,

11 / *Senate Documents*, 24th Cong., 1st Sess., No. 17, Serial 280.
12 / U.S. Public Lands Commission, *Report*, 1904, p. 140; Herndon, *Annals of Arkansas*, I, 53–65.
13 / 3 *Statutes* 406, 554; 4 *Statutes* 153.
14 / Clarence E. Carter (ed.), *The Territory of Arkansas, 1819–1836* (Washington, D.C.,

1832, incorporated this plan, and accordingly new land offices were set up at Washington and Fayetteville, and the boundaries of the old districts were altered.[15] This rearrangement necessitated the transcribing and transferring of the records of the old districts—a task that was completed by the beginning of 1834.[16] The Mississippi land district with its office at Helena, Arkansas, was established by the act of June 26, 1834. Instructions about the records that were to be kept by the receiver at Batesville and others that were to be sent to the General Land Office and the secretary of the treasury are in print.[17]

The federal land offices in Arkansas, which had been closed at the beginning of the Civil War, were reopened after its termination. A register, a receiver, and land commissioners were appointed to the office at Little Rock in 1866, and in 1867 others were designated for Washington and Clarksville. As the land office business declined in Arkansas in later years, offices were closed and their records transferred to the office at Little Rock. When that office closed in 1933, its records were transferred to the General Land Office in Washington, D.C.[18] After the Arkansas legislature made provision by the act of March 25, 1933, for the proper care of them, the records were returned to Little Rock and placed in the office of the state land commissioner. Later in the 1930s the records in that office were inventoried by the Survey of Federal Archives. The collection includes U.S. government land plats, from about 1815 to 1930, in fifty-five volumes, 8 feet, containing originals and copies of township plats showing the dates of survey, the names of the surveyors, the character of the land, its original ownership, and private land claims recognized by the United States; tract books from the district land office, from about 1815 to 1931, in ninety-seven volumes, 19 feet, with the dates of entry, the names of owners, and the locations of mineral, coal, swamp, and railroad lands; original survey field notes, October 27, 1815–June 9, 1934, in bound volumes, envelopes, pockets, and folded papers, 73 feet, with an index volume; original land plats of U.S. government surveys, March 6, 1816–

1953–54), XXI, 488–89, Vols. XIX–XXI of Carter (ed.), *The Territorial Papers of the United States,* 26 vols.

15 / 4 *Statutes* 549. Documents relating to the appointments of land officers are in Carter's volumes on the Arkansas Territory.

16 / Elijah Hayward to Joseph Duncan, January 24, 1834, in Carter (ed.), *Territory of Arkansas,* XXI, 888–89.

17 / 4 *Statutes* 687–88; George Graham to William Noland, January 22, 1824, in Carter (ed.), *Territory of Arkansas,* XXI, 601.

18 / Report of the Commissioner of the General Land Office, 1866, *House Executive Documents,* 39th Cong., 2nd Sess., No. 1, p. 363, Serial 1284.

August 6, 1849, in 4 feet, 2 inches, covering townships and fractional townships; copies of field notes, no date, in eleven volumes, 2½ feet; and records relating to Spanish claims.[19]

For many years, surveying in Arkansas was done under the direction of William Rector and his successors as surveyor general at St. Louis. The fifth principal meridian and the base line that were surveyed under Rector's direction in 1815, mentioned above, served for both Arkansas and Missouri.[20] As the summer season proved to be too dangerous to the health of the deputies, who contracted fevers, they were sent out during the winter. By the middle of 1818, Rector was receiving returns from deputies on surveys of confirmed private claims between the St. Francis and Arkansas rivers.[21] In February, 1819, Rector reported that extensive surveys were under way in Arkansas County, and in April he forwarded a sketch of surveys that had been done there. Field notes of surveys and township plats were certified by the deputy surveyors and sent to the General Land Office. Plats also had to be furnished to the local land offices for use in managing public land sales. In the field, surveyed tracts were marked with stakes, mounds of stones, and carvings on trees. By March, 1822, more than five million acres of land in what were then Lawrence and Arkansas counties had been surveyed.[22] A report submitted in May, 1826, concerned surveys made during the preceding winter on the White River by Charles Pelham, south of the Arkansas River by Nicholas Rightor, and by the Rector brothers (Elias, Stephen, Wharton, and William) in other places, as well as surveys by James S. Conway and deputy surveyors named Greenup and Smith.[23] Some of these surveys were not accepted, and corrections sometimes necessitated a return to Arkansas.

After Arkansas became a separate territory in 1819, sentiment developed for the appointment of a surveyor general there.[24] A bill to accom-

19 / Survey of Federal Archives, Arkansas, *Inventory of Federal Archives in the States, Series VIII, The Department of the Interior, No. 4, Arkansas* (New Orleans, 1941), 1–2.

20 / Robert R. Logan, "Notes on the First Land Surveys in Arkansas," *Arkansas Historical Quarterly*, XIX (Autumn, 1960), 266–68.

21 / William Rector to Josiah Meigs, June 5, July 20, 1818 Carter (ed.), *Territory of Louisiana-Missouri*, XV, 398, 418.

22 / *American State Papers, Public Lands*, IV, 1922, contains a list of surveying contracts made by William Rector between January, 1819, and April, 1822, and a copy of his instructions to deputies.

23 / William McRee to George Graham, May 26, 1826, in Carter (ed.), *Territory of Arkansas*, XX, 254.

24 / Memorial to Congress by the Territorial Assembly, October 8, 1820, Governor James Miller, William Bradford, and William Russell to David Barton, Senate Committee on Lands, March 25, 1824, both in Carter (ed.), *Territory of Arkansas*, XIX, 224, 630.

plish that object introduced in the Senate on March 24, 1824, was indefinitely postponed on May 21. On June 15, 1832, Congress finally adopted a statute providing for a surveyor general for the Arkansas Territory.[25] The appointment went to James S. Conway, who had been a deputy surveyor and surveyor of Lafayette County, Arkansas Territory, since 1828; he was commissioned on June 21, 1832.[26] That statute also provided that the surveyor for Missouri and Illinois was to deliver to the surveyor for the Arkansas Territory all the maps, papers, records, and documents or copies thereof relating to public lands and private land claims in Arkansas. Toward the end of 1832, Conway went to St. Louis to receive the records but had to wait while they were prepared. He received them on January 7, 1833, and conveyed them by wagon to Little Rock, where he made his headquarters. During the years 1833–1835, his staff was occupied in preparing plats and descriptions of townships, surveying instructions, diagrams, and the manuscript of printed bonds.

Under a succession of surveyors general and with appropriations made by Congress, surveying continued in the different districts of Arkansas. Pamphlets containing *Instructions to Deputy Surveyors*, printed at Little Rock in 1833 and 1837, contained detailed directions for the preparation of field notebooks.[27] In November, 1848, the General Land Office reported to Congress that surveys in Arkansas with an area of 33,406,720 acres had been executed or were being executed and that the closing of the surveyor general's office was planned for the next June 30. But the discovery of frauds in surveying in earlier years necessitated keeping the office open to direct some resurveying. The office was finally closed on March 12, 1859, and the records placed in the custody of the register of the land office at Little Rock. During the Civil War, the records were transferred to the office of the state auditor, and in 1869 they were placed in the newly created office of the state land commissioner. The collection includes survey plats and field notes of surveys, including boundary surveys dating from 1815, and maps.[28]

25 / 4 *Statutes* 531.

26 / White, *Rectangular Survey System*, 198, lists the successive surveyors general of Arkansas.

27 / Reprinted in White, *Rectangular Survey System*, 283–90, 313–20.

28 / Report of the Commissioner of the General Land Office, November 30, 1848, *Senate Executive Documents*, 30th Cong., 2nd Sess., No. 2, pp. 5–6, Serial 530; Report of the Commissioner of the General Land Office, November 30, 1859, *Senate Executive Documents*, 36th Cong., 1st Sess., No. 2, pp. 182–83, Serial 1023; John H. Reynolds, "An Account of Books, Manuscripts, Papers and Documents Concerning Arkansas in Public Repositories," *Arkansas Historical Association Publications* (Fayetteville, Ark., 1906), I, 121–23.

Land entry papers and other records of the Bureau of Land Management relating to the adjudication and survey of private land claims in the territories and states are described in this book at the end of the chapter on Land Records in Louisiana. An index to the private land claim dockets is in print.[29] Records of the bureau relating to Arkansas include files entitled the following: the claim of Colonel William Russell to land in Arkansas, 1840–1848, in four inches; private land claim records, territories of Louisiana, Arkansas, and Missouri, 1804, in three inches; records relating to the Bowie claims, fraudulent claims in Arkansas, 1827–1843, in half an inch; letters received relating to private land claims in Arkansas, 1828–1830, in eight inches; the claim of the heirs of Nathaniel Philbrook to land in Arkansas, 1877–1879, in four inches; a record of testimony in private land claims cases in Missouri and Arkansas, 1824–1859, in one volume; and record copies of letters received by the surveyor general of Arkansas from the commissioner of the General Land Office, 1834–1840, in one volume. Letters to and from the surveyor general, 1840–1858, in four volumes, and an inventory of books, plats, etc., 1853, in the surveyor general's office were transferred from the National Archives to the Federal Records Center in Fort Worth in 1984.

29 / Ainsworth, *Private Land Claims*, 1–10.

25

ða

Ecclesiastical Records

After the establishment of Arkansas Post, a mission was set up by the Jesuits on land granted by Tonti. Priests served there irregularly during the French and Spanish periods, and sometimes others from Ste. Geneviève and New Madrid made brief visits during which they made recordings in the registers.

About 1900, Myra McAlmont Vaughan, a collector of historical materials relating to Arkansas, copied the registers of the Catholic church at Arkansas Post, which were then in the custody of the circuit clerk of Arkansas County in the courthouse at De Witt, Arkansas. An abstract of these transcripts that was published later includes marriages, baptisms, and burials, 1764–1799, marriages of whites, October 25, 1799–August 9, 1802, and burials of whites, September 15, 1796–September 24, 1799.[1] A record of the births of four girls at Arkansas Post on July 10, 1744, made by a visiting missionary is in the Public Archives of Canada. Copies of the registers are in the Quebec Archives, the Public Archives of Canada, and the repository of the Missouri Historical Society. The registers of the church of St. Francis of Assisi at Pointe Coupee, 1727–1756, contain entries for Arkansas Post.

---

1 / Dorothy J. Core (comp. and ed.) and Nicole W. Hatfield (trans.), *Abstract of Catholic Register of Arkansas (1764–1858)* (De Witt, Ark., 1976), 10–85.

Bibliography

I. Bibliographies

Child, Sargent B., and Dorothy O. Holmes. *Bibliography of Research Projects Reports: Check List of Historical Records Survey Publications.* Washington, D.C., 1943.

Clark, Thomas D., ed. *The Expanding South, 1750–1825: The Ohio Valley and the Cotton Frontier.* Norman: University of Oklahoma Press, 1959. Vol. II of Clark, ed., *Travels in the Old South: A Bibliography.* 3 vols.

——, ed. *The Formative Years, 1527–1783: From the Spanish Exploration Through the American Revolution.* Norman: University of Oklahoma Press, 1956. Vol. I of Clark, ed., *Travels in the Old South: A Bibliography.* 3 vols.

Conrad, Glenn R., and Carl A. Brasseaux. *A Selected Bibliography of Scholarly Literature on Colonial Louisiana and New France.* Lafayette, La.: Center for Louisiana History, 1983.

Faÿ, Bernard. *Bibliographie critique des ouvrages français relatifs aux Etats-Unis (1770–1800).* Paris: E. Champion, 1925.

Ford, Worthington C. "French Royal Edicts, etc. on America." *Massachusetts Historical Society Proceedings,* LX (April, 1927), 250–304.

Hale, Richard W., Jr., ed. *Guide to Photocopied Historical Materials in the United States and Canada.* Ithaca, N.Y.: Cornell University Press, 1961.

Hefner, Loretta L. *The WPA Historical Records Survey: A Guide to the Unpublished Inventories, Indexes and Transcripts.* Chicago: Society of American Archivists, 1980.

Hilton, Ronald, ed. *Handbook of Hispanic Source Materials and Research Organizations in the United States.* Stanford: Stanford University Press, 1956.

Holmes, Jack D. L. *A Guide to Spanish Louisiana, 1762–1806.* Birmingham, Ala.: Jack D. L. Holmes, 1970.

Hubach, Robert R. *Early Midwestern Travel Narratives: An Annotated Bibliography, 1634–1850.* Detroit: Wayne State University Press, 1961.

Matthews, William. *American Diaries: An Annotated Bibliography of American Diaries Written Prior to the Year 1861.* Berkeley and Los Angeles: University of California Press, 1945.

——. *Canadian Diaries and Autobiographies.* Berkeley and Los Angeles: University of California Press, 1950.

McDermott, John F., ed. *Travelers on the Western Frontier.* Urbana: University of Illinois Press, 1970.

McMurtrie, Douglas C. *Early Printing in New Orleans, 1764–1810, with a Bibliography of the Issues of the Louisiana Press.* New Orleans: Searcy and Pfaff, 1929.

——. *Louisiana Imprints, 1768–1810; in Supplement to the Bibliography in "Early Printing in New Orleans."* Heartman's Historical Series, no. 62. Hattiesburg, Miss.: Book Farm, 1942.

Monaghan, Frank. *French Travellers in the United States, 1765–1932: A Bibliography.* Supplement by Samuel J. Marino. New York: Antiquarian Press, 1961.

Moncton, Université de, Centre d'Études Acadiennes. *Bibliographie Acadienne. Liste de volumes, brochures et theses concernant L'Acadie et les Acadiens.* Rédigée

sous la direction de R. P. Anselme Chiasson, compilée par Claude Guilbeault
(Publications du Centre d'Études Acadiennes, t. II). Moncton, Canada, 1976.
————. *Bibliographie Acadiennes. Liste des articles de periodiques concernant l'Acadie et
les Acadiens des débuts à 1976 (Inventaire general des sources documentaires sur les
Acadiens*, t. III). Moncton, Canada, 1977.
Parker, John, and Carol Urness. *The James Ford Bell Collection, a List of Additions,
1960–1964.* Minneapolis: University of Minnesota Press, 1967.
Roaten, Darnell. "Denis Braud: Some Imprints in the Bancroft Library." *Biblio-
graphic Society of America Papers*, LXII (1968), 252–54.
Thomas Gilcrease Institute of American History and Art. *A Catalog of Hispanic
Documents in the Thomas Gilcrease Institute.* Compiled by Clevy L. Strout.
Tulsa, Okla.: Thomas Gilcrease Institute, 1962.
U.S. Work Projects Administration, Division of Service Projects. *Bibliography of
Research Projects Reports. Check List of Historical Records Survey Publications.*
Prepared by Sargent B. Childs, Dorothy P. Holmes and Cyril E. Paquin.
Washington, D.C.: Work Projects Administration, 1943.
Vollmar, Edward R., S.J. *The Catholic Church in America: An Historical Bibliography.*
New Brunswick, N.J.: Scarecrow Press, 1956.

II. Manuscripts and Archives

Beers, Henry P. Correspondence, 1939–85. Numerous letters to and from archival and manuscript repositories, libraries, historians, and others.
Carnegie Institution of Washington, Department of Historical Research. Correspondence, 1905–29. Since this file was used, it has been interfiled with the
papers of John Franklin Jameson, who was the director of the department
from 1905 to 1928, in the Manuscript Division of the Library of Congress.
Hill Memorial Library, Louisiana State University, Baton Rouge Survey of Federal Archives, Louisiana. Reports on Serials, no. 861.
National Archives, Washington, D.C.
    U.S. Department of the Interior. Records of the Bureau of Land Manage-
    ment (Record Group 49).
    Letters Received.
    Letters Received from Registers and Receivers.
    Letters Received from Surveyors General.
    Missouri Miscellaneous Private Land Claims Correspondence.
    U.S. Department of the Interior. Records of the Office of the Secretary of the
    Interior (Record Group 48).
    Lands and Railroads Division. Letter Book.
    U.S. Department of Justice. Letters Sent Book, General Records of the De-
    partment of Justice (Record Group 60).
    U.S. Department of State. General Records of the Department of State
    (Record Group 59).
    Florida Territory Papers, 1821–1845.

Louisiana Territory Papers, 1796–1812.
Miscellaneous Permanent Commissions, 1823–1848.
Mississippi Territory Papers, 1797–1817.
Orleans Territory Papers, 1764–1813.
U.S. Work Projects Administration. Records of the Work Projects Administration (Record Group 69).

III. Printed Archives and Manuscripts

A. *Alabama*

Borja Medina, Francisco Rojos de. *José de Ezpeleta, Governador de la Mobile, 1780–1781*. Seville: Escuela de Estudios Hispánico Americanos de Sevilla, 1980.

Carter, Clarence E., ed. *The Territory of Alabama, 1817–1819*. Washington, D.C.: Government Printing Office, 1952. Vol. XVIII of Carter, ed., *The Territorial Papers of the United States*. 26 volumes.

"Census of the Habitants of Fort Louis de la Mobile and the Surrounding Villages, June 28, 1721." *Deep South Genealogical Quarterly*, I (March, 1964), 136–39.

"Census of the Inhabitants of Dauphine Island, Mobile, and Pascagoula taken by Monsieur Perry, March, 1725." *Deep South Genealogical Quarterly*, I (December, 1963), 86.

De Ville, Winston. "Fort St. Stephens in 1797." *Deep South Genealogical Quarterly*, V (February, 1968), 159–60.

———. "Some Non-French Inhabitants of Alabama, 1787." *Louisiana Genealogical Register*, XXI (March, 1974), 42–44.

Hahn, Marilyn D. *Old Cahaba Land Office Records & Military Warrants, 1817–1853*. Mobile, Ala.: Old South Printing & Publishing Co., 1981.

———. *Old Sparta & Elba Land Office Records & Military Warrants, 1822–1860*. Easley, S.C.: Southern Historical Press, 1983.

———. *Old St. Stephen's Land Office Records & American State Papers, Public Lands, Vol. I, 1768–1888*. Easley, S.C.: Southern Historical Press, 1983.

Holmes, Jack D. L., comp. "1797 Alabama Census According to Spanish Records." *Alabama Genealogical Quarterly*, VIII (September, 1966), 123–24.

Mallon, Mrs. John H., Jr. "Mobile Translated Records, 1781–1785." *Deep South Genealogical Quarterly*, V (February, 1968), 144–59.

"1706 Census at Fort Louis de la Louisiane (Mobile)." *Deep South Genealogical Quarterly*, I (August, 1963), 30.

Villeré, Sidney L. "List of French Inhabitants of Mobile in West Florida, Who Took the Oath of Allegiance and Fidelity to His Britannic Majesty King George III, October 2, 1764." *New Orleans Genesis*, VI (March, 1967), 117–18.

Warren, Ruth. "List of Inhabitants of Mobile [1764]." *Deep South Genealogical Quarterly*, III (May, 1966), 629–30.

B. *Louisiana*

1. BOOKS

Acosta Rodríquez, Antonio. *La población de Luisiana española (1763–1803).* Madrid: Ministerio de Asuntos Exteriores, 1979.

Ardoin, Robert B. L. *Louisiana Census Records: Avoyelles and St. Landry Parishes, 1810 & 1820.* 2 vols. Baltimore: Genealogical Publishing Co., 1970.

Arthur, Stanley C. *Index to the Dispatches of the Spanish Governors of Louisiana, 1766–1792.* New Orleans, 1975.

Baillardel, A., and A. Prioult. *Le Chevalier de Pradel: Vie d'un colon français en Louisiane au xviiiᵉ siècle d'après sa correspondance et celle de sa famille.* Paris: Maisonneuve, 1928.

Barron, Bill, ed. *Census of Pointe Coupee, Louisiana, 1745.* New Orleans: Polyanthos, 1978.

———, ed. *The Vaudreuil Papers: A Calendar and Index of the Personal and Private Records of Pierre de Rigaud de Vaudreuil, Royal Governor of the French Province of Louisiana, 1743–1753.* New Orleans: Polyanthos, 1975.

Behrman, Eileen L., comp. *St. James Parish, Louisiana, Colonial Records, 1782–1787.* Conroe, Tex.: Behrman, 1980.

Bolton, Herbert E., trans. and ed. *Athanese de Mézières and the Louisiana-Texas Frontier, 1768–1780. Documents Published for the First Time, from the Original Spanish and French Manuscripts, Chiefly in the Archives of Mexico and Spain.* 2 vols. Cleveland: Arthur H. Clark, 1914.

Conrad, Glenn R., comp. and trans. *The First Families of Louisiana.* Baton Rouge: Claitor's, 1970.

De Ville, Winston. *Gulf Coast Colonials: A Compendium of French Families in Early Eighteenth Century Louisiana.* Introduction by James D. Hardy, Jr. Baltimore: Genealogical Publishing Co., 1968.

———. *Louisiana Colonials: Soldiers and Vagabonds.* Baltimore: Genealogical Publishing Co., 1963.

———. *Louisiana Recruits, 1752–1758: Ship Lists of Troops from the Independant [sic] Companies of the Navy Destined for Service in the French Colony of Louisiana.* Preface by René Chartrand. Cottonport, La.: Polyanthos, 1973.

———. *Louisiana Troops, 1720–1770.* Fort Worth: American Reference Publishers, [1965?].

———. *Marriage Contracts of Natchitoches, 1739–1803.* Introduction by Edwin A. Davis [Nashville?], 1961.

De Ville, Winston, and Jane G. Bulliard, trans. and eds. *Marriage Contracts of the Attakapas Post, 1760–1803: Colonial Louisiana Marriage Contracts and the 1774 Census of Attakapas Post.* St. Martinville, La.: Attakapas Historical Association, 1966.

Documents Relative to Louisiana and Florida, Received at the Department of State from the Secretary of State of Spain Through the Hon. C. P. Van Ness. [Washington? 1833?].

Forsyth, Alice D., and Ghislaine Pleasonton. *Louisiana Marriage Contracts: A Compilation of Abstracts from the Records of the Superior Council of Louisiana during the French Regime, 1725–1758*. Introduction by Hans W. Baade. New Orleans: Polyanthos, 1980.

Forsyth, Alice D., and Earline L. Zeringue, comps. and trans. *German "Pest Ships," 1720–1721*. New Orleans: Genealogical Research Society of New Orleans, 1969.

French, Benjamin F., ed. *Historical Collections of Louisiana and Florida, Including Translations of Original Manuscripts Relating to Their Discovery and Settlement, with Numerous Historical and Biographical Notes, New Series*. New York: J. Sabin & Sons, 1869. *Second Series, Historical Memoirs and Narratives, 1527–1702*. New York: A. Mason, 1875. Reprint. New York: AMS Press, 1976.

———, ed. *Historical Collections of Louisiana, Embracing Translations of Many Rare and Valuable Documents Relating to the Natural, Civil and Political History of That State*. 5 vols. New York: Wiley and Putnam, 1846–53. Reprint. New York: AMS Press, 1976.

Gaudet, Placide. *Acadian Genealogy and Notes* [With Documents Concerning the Expulsion of the Acadians]. Canada, Public Archives. *Report Concerning Canadian Archives for the year 1905*, Vol. II. Ottawa: S. E. Dawson, 1906. Appendix A, Part III.

Gianelloni, Elizabeth B. *Love, Honor, and Betrayal: The Notarial Acts of Estevan De Quiñones, 1778–1784*. [Baton Rouge?], 1964.

———. *Love, Honor, and Betrayal: The Notarial Acts of Estevan de Quiñones, 1785–1786*. Baton Rouge: Elizabeth B. Gianelloni, 1964–65.

Hackett, Charles W., ed., and Charmion C. Shelby and Mary R. Splawn, trans. *Pichardo's Treatise on the Limits of Louisiana and Texas: An Argumentative Historical Treatise with Reference to the Verification of the True Limits of the Provinces of Louisiana and Texas: Written by Father Jose Antonio Pichardo . . .* 4 vols. Austin: University of Texas Press, 1931–46.

Holmes, Jack D. L. *Honor and Fidelity: The Louisiana Infantry Regiment and the Louisiana Militia Companies, 1766–1821*. Birmingham, Ala., 1965.

Holmes, Jack D. L., ed. *Documentos inéditos para la historia de la Luisiana, 1792–1810. Colección Chimalistac de libros y documentos acerca de la Nueva España*, no. 15. Madrid: Ediciónes José Porrúa Turanzas, 1963.

———, ed. *José de Evía y sus reconocimientos del Golfe de México, 1783–1796. Colección Chimalistac de libros y documentos de la Nueva España*, no. 26. Madrid: Ediciónes José Porrúa Turanzas, 1968.

Kinnaird, Lawrence, ed. *Spain in the Mississippi Valley, 1765–1794*. 3 vols. American Historical Association, *Annual Report*, 1945, Vols. II–IV. Washington, D.C., Government Printing Office, 1949.

Le Gac, Charles. *Immigration and War: Louisiana, 1718–1721, from the Memoir of Charles Le Gac*. Translated, edited, and annotated by Glenn R. Conrad. Lafayette: University of Southwestern Louisiana, [1970].

Maduell, Charles R., Jr. *Marriage Contracts, Wills, and Testaments of the Spanish*

Colonial Period in New Orleans, 1770–1804. [New Orleans]: C. R. Maduell, Jr., 1969.

———, comp. and trans. *The Census Tables for the French Colony of Louisiana from 1699 through 1732.* Baltimore: Genealogical Publishing Co., 1972.

Margry, Pierre, ed. *Découvertes et établissements des français dans l'ouest et dans le sud de l'Amérique Septentrionale (1614–1754): Mémoires et documents originaux.* 6 vols. Paris: Imprimerie D. Jouaust, 1876–86.

Medina Encina, Parificación. *Documentos relativos a la independencia de Norteamérica existentes en archivos españoles, Vol. I, Archivo General de Indias, sección de gobierno, años 1752–1822.* Pts. 1 and 2. Introduction by Rosario Parra Cala. Madrid: Ministerio de Asuntos Exteriores, Dirección General de Relaciones Culturas, 1976.

Mills, Elizabeth S. *Natchitoches Colonials: Censuses, Military Rolls, and Tax Lists, 1722–1803.* Chicago: Adams Press, 1981.

Morazán, Ronald B., trans. and ed. "Letters, Petitions and Decrees of the Cabildo of New Orleans, 1800–1803." Ph.D. dissertation, Louisiana State University, 1972.

Nasatir, Abraham P. *Spanish War Vessels on the Mississippi, 1792–1796.* New Haven: Yale University Press, 1968.

Pease, Theodore C., and Ernestine Jenison, eds. *Illinois on the Eve of the Seven Years' War, 1747–1755.* Collections of the Illinois State Historical Library, Volume XXIX, French Series, Volume III. Springfield, Ill., 1940.

Portré-Bobinski, Germaine, trans. *Natchitoches: Translations of Old French and Spanish Documents.* [Rutland, Ill.], 1928.

Robertson, James A., ed. *Louisiana Under the Rule of Spain, France, and the United States, 1785–1807, as Portrayed in Hitherto Unpublished Contemporary Accounts.* 2 vols. Cleveland: Arthur H. Clark Co., 1911.

Robichaux, Albert J., Jr., comp., trans., and ed. *Colonial Settlers Along Bayou Lafourche: Louisiana Census Records, 1770–1798.* Harvey, La.: Robichaux, 1974.

———, comp., trans., and ed. *Louisiana Census and Militia Lists, 1770–1789, Volume I, German Coast, New Orleans, Below New Orleans and Lafourche, Volume II, Colonial Settlers Along the Bayou Lafourche.* Harvey, La.: Dumas Printing, 1973–74.

Serrano y Sanz, Manuel. *Documentos históricos de la Florida y la Luisiana, siglos XVI al XVIII.* Madrid: V. Suárez, 1912.

Toups, Neil J. *Mississippi Valley Pioneers.* Lafayette, La.: Neilson Publishing Co., [1970].

Vidrine, Jacqueline O., and Winston De Ville, comps. *Marriage Contracts of the Opelousas Post, 1766–1803.* Introduction by John C. L. Andreassen. [Ville Platte?], 1960.

Villeré, Sidney L. *The Canary Islands Migration to Louisiana, 1778–1783. The History and Passenger Lists of the Isleños Volunteer Recruits and Their Families.* New Orleans: Genealogical Research Society of New Orleans, [1971].

Voorhies, Jacqueline K., comp. and trans. *Some Late Eighteenth-Century Louisia-*

nians: Census Records of the Colony, 1758–1796. Lafayette: University of Southwestern Louisiana, 1973.

Whitaker, Arthur P., trans. and ed. *Documents Relating to the Commercial Policy of Spain in the Floridas, with Incidental References to Louisiana.* De Land: Florida State Historical Society, 1931.

Woodward, Ralph L., Jr., trans. and ed. *Tribute to Don Bernardo de Gálvez.* New Orleans: Historic New Orleans Collection, 1979.

2. ARTICLES

Anderson, Sherburne, ed. "Brand Books of Iberville Parish, Louisiana." *Louisiana Genealogical Register,* XI (June, 1964), 15–20.

"Attakapas Militia List." *Louisiana Genealogical Register,* IX (September, 1962), 39–40.

Boling, Yvette G. "The German Coast of Louisiana in 1749." *Louisiana Genealogical Register,* XXIX (December, 1982), 373–90.

Brasseaux, Carl A. "Official Correspondence of Spanish Louisiana, 1770–1803." *Revue de Louisiane,* VI– (Winter, 1977–).

Bridges, Katherine, and Winston De Ville. "Natchitoches in 1766." *Louisiana History,* IV (Spring, 1963), 145–59.

Bulliard, Jane G., and Leona T. David, eds. "1774 Census of Attakapas Post, St. Martinville, La." *Attakapas Historical Association Special Publication,* no. 1 (1966), 33–72.

Burnet, Edmund C., ed. "Papers Relating to Bourbon County, Georgia, 1785–1786." *American Historical Review,* XV (October, 1909, January, 1910), 66–111, 297–353.

Centanni, Irna A., and Sidney L. Villeré. "Early Census of the Louisiana Province." *New Orleans Genesis,* V (June, September, 1966), 221–25, 349–51; VI (January, 1967), 35–41.

Chandler, R. E. "A Shipping Contract: Spain Brings Acadians to Louisiana." *Revue de Louisiane,* VIII (Summer, 1979), 73–81.

Churchill, Charles R. "The Gálvez Expedition, 1779–1783, Register of Infantry Regiment of Louisiana, Roster." *New Orleans Genesis,* XVI (September, 1976), 321–23.

Corbitt, Duvon C. "Papers Relating to the Georgia-Florida Frontier, 1784–1800." *Georgia Historical Quarterly,* XX–XXXV (1936–51).

Corbitt, Duvon C., ed., and Roberta D. Corbitt, trans. "Papers from the Spanish Archives Relating to Tennessee and the Old Southwest, 1783–1800." *East Tennessee Historical Society Publications,* nos. 9–50 (1937–78).

Cruzat, Heloise H., trans. "Documents Concerning Sale of Chaouachas Plantation in Louisiana, 1737–38." *Louisiana Historical Quarterly,* VIII (October, 1925), 594–646.

———, trans. "Louisiana in 1724: Banet's Report to the Company of the Indies, Dated Paris, December 20, 1724." *Louisiana Historical Quarterly,* XII (January, 1929), 121–33.

Cruzat, Heloise H., trans., and Henry P. Dart, ed. "Documents Concerning Bien-ville's Lands in Louisiana, 1719–1737." *Louisiana Historical Quarterly*, X (Jan-uary–October, 1927), 5–24, 161–84, 364–80, 538–61; XI (January–July, 1928), 87–111, 209–32, 463–65.

Dart, Albert L., trans. "Ship Lists of Passengers Leaving France for Louisiana, 1718–1724." *Louisiana Historical Quarterly*, XIV (October, 1931), 516–20; XV (January, July, 1932), 68–77, 453–67; XXI (October, 1938), 965–78.

Dart, Henry P., ed. "The First Law Regulating Land Grants in French Colonial Louisiana [October 12, 1716]." *Louisiana Historical Quarterly*, XIV (April, 1931), 346–48.

———, ed. "The Oath of Allegiance to Spain." *Louisiana Historical Quarterly*, IV (April, 1921), 205–15.

Dart, Henry P., ed., and Heloise H. Cruzat, trans. "The Cabildo Archives— French Period." *Louisiana Historical Quarterly*, III (January–October, 1920), 71–99, 279–321, 322–60, 506–69; IV (April–July, 1921), 216–17, 361–68.

Delanglez, Jean, S.J., ed. "Mémoire [by François Le Maire] sur la Louisiane, 1717." *Revue d'histoire de l'Amérique française*, III (June, September, December, 1949), 94–110, 256–69, 423–46.

———, trans. and ed. "M. Le Maire on Louisiana [January 15, 1714]." *Mid-America*, XIX (April, 1937), 124–54.

De Ville, Winston. "Census of the Opelousas Post, 28 May 1796." *Louisiana Gene-alogical Register*, XIII (March, 1966), 7–8.

———. "Census of the Ouachita Post in Louisiana: 1790." *Louisiana Genealogical Register*, XXIX (March, 1982), 21–24.

———. "Land Census of the Inhabitants of the Opelousas, 1793." *Louisiana Gene-alogical Register*, VII (March, June, 1960), 8–9, 26–28.

———. "Louisiana Officers in 1750." *Louisiana Genealogical Register*, XVII (De-cember, 1970), 314, 321.

———, trans. "French Soldiers in Louisiana–1751." *Louisiana Genealogical Regis-ter*, XV (September, 1968), 85–87.

———, trans. "Natchitoches Tax List for 1793." *Louisiana Genealogical Register*, XXVII (September, 1980), 245–48.

De Ville, Winston, ed., and Mrs. Drouet W. Vidrine, trans. "Spanish Census of Point Coupee—1766." *Louisiana Genealogical Register*, VII (September, De-cember, 1960), 33, 55.

Devron, Gustavus. "Two Original and Newly-Found Documents of the Depar-ture, Shipwreck and Death of Mr. Aubry, the Last French Governor of Loui-siana." *Louisiana Historical Society Publications*, II (1897), 28–35.

Ditchy, Jay K., trans. "Early Census Tables of Louisiana." *Louisiana Historical Quarterly*, XIII (April, 1930), 205–29.

Ducote, Mrs. Joseph. "The Names of Those Who Sold Lands Situated in the Post of Opelousas [1765–1805]." *Louisiana Genealogical Register*, XIX (March, 1972), 82–85.

Hebert, Gladys, ed., and Sidney L. Villeré, trans. "A Partial Colonial Census of

Saint Charles Parish—Louisiana." *New Orleans Genesis*, VII (January, 1968), 30–34.

Kendall, John S., ed. "Documents Concerning the West Florida Revolution, 1810." *Louisiana Historical Quarterly*, XVII (January–July, 1934), 81–95, 306–14, 474–501.

"Loyalty Oath List for Pointe Coupee to the Government of Spain, 1769." *Louisiana Genealogical Register*, XI (March, 1964), 10–11.

Mills, Elizabeth S. "Natchitoches Militia of 1782." *Louisiana Genealogical Register*, XX (September, 1973), 216–18.

Miró, Esteban, and Martin Navarro. "Report of Governor Esteban Miró and Intendente Martin Navarro on the Fire Which Destroyed New Orleans, March 21, 1788 [April 1, 1788]." *Louisiana Historical Society Publications*, VIII (1914–15), 59–62.

Padgett, James A., ed. "The Constitution of the West Florida Republic." *Louisiana Historical Quarterly*, XX (October, 1937), 881–94.

————, ed. "Official Records of the West Florida Revolution and Republic." *Louisiana Historical Quarterly*, XXI (July, 1938), 685–805.

————, ed. "The West Florida Revolution of 1810, as Told in the Letters of John Rhea, Fulwar Skipwith, Reuben Kemper and Others." *Louisiana Historical Quarterly*, XXI (January, 1938), 76–202.

Portré-Bobinski, Germaine, trans., and Sarah L. C. Clapp, comp. "Index to Natchitoches: Translation of Old French and Spanish Documents." *Deep South Genealogical Quarterly*, IV (August, November, 1966, February, May, 1967), 713–17, 758–64, 826–34, 870–78; V (August, November, 1967, May, 1968), 38–42, 79–83, 209–14.

Préjean, Harold. "The Passenger List of the *Beaumont.*" *Attakapas Gazette*, VIII (December, 1973), 165–73.

Sanders, Albert G., trans., and Henry P. Dart, ed. "Documents Concerning the Crozat Regime in Louisiana, 1712–1717." *Louisiana Historical Quarterly*, XV (July, 1932), 589–609; XVI (April, 1933), 293–308; XVII (April, July, 1934), 268–93, 452–73.

Tate, Albert J. "Spanish Census of the Baton Rouge District for 1786." *Louisiana History*, XXIV (Winter, 1983), 70–84.

"Translation of Some Documents Bearing on General Collot's Arrest." *Louisiana Historical Quarterly*, I (April, 1918), 321–26.

Vidrine, Jacqueline O. "Attakapas Area Families (Non-Acadians)." *Louisiana Genealogical Register*, XXI (March, 1974), 57–63.

Vidrine, Mrs. Druet W. "Recensement General des Attakapas, October 30, 1774." *Louisiana Genealogical Register*, XIII (March, 1966), 65–66.

Villeré, Sidney L. "General Census of the First German Coast Province of Louisiana [May 1, 1804]." *New Orleans Genesis*, VI (September, 1967), 337–40.

Wells, Carol, trans. and ed. "The Succession of François Clauseau." *Louisiana Studies*, XI (Spring, 1972), 70–83.

C. *Mississippi*

Centanni, Irna A. "Louisiana, État Civil 1720–1724. Registre de ceux qui sont morts au vieux Fort Biloxi pendant l'administration de M. Damion depuis le huit août 1720." *New Orleans Genesis*, VI (September, 1967), 388–90.

Dunbar, William. "Report of Sir William Dunbar to the Spanish Government at the Conclusion of His Services in Locating and Surveying the Thirty-First Degree of Latitude." Edited by Franklin L. Riley. *Mississippi Historical Society Publications*, III (1900), 185–205.

Edwards, Mrs. Boyd C., and Bickham Christian. "Lists of Persons Taking the Oaths of Allegiance in the Natchez District, 1798–99." *National Genealogical Society Quarterly*, XLII (September, 1954), 108–16.

Gillis, Norman E. *Early Inhabitants of the Natchez District.* [Baton Rouge, 1963].

Holmes, Jack D. L., ed. "William Dunbar's Correspondence on the Southern Boundary of Mississippi, 1798." *Journal of Mississippi History*, XXVII (May, 1965), 187–90.

Jackson, Ronald V., Altha Polson, and Shirley P. Zachrison. *Early American Series, Early Mississippi Census, Volume I, 1788–1819.* Bountiful, Utah: Accelerated Indexing Systems, 1980.

McBee, May Wilson, ed. *The Natchez Court Records, 1767–1805: Abstracts of Early Records.* Ann Arbor, Mich.: Edwards Brothers, 1953. Reprint. Baltimore: Genealogical Publishing Co., 1979.

Mills, Elizabeth S. "Deaths at Biloxi, 1699–1700." *Louisiana Genealogical Register*, XXII (June, 1974), 130.

Rowland, Dunbar, and Albert G. Sanders, trans. and eds. *Mississippi Provincial Archives [1701–1743], French Dominion.* 3 vols. Jackson: Press of the Mississippi Department of Archives and History, 1927–32.

———, trans. and eds. *Mississippi Provincial Archives, French Dominion, Volume IV, 1729–1748, Volume V, 1749–1763.* Revised and edited by Patricia K. Galloway. Baton Rouge: Louisiana State University Press, 1984.

Rowland, Mrs. Dunbar. "Mississippi's Colonial Population and Land Grants." *Mississippi Historical Society Publications, Centenary Series, Volume I.* Jackson, Miss.: The Society, 1916, pp. 405–28.

D. *Missouri*

Barker, Eugene C., ed. *The Austin Papers.* American Historical Association, *Annual Report* [1919], pts. 1 and 2; [1928], pt. 2. 3 vols. Washington, D.C.: Government Printing Office, 1924, 1928.

Barnhart, Warren L. "The Letterbooks of Charles Gratiot, Fur Trader: The Nomadic Years, 1769–1797." Ph.D. dissertation, St. Louis University, 1972.

Ericson, Carolyn, and Frances Ingmire. *First Settlers of the Missouri Territory, Volume I, Grants from American State Papers, Class VIII, Public Lands.* Nacogdoches, Tex.: Ericson Books, 1983.

———. *First Settlers of the Missouri Territory, Containing Grants in the Present States* of Missouri, Arkansas, and Oklahoma, Volume II. Nacogdoches, Tex.: Ericson Books, [1983].

Forsyth, Alice D. "Earliest Missouri Records." New Orleans Genesis, XVI (January, 1977), 77–80.

————. "The Spanish Regime in Missouri—(Part I—Saint Geneviève) (Part II—Saint Louis) Upper Louisiana." New Orleans Genesis, XIV (March, June, September, 1975), 116–22, 267–71, 357–64.

Holmes, Jack D. L. "A 1795 Inspection of Spanish Missouri." Missouri Historical Review, LV (October, 1960), 5–7.

Houck, Louis, ed. The Spanish Regime in Missouri. 2 vols. Chicago: R. R. Donnelley & Sons, 1909.

Laussat, Pierre Clément de. "Laussat to Pierre Chouteau." Missouri Historical Society Bulletin, IX (April, 1953), 311–14.

Nasatir, Abraham P., trans., and ed. Before Lewis and Clark: Documents Illustrating the History of Missouri, 1785–1804. 2 vols. Joseph Desloge Fund Publication, no. 3. St. Louis: St. Louis Historical Documents Foundation, 1952.

"Transfer of Upper Louisiana, Papers of Captain Amos Stoddard." Missouri Historical Society Glimpses of the Past, II (May–September, 1935), 76–122.

E. Ecclesiastical Publications

1. BOOKS

Bodin, George A., Rt. Rev. Msgr. Selected Acadian and Louisiana Church Records. 2 vols. Attakapas Historical Association Special Publication, nos. II–III. St. Martinville, La.: Attakapas Historical Association, 1968, 1970.

Bourquard, Shirley C. Marriage Dispensations in the Diocese of Louisiana and the Floridas, 1786–1803. Introduction by Charles E. Nolan. New Orleans: Polyanthos, 1980.

Catholic Church, Archdiocese of Québec. Mandements, lettres pastorales et circulares des évêques de Québec. Edited by Henri Têtu and l'Abbé C.-O. Gagnon. 4 vols. Québec: Imprimerie Générale A. Coté, 1887–88.

Catholic Church, Diocese of Baton Rouge. Diocese of Baton Rouge Catholic Church Records, Volume I, 1707–1769. Baton Rouge: Diocese of Baton Rouge, 1978.

————. Diocese of Baton Rouge Catholic Church Records, Volume II, 1770–1803. Baton Rouge: Diocese of Baton Rouge, 1980.

————. Diocese of Baton Rouge Catholic Church Records, Volume III, 1804–1819. Baton Rouge: Diocese of Baton Rouge, 1982.

Catholic Church, Diocese of Louisiana and the Floridas. Confirmaciones, the "First Book of Confirmations of this Parish of St. Louis of New Orleans, Containing Folios from the Beginning up to the Present" by the Bishop of Louisiana and the Floridas. New Orleans: Genealogical Society of New Orleans, 1967.

Core, Dorothy, J., ed. Abstract of Catholic Register of Arkansas (1764–1858). Translated by Nicole W. Hatfield. De Witt, Ark.: De Witt Publishing Co., 1976.

Costa, Myldred M., trans. The Letters of Marie Madeleine Hachard, 1727–28. New Orleans: Privately Printed, 1974.

D'Antoni, Blaise C., comp. and trans. *The Natchitoches Registers, 1734–1764, Volume One, Being a Compilation of Baptismal, Marriage and Funeral Records of the Poste Saint Jean Baptiste de Natchitoches for the Years 1734–1764*. New Orleans, 1970.

De Ville, Winston, comp. and trans. *Acadian Church Records, 1679–1757*. Mobile, Ala., 1964.

———, ed. *First Settlers of Pointe Coupee: A Study, Based on Early Louisiana Church Records, 1737–1750*. New Orleans: Polyanthos, 1974.

———. *The New Orleans French, 1720–1733; a Collection of Marriage Records Relating to the First Colonists of Louisiana Province*. Baltimore: Genealogical Publishing Co., 1973.

De Villier, Gladys. *The Opelousas Post: A Compendium of Church Records Relating to the First Families of Southwest Louisiana, 1776–1806*. New Orleans: Polyanthos, 1972.

Forsyth, Alice D., ed. *Louisiana Marriages, Volume I, A Collection of Marriage Records from the St. Louis Cathedral in New Orleans During the Spanish Regime and the Early American Period, 1784–1806*. New Orleans: Polyanthos, 1977.

Hanley, Thomas O., ed. *The John Carroll Papers*. 3 vols. Notre Dame, Ind.: University of Notre Dame Press, 1976.

Hébert, Donald J. *South Louisiana Records: Church and Civil Records of Lafourche-Terrebonne Parishes, Volume I, 1794–1840*. Cecelia, La.: Hébert, 1978.

Mills, Elizabeth S., trans. and ed. *Natchitoches, 1729–1803; Abstracts of the Catholic Church Registers of the French and Spanish Post of St. Jean Baptiste des Natchitoches in Louisiana*. New Orleans: Polyanthos, 1977.

———, trans. and ed. *Natchitoches, 1800–1826. Translated Abstracts of Register Number Five of the Catholic Church Parish of St. François des Natchitoches in Louisiana*. New Orleans, Polyanthos, 1980.

Morrison, Veneta de Graffenried, comp. *Index—Early Marriages of Point Coupee, 1771–1843*. New Roads, La., [1971?].

Murray, Nicholas R. *Ascension Parish, Louisiana, 1768–1899. Computer-Indexed Marriage Records*. Hammond, La., [1980?].

———. *Iberville Parish, Louisiana, 1777–1900. Computer-Indexed Marriage Records*. Hammond, La., [1981].

———. *Pointe Coupee Parish, Louisiana, 1763–1872. Computer-Indexed Marriage Records*. Hammond, La., [1982].

———. *St. Charles Parish, Louisiana, 1778–1900. Computer-Indexed Marriage Records*. Hammond, La., [1981].

———. *St. Martin Parish, Louisiana, 1760–1900. Computer-Indexed Marriage Records*. Hammond, La., 1982.

———. *St. Mary Parish, Louisiana, 1739–1892. Computer-Indexed Marriage Records*. Hammond, La., 1981.

———. *West Feliciana Parish, Louisiana, 1791–1875. Computer-Indexed Marriage Records*. Hammond, La., [1980?].

Rieder, Milton P., Jr., and Norma G. Rieder, trans. and eds. *Beaubassin,*

1712–1748. Metairie, La.: Milton and Norma Rieder, 1976. Vol. II of Rieder and Rieder, eds., *Acadian Church Records*. 3 vols.

———, trans. and eds. *Port Royal, 1702– 1721*. Metairie, La.: Milton and Norma Rieder, 1977. Vol. III of Rieder and Rieder, eds., *Acadian Church Records*. 3 vols.

St. Louis Cathedral, New Orleans. *Confirmaciónes—Libro primero de confirmaciones de esta parroquis de Sn. Luis de la Nueva Orleans*. New Orleans: Genealogical Research Society of New Orleans, 1967.

Thwaites, Reuben G., ed. *The Jesuit Relations and Allied Documents: Travels and Explorations of the Jesuit Missionaries in New France, 1610–1791; the Original French, Latin, and Italian Texts, with English Translations and Notes: Illustrated by Portraits, Maps, and Facsimiles*. 73 vols. Cleveland: Burrows Brothers, 1896–1901.

Vidrine, Jacqueline O. *Love's Legacy. The Mobile Marriages Recorded in French, Transcribed, with Annotated Abstracts in English, 1724–1786*. Lafayette, La.: Center for Louisiana Studies, University of Southwestern Louisiana, 1985.

2. ARTICLES

Allain, Mathé, trans. "Records of Belle-Isle-en-Mer." *Attakapas Gazette*, XVI (Winter, 1981), 165–71; XVII (Summer, Fall, Winter, 1982), 76–83, 123–31, 183–92.

Belsom, Jack. "Index to Confirmaciónes." *New Orleans Genesis*, X (January, 1971), 96–98.

Bernard, Paul H. F. "St. Louis Cathedral Baptismal Register 4—1802–1806." *New Orleans Genesis*, X (June, September, 1971), 220–27, 364–68.

Broders, Mrs. Edwin A. "A First Book of Burials of Natchez, Miss." *Louisiana Genealogical Register*, XI (June, 1964), 20–21.

———. "Funerals from Sept. 12, 1793, to Dec. 17, 1815, Our Lady of Sorrows Church, Baton Rouge, La." *Louisiana Genealogical Register*, XI (June, 1964), 21–24.

Broders, Mrs. Edwin A., Catherine Futch, and Marguerite W. Webb. "Acadian Records from the Parish of St. Charles-au-Mines, Grandpré, St. Gabriel Church." *New Orleans Genesis*, IX–XIV (September, 1970–January, 1975).

Campbell, Mrs. S. R. "Some Vital Records of the St. Louis Cathedral, New Orleans, La." *New Orleans Genesis*, IV (June, 1965), 186–93.

Caron, Ivanhoë. "Les Archives de l'Archevêché de Québec." Société canadienne d'histoire de l'église catholique, *Rapport* (1934–1935), 65–73.

———. "Lettres et mémoires de l'Abbé de l'Isle Dieu [1742–74]." *Rapport de l'archiviste de la province de Québec, 1935–36* [1936–37, 1937–38]. Quebec, 1936–38, pp. 275–410, 331–459, 147–253.

Centanni, Irna A. "Baptismal Register of St. John the Baptist Church [1772–1817, title varies]." *New Orleans Genesis*, IX (March, 1970), 114–31; XI (January, September, 1972), 46–49, 378–83; XII (January, March, 1973), 57–68, 176–81.

———. "Extracts from the Register of Burials in New Orleans, 1724–1726,

1729–30, 1734." *New Orleans Genesis*, VI (January–June, 1967), 27–28, 105–106, 220–21.

———. "Index to First Book of Baptisms of St. John the Baptist Parish, Edgard, Louisiana, August 1772 to December 1791." *New Orleans Genesis*, IX (March, June, 1970), 114–31, 212–21.

———. "St. John the Baptist Church, Edgard, Louisiana, Second Book of Baptisms, January 1792 to February 1796." *New Orleans Genesis*, XI (January, September, 1972), 46–49, 378–83.

———. "St. John the Baptist Church, Edgard, Louisiana, Third Book of Baptisms, March 12, 1796–April 8, 1817." *New Orleans Genesis*, XII (January, March, 1973), 57–62, 170–75.

———. "St. Louis Cathedral Baptismal Book 2, May 12, 1786, to June 5, 1796." *New Orleans Genesis*, VIII (June, September, 1969), 221, 317–23; IX (January, March, 1970), 27–33, 142–46.

"Correspondence between Abbé Gibault and Bishop Briand, 1768–1788." *American Catholic Historical Society of Philadelphia Records*, XX (December, 1909), 406–30.

"Correspondence between the Sees of Quebec and Baltimore, 1788–1847." *American Catholic Historical Society Records*, XVIII (March–December, 1907), 154–90, 282–305, 435–67.

Dart, Mrs. Stephen. "West Feliciana Parish Marriage Index, 1791–1875." *Louisiana Genealogical Register*, XVI (June, September, 1969), 177–78, 242–43; XVII (June, 1970), 193–96; XVIII (March, December, 1971), 52–54, 314–16.

De Ville, Winston. "List of Children Baptized in the Parish of New Orleans in 1728." *Louisiana Genealogical Register*, X (June, 1963), 32.

———. "Register of Deaths at Old Fort Biloxi, Mississippi, 1720–1723." *National Genealogical Society Quarterly*, LV (March, 1967), 45–48.

DeVitt, E. I., ed. "Propaganda Documents: Appointment of the First Bishop of Baltimore, [1783–89]." *American Catholic Historical Society Records*, XXI (December, 1910), 185–236.

Forsyth, Alice D. "Baptismal Book, V–VI, 1763–1771, St. Louis Cathedral Archives." *Louisiana Genealogical Register*, XXII (June, 1975), 173–79.

———. "Baptismal Register [St. Bernard Church at] Our Lady of Lourdes Church—Violet, La., 1801–1851." *New Orleans Genesis*, V (January–September, 1966), 47–50, 164–68, 238–40, 352–55; VI (March, 1967), 121.

———. "Marriages, Baptisms, and Deaths of the Little Red Church [1739–55]." *New Orleans Genesis*, I (January–September, 1962), 64–82, 172–83, 258–72, 356–60; II (January, June, 1963), 35–42, 249–52; IV (March, 1965), 153–61; V (January, 1966), 51–58.

———. "St. Louis Cathedral Archives, Marriages Entered in Baptismal Register IV–May 1, 1759, to November 15, 1762." *New Orleans Genesis*, VI (June, 1967), 226–30.

———. "St. Louis Cathedral Funeral Register, 1772–1790—Excerpts." *Louisiana Genealogical Register*, XXII (September, 1975), 207–12.

————. "St. Louis Cathedral Funeral Register, 1793–1803." *Louisiana Genealogical Register*, XXII (June, 1975), 125–31.

Forsyth, Alice D., and Hewitt L. Forsyth. "Extrait des registres pour les baptêmes de l'église paroissialle de la Nouvelle Orleans de l'année 1729–30." *New Orleans Genesis*, VI (March, 1967), 103–105.

Forsyth, Hewitt L. "Funeral Records—St. Louis Cathedral—1803–1807." *New Orleans Genesis*, VI (September, 1967), 328–29; VII (January, March, 1968), 52–57, 140–45.

Forsyth, Hewitt L., and Alice D. Forsyth. "Marriage Register of St. Louis Basilica—Volume 1, February 6, 1777–April 13, 1784." *New Orleans Genesis*, V (September, 1966), 309–12.

————. "Marriage Register of St. Louis Basilica Archives, January 17, 1764, to January 22, 1774, Register B." *New Orleans Genesis*, V (September, 1966), 305–309.

————. "Marriage Register of St. Louis Cathedral, May 1784 to June 1806." *New Orleans Genesis*, VI (January, 1967), 19–23.

————. "Saint Louis Basilica Marriage Records, July 1st 1720 to December 4th 1730." *New Orleans Genesis*, V (June, 1966), 190–211.

Fortier, Lucille M. B. "Funeral Records—St. Louis Cathedral, 1772–1793." *New Orleans Genesis*, V (June, September, 1966), 211–14, 313–17; VI (January, 1967), 24–26.

————. "Our Lady of Lourdes Catholic Church, Violet, La.—Interment Records [1787–91]." *New Orleans Genesis*, IV (March, 1966), 319–20.

Futch, Catherine B., comp. and trans. "Baptisms Recorded at the Church of St. Francis of Assisi—Now the Church of the Immaculate Conception, Natchitoches, Louisiana, 1734–1743." *New Orleans Genesis*, VIII (June, 1969), 243–52.

————, comp. and trans. "Burials from the Santiago de Cabanoce Church, Now Known as St. James Catholic Church, St. James Parish, Louisiana, for the Year 1796." *New Orleans Genesis*, VIII (January, 1969), 47–49.

————, comp. and trans. "Marriages Performed at the Church of Santiago de Cabanoce, Known Now as St. James Catholic Church, St. James Parish, Louisiana, for the Year 1796." *New Orleans Genesis*, VIII (January, 1969), 47.

Futch, Catherine B., and Mrs. Edwin A. Broders. "Marriages of Early Natchez Settlers Primarily Protestant Performed at Natchez, Mississippi, by Father Francis Lennan of the Order of Franciscan Irish Capuchins." *New Orleans Genesis*, VI (January, June, 1967), 84–87, 222–25.

Gianelloni, Elizabeth B. "Earliest Baptismal Records (1793–1806) of St. Joseph Cathedral, Baton Rouge." *Louisiana Genealogical Register*, XVIII (March, 1971), 89–93.

————. "Earliest Records of Ascension Church, Donaldsonville." *New Orleans Genesis*, IX (January, 1970), 11–22.

————. "Genealogical Data from the Records of the Diocese of Louisiana and the Floridas." *Louisiana Genealogical Register*, XVIII (September, December, 1971), 201–10, 302–309; XIX (March, 1972), 1–18.

———. "'Miscellaneous' Records of St. Joseph Cathedral, Baton Rouge." *Louisiana Genealogical Register*, XVI (June–December, 1969), 121–25, 283–87, 329–30.
———. "St. James Parish Church Records: Baptisms, 1757–1783." *New Orleans Genesis*, VII (January, 1968), 7–13.
———. "St. James Parish Church Records: Burials, 1773–1783." *New Orleans Genesis*, VII (January, 1968), 14–15.
———. "St. James Parish Church Records: Marriages, 1770–1781." *New Orleans Genesis*, VII (January, 1968), 1–6.
Hébert, Donald J., trans. "St. Landry Catholic Church—Opelousas, Louisiana, Marriages, Volume I, 1787–1830." *New Orleans Genesis*, XII (September, 1973), 385–94; XIII (January–September, 1974), 11–20, 191–96, 283–88, 365–70; XIV (January–September, 1975), 73–78, 124–29, 231–36, 384–86.
———, trans. "St. Martin of Tours Church, St. Martinville, La., Index of Marriages [1756–1816]." *New Orleans Genesis*, X (September, 1971), 330–34; XI (January, March, 1972), 33–39, 114–29; XIII (January, September, 1974), 59–64, 385–90; XIV (January, March, 1975), 13–18, 202–206.
———, trans. "St. Martin of Tours Church—St. Martinville, Louisiana, Index of Marriages—Volume 1–4, June 5, 1756 to July 16, 1802." *New Orleans Genesis*, X (September, 1971), 330–33; XI (January, March, 1972), 33–39, 114–19.
———, trans. "St. Martin of Tours Church—St. Martinville, Louisiana, Information Produced on the Single State of Persons Marrying by Fr. Michel Bernard Barrière." *New Orleans Genesis*, XI (June, 1972), 277–83.
James, Mrs. Fred O. "Baptismal and Marriage Register—No. 1, Jan. 1, 1731–Dec. 27, 1733, St. Louis Cathedral—New Orleans." *New Orleans Genesis*, V (September, 1966), 297–302; VI (June, 1967), 206–207.
———. "St. Louis Cathedral Baptismal Book IV, Jan. 1, 1759, to Apr. 27, 1762." *New Orleans Genesis*, VII (January, 1968), 37–43.
———. "St. Louis Cathedral Baptismal Register—Book III, March 3, 1753, to March 30, 1759." *New Orleans Genesis*, VI (June, September, 1967), 206–207, 305–11; VII (January, March, 1968), 35–37.
———. "St. Louis Cathedral Baptismal Register, Vol. VII, Jan. 3, 1772–Dec. 30, 1776." *New Orleans Genesis*, VII (June, September, 1968), 219–20, 323–28; VIII (January, 1969), 5–9.
———. "St. Louis Cathedral, New Orleans, Louisiana, Baptismal Book VI—June 21, 1767, to December 31, 1771." *New Orleans Genesis*, VII (January–June, 1968), 43, 122–27, 215–19.
James, Mrs. Fred O., and Albert Robichaux, Jr. "St. Louis Cathedral Baptismal Book I, Jan. 9, 1777, to May 11, 1786." *New Orleans Genesis*, VIII (March, June, 1969), 122–29, 215–21.
"Letters from the Archiepiscopal Archives at Baltimore, 1787–1815." *American Catholic Historical Society of Philadelphia Records*, XX (March–September, 1909), 49–74, 193–208, 250–89.
Lindsay, Lionel St. G., ed. "Letters from the Archdiocesan Archives at Quebec, 1768–1788." *American Catholic Historical Society of Philadelphia Records*, XX (December, 1909), 406–30.

"List of Persons Confirmed at Cabahanoce, by the First Bishop of Louisiana and the Floridas (Cabanhanoce, Parish of St. Jacques de Cabahanoce) May 11, 1800." *New Orleans Genesis*, IV (June, 1965), 191–92.

Mackie, Charles L. "St. Louis Cathedral Baptismal Register 3—1796–1802." *New Orleans Genesis*, X (January, March, 1971), 22–31, 128–35.

Melancon, Mrs. Harold. "Little Red Church [Baptisms, Deaths, 1741–55]." *New Orleans Genesis*, VI (Mach, 1967), 128–39.

Mills, Elizabeth S. "Selected Extracts from the Registers of the Parish of St. François des Natchitoches." *Louisiana Genealogical Register*, XXIII (June, 1976), 151–61.

Nolan, Charles E. "The Bicentennial Archival Project of the Catholic Province of New Orleans." In *Genealogical Institute, 19th, Proceedings, 20 March 1976*. Baton Rouge: Louisiana Genealogical and Historical Society, 1976.

Ortiz, Mrs. Arthur F. "St. Ann's Church Records, Morganza, Louisiana." *New Orleans Genesis*, VII (January, 1968), 68–74.

Ortiz, Mrs. Arthur F., and Hazel B. Bello. "Pointe Coupee Marriages—1728–1785." *Louisiana Genealogical Register*, XXIII (December, 1976), 339–50.

Robichaux, Albert J. "Marriage Records, 1785–1861, St. James Church, St. James, Louisiana." *New Orleans Genesis*, X (September, 1971), 310–29; XI (January, 1972), 50–69.

"St. Louis Cathedral Marriage Book B, 1764–1774." *Louisiana Genealogical Register*, XXII (June, 1975), 180–82.

"Statutes of the Diocese of Louisiana and the Floridas Issued by Rt. Rev. Luis Ignatius Peñalver y Cardenas in 1795." *United States Catholic Historical Magazine*, I (October, 1887), 417–43.

Vidrine, Jacqueline O. "Marriages Entered in Baptismal Book 1, Archives of the Archdiocese of Mobile-Birmingham Chancery Office—Mobile, Alabama." *New Orleans Genesis*, IX (March, 1970), 198.

Walker, Fintan G., ed. "Some Correspondence of an Eighteenth Century Bishop with His Missionaries, 1767–1778." *Catholic Historical Review*, XXVII (July, 1941), 186–200.

Zeringue, Mrs. Lionel J. "St. John the Baptist Church, Edgard, Louisiana, Index of Funerals, Book 1, September 6, 1772, to December 21, 1815." *New Orleans Genesis*, IX (September, 1970), 321–38.

· F. *Journals*

Chouteau, Auguste. "Chouteau's Journal of the Founding of St. Louis." *Missouri Historical Society Collections*, III (1911), 335–66. Also in *Early Histories of the Founding of St. Louis*, edited by John F. McDermott. St. Louis: Historical Documents Foundation, 1952.

Ellicott, Andrew. *The Journal of Andrew Ellicott, Late Commissioner . . . for Determining the Boundary Between the United States and the Possessions of His Catholic Majesty in America*. Philadelphia: Budd & Bartram for Thomas Dobson, 1803.

Guion, Isaac. "Military Journal of Captain Isaac Guion, 1797–1799." Mississippi

Department of Archives and History, *Seventh Annual Report, 1907–1908.* Nashville, 1909.

Hachard de Stanislaus, Marie Magdeleine. *Relation of the Voyage of the Dames Religieuses Ursulines of Rouen to New Orleans.* Rouen: Antoine Le Prevost, 1728.

Mereness, Newton D., ed. *Travels in the American Colonies.* New York: Macmillan, 1916.

Pittman, Philip. *The Present State of the European Settlements on the Mississippi.* Edited by Frank H. Hodder. Cleveland: Arthur H. Clark Co., 1906. Reprint. Memphis: Memphis State University, 1977.

Tranchepain de St. Augustin, Marie. *Relation du voyages des premières Ursulines à la Nouvelle Orleans et de leur établissement en cette ville.* New York: Presse Cramoisy de Jean-Marie Shea, 1859. Translated by John Gilmary Shea in *United States Catholic Historical Magazine,* I (January, 1887), 28–41; and by Marion Ware in *Louisiana History,* I (Summer, 1960), 212–29.

IV. Printed Sources

American State Papers: Documents, Legislative and Executive of the Congress of the United States. Edited by Walter Lowrie and Matthew St. Clair Clarke. 38 vols. Washington, D.C.: Gales and Seaton, 1832–61.

American State Papers, Miscellaneous Affairs (1789–1823). Edited by Walter Lowrie and Matthew St. Clair Clarke. 2 vols. Washington, D.C., 1834.

American State Papers, Public Lands (1789–1837). Edited by Walter Lowrie and Matthew St. Clair Clarke. 8 vols. Washington, D.C., 1832–61.

Carnegie Institution of Washington. *Report of the Department of Historical Research.* [Washington, D.C., 1905–29]. Extracted from the *Yearbook of the Carnegie Institution.*

Carter, Clarence E., ed. *The Territory of Mississippi, 1798–1817.* Washington, D.C.: Government Printing Office, 1937–38. Vols. V–VI of Carter, ed., *The Territorial Papers of the United States.* 26 volumes.

———, ed. *The Territory of Orleans, 1803–1812.* Washington, D.C.: Government Printing Office, 1940. Vol. IX of Carter, ed., *The Territorial Papers of the United States.* 26 volumes.

———, ed. *The Territory of Louisiana-Missouri, 1803–1821.* Washington, D.C.: Government Printing Office, 1943–51. Vols. XIII–XV of Carter, ed., *The Territorial Papers of the United States.* 26 volumes.

———, ed. *The Territory of Arkansas, 1819–1836.* Washington, D.C.: Government Printing Office, 1953–54. Vols. XIX–XXI of Carter, ed. *The Territorial Papers of the United States.* 26 volumes.

Clarke, Matthew St. Clair, comp. *Laws of the United States, Resolutions of Congress under the Confederation, Treaties, Proclamations, Spanish Regulations, and Other Documents Respecting the Public Lands.* 2 vols. Washington, D.C., 1828.

France, Laws, Statutes, etc. *Recueil des édits, declarations, lettres patentes, arrests, et autres pièces concernant la Compagnie des Indes.* 3 vols. Paris: Le Veuve, Saugrain et P. Prault, 1720.

Laussat, Pierre Clément de. *Memoirs of My Life to My Son During the Years 1803 and After, Which I Spent in Public Service in . . . the United States.* Edited by Robert D. Bush. Translated by Agnes-Josephine Pastwa. Baton Rouge: Louisiana State University Press, 1978.

Maduell, Charles R., Jr. *Federal Land Grants in the Territory of Orleans: The Delta Parishes . . . in 1812.* New Orleans: Polyanthos, 1975.

Manning, William R., ed. *Diplomatic Correspondence of the United States: Inter-American Affairs, 1831–1860.* 12 vols. Washington, D.C.: Carnegie Endowment for International Peace, 1932–39.

Marshall, Thomas M., ed. *The Life and Papers of Frederick Bates.* 2 vols. St. Louis: Missouri Historical Society, 1926.

Miller, David Hunter, ed. *Treaties and Other International Acts of the United States of America.* 8 vols. Washington, D.C.: Government Printing Office, 1931–48.

Missouri Land Claims. Introduction by Anton Pregaldin. New Orleans: Polyanthos, 1976. Reprint. *Senate Documents,* 24th Cong., 1st Sess., No. 16. Serial 280.

Moreau Lislet, Louis, and Henry Carleton, trans. *The Laws of Las Siete Partidos, Which Are Still in Force in the State of Louisiana.* 2 vols. New Orleans: James M'Karaher, 1820.

Rieder, Milton P., Jr., and Norma G. Rieder, comps. *The Crew and Passenger Registration Lists of the Seven Acadian Expeditions of 1785.* Metairie, La.: Milton and Norma Rieder, 1965.

———, comps. and eds. *The Acadians in France, 1762–1776. Volume I, Rolls of the Acadians Living in France Distributed by Towns for the Years 1762 to 1776. Volume II, Belle-Isle-en-Mer Registers, La Rochelle Papers. Volume III, Archives of the Port of Saint Servan.* Metairie, La.: Milton and Norma Rieder, 1967–73.

Robichaux, Albert J., Jr. *The Acadian Exiles in Nantes, 1775–1785.* Harvey, La.: Robichaux, 1978.

———. *Acadian Marriages in France, Departmente of Ille-et-Vilaine 1759–1776.* Harvey, La.: Robichaux, 1976.

Rowland, Dunbar, ed. *The Mississippi Territorial Archives, 1798–1803. Executive Journals of Governor Winthrop Sargent and Governor William Charles Cole Claiborne.* 2 vols. Nashville: Brandon Printing Co., 1905.

———, ed. *Official Letter Books of W. C. C. Claiborne, 1801–1816.* 6 vols. Jackson: Mississippi State Department of Archives and History, 1917.

U.S. Congress (Congressional series arranged by serial numbers):

Letter from the Commissioner of the General Land Office, Transmitting Reports of the Land Commissioners at Jackson Court House, November 17, 1820. *Senate Documents,* 16th Cong., 2nd Sess., No. 3. Serial 42.

Letter from the Commissioner of the General Land Office, Transmitting a Report of the Commissioner at St. Helena, January 28, 1822. *Senate Documents,* 17th Cong., 1st Sess., No. 24. Serial 59.

Report of the Register of the Land Office in the Eastern District of Louisiana, March 4, 1824. *House Documents,* 18th Cong., 1st Sess., No. 103. Serial 97.

Land Claims, St. Helena District. Letter from the Secretary of the Treasury, Transmitting a Supplementary Report of the Register and Receiver of the

Land Office for the District of St. Helena, . . . January 24, 1826. *House Documents*, 19th Cong., 1st Sess., No. 56. Serial 134.

Land Claims in the St. Helena District. Letter from the Secretary of the Treasury, Transmitting a Report of the Register and Receiver of the District of St. Helena, on Land Claims in That District, December 29, 1825. *House Documents*, 19th Cong., 1st Sess., No. 70. Serial 134.

Report [of the] Register of Opelousas. Letter from the Secretary of the Treasury, Transmitting a Report of the Register of Opelousas [October 1, 1825] . . . *House Documents*, 19th Cong., 1st Sess., No. 80. Serial 134.

Francis Valle *et al*. February 15, 1826 . . . Report: The Committee on the Public Lands . . . *House Reports*, 19th Cong., 1st Sess., No. 75. Serial 141.

Land Claims between the Rio Hondo and Sabine, January 13, 1826 . . . Committee on the Public Lands . . . Report. *House Reports*, 19th Cong., 1st Sess., No. 33. Serial 141.

Claim of the Marquis de Maison Rouge, December 19, 1825. *House Reports*, 19th Cong., 1st Sess., No. 2. Serial 141.

Land Claims in Opelousas, January 17, 1827 . . . Report . . . of the Register of the Land Office at Opelousas, in the State of Louisiana, of the 1st of October, 1825 . . . *House Reports*,19th Cong., 2nd Sess., No. 49. Serial 159.

Report of the Secretary of the Treasury, with Statements of the Register and Receiver of the Land Office at St. Stephens in Alabama . . . a Supplemental Report on the Claim of Lewis Judson, and the Names of the Spanish Commandants of Mobile, March 28, 1828. *Senate Documents*, 20th Cong., 1st Sess., No. 159. Serial 166. Also printed in *House Documents*, 20th Cong., 1st Sess., No. 285. Serial 175.

Land District—South of Tennessee. Letter from the Secretary of the Treasury, Transmitting the Information . . . in Relation to the Survey of the Public Lands South of Tennessee, February 2, 1828. *House Documents*, 20th Cong., 1st Sess., No. 110. Serial 171.

Land Claims in Mississippi. Documents Accompanying the Bill (No. 169.) Supplementary to the Several Acts, for the Adjustment of Land Claims in the State of Mississippi. February 18, 1828. *House Documents*, 20th Cong., 1st Sess., No. 114. Serial 172.

Report—Registers &c. St. Stephens. Letter from the Secretary of the Treasury, Transmitting Two Reports, Made by the Register and Receiver of the Land Office for the District of St. Stephens, in the State of Alabama, March 28, 1828. *House Documents*, 20th Cong., 1st Sess., No. 285. Serial 175.

Report from the Commissioner of the General Land Office, with Reports from the Register and Receiver of the Land Office for the District of Jackson Court House . . . Mississippi, February 18, 1829. *Senate Documents*, 20th Cong., 2nd Sess., No. 85. Serial 182.

Land Claims—St. Helena District. Letter from the Commissioner of the General Land Office, Transmitting a Report of the Register and Receiver of the St. Helena Land District . . . January 4, 1831. *House Documents*, 21st Cong., 2nd Sess., No. 23. Serial 206.

Land Claims, St. Stephens, Alabama. Letter from the Secretary of the Treasury, Transmitting a Report of the Register and Receiver of the Land Office at St. Stephens . . . April 6, 1832. *House Documents*, 22nd Cong., 1st Sess., No. 197. Serial 220.

Land Claims Derived from Spain. Letter from the Secretary of State . . . on the Expediency of Providing by Law for the Final Disposition of All the Land Claims Derived from the Former Government of Spain, &c. &c. June 14, 1832. *House Documents*, 22nd Cong., 1st Sess., No. 274. Serial 221.

Report from the Secretary of the Treasury, with Reports of the Register and Receiver of the Land Office at St. Stephens, Alabama, June 11, 1834. *Senate Documents*, 23rd Cong., 1st Sess., No. 434. Serial 243.

Land Claims, S.E. Land District, Louisiana [to accompany Bill H.R. No. 290]. Letter from the Secretary of the Treasury, Transmitting Reports of the Register and Receiver of the Land Office at New Orleans, on Private Land Claims . . . January 31, 1834. *House Documents*, 23rd Cong., 1st Sess., No. 73. Serial 255.

Private Land Claims in Missouri. Letter from the Commissioner of the General Land Office, upon the subject of Private Land Claims in Missouri, February 5, 1834. *House Documents*, 23rd Cong., 1st Sess., No. 79. Serial 255.

Reports—Register and Receiver St. Stephens Land District. Letter from the Secretary of the Treasury, Transmitting a Copy of Two Reports by the Register and Receiver of the Land Office for the District of St. Stephens, Alabama, June 13, 1834. *House Documents*, 23rd Cong., 1st Sess., No. 496. Serial 259. Also in *Senate Documents*, 23rd Cong., 1st Sess., No. 434. Serial 243.

Land Claims in Missouri. Letter from the Commissioner of the General Land Office, Transmitting the Report (Supplemental) of the Board of Commissioners for the Settlement of Land Claims in Missouri, March 3, 1835. *House Documents*, 23rd Cong., 2nd Sess., No. 197. Serial 275. Also printed in *House Documents*, 24th Cong., 1st Sess., No. 59. Serial 288.

Report from the Commissioner of the General Land Office. With Final Reports from the Board of Commissioners at St. Louis, under the Act of the 9th July, 1832. *Senate Documents*, 24th Cong., 1st Sess., No. 16. Serial 280.

Report of the Recorder of Land Titles and Commissioner for the Adjustment of Private Land Claims in Missouri, on Certain Land Claims in the Territory of Arkansas, December 21, 1835. *Senate Documents*, 24th Cong., 1st Sess., No. 17. Serial 280.

Documents Relating to the Re-organization of the General Land Office, March 3, 1836. *Senate Documents*, 24th Cong., 1st Sess., No. 216. Serial 281.

Land Claims—Between the Rio Hondo and the Sabine . . . Report of the Register and Receiver of the Land District South of Red River, in Louisiana upon the Land Claims Situated Between the Rio Hondo and the Sabine [January 9, 1836]. *House Documents*, 24th Cong., 1st Sess., No. 49. Serial 287.

Report of the Register and Receiver of the Land Office at New Orleans [December 1, 1835]. Letter from the Secretary of the Treasury, Transmitting the Report of the Register and Receiver of the Land Office at New Orleans, &c. &c. January 12, 1836. *House Documents*, 24th Cong., 1st Sess., No. 55. Serial 287.

John Sibley and John W. Butler. Letter from the Secretary of the Treasury, Transmitting a Report of the Register and Receiver of the Land Office at Ouachita, Louisiana, upon Certain Claims to Land Therein Mentioned, February 16, 1836. *House Documents*, 24th Cong., 1st Sess., No. 114. Serial 289.

Land Claims in Missouri—Arguments, &c. Letter from the Secretary of the Treasury, Transmitting a Communication from the Commissioner of the General Land Office, Accompanied by Opinions and Arguments Respecting Claims to Land in Missouri, Embraced in the Reports of the Board of Commissioners at St. Louis, &c. June 3, 1836. *House Documents*, 24th Cong., 1st Sess., No. 270. Serial 292.

Land Claims in Opelousas, January 7, 1836 . . . Report: The Committee on the Public Lands to Which Was Referred the Report of the Register of the Land Office at Opelousas, in the State of Louisiana, of the 1st of October, 1825. *House Report*, 24th Cong., 1st Sess., No. 93. Serial 293.

New Land Office—Louisiana [to accompany Bill H.R. No. 241] January 27, 1836 . . . Report: The Committee on the Public Lands . . . *House Report*, 24th Cong., 1st Sess., No. 229. Serial 293.

Memorial of the Heirs of Carlos de Vilemont Praying the Confirmation of Their Claim to a Tract of Land, January 20, 1837. *Senate Documents*, 24th Cong., 2nd Sess., No. 89. Serial 298.

Land Claims—Southeastern District of Louisiana. Letter from the Secretary of the Treasury, Transmitting a Report of the Register and Receiver of the Land Office for the Southeastern District of Louisiana, &c. January 4, 1837. *House Documents*, 24th Cong., 2nd Sess., No. 64. Serial 302.

Report of the Secretary of the Treasury, with Statement of the Claims Presented to the Register and Receiver of the Land Office at Greensburgh . . . January 12, 1838. *Senate Documents*, 25th Cong., 2nd Sess., No. 97. Serial 315.

Report from the Secretary of the Treasury, Transmitting a Report from the Register and Receiver of the Land Office at Ouachita [July 24, 1837], with a Statement of the Claims Presented to Them . . . February 14, 1838. *Senate Documents*, 25th Cong., 2nd Sess., No. 196. Serial 316.

Report from the Secretary of the Treasury, Transmitting a Report from the Register and Receiver of the Land Office at New Orleans [November 22, 1837] with a Statement of the Claims Presented to Them . . . February 14, 1838. *Senate Documents*, 25th Cong., 2nd Sess., No. 197. Serial 316.

In the Senate of the United States, April 16, 1838 . . . Report [to accompany Bill S. No. 303]. The Committee on Private Land Claims . . . Report of the Register and Receiver of the New Orleans Land District [December 14, 1836, and November 2, 1837]. *Senate Documents*, 25th Cong., 2nd Sess., No. 379. Serial 317.

Supplement to the Annual Report of the Commissioner of the General Land Office [to be annexed to document no. 23], March 27, 1838. *House Documents*, 25th Cong., 2nd Sess., No. 23. Serial 322.

Fire-Proof Buildings in Each Surveying District . . . Report: The Committee on the Public Lands, July 5, 1838. *House Reports*, 25th Cong., 2nd Sess., No. 1042. Serial 336.

Report from the Secretary of the Treasury, Transmitting a Report from the Regis-

ter and Receiver of the District of St. Stephen's, Alabama . . . February 28, 1839. *Senate Documents*, 25th Cong., 3rd Sess., No. 278. Serial 342.
Land Claims—Opelousas, Louisiana. Letter from the Secretary of the Treasury, Transmitting a Report from the Commissioner of the General Land Office . . . January 6, 1842. *House Documents*, 27th Cong., 2nd Sess., No. 33. Serial 402.
Maison Rouge Land Claims. Transcript of Proceedings in the Case of Lauderneau vs. Coxe and Turner, Containing Evidence in Relation to the Maison Rouge Land Claims, March 14, 1842. *House Documents*, 27th Cong., 2nd Sess., No. 151. Serial 403.
Land Claims in Louisiana, &c. Letter from the Secretary of the Treasury . . . [December 16, 1842] Transmitting a Communication from the General Land Office with Evidence . . . to Confirm Certain Land Claims in Louisiana. *House Documents*, 27th Cong., 3rd Sess., No. 21. Serial 419.
Report of the Secretary of the Treasury, Communicating . . . Information in Relation to the Claim to Land in the State of Louisiana called the "Houmas Claim," January 13, 1845. *Senate Reports*, 28th Cong., 2nd Sess., No. 45. Serial 450.
In the Senate of the United States, March 30, 1846 . . . Report . . . Committee on Private Land Claims . . . to a Certain Tract of Land Situated in the Territory of Iowa and Known as the "Dubuque Claim" . . . *Senate Documents*, 29th Cong., 1st Sess., No. 256. Serial 474.
Resolution of the Legislature of Louisiana, in Favor of the Reimbursement of Money Paid for the Purchase of Certain Land Records, April 28, 1848. *Senate Miscellaneous Documents*, 30th Cong., 1st Sess., No. 127. Serial 511.
Reports of Surveyor General of Illinois, Missouri and Oregon. Letter from the Secretary of the Interior, Transmitting Reports of the Surveyors General of Illinois, Missouri and Oregon, February 4, 1852. *House Executive Documents*, 32nd Cong., 1st Sess., No. 52. Serial 640.
Report of the Commissioner of the General Land Office . . . for the Settlement of Certain Classes of Private Land Claims Within the Bastrop Grant, a Report of the Register and Receiver of the Land Office at Monroe, Louisiana, July 30, 1852. *Senate Executive Documents*, 32nd Cong., 2nd Sess., No. 4. Serial 661.
Inhabitants of St. Louis County, Missouri. [To accompany Bill H.R. No. 403] March 3, 1857. Mr. Porter . . . Report for the Relief of the Inhabitants of St. Louis County . . . *House Reports*, 34th Cong., 2nd Sess., No. 268. Serial 914.
Location of Confirmed Private Land Claims in Missouri [to accompany Bill S. 41], May 29, 1858 . . . *House Reports*, 35th Cong., 1st Sess., No. 463. Serial 968.
Special Report by Joseph S. Wilson in Regard to Surveying Archives of Missouri, Iowa and Wisconsin [May 26, 1866]. Report of the Secretary of the Interior, November 19, 1866. *House Executive Documents*, 39th Cong., 2nd Sess., No. 2. Serial 1284.
Rio Hondo Claims. Letter from the Secretary of the Interior Transmitting a Copy of the Report on the Rio Hondo Claims, Louisiana, February 22, 1870. *House Executive Documents*, 41st Cong., 2nd Sess., No. 157. Serial 1418.
Digested Summary and Alphabetical List of Private Claims Which Have Been

Presented to the House of Representatives from the Thirty-Second to the Forty-First Congress, Inclusive. *House Miscellaneous Documents,* 42nd Cong., 3rd Sess., No. 109. Serial 1574.

Private Land Claims in Louisiana. Letter from the Secretary of the Interior, Relative to Certain Private Land-Claims in Louisiana, December 18, 1873. *House Executive Documents,* 43rd Cong., 1st Sess., No. 60. Serial 1607.

Confirmation of Land Claims in Missouri, January 28, 1876 . . . Committee on Private Land Claims . . . Report: The Committee on Private Land Claims. *House Reports,* 44th Cong., 1st Sess., No. 24. Serial 1708.

Rio Hondo Land Claims, February 15, 1878 . . . Committee on Private Land-Claims, Submitted the Following Report . . . *House Reports,* 45th Cong., 2nd Sess., No. 222. Serial 1822.

Letter from the Secretary of the Interior, Transmitting . . . Information Concerning Located but Unconfirmed Private Land Claims in the State of Louisiana, March 8, 1880. *Senate Executive Documents,* 46th Cong., 2nd Sess., No. 111. Serial 1885.

Letter from the Secretary of the Interior, Transmitting . . . Report of the Commissioner of the General Land Office Relative to Private Land Claims in Louisiana, December 16, 1886. *Senate Executive Documents,* 49th Cong., 2nd Sess., No. 67. Serial 2448.

U.S. Congress. *The New American State Papers: Public Lands.* Introduction by Margaret B. Bogue and Thomas C. Cochran, General Editors. Irwin F. Greenberg and Graham D. Taylor, Research Editors. 8 vols. Wilmington, Del.: Scholarly Resources, 1973.

U.S. Congress. *Reports of the Committee on Private Land Claims of the . . . Congress. Senate Miscellaneous Documents,* 45th Cong., 3rd Sess., No. 81. Serial 1836. 2 vols.

U.S. Congress, House of Representatives. *Digested Summary and Alphabetical List of Private Claims . . . Elucidating Its Progress [1789–1851]. House Miscellaneous Documents,* 32nd Cong., 1st Sess., unnumbered series. Serials 653–55. 3 vols. Reprint. Baltimore: Genealogical Pubishing Co., 1970.

———. *Digested Summary and Alphabetical List of Private Claims . . . Inclusive [1851–71]. House Miscellaneous Documents,* 42nd Cong., 3rd Sess., No. 109. Serial 1574.

———. *Digested Summary and Alphabetical List of Private Claims . . . Inclusive [1871–81]. House Miscellaneous Documents,* 47th Cong., 1st Sess., No. 53. Serial 2036.

U.S. Department of the Interior. *Annual Report of the Secretary of the Interior.* Washington, D.C.: Government Printing Office, 1849–1963.

U.S. General Land Office. *Annual Report.* The reports for 1817 through 1848 are in the *Annual Report of the Secretary of the Treasury* in the Congressional series, and the reports for 1849 through 1963 are in the *Annual Report of the Secretary of the Interior.*

U.S. Laws, Statutes, etc. *The Statutes at Large of the United States of America,* 1789–date. Boston: C. C. Little and J. Brown, 1845–51; Boston: Little, Brown and

Company, 1855–73; Washington, D.C.: Government Printing Office, 1875–.
U.S. Library of Congress. *Annual Report of the Librarian of Congress, 1866–1979.* Washington, D.C.: Government Printing Office, 1866–1980.
U.S. Public Lands Commission. *Report of the Public Lands Commission with Appendix. Senate Documents,* 58th Cong., 3rd Sess., No. 189. Serial 4766.
White, Joseph M., ed. *A New Collection of Laws, Charters, and Local Ordinances of the Governments of Great Britain, France and Spain . . . Together with the Laws of Mexico and Texas on the Same Subject.* 2 vols. Philadelphia: T. & J. W. Johnson, 1839.

V. Guides, Inventories, Catalogs, Calendars

Alabama, Department of Archives and History. List of U.S. General Land Office Records in the Department of Archives and History, State of Alabama, Montgomery, Alabama. Xerographic copy supplied to Henry P. Beers, October, 1984.
Alabama History Commission. *Report of the Alabama History Commission . . . 1900.* Edited by Thomas M. Owen. Montgomery, Ala.: Brown Printing Co., 1901.
Andreassen, John C. L., and Edwin A. Davis. *Louisiana Archives Survey Report No. 1 (Under Act No. 381, 1954).* [Baton Rouge? La., 1956].
———. *Louisiana Archives Survey Report No. 2, Findings and Recommendations.* [Baton Rouge, 1956].
Beer, William. "Calendar of Documents in a Volume Having on Back: French Mss., Mississippi Valley, 1679–1769." *Louisiana Historical Society Publications,* IV (1908), 4–120.
Beers, Henry P. *The French & British in the Old Northwest: A Bibliographical Guide to Archive and Manuscript Sources.* Detroit: Wayne State University Press, 1964.
———. *Spanish & Mexican Records of the American Southwest: A Bibliographical Guide to Archive and Manuscript Sources.* Tucson: University of Arizona Press, 1979.
Bush, Robert D., and Blake Touchstone. "A Survey of Manuscript Holdings in the Historic New Orleans Collection." *Louisiana History,* XVI (Winter, 1975), 89–96.
Butler, Ruth L. *A Check List of Manuscripts in the Edward E. Ayer Collection.* Chicago, 1937.
California, University, Berkeley. Bancroft Library. *A Guide to the Manuscript Collections of the Bancroft Library, Volume I: Pacific and Western Manuscripts, Except California.* Edited by Dale L. Morgan and George P. Hammond. (Bancroft Library, *Publications, Bibliography Series, Vol. I*). Berkeley and Los Angeles, University of California Press, 1963.
Coutts, Brian E., and Merna Whitley. "An Inventory of Sources in the Department of Archives and Manuscripts, Louisiana State University, for the History of Spanish Louisiana and West Florida." *Louisiana History,* XIX (Spring, 1978), 213–50.
Cummins, Light T., and Glen Jeansonne, eds. *A Guide to the History of Louisiana.* Westport, Conn.: Greenwood Press, 1982.

De Ville, Winston. "A Partial Calendar of Non-Extant Pointe Coupee Post Records, 1762–1769." *Louisiana Genealogical Register*, XV (December, 1968), 129–38.

Falcón, Guillermo Nañez, comp. *The Rosemunde E. and Emile Kuntz Collection: A Catalogue of the Manuscripts and Printed Ephemera.* New Orleans: Howard-Tilton Memorial Library, Tulane University, 1981.

Forstall, Edmund J. "An Analytical Index of the Whole of the Public Documents Relative to Louisiana, Deposited in the Archives of the Department 'de la marine et des colomes [sic]' et 'Bibliothèque du roi' at Paris." In *Historical Collections of Louisiana,* by Benjamin F. French. Philadelphia: Daniels & Smith, 1850.

Hamer, Philip M., ed. *A Guide to Archives and Manuscripts in the United States.* New Haven: Yale University Press, 1961.

Henry E. Huntington Library and Art Gallery. *American Manuscript Collections in the Huntington Library for the History of the Seventeenth and Eighteenth Centuries.* Compiled by Norma B. Cuthbert. Huntington Library Lists, no. 5. San Marino: Huntington Library, 1941.

Historical Records Survey. [Typescript; Inventory of Entries Covering the Colonial Records of Louisiana. Washington, D.C., 1939].

Historical Records Survey, Louisiana. *Guide to Depositories of Manuscript Collections in Louisiana.* University, La.: Department of Archives, Louisiana State University, 1941.

———. *Guide to Manuscript Collections in Louisiana: The Department of Archives, Louisiana State University, Volume I.* Edited by William R. Hogan. University, La.: Department of Archives, Louisiana State University, 1940.

———. *Inventory of the Parish Archives of Louisiana, No. 4, Assumption Parish (Napoleonville).* Baton Rouge: Department of Archives, Louisiana State University, 1942.

———. *Inventory of the Parish Archives of Louisiana, No. 28, Lafayette Parish (Lafayette).* University, La.: Department of Archives, Louisiana State University, 1938.

———. *Inventory of the Parish Archives of Louisiana, No. 29, Lafourche Parish (Thibodaux).* Baton Rouge: Department of Archives, Louisiana State University, 1942.

———. *Inventory of the Parish Archives of Louisiana, No. 35, Natchitoches Parish (Natchitoches).* University, La.: Department of Archives, Louisiana State University, 1938.

———. *Inventory of the Parish Archives of Louisiana, No. 37, Ouachita Parish (Monroe).* Baton Rouge: Department of Archives, Louisiana State University, 1942.

———. *Inventory of the Parish Archives of Louisiana, No. 38, Plaquemines Parish (Point a la Hache).* University, La.: Department of Archives, Louisiana State University, 1939.

———. *Inventory of the Parish Archives of Louisiana, No. 44, St. Bernard Parish (Chalmette).* University, La.: Department of Archives, Louisiana State University, 1938.

————. *Inventory of the Parish Archives of Louisiana, No. 45, Saint Charles Parish (Hahnville)*. University, La.: Department of Archives, Louisiana State University, 1937.

————. *Title-Line Inventory of the Parish Archives of Louisiana, Parts 1 and 2, Acadia Through Winn*. New Orleans, 1939.

Historical Records Survey, Missouri. *Early Missouri Archives, [Volume I, Ste. Geneviève, St. Charles]*. St. Louis: Missouri Historical Records Survey, 1941.

————. *Early Missouri Archives (New Madrid, 1791–1804), Vol. II*. St. Louis: Missouri Historical Records Survey, 1942.

————. *Guide to Depositories of Manuscript Collections in the United States: Missouri*. St. Louis: Missouri Historical Records Survey, 1940.

Historical Society of Pennsylvania. *Guide to the Manuscript Collections of the Historical Society of Pennsylvania*. Philadelphia, 1949.

Louisiana State Archives and Records Service. *Calendar of Documents of the Opelousas Post, 1764–1789*. Compiled by Arthur W. Bergeron, Jr. Baton Rouge: Le Comité des Archives de la Louisiane, 1979.

————. *Calendar of Louisiana Colonial Documents, Volume I, Avoyelles Parish*. Compiled by Winston De Ville. [Baton Rouge], 1961.

————. *Calendar of Louisiana Colonial Documents, Volume II, St. Landry Parish*. Compiled by Winston De Ville. [Baton Rouge], 1964.

————. *Calendar of Louisiana Colonial Documents, Volume III, St. Charles Parish, Part I: The D'Arensbourg Records, 1734–1769*. Compiled by Elizabeth B. Gianelloni. Baton Rouge, 1967.

Massachusetts Historical Society Library. *Guide to the Microfilm Edition of the Winthrop Sargent Papers*. Edited by Frederick S. Allis, Jr., and Roy Bartolomee. Boston: Massachusetts Historical Society, 1965.

Michigan, University. William L. Clements Library of American History. *Guide to the Manuscript Collections in the William L. Clements Library*. Compiled by Howard Henry Peckham. Ann Arbor: University of Michigan Press, 1942.

Mississippi Department of Archives and History. *Guide to Official Records in the Mississippi Department of Archives and History*. Compiled by Thomas W. Henderson and Ronald E. Tomlin. Jackson: The Department, [1975].

Mississippi Historical Commission. "An Account of the Manuscripts, Papers, and Documents Pertaining to Mississippi in the Public Repositories Within the State of Mississippi." *Mississippi Historical Society Publications*, V (1902), 121–227.

Missouri, Office of the Secretary of State. *A Guide to the Missouri State Archives, 1975*. Jefferson City: Office of the Secretary of State of Missouri, 1975.

Newberry Library, Edward E. Ayer Collection. *A Check List of Manuscripts in the Edward E. Ayer Collection*. Compiled by Ruth L. Butler. Chicago: Newberry Library, 1937.

Pargellis, Stanley M., and Norman B. Cuthbert. "Loudoun Papers: (a) Colonial, 1756–58, (b) French Colonial, 1742–53." *Huntington Library Bulletin*, no. 3 (February, 1933), 97–107.

Parkin, Robert E. *Parkin's Guide to Tracing Your Family Tree in Missouri*. St. Louis: Genealogical Research & Productions, 1979.

Reynolds, John H. "An Account of Books, Manuscripts, Papers and Documents Concerning Arkansas in Public Repositories." *Arkansas Historical Association Publications*, I. Fayetteville, Ark., 1906, pp. 43–273.

Smith, Clifford N. *Federal Land Series: A Calendar of Archival Materials on the Land Patents Issued by the United States Government, with Subject, Tract, and Name Indexes, Volume I, 1788–1810*. Chicago: American Library Association, 1972.

Survey of Federal Archives, Alabama. *Inventory of Federal Archives in the States, Series VIII, The Department of the Interior, No. 2, Alabama*. Birmingham, Ala., 1941.

Survey of Federal Archives, Arkansas. *Inventory of Federal Archives in the States, Series VIII, The Department of the Interior, No. 4, Arkansas*. New Orleans, 1941.

Survey of Federal Archives, Louisiana. *Index to the Archives of Spanish West Florida, 1782–1810*. Introduction by Stanley C. Arthur. New Orleans: Polyanthos, 1975.

———. *Index to the Dispatches of the Spanish Governors of Louisiana, 1766–1792*. Prepared by Stanley C. Arthur. New Orleans: Polyanthos, 1975.

———. *Inventory of Federal Archives in the States, Series VIII, The Department of the Interior, No. 17, Louisiana*. New Orleans, 1941.

Survey of Federal Archives, Mississippi. *Inventory of Federal Archives in the States, Series VIII, The Department of the Interior, No. 23, Mississippi*. New Orleans, 1941.

Survey of Federal Archives, Missouri. *Inventory of Federal Archives in the States, Series VIII, The Department of the Interior, No. 24, Missouri*. St. Louis, 1938.

Texas, University, Austin. Library. *The University of Texas Archives: A Guide to the Historical Manuscripts in the University of Texas Library*. Compiled by Chester V. Kielman. Austin: University of Texas Press, 1967.

Thomas Gilcrease Institute of American History and Art. *A Guidebook to Manuscripts in the Library of the Thomas Gilcrease Institute of American History and Art*. Compiled by Mrs. H. H. Keene. [Tulsa, Okla., 1969].

U.S. Library of Congress. *The National Union Catalog of Manuscripts, 1959 / 61*. Ann Arbor, Mich.: J. W. Edwards, 1962.

———. *The National Union Catalog of Manuscripts, 1962*. Hamden, Conn.: Shoe String Press, 1964.

———. *The National Union Catalog of Manuscripts, 1963 / 64–84*. 21 vols. Washington, D.C., 1965–84.

U.S. Library of Congress, Manuscript Division. Dictionary Catalog of Collections. Unpublished catalog in the library.

U.S. Library of Congress, Photoduplication Service. *A Guide to the Microfilm Collection of Early State Records*. Compiled under the direction of William S. Jenkins. Edited by Lillian A. Hamrick. Washington, D.C., 1950.

———. *A Guide to the Microfilm Collection of Early State Records, a Supplement*. Compiled and edited by W. S. Jenkins. Washington, D.C., 1961.

U.S. National Archives. The General Land Office (Record Group 49), Administrative Records of the General Land Office, 1785–1955. Typescript; Washington, D.C., 1973.
———. *Guide to Genealogical Research in the National Archives*. Washington, D.C.: National Archives and Records Service, 1982.
———. *Guide to the National Archives of the United States*. Washington, D.C.: Government Printing Office, 1974.
———. *List of Cartographic Records of the General Land Office (Record Group 49)*. Compiled by Laura E. Kelsay. Special List, no. 19. Washington, D.C., 1964.
———. *Preliminary Inventory of the Land-Entry Papers of the General Land Office*. Compiled by Harry P. Yoshpe and Philip P. Brower. Preliminary Inventories, no. 22. Washington, D.C., 1949.
———. *Preliminary Inventory of the Records of the United States House of Representatives, 1789–1946 (Record Group 233)*. Compiled by Buford Rowland, Handy B. Fant, and Harold E. Hufford. 2 vols. Preliminary Inventories, no. 113. Washington, D.C.: National Archives, 1959.
———. *Preliminary Inventory of the Records of the United States Senate (Record Group 46)*. Compiled by Harold E. Hufford and Watson G. Caudill. Preliminary Inventories, no. 23. Washington, D.C.: National Archives, 1950.
———. *Preliminary Inventory of Records Relating to International Boundaries (Record Group 76)*. Compiled by Daniel T. Goggin. Preliminary Inventories, no. 170. Washington, D.C.: National Archives, 1968.
Vidrine, Jacqueline O. *The Opelousas Post, 1764–1789: Guide to the St. Landry Parish Archives Deposited at Louisiana State Archives*. Baton Rouge: Le Comité des Archives de la Louisiane, 1979.
Western Reserve Historical Society, Cleveland. *A Guide to the Manuscripts and Archives of the Western Reserve Historical Society*. Compiled by Kermit J. Pike. Cleveland, 1972.
Wisconsin, State Historical Society. *Guide to the Manuscripts of the State Historical Society of Wisconsin, Supplement Number One*. Compiled by Josephine L. Harper and Sharon C. Smith. Madison: State Historical Society of Wisconsin, 1957.
———. *Guide to the Manuscripts of the State Historical Society of Wisconsin, Supplement Number Two*. Compiled by Josephine L. Harper. Madison: State Historical Society of Wisconsin, 1966.
———. *Guide to the Manuscripts of the Wisconsin Historical Society*. Edited by Alice E. Smith. Madison: State Historical Society of Wisconsin, 1944.

A. Abstracts

Conrad, Glenn R. *The German Coast: Abstracts of the Civil Records of St. Charles and St. John the Baptist Parishes, 1804–1812*. Lafayette: University of Southwestern Louisiana, 1981.
———. *St. Charles: Abstracts of the Civil Records of St. Charles Parish, 1770–1803*. Lafayette: University of Southwestern Louisiana, 1974.

———. *Saint-Jean-Baptiste des Allemands: Abstracts of the Civil Records of St. John the Baptist Parish, with Genealogy and Index, 1753–1803*. Lafayette: University of Southwestern Louisiana, 1972.

Core, Dorothy J., comp. and ed., and Nicole W. Hatfield, trans. *Abstract of Catholic Register of Arkansas (1764–1858)*. De Witt, Ark.: De Witt Publishing Co., 1976.

Gianelloni, Elizabeth B. "Spanish West Florida Records: Index to Abstracts of Translations." *Louisiana Genealogical Register*, XVI–XX (December, 1969–December, 1973).

Hébert, Donald J. *Southwest Louisiana Records: Church and Civil Records of Settlers, Volume I, 1756–1810*. Eunice, La.: Hébert, 1974.

Maduell, Charles R., Jr. *Federal Land Grants in the Territory of Orleans: The Delta Parishes*. New Orleans: Polyanthos, 1976.

Maduell, Charles R., Jr., and Agnes H. Anzalone, eds. "Abstracts of Land Grants in the County of German Coast (Now St. Charles and St. John the Baptist Parish), Territory of Orleans." *New Orleans Genesis*, XV (June, 1976), 251–56; XVI (January, 1977), 24–30.

———, eds. "Abstracts of Land Grants in the County of Orleans Comprising the Present Parishes of Orleans, Jefferson, St. Bernard, and Plaquemines." *New Orleans Genesis*, XIV (January–September, 1975), 49–54, 207–12, 275–80, 389–94; XV (January–June, 1976), 11–16, 153–54, 251–56.

Robichaux, Albert J., Jr. *The Acadian Exiles in Saint-Malo, 1758–1785*. 3 vols. Eunice, La.: Hébert, 1981.

Sanders, Mary E. *Records of Attakapas District, La., 1739–1811*. [Lafayette, La. ?], 1962.

Young, Clyde P., comp., E. Russ Williams, Jr., ed. *Succession Records of St. Helena Parish, Louisiana, 1804–1854, Abstracted from the Original Files*. Bogalusa, La., 1966.

B. *Indexes*

Ainsworth, Fern. *Private Land Claims: Alabama, Arkansas, Florida*. Natchitoches, La.: Fern Ainsworth, 1978.

Baton Rouge Genealogical Society. "Index to Pintado Papers." *Louisiana Genealogical Register*, XV–XIX (September, 1968–June, 1972).

Broders, Mrs. Edwin A. "Index of Spanish West Florida Archives, East Baton Rouge Parish Courthouse." *Louisiana Genealogical Register*, XI–XVII (September, 1964–December, 1970).

———. "List of Successions Found in the Records of the Spanish West Florida Archives, East Baton Rouge Parish Courthouse." *Louisiana Genealogical Register*, XI (September, December, 1964), 42–44, 57–60.

James, Mrs. Fred O. "Index to French and Spanish Translations of Original Documents from Louisiana State Museum Library, New Orleans." *New Orleans Genesis*, I–IV (1962–March, 1965).

James, Mrs. Fred O., Mrs. Larry J. Dupuy, and Irene Owen. "Index to the Black Boxes." *New Orleans Genesis*, IV–XVI (September, 1965–January, 1977).

Konikoff, Mrs. Ben S. "Special Index for Special Marriage Contracts, Book #1, 1770–1798, Iberville Parish, Louisiana." *Louisiana Genealogical Register,* XXII (March, 1975), 55–63.

McAnelly, Shelton B. "State Land Office Records, U.S. Tract Book Indexes: Greensburg District, Southwestern Land District, District North of the Red River, Southeastern Land District, Northwestern Land District." *Louisiana Genealogical Register,* XIX (March, 1972), 62–76.

McMullin, Philip W., ed. *Grassroots of America: A Computerized Index to the American State Papers, Land Grants and Claims (1789–1837), with Other Aids to Research (Government Documents Serial Set Numbers 2 Through 36).* Salt Lake City: Gendex Corp., 1972.

Murray, Nicholas R. *Louisiana Surname Index, Computer-Indexed Marriage Records.* 2 vols. Hammond, La.: Hunting for Bears, 1984.

St. Louis Genealogical Society. *StLGS Index of St. Louis Marriages, 1804–1876.* 2 vols. St. Louis, [1973].

Tipton, Ennis M. *Index to U.S. Tract Books, Northwestern Land District (Old Natchitoches District) in the Louisiana State Land Office, Baton Rouge, Louisiana.* Bossier City, La.: Tipton Printing and Publishing Co., 1981.

Wells, Carolyn M. *Index and Abstracts of Colonial Documents in the Eugene P. Watson Memorial Library* [Northwestern State University]. Natchitoches, La.: Watson Memorial Library, 1980.

Williams, E. Russ, Jr. "Index of the Private Land Claims, State of Louisiana." *Louisiana Genealogical Register,* VII (June–December, 1960); IX–XIII (March, 1962–December, 1967).

Wright, Margery, and Benjamin E. Achee. *Index of Ouachita Parish, Louisiana, Probate Records, 1800–1870.* Shreveport, La.: Wright and Achee, 1969.

C. Guides to Foreign Archival Materials

1. BOOKS

Beers, Henry P. *The French in North America: A Bibliographical Guide to French Archives, Reproductions, and Research Missions.* Baton Rouge: Louisiana State University Press, 1957.

Canada. Public Archives. *General Inventory: Manuscripts. Inventaire général: manuscrits.* 5 vols. Ottawa: Public Archives, 1971–72.

———. *Union List of Manuscripts in Canadian Repositories.* Rev. ed. Ottawa: Public Archives, 1975.

Cuba. Archivo Nacional. *Catálogo de los Fondos de las Floridas.* Publicationes del Archivo Nacional de Cuba, III. Havana: Archivo Nacional, 1944.

———. "Inventario de las copias fotostaticas de documentos existentes en el Archivo Nacional de la Republica de Cuba donados al Archivo Nacional de Washington, que se refieren a los Estados Unidos de América." 65 vols. Havana, [1946]. Typescript in the National Archives Library, Washington, D.C.

France. Archives de la Marine. *Inventaire des Archives de la Marine: Service Hydrographique, sous-série 4 JJ (journaux de bord) déposée aux Archives Nationales.* Par

Georges Bourgin, revu et complété par Étienne Taillemite. Paris: Imprimerie Nationales, 1963.

France. Archives Nationales. *Inventaire des Archives coloniales: Correspondance à l'arrivée en provenance de la Louisiane* [1678–1753]. Par Marie-Antoinette Menier, Étienne Taillemite, et Gilberto de Forges. Paris: Archives Nationales, 1976.

———. *Les Archives Nationales: État général des fonds.* Publié sous la direction de Jean Favier. *Tome III, Marine et outre-mer,* sous la direction de Pierre Boyer, Marie-Antoinette Menier, Étienne Taillemite. Paris: Archives Nationales, 1980.

France. Direction des Archives. *Catalogue des inventaires, répertoires, guide de recherche et autres instruments de travail des archives départementales, communales et hospitalières en vente dans les services départmentaux d'archives à la date du 31 décember 1961.* Paris: Imprimerie Nationale, 1962.

———. *Guide des recherches généalogiques aux Archives Nationales.* Par Jacques Meugrey de Tupigny. Paris: Imprimeur Nationale, 1953.

———. *Guide des sources de l'histoire des États-Unis dans les archives françaises.* Paris: France Expansion, 1976.

France. Ministère de la France d'Outre-Mer, Service des Archives. *Inventaire analytique de la correspondance générale avec les colonies, départ, série B (déposée aux Archives Nationales), Tome I, Registres 1 à 37 (1654–1715).* Par Étienne Taillemite. Paris, 1959.

Hale, Richard W., Jr. *Guide to Photocopied Historical Materials in the United States and Canada.* Ithaca, N.Y.: Cornell University Press, 1961.

Hill, Roscoe R. *Descriptive Catalogue of the Documents Relating to the United States in the Papeles Procedentes de Cuba Deposited in the Archivo General de Indies at Seville.* Washington, D.C.: Carnegie Institution of Washington, 1916.

———. *The National Archives of Latin America.* Cambridge, 1945.

Historical Records Survey, North Carolina. *List of the Papeles Procedentes de Cuba in the Archives of the North Carolina Historical Commission.* Raleigh, 1942.

Jensen, C. Russell. *Preliminary Survey of the French Collections.* Finding Aids to the Microfilmed Manuscript Collection of the Genealogical Society of Utah. Salt Lake City: University of Utah Press, 1980.

Leland, Waldo G. *Guide to Materials for American History in the Libraries and Archives of Paris, Volume I, Libraries.* Washington, D.C.: Carnegie Institution of Washington, 1932.

Leland, Waldo G., John J. Meng, and Abel Doysié. *Guide to Materials for American History in the Libraries and Archives of Paris, Volume II, Archives of the Ministry of Foreign Affairs.* Washington, D.C.: Carnegie Institution of Washington, 1943.

Matteson, David M. *List of Manuscripts Concerning American History Preserved in European Libraries and Noted in Their Published Catalogues and Similar Printed Lists.* Washington, D.C.: Carnegie Institution of Washington, 1925.

Moncton, Université de, Centre d'Études Acadiennes. *Inventaire général des sources documentaires sur les Acadiens.* 3 vols. Moncton, Canada, 1975. Translated in Donald J. Hébert, *Acadians in Exile.* Cecelia, La.: Hebért, 1980.

322 / Bibliography

Parker, David W. *Guide to Materials for United States History in Canadian Archives.* Washington, D.C.: Carnegie Institution of Washington, 1913.
Peña y Camara, José de la, *et al. Catálogo de documentos del Archivo General de Indias (sección V, Gobierno, Audiencia de Santo Domingo) sobre la época española de Luisiana.* 2 vols. New Orleans: Loyola University, 1968.
Pérez, Luis M. *Guide to Materials for American History in Cuban Archives.* Washington, D.C.: Carnegie Institution of Washington, 1907.
Robertson, James A. *List of Documents in Spanish Archives Relating to the History of the United States, Which Have Been Printed or of Which Transcripts Are Preserved in American Libraries.* Washington, D.C.: Carnegie Institution of Washington, 1910.
Roy, Joseph E. *Rapport sur les archives de France relatives à l'histoire du Canada.* Ottawa: C. H. Parmelee, 1911.
Shepherd, William R. *Guide to the Materials for the History of the United States in Spanish Archives (Simancas, the Archivo Nacional, and Seville).* Washington, D.C.: Carnegie Institution of Washington, 1907.
Sociedad Colombista Panamericana. *Documents Pertaining to the Floridas Which Are Kept in Different Archives of Cuba. Appendix Number 1: Official List of Documentary Funds of the Floridas—Now Territories of the States of Louisiana, Alabama, Mississippi, Georgia and Florida—Kept in the National Archives.* Havana, 1945.
Spain. Archivo General de Simancas. *Guía del Archivo General de Simancas.* (Junta Técnica de Archivos, Bibliotecas y Museos, *Ediciones conmemorativas del centenario del Cuerpo Facultativo,* 1858–1958, XI). [Madrid]: Dirección General de Archivos y Bibliotecas; Valencia: Tipografía Moderna, 1958.
Spain. Archivo Histórico Nacional, Madrid. *Guía del Archivo Histórico Nacional.* Por Luis Sánchez Belda. (Junta Técnica de Archivos, Bibliotecas y Museos, Ediciones conmemorativas del centenario del Cuerpo Facultativo, 1858–1958, XII). [Madrid], 1958.
Surrey, Nancy Maria (Miller), ed. *Calendar of Manuscripts in Paris Archives and Libraries Relating to the History of the Mississippi Valley to 1803.* 2 vols. Washington, D.C: Carnegie Institution of Washington, 1926–28.
U.S. Library of Congress, Manuscripts Division. *Manuscripts on Microfilm: A Checklist of the Holdings in the Manuscript Division.* Compiled by Richard B. Bickel. Washington, D.C.: Government Printing Office, 1975.
Waldo, Rudolph H. *Notarial Archives of New Orleans Parish, 1731–1953.* [New Orleans, 1953].
Welsch, Edwin K., ed. *Libraries and Archives in France: A Handbook.* New York: Council for European Studies, 1979.

2. ARTICLES

Beerman, Eric C. "A Check-list of Louisiana Documents in the Servicio Histórico Militar in Madrid." *Louisiana History,* XX (Spring, 1979), 221–22.
———. "French Maps of Mississippi in Spanish Archives." *Journal of Mississippi History,* XLVII (February, 1980), 43–48.
Bonnel, Ulane Z. "Resources in France for the American Historian: Maps and

Rare Books at the Library of the Ministère d'Etat chargé de la Défense nationale." *Library of Congress Quarterly Journal*, XXX (October, 1973), 256–61.

Burrus, Ernest J., S.J. "An Introduction to Bibliographical Tools in Spanish Archives and Manuscript Collections Relating to Hispanic America." *Hispanic American Historical Review*, XXXV (November, 1955), 443–83.

Campillo, Don Miguel Gomez del. "Madrid Archives, Chronological Statement of Papers and Documents Relative to Louisiana in the National Historical Archives of Madrid (1740–1832.)" *Louisiana Historical Society Publications*, IV (1908), 121–44.

Holmes, Jack D. L. "Maps, Plans and Charts of Louisiana in Paris Archives: A Checklist." *Louisiana Studies*, IV (Fall, 1965), 200–21.

————. "Maps, Plans and Charts of Louisiana in Spanish and Cuban Archives: A Checklist." *Louisiana Studies*, II (Winter, 1963), 183–203.

Legrand, Albert. "Inventaire des archives de la Compagnie des Indes." *Bulletin de la section de géographie* (France, Comité des travaux historiques et scientifiques), XXVIII (1913), 160–251.

Maheux, Arthur. "Les Archives du Séminaire de Québec." *Le Canada français*, XXVII (February, 1940), 503–508.

Mississippi Department of Archives and History. "[List of Documents in England, France, and Spain, 1540–1798, of Value for Mississippi History]." In *Fifth Annual Report of the Mississippi Department of Archives and History*, by Dunbar Rowland. Nashville: Brandon Printing Co., 1907.

Moël, Michelle. "Resources in France for the American Historian: Maps and Plans of the United States in the Archives Nationales." *Library of Congress Quarterly Journal*, XXX (October, 1973), 245–47.

O'Neill, James E. "Copies of French Manuscripts for American History in the Library of Congress." *Journal of American History*, LI (March, 1965), 674–91.

Pognon, Edmond, and Edwige Archier. "Resources in France for the American Historian: Maps and Plans in the Bibliothèque Nationale." *Library of Congress Quarterly Journal*, XXX (October, 1973), 248–51.

Roussier, Paul. "Les Origines du Dépôt des Papiers Publics des Colonies: Le Dépôt de Rochefort (1763–1790)." *Revue de l'histoire des colonies françaises*, XVIII (1925), 21–50.

Weilbrenner, Bernard. "Archival Resources in Quebec for the History of the Mississippi Valley." *French Canadian and Acadian Genealogical Review*, II (Winter, 1969), 279–83.

D. *Ecclesiastical Materials*

Caron, Ivanhoë. "Inventaire de la correspondance de Mgr. Jean-Olivier Briand, Évêque de Québec, 1741 à 1794." *Rapport de l'archiviste de la province de Québec, 1929–30.* Québec: Rédempti Paradis, 1930, pp. 47–136.

————. "Inventaire de la correspondance de Mgr. Jean-François Hubert, Évêque de Québec, et de Mgr. Charles-François Bailley de Messein, son coadjuteur." *Rapport de l'archiviste de la province de Québec, 1930–31.* [Québec]: Rédempti Paradis, 1931, pp. 199–351.

————. "Inventaire de la correspondance de Mgr. Louis-Philippe Mariaucheau d'Esgly, Évêque de Québec." *Rapport de l'archiviste de la province de Québec, 1930–31.* Québec: Rédempti Paradis, 1931, pp. 185–98.

Catholic Church, Diocese of Baton Rouge. *A Guide to Archival Material Held by the Catholic Diocese of Baton Rouge.* Compiled by Elizabeth J. Doyle. Baton Rouge: Diocese of Baton Rouge, Department of History and Archives, 1964.

Catholic Church, Diocese of Louisiana and the Floridas. *Guide to the Microfilm Edition of the Records of the Diocese of Louisiana and the Floridas, 1576–1803.* Thomas T. McAvoy, project director; Lawrence J. Bradley, manuscripts preparator. Notre Dame, Ind.: University of Notre Dame Archives, 1967.

Centanni, Irna A. "Index to the First Book of Marriages, St. John the Baptist Parish, Edgard, Louisiana, November 14, 1772, to August 18, 1807." *New Orleans Genesis,* IX (September, 1970), 321–38.

Curry, Cora C. *Records of the Roman Catholic Church in the United States as a Source for Authentic Genealogical and Historical Material.* National Genealogical Society, Genealogical Publications, no. 5. Washington, D.C., 1935.

Ellis, John T. "A Guide to the Baltimore Cathedral Archives." *Catholic Historical Review,* XXXII (October, 1946), 341–60.

Hébert, Donald J. *A Guide to Church Records in Louisiana, (1720–1975).* Eunice, La.: Donald J. Hébert, 1975.

Nolan, Charles E. *A Southern Catholic Heritage, Volume I, Colonial Period, 1704–1813.* New Orleans: Archdiocese of New Orleans, 1976.

VI. Secondary Publications

A. *Books*

Alvord, Clarence W. *The Illinois Country, 1673–1818. The Centennial History of Illinois,* Vol. I. Springfield: Illinois Centennial Commission, 1920.

Arkansas Historical Association. *Publications.* 4 vols. Fayetteville, 1906–17.

Arsenault, Bona. *Histoire et généalogie des Acadiens.* 6 vols. [Montréal]: Leméac, 1978.

Arthur, Stanley C. *The Story of the West Florida Rebellion.* [St. Francisville, La.]: St. Francisville Democrat, 1935.

Basler, Lucille. *The District of Ste. Geneviève, 1725–1980.* Greenfield, Mo.: Vedette Printing Co., 1980.

Baudier, Roger. *The Catholic Church in Louisiana.* New Orleans: [A. W. Hyatt], 1939.

Billon, Frederic L. *Annals of St. Louis in Its Early Days Under the French and Spanish Dominations, 1764–1804.* St. Louis: G. I. Jones, 1886.

Bourgeois, Lillian C. *Cabonocey: The History, Customs and Folklore of St. James Parish.* New Orleans: Pelican Publishing Co., [1957].

Brasseaux, Carl A., Glenn R. Conrad, and R. Warren Robison. *The Courthouses of Louisiana.* Lafayette: Center for Louisiana Studies, University of Southwestern Louisiana, 1977.

Burson, Caroline M. *The Stewardship of Don Esteban Miró, 1782–1792; a Study of Louisiana Based Largely on the Documents in New Orleans*. New Orleans: American Printing Co., 1940.

Bushman, Katherine G., comp. *Index of the First Plat Book of Clay County, Missouri, 1819–1875*. [Staunton, Va.?, 1967].

Cadden, John P. *The Historiography of the American Catholic Church, 1785–1943*. Washington, D.C.: Catholic University of America Press, 1944.

Carleton, Roderick L. *Local Government and Administration in Louisiana*. Baton Rouge: Louisiana State University Press, 1935.

Caruso, John A. *The Southern Frontier*. Indianapolis: Bobbs-Merrill, [1963].

Casey, Albert E., Frances P. Otken, *et al. Amite County, Mississippi, 1699–[1865]*. 4 vols. Birmingham, Ala.: Published privately through the Amite County Historical Fund, 1948–69.

Caughey, John W. *Bernardo de Gálvez in Louisiana, 1776–1783*. Berkeley: University of California Press, 1934.

Chambon, Celestin M. *In and Around the Old St. Louis Cathedral of New Orleans*. New Orleans: Philippe's Printery, 1908.

Cole, Cyrenus. *Iowa Through the Years*. Iowa City: State Historical Society of Iowa, 1940.

Coleman, James J., Jr. *Gilbert Antoine de St. Maxent; the Spanish-Frenchman of New Orleans*. New Orleans: Pelican Publishing House, 1968.

Coles, Harry L., Jr. "A History of the Administration of the Federal Land Policies and Land Tenure in Louisiana, 1803–1860." Ph.D. thesis, Vanderbilt University, 1949. Typewritten copy in National Archives Library.

Cowart, Margaret M. *Old Land Records of Madison County, Alabama*. Huntsville, Ala., 1979.

Cox, Isaac J. *The West Florida Controversy, 1798–1813: A Study in American Diplomacy*. Baltimore: Johns Hopkins University Press, 1918.

Cunningham, Mary B., and Jeanne C. Blythe. *The Founding Family of St. Louis*. St. Louis: Midwest Technical Publications, 1977.

Davis, Edwin A. *Louisiana, the Pelican State*. Baton Rouge: Louisiana State University Press, 1959.

De Conde, Alexander. *This Affair of Louisiana*. New York: Charles Scribner's Sons, 1976.

De Ville, Winston. *Gulf Coast Colonials: A Compendium of French Families in Early Eighteenth Century Louisiana*. Introduction by James D. Hardy, Jr. Baltimore: Genealogical Publishing Co., 1968.

———. *Opelousas: The History of a French and Spanish Military Post in America, 1716–1803*. Cottonport, La.: Polyanthos, 1973.

Din, Gilbert C., and Abraham P. Nasatir. *The Imperial Osages: Spanish-Indian Diplomacy in the Mississippi Valley*. Norman: University of Oklahoma Press, 1983.

Doherty, William T., Jr. *Louis Houck: Missouri Historian and Entrepreneur*. University of Missouri Studies, Vol. XXXIII. Columbia: University of Missouri Press, [1960].

Donaldson, Thomas. *The Public Domain: Its History, with Statistics. House Miscella-*

neous Documents, 47th Cong., 2nd Sess., No. 45. Washington, D.C.: Government Printing Office, 1884. Serial 2158.

Donnelly, Joseph P. *Pierre Gibault Missionary, 1737–1802.* Chicago: Loyola University Press, 1971.

Doughty, Arthur G. *The Acadian Exiles: A Chronicle of the Land of Evangeline.* Toronto: Brook & Co., 1916.

Eccles, William J. *France in America.* New York: Harper & Row, 1972.

Evans, Melvin. *A Study in the State Government of Louisiana.* Louisiana State University *Studies,* no. 4. Baton Rouge: Louisiana State University Press, 1931.

Ferguson, John L., and J. H. Atkinson. *Historic Arkansas.* Little Rock: Arkansas Historical Commission, 1966.

Fisher, Lillian E. *The Intendant System in Spanish America.* Berkeley: University of California Press, 1929.

Fletcher, John G. *Arkansas.* Chapel Hill: University of North Carolina Press, 1947.

Fortier, Alcée. *A History of Louisiana.* Edited by Jo Ann Carrigan. 4 vols. 1904; rpr. Baton Rouge, La.: Claitor's, 1966.

―――, ed. *Louisiana: Comprising Sketches of Counties, Towns, Events, Institutions, and Persons, Arranged in Cyclopedic Form.* 2 vols. Atlanta: Southern Historical Association, 1909.

Franzwa, Gregory M. *The Story of Ste. Geneviève.* St. Louis: Patrice Press, 1967.

Garraghan, Gilbert J. *Saint Ferdinand de Florissant: The Story of an Ancient Parish.* Chicago: Loyola University Press, 1923.

Gayarré, Charles E. A. *History of Louisiana.* 4 vols. New York: Redfield, 1854–66. Reprint. New York: AMS Press, 1972.

Gerow, Richard O. *Catholicity in Mississippi.* Natchez, Miss.: n.p., 1939.

―――. *Cradle Days of St. Mary's at Natchez.* Natchez, Miss.: n.p., 1941.

Gibson, Charles. *Spain in America.* New York: Harper & Row, 1906.

Gillis, Norman E. *Early Inhabitants of the Natchez District.* [Baton Rouge? La., 1963].

Grace, Albert L. *The Heart of the Sugar Bowl: The Story of Iberville.* Plaquemine, La.: [Franklin Press], 1946.

Griffin, Harry L. *The Attakapas Country: A History of Lafayette Parish, Louisiana.* New Orleans: Pelican Publishing Co., 1959.

Hamilton, Peter J. *Colonial Mobile: An Historical Study Largely from Original Sources, of the Alabama-Tombigbee Basin and the Old South West . . .* Boston: Houghton, Mifflin and Co., 1897.

Hammang, Francis H. *The Marquis de Vaudreuil: New France at the Beginning of the Eighteenth Century.* Bruges, Belgium: Descleé de Brouwer, 1938.

Háring, Clarence H. *The Spanish Empire in America.* New York: Oxford University Press, 1947.

Harlan, Edgar R. *A Narrative History of the People of Iowa.* 5 vols. Chicago: American Historical Society, 1931.

Hébert, Donald J. *Acadians in Exile.* Cecelia, La.: Hébert, 1980.

Heinrich, Pierre. *La Louisiane sous le Compagnie des Indes, 1717–1731.* Paris: E. Guilmoto, [1908]. Reprint. New York: Burt Franklin, 1970. Typewritten English translation in National Archives Library.

Herndon, Dallas T. *Annals of Arkansas, 1947: A Narrative Historical Edition.* 4 vols. Hopkinsville, Ky.: Historical Records Association, [1947].

Higginbotham, Jay. *Old Mobile: Fort Louis de la Louisiane, 1702–1711. Museum Publication, no. 4.* [Mobile, Ala.]: Museum of the City of Mobile, 1977.

Hill, Roscoe R. *American Missions in European Archives.* Instituto Panamericana de Geografia et Historia, Comisión de Historia 22 Publicación, núm. 108. México, D.F., 1951.

Historical Records Survey, Louisiana. *County-Parish Boundaries in Louisiana.* New Orleans: Department of Archives, Louisiana State University, 1939.

Historical Records Survey, Mississippi. *State and County Boundaries of Mississippi.* Jackson, Miss., 1942.

Historic New Orleans Collection. *Guide to Research at the Historic New Orleans Collection.* New Orleans, 1978.

Holmes, Jack D. L. *Gayoso, the Life of a Spanish Governor in the Mississippi Valley, 1789–1794.* Baton Rouge: Louisiana State University Press, 1965.

Houck, Louis. *A History of Missouri, from the Earliest Explorations and Settlements Until the Admission of the State into the Union.* 3 vols. Chicago: R. R. Donnelley, & Sons Co., 1908.

Huber, Leonard V., and Samuel Wilson, Jr. *The Basilica on Jackson Square and Its Predecessor Churches Dedicated to St. Louis, King of France, 1727–1965.* New Orleans: St. Louis Basilica, 1965.

Jehn, Janet. *Acadian Descendants.* 6 vols. Covington, Ky.: Janet Jehn, 1972–1984.

———. *Acadian Exiles in the Colonies.* Covington, Ky.: Janet Jehn, 1977.

Johnson, Charles O., ed. *The Order of the First Families of Mississippi, 1699–1817.* Ann Arbor, Mich.: Edwards Brothers, 1981.

Kane, Harnet T. *The Ursulines, Nuns of Adventure: The Story of the New Orleans Community.* New York: Vision Books, 1959.

Kendall, John S. *History of New Orleans.* 3 vols. Chicago: Lewis Publishing Co., 1922.

Kenny, Michael. *Catholic Culture in Alabama: Centenary Stories of Spring Hill College.* New York: America Press, 1931.

Llaverías y Martínez, Joaquin. *Historia de los archivos de Cuba.* Archivo Nacional, Cuba, *Publicaciones,* Vol. XXIV. Havana: Imp. de Ruiz y Comp., 1942.

Louisiana State Museum. *Biennial Report, 1906/08–1932/33.* New Orleans, 1908–34.

———. *Handbook of Information Concerning Its Historic Buildings and the Treasures They Contain,* by Robert Glenk. New Orleans: n.p., 1934.

Lyon, E. Wilson. *Louisiana in French Diplomacy, 1759–1804.* Norman: University of Oklahoma Press, 1934.

March, David D. *History of Missouri,* 4 vols. New York: Lewis Historical Publishing Co., 1967.

Marchand, Sidney A. *Acadian Exiles in the Golden Coast of Louisiana.* Donaldsonville, La.: n.p., 1943.

———. *An Attempt to Re-assemble the Old Settlers in Family Groups.* Baton Rouge: Claitor's Book Store, 1965.

———. *The Story of Ascension Parish.* [Baton Rouge]: J. E. Ortlieb Printing Co., 1931.

Martínez, Raymond, J. *Pierre George Rousseau, Commanding General of the Galleys of the Mississippi.* New Orleans, 1964.

Mathews, Catharine Van Cortlandt. *Andrew Ellicott, His Life and Letters.* New York: Grafton Press, [1908].

McAvoy, Thomas T., C.S.C. *A History of the Catholic Church in the United States.* Notre Dame, Ind.: University of Notre Dame Press, 1969.

McDermott, John F., ed. *The French in the Mississippi Valley.* Urbana: University of Illinois Press, 1965.

———. *Frenchmen and French Ways in the Mississippi Valley.* Urbana: University of Illinois Press, 1969.

———. *The Spanish in the Mississippi Valley, 1762–1804.* Urbana: University of Illinois Press, [1974].

McMurtrie, Douglas C. *Denis Braud, imprimeur du roi à la Nouvelle Orléans.* Paris, 1929.

Mississippi, Department of Archives and History, *Annual Report, 1902–80.* Nashville, Tenn., Jackson, Miss., 1902–80.

Mississippi Historical Commission. *Report of the Mississippi Historical Commission, 1901.* Edited by Franklin L. Riley. Mississippi Historical Society *Publications,* Vol. V. Oxford, Miss.: Printed for the Society, 1902.

Moore, Albert B. *History of Alabama.* University, Ala.: University Supply Store, 1934.

New Catholic Encyclopedia. 15 vols. New York: McGraw-Hill, 1967.

Noggle, Burl. *Working with History: The Historical Records Survey in Louisiana and the Nation, 1936–1942.* Baton Rouge: Louisiana State University Press, 1981.

Oglesby, Richard E. *Manuel Lisa and the Opening of the Fur Trade.* Norman: University of Oklahoma Press, 1963.

O'Neill, Charles E. *Church and State in French Colonial Louisiana; Policy and Politics to 1732.* New Haven: Yale University Press, 1966.

Owen, Thomas M. *History of Alabama and Dictionary of Alabama Biography.* 4 vols. Chicago: S. J. Clarke Publishing Co., 1921.

Posner, Ernst. *American State Archives.* Chicago: University of Chicago Press, 1964.

Riffel, Judy, ed. *A History of Pointe Coupee Parish and Its Families.* Baton Rouge: Le Comité des Archives de la Louisiane, 1983.

Rohrbough, Malcolm J. *The Land Office Business; the Settlement and Administration of American Public Lands, 1789–1837.* New York: Oxford University Press, 1968.

Rowland, Dunbar. *History of Mississippi, the Heart of the South.* 4 vols. Chicago: S. J. Clarke Publishing Co., 1925. Reprint. Spartanburg, S.C.: Reprint Co., 1978.

———. *Mississippi: Comprising Sketches of Counties, Towns, Events, Institutions, and Persons, Arranged in Cyclopedia Form.* 3 vols. Atlanta: Southern Historical Publishing, 1907.

Rowland, Mrs. Dunbar. *Life, Letters and Papers of William Dunbar . . .* Jackson: Mississippi Historical Society, 1930.

Saucier, Corinne L. *The History of Avoyelles Parish, Louisiana.* New Orleans: Pelican Publishing Co., [1943].
Savelle, Max. *George Morgan, Colony Builder.* New York: Columbia University Press, 1932.
Semple, Henry C., ed. *The Ursulines in New Orleans and Our Lady of Prompt Succor; a Record of Two Centuries, 1727–1925.* New York: P. J. Kenedy & Sons, 1925.
Shea, John D. G. *The History of the Catholic Church Within the Limits of the United States.* 4 vols. New York: J. G. Shea, 1886–92. Reprint. New York: Arno Press, 1978.
Shoemaker, Floyd C. *Missouri and Missourians: Land of Contrasts and People of Achievements.* 5 vols. Chicago: Lewis Publishing Co., 1943.
Soniat du Fossat, Guy. *Synopsis of the History of Louisiana, from the Founding of the Colony to the End of the Year 1791.* Translated by Charles T. Soniat. 1903; rpr. New Orleans, Polyanthos, 1976.
Stoddard, Amos. *Sketches, Historical and Descriptive, of Louisiana.* Philadelphia: Mathew Carey, 1812. Reprint. New York: AMS Press, 1973.
Thomas, David Y. *Arkansas and Its People: A History, 1541–1930.* 4 vols. New York: American Historical Society, 1930.
Troen, Selwyn K., and Glen Holt. *St. Louis.* New York: New Viewpoints, 1977.
Van Zandt, Franklin K. *Boundaries of the United States and of the Several States.* U.S. Geological Survey *Professional Paper,* no. 909. Washington, D.C.: Government Printing Office, 1976.
Villiers du Terrage, Marc, Baron de. *Les Dernières années de la Louisiane française: Le Chevalier de Kerlérec, D'Abbadie, Aubry, Laussat.* Paris: E. Guilomoto, [1904].
Whitaker, Arthur P. *The Mississippi Question, 1795–1803: A Study in Trade, Politics, and Diplomacy.* New York: D. Appleton-Century Co., [1934].
———. *The Spanish-American Frontier, 1783–1795: The Westward Movement and the Spanish Retreat in the Mississippi Valley.* Boston: Houghton Mifflin Co., 1927.
White, C. Albert. *A History of the Rectangular Survey System.* Washington, D.C.: Government Printing Office, [1983].
Wilson, Samuel, Jr. *The Capuchin School in New Orleans, 1725: The First School in Louisiana.* New Orleans: Archdiocesan School Board, 1961.
Wilson, Samuel, Jr., and Leonard V. Huber. *The Cabildo on Jackson Square: The Colonial Period, 1723–1803, The American Period, 1803 to the Present.* New Orleans: Friends of the Cabildo, 1970.
Winzerling, Oscar W. *Acadian Odyssey.* Baton Rouge: Louisiana State University Press, 1955.

B. *Articles*

Andreassen, John C. L. "Check List of Historical Records Survey and Survey of Federal Archives Publications for Louisiana." *Louisiana Historical Quarterly,* XXVII (April, 1944), 613–23.
Arena, C. Richard. "Land Settlement Policies and Practices in Spanish Louisiana." In *The Spanish in the Mississippi Valley, 1762–1804,* edited by John F. McDermott. Urbana: University of Illinois Press, 1974.
Barras, Mrs. M. A. "Records of St. Martin Parish Courthouse, St. Martinville,

Louisiana." In *Genealogical Institute, 16th, Proceedings, 31 March 1973*. Baton Rouge: Louisiana Genealogical and Historical Society, 1974.

Beer, William, ed. "Early Census Tables of Louisiana." *Louisiana Historical Society Publications*, V (1911), 79–103.

Belsom, Jack. "St. John the Baptist Parish Church, Edgard, Louisiana." *New Orleans Genesis*, IX (March, 1970), 110–11.

Bennett, Archibald F. "The Microfilming Activities of the Genealogical Society of the Church of Jesus Christ of Latter-Day Saints." *Archivum*, IX (1959), 121–23.

Bergeron, Arthur W. "Genealogical Resources and Services of the Louisiana State Archives." *Attakapas Gazette*, XIII (Spring, 1978), 14–16.

Bitton, Davis. "Research Materials in the Mormon Genealogical Society." *French Historical Studies*, VIII (Spring, 1973), 172–74.

Bonnel, Ulane Z. "La Déléguée à Paris: The Library of Congress Foreign Copying Program in France." *Library of Congress Quarterly Journal*, XXIII (July, 1966), 187–203.

Brasseaux, Carl A. "The Colonial Records Collection of the Center for Louisiana Studies." *Louisiana History*, XXV (Spring, 1984), 181–88.

Briceland, Alan V. "The Mississippi Territorial Land Board East of the Pearl River, 1804." *Alabama Review*, XXXII (January, 1979), 38–68.

Briede, Kathryn C. "A History of the City of Lafayette." *Louisiana Historical Quarterly*, XX (October, 1937), 895–964.

Broders, Mrs. E. A. "List of Successions Found in the Records of the Spanish West Florida Archives." *Louisiana Genealogical Register*, XI (September, December, 1964), 42–44, 57–60.

Brooks, George R. "The First Century of the Missouri Historical Society." *Missouri Historical Society Bulletin*, XXII (April, 1966), 274–301.

Browne, Henry J. "Report of the Committee on the John Carroll Papers." *Catholic Historical Review*, XXXIX (April, 1953), 40–43.

Bush, Evelyn. "United States Land Offices in Alabama, 1803–1879." *Alabama Historical Quarterly*, XVII (Fall, 1955), 146–53.

Bush, Robert D. "Documents on the Louisiana Purchase: The Laussat Papers." *Louisiana History*, XVIII (Winter, 1977), 104–107.

———. "L'Abandon de la Louisiane: The Last Days of Prefect Laussat, 1803–1804." *Revue de Louisiane/Louisiana Review*, VIII (Winter, 1979), 120–29.

Calhoun, Robert D. "A History of Concordia Parish, Louisiana." *Louisiana Historical Quarterly*, XV (January–October, 1932), 44–67, 214–33, 428–52, 618–45; XVI (January–October, 1933), 92–124, 309–29, 454–78, 598–607; XVII (January, 1934), 96–111.

———. "The Origin and Development of County-Parish Government in Louisiana (1805–1845)." *Louisiana Historical Quarterly*, XVIII (January–October, 1935), 56–160.

Carrigan, Jo Ann. "Government in Spanish Louisiana." *Louisiana Studies*, XI (Fall, 1972), 215–29.

Carroll, Joseph W., *et al.* "In Memoriam Henry Plauché Dart." *Louisiana Historical Quarterly*, XVIII (April, 1935), 255–66.

Case, Conrad W. "Franklin L. Riley and the Historical Renaissance in Missis-
sippi, 1897–1914." *Journal of Mississippi History*, XXXII (August, 1970),
195–227.
Chappell, Gordon T. "John Coffee: Surveyor and Land Agent." *Alabama Review*,
XIV (July–October, 1961), 180–95, 243–50.
"The Church of the Attakapas, 1750–1889." *American Catholic Quarterly Review*,
XIV (July, 1889), 462–87.
Coker, William S. "Research in the Spanish Borderlands: Mississippi, 1779–
1798." *Latin American Research Review*, VII (Summer, 1972), 40–54.
Coker, William S., and Jack D. L. Holmes. "Sources for the History of the Span-
ish Borderlands." *Florida Historical Quarterly*, XLIX (April, 1971), 380–93.
Coles, Harry L., Jr. "Applicability of the Public Land System to Louisiana." *Mis-
sissippi Valley Historical Review*, XLVIII (June, 1956), 39–58.
———. "The Confirmation of Foreign Land Titles in Louisiana." *Louisiana His-
torical Quarterly*, XXXVIII (October, 1955), 1–22.
Corbitt, Duvon C. "The Administrative System in the Floridas, 1781–1821." *Te-
questa*, I (August, 1942, July, 1943), 41–62, 57–67.
———. "Exploring the Southwest Territory in the Spanish Archives." *East Ten-
nessee Historical Society Publications*, XXXVIII (1966), 109–18.
———. "Señor Joaquin Llaverias and the Archivo Nacional de Cuba." *Hispanic
American Historical Review*, XX (May, 1940), 283–86.
Coutts, Brian E. "The Cuban Papers." *Louisiana Genealogical Register*, XXVII (De-
cember, 1980), 354–68.
Cruzat, Heloise H. "The Ursulines of Louisiana." *Louisiana Historical Quarterly*, II
(January, 1919), 5–23.
D'Antoni, Blaise C. "The Church Records of North Louisiana." *Louisiana History*,
XV (Winter, 1974), 59–67.
Dart, Henry P. "The Archives of Louisiana." *Louisiana Historical Quarterly*, II (Oc-
tober, 1919), 351–67.
———. "The Cabildo of New Orleans." *Louisiana Historical Quarterly*, V (April,
1922), 279–81.
———. "Courts and Law in Colonial Louisiana." *Louisiana Bar Association Re-
ports*, XXII (1921), 17–63.
———. "The Index to the French and Spanish Archives of Louisiana." *Louisiana
Historical Quarterly*, X (July, 1927), 407–408.
———. "The Legal Institutions of Louisiana." *Louisiana Historical Quarterly*, II
(January, 1919), 72–103.
———. "The Legal Institutions of Louisiana." *Southern Law Quarterly*, III (No-
vember, 1918).
———. "Marriage Contracts of French Colonial Louisiana." *Louisiana Historical
Quarterly*, XVII (April, 1934), 229–41.
———, ed. "Civil Procedure in Louisiana Under the Spanish Regime as Illus-
trated in Loppinot's Case, 1774." *Louisiana Historical Quarterly*, XII (January,
1929), 33–120.

Dart, Mrs. Stephen P. "West Feliciana Parish Marriage Index, 1791–1875." *Louisiana Genealogical Register*, XVI (June–September, 1969), 177–78, 242–45; XVII (June, 1970), 193–96; XVIII (March, December, 1971), 52–54, 314–16.

Delanglez, Jean. "A French Bishop for Louisiana (1722–1763)." *Catholic Historical Review*, XX (January, 1935), 411–19.

De Ville, Winston. "Manuscript Sources in Louisiana for the History of the French in the Mississippi Valley." In *The French in the Mississippi Valley*, edited by John F. McDermott. Urbana: University of Illinois Press, 1965.

Din, Gilbert C. "The Irish Mission to West Florida." *Louisiana History*, XII (Fall, 1971), 315–34.

————. "The Spanish Fort on the Arkansas, 1763–1803." *Arkansas Historical Quarterly*, XLII (Autumn, 1983), 270–93.

————. "Spanish Immigration to a French Land." *Revue de Louisiane*, V (Summer, 1976), 63–80.

Ducote, Alberta R. "Mark and Brand Book I, Avoyelles Parish." *Louisiana Genealogical Register*, XVII (September, 1970), 254–56.

Dunn, Milton. "History of Natchitoches Parish." *Louisiana Historical Quarterly*, III (January, 1920), 26–56.

Eastwood, Sidney K. "The Pintado Papers." *New Orleans Genesis*, III (March, 1964), 137–47.

Eaton, Joy D. "Early Louisiana Land Records." In *Eighteenth Annual Genealogical Institute Proceedings, 22 March 1975*. Baton Rouge: Louisiana Genealogical and Historical Society, 1975.

Favrot, H. Mortimer. "Colonial Forts of Louisiana." *Louisiana Historical Quarterly*, XXV (July, 1943), 722–54.

Favrot, J. St. Clair. "Baton Rouge, the Historic Capital of Louisiana." *Louisiana Historical Quarterly*, XII (October, 1929), 611–29.

Forsyth, Alice D. "Saint Gabriel of Iberville—Iberville Parish, Louisiana." *Louisiana Genealogical Register*, XXII (June, 1974), 137–43.

Fortier, Alcée. "Report of Prof. Fortier." *Louisiana Historical Society Publications*, I (1895), 3–9.

Gannon, Michael V. "Documents of the Spanish Florida Borderlands: A Calendaring Project at the University of Florida." *William and Mary Quarterly*, XXXVIII (October, 1981), 718–22.

Garraghan, Gilbert J. "The Ecclesiastical Rule of Old Quebec in Mid-America." *Catholic Historical Review*, XIX (April, 1933), 17–32.

Garrett, Mitchell B. "The Preservation of Alabama History." *North Carolina Historical Review*, V (January, 1928), 3–19.

Gass, Conrad W. "Franklin L. Riley and the Historical Renaissance in Mississippi, 1897–1914." *Journal of Mississippi History*, XXXII (August, 1970), 195–227.

Gates, Paul W. "Private Land Claims in the South." *Journal of Southern History*, XXII (May, 1956), 183–204.

Gianelloni, Elizabeth B. "Tour of Department Archives of the Catholic Diocese of Baton Rouge." In *Genealogical Institute, 14th, Proceedings, 17 April 1971*. Baton Rouge: Louisiana Genealogical and Historical Society, 1972.

Grégorie, Jeanne. "Les Acadiennes dans une seconde patrie: La Louisiane." *Revue d'histoire de l'Amérique française*, XV (March, 1962), 572–93; XVI (June, September, December, 1962), 105–16, 254–66, 428–35.
Griffith, Connie G. "Collections in the Manuscript Section of Howard-Tilton Memorial Library, Tulane University." *Louisiana History*, I (Fall, 1960), 320–27.
———. "Summary of Inventory: Louisiana Historical Association Collection." *Louisiana History*, IX (Fall, 1968), 365–70.
Grima, Edgar. "The Notarial System of Louisiana." *Louisiana Historical Quarterly*, X (January, 1927), 76–81.
Hamer, Collin B., Jr. "Library Additions, New Orleans Public Library [List of New Orleans Notarial Records Available on Microfilm]." *New Orleans Genesis*, XI (September, 1972), 406–409.
———. "Recent Genealogical Acquisitions in the New Orleans Public Library." In *Eighteenth Annual Genealogical Institute Proceedings, 22 March 1975*. Baton Rouge: Louisiana Genealogical and Historical Society, 1975.
Hardcastle, David. "The Military Organization of French Colonial Louisiana." In *The Military Presence on the Gulf Coast; Proceedings of the Gulf Coast History and Humanities Conference, 7th, Pensacola, 1977*, edited by William S. Coker. Pensacola, 1978.
Hardin, J. Fair. "Don Juan Filhiol and the Founding of Fort Miro, the Modern Monroe, Louisiana." *Louisiana Historical Quarterly*, XX (April, 1937), 463–86.
Hardy, James D., Jr. "The Superior Council in Colonial Louisiana." In *Frenchmen and French Ways in the Mississippi Valley*, edited by John F. McDermott. Urbana: University of Illinois Press, 1969.
Harlan, Edgar R. "Claim of Bazil Giard." *Annals of Iowa*, 3d ser., XVI (April, 1929), 622–27.
Harrell, Mrs. W. O. "A List of Claims on Spanish Patents in Mississippi, 1806." *Journal of Mississippi History*, VIII (July, 1946), 148–51.
Harrison, Robert W. "Public Land Records of the Federal Government." *Mississippi Valley Historical Review*, XLI (September, 1954), 277–88.
Haynes, Robert V. "The Disposal of Lands in the Mississippi Territory." *Journal of Mississippi History*, XXIV (October, 1962), 226–52.
Hébert, A. Otis, Jr. "Keeping Louisiana's Records." *McNeese Review*, XVIII (1967), 27–38.
———. "Resources in Louisiana Depositories for the Study of Spanish Activities in Louisiana." In *The Spanish in the Mississippi Valley, 1762–1804*, edited by John F. McDermott. Urbana: University of Illinois Press, [1974].
Henshaw, Francis G. "A Brief History of the Library of Congress Microreproduction Projects." In *National Microfilm Association Proceedings, 8th Annual Meeting, Washington* (1959), 211–27.
Holmes, Jack D. L. "Alabama's Forgotten Settlers: Notes on the Spanish Mobile District, 1780–1813." *Alabama Historical Quarterly*, XXXIII (Summer, 1971), 87–97.
———. "Father Francis Lennan and His Activities in Spanish Louisiana and West Florida." *Louisiana Studies*, V (Winter, 1966), 255–68.

———. "Genealogical and Historical Sources for Spanish Alabama, 1780–1813." *Deep South Genealogical Quarterly,* V (February, 1968), 130–38.

———. "The Historiography of the American Revolution in Louisiana." *Louisiana History,* XIX (Summer, 1978), 309–26.

———. "Interpretations and Trends in the Study of the Spanish Borderlands: The Old Southwest." *Southwestern Historical Quarterly,* LXXIV (April, 1971), 461–77.

———. "A New Look at Spanish Louisiana Census Accounts: The Recent Historiography of Antonio Acosta." *Louisiana History,* XXI (Winter, 1980), 77–86.

———. "Stephen Minor: Natchez Pioneer." *Journal of Mississippi History,* XLII (February, 1980), 17–26.

Jacobs, John H. "Keeping Archives Widens Library Community Service." *Library Journal,* XLVII (June, 1947), 950.

Jennings, Mrs. Robert B. "Genealogical Research in East Baton Rouge and the Florida Parishes." *New Orleans Genesis,* V (March, 1966), 95–103.

Kendall, John S. "Historical Collections in New Orleans." *North Carolina Historical Review,* VII (October, 1930), 463–76.

Kernion, George C. H. "Reminiscences of the Chevalier Bernard de Verges, an Early Colonial Engineer of Louisiana." *Louisiana Historical Quarterly,* VII (January, 1924), 56–86.

King, Grace. "The Preservation of Louisiana History." *North Carolina Historical Review,* V (October, 1928), 363–71.

Lacrocq, Nelly. "Resources in France for the American Historian: Maps and Drawings at the Bibliothèque de l'Inspection du Génie." *Library of Congress Quarterly Journal,* XXX (October, 1973), 253–55.

Lafargue, André. "Pierre Clément de Laussat, Colonial Prefect and High Commissioner of France in Louisiana: His Memoirs, Proclamations and Orders." *Louisiana Historical Quarterly,* XX (January, 1937), 159–82.

Landry, Louis C., Jr. "Louisiana Colonial Militia Lists." *Louisiana Genealogical Register,* IX (June–December, 1962), 20–25, 33–40, 51–54; X (March, 1963), 11–16.

Laurent, Lubin F. "History of St. John the Baptist Parish." *Louisiana Historical Quarterly,* VII (April, 1924), 316–31.

Levron, Jacques. "Les Registres paroissiaux et d'état civil en France." *Archivum,* IX (1959), 55–100.

Lightner, David. "Private Land Claims in Alabama." *Alabama Review,* XX (July, 1967), 187–204.

Lindsay, Lionel St. G. "The Archives of the Archbishopric of Quebec." *American Catholic Historical Society of Philadelphia Records,* XVIII (March, 1907), 8–11.

"Lists of Persons Taking the Oaths of Allegiance in the Natchez District, 1798–99." Copied by Mrs. Boyd C. Edwards. *National Genealogical Society Quarterly,* XLII (September, 1954), 108–16.

Logan, Robert R. "Notes on the First Land Surveys in Arkansas." *Arkansas Historical Quarterly,* XIX (Autumn, 1960), 260–70.

Martin, Wade O., Jr. "Archives." In *Eighteenth Annual Genealogical Institute Pro-*

ceedings, 22 March 1975. Baton Rouge: Louisiana Genealogical and Historical Society, 1975.

McMurtrie, Douglas C. "Three Louisiana Broadsides, 1778–1779." *American Book Collector*, VI (May–June, 1935), 195–200.

Micelle, Jerry A. "From Law Court to Local Government: Metamorphosis of the Superior Council of French Louisiana." *Louisiana History*, IX (Spring, 1968), 85–108.

Miller, W. James. "The Militia System of Spanish Louisiana, 1769–1783." In *The Military Presence on the Gulf Coast; Proceedings of the Gulf Coast History and Humanities Conference, 7th, Pensacola, 1977*, edited by William S. Coker. Pensacola, 1978.

Mills, Elizabeth S. "Land Titles: A Neglected Key to Solving Genealogical Problems. A Case Study at Natchitoches." *Louisiana Genealogical Register*, XXXI (June, 1984), 103–23.

Mitchell, Jennie O., and Robert D. Calhoun. "The Marquis de Maison Rouge, the Baron de Bastrop, and Colonel Abraham Morhouse, Three Ouachita Valley Soldiers of Fortune, the Maison Rouge and Bastrop Spanish Land Grants." *Louisiana Historical Quarterly*, XX (April, 1937), 289–462.

Moore, Ellen B. "Report from the State Land Office." *Louisiana Genealogical Register*, XVI (March, 1969), 1–4.

Morazán, Ronald R. "The Cabildo of Spanish New Orleans, 1769–1803: The Collapse of Local Government." *Louisiana Studies*, XII (Winter, 1973), 589–606.

Motley, Archie. "Chicago Historical Society [Manuscripts]." *Illinois Libraries*, LVII (March, 1975), 223–26.

Nasatir, Abraham P. "Jacques Clamorgan: Colonial Promoter of the Northern Border of New Spain." *New Mexico Historical Review*, XVII (April, 1942), 101–12.

Owen, Thomas M. "Alabama Archives." In American Historical Association, *Annual Report, 1904*. Washington, D.C.: Government Printing Office, 1905.

Pargellis, Stanley M., and Norman B. Cuthbert. "Loudoun Papers: (a) Colonial, 1756–58, (b) French Colonial, 1742–53." *Huntington Library Bulletin*, no. 3 (February, 1933), 97–107.

Parkhurst, Helen H. "Don Pedro Favrot, a Creole Pepys, New Orleans, La." *Louisiana Historical Quarterly*, XXVIII (July, 1945), 680–734.

Parkin, Robert E. "Index of U.S. Government Surveys of Land Grants in St. Charles County." *St. Louis Genealogical Society Quarterly*, VII (December, 1974), 77.

Pattison, William D. "Use of the U.S. Public Land Survey Plats and Notes as Descriptive Sources." *Professional Geographer*, n.s., VIII (January, 1956), 10–14.

Pérez, Luis M. "French Immigrants to Louisiana, 1796–1800." *Southern History Association Publications*, XI (March, 1907), 106–12.

Peterson, Charles E. "Colonial St. Louis." *Missouri Historical Society Bulletin*, IV (April, 1947), 94–111.

Post, Lauren C. "Cattle Branding in Southwest Louisiana." *McNeese Review*, X (Winter, 1958), 101–17.

———. "The Od Cattle Industry of Southwest Louisiana." *McNeese Review*, IX (Winter, 1957), 43–55.

Price, William. "Work of Indexing Louisiana Black Boxes." *Louisiana Historical Society Publications*, VIII (1914–15), 7–20.

Rees, Grover. "The Missing Sixty-one Bundles." *New Orleans Genesis*, V (January, 1966), 11–12.

"Research in the Archives of the Archdiocese of New Orleans." *Louisiana Genealogical Register*, XXIX (September, 1982), 290–93.

Richardson, Lamont K. "Private Land Claims in Missouri." *Missouri Historical Review*, L (January–July, 1956), 133–44, 271–86, 387–99.

Riley, Franklin L. "The Department of Archives and History of the State of Mississippi." American Historical Association, *Annual Report*, 1903, I, pp. 475–78.

Rothensteiner, John. "Historical Sketch of Catholic New Madrid." *St. Louis Catholic Historical Review*, IV (July, October, 1922), 113–29, 206–18.

Rowsell, Kent. "Talk Given by Mr. Kent Rowsell, Field Operator for the Genealogical Society of the Church of Jesus Christ of Latter-Day Saints." *New Orleans Genesis*, VI (March, 1967), 100–102.

Ruckert, Margaret. "Archive Preservation in New Orleans." *Library Journal*, LXXXIII (July, 1958), 2000–2002.

———. "Archives Department, New Orleans Public Library." *Louisiana Library Association Bulletin*, XII (January, 1949), 45–49.

"St. Louis Real Estate in Review." Missouri Historical Society *Glimpses of the Past*, IV (October–December, 1937), 117–77.

"St. Martin Parish Library Microfilm Collection as of March, 1973." *Genealogical Institute, 16th, Proceedings, 31 March 1973.* Baton Rouge: Louisiana Genealogical and Historical Society, 1974.

Scanlan, P. L., and Marian Scanlan. "Basil Giard and His Land Claim in Iowa." *Iowa Journal of History*, XXX (April, 1932), 219–47.

Schaaf, Ida M. "Sainte Geneviève, Missouri, Catholic Records." *National Genealogical Society Publications*, 5 (1935), 6–9.

Scramuzza, V. M. "Galveztown: A Spanish Settlement of Colonial Louisiana." *Louisiana Historical Quarterly*, XIII (October, 1930), 553–609.

Scroggs, William O. "The Archives of the State of Louisiana." American Historical Association, *Annual Report*, 1912, pp. 279–93.

Segura, Pearl M. "Infantry Regiment of Louisiana. Book of Life and Customs and Services of Commissioned Officers, First Sergeants, and Cadets of Said Regular Regiment up to the End of December of 1781." *Louisiana Genealogical Register*, VII (March–December, 1960), 9–12, 24–26, 41–43, 57–58; IX (March, December, 1962), 7–9, 55–56.

Simpson, Robert R. "The Origin of the Mississippi Department of Archives and History." *Journal of Mississippi History*, XXXV (February, 1973), 1–14.

"State Land Office Records—U.S. Tract Book Index District North of the Red River." *Louisiana Genealogical Register*, XVIII (December, 1971), 404–405.

Sydnor, Charles S. "Historical Activities in Mississippi in the Nineteenth Century." *Journal of Southern History*, III (May, 1937), 139–60.

Taylor, James W. "Louisiana Land Survey Systems." *Southwestern Social Science Quarterly*, XXXI (March, 1951), 275–82.

Thayer, Mrs. Walter W., Sr. "Marriage Contracts, Index Volume 15 Sundry Dispensations, Acts of Narcisse Broutin." *New Orleans Genesis*, VII (January, 1968), 96–98; VIII (September, 1969), 399–406.

U.S. State Department. "Despatches from the United States Consulate in New Orleans, 1801–1803." *American Historical Review*, XXXII (July, 1927), 801–24; XXXIII (January, 1928), 331–59.

Utley, George B. "Source Material for the Study of American History in the Libraries of Chicago." Bibliographic Society of America *Papers*, XVI, pt. 1 (1922), 17–46.

Verges, Mrs. Edwin X. de. "The French and Spanish Colonial Archives of Louisiana." *New Orleans Genesis*, IV (January, 1965), 6–8.

Viles, Jonas. "Population and Extent of Settlement in Missouri before 1804." *Missouri Historical Review*, V (July, 1911), 189–212.

——. "Report on the Archives of the State of Missouri." American Historical Association, *Annual Report*, 1908, Vol. I. Washington, D.C., 1909.

Violette, E. M. "Spanish Land Claims in Missouri." *Washington University Studies*, VIII, Humanistic Series, no. 2 (April, 1921), 167–200.

Whittington, G. P. "Rapides Parish, Louisiana—a History." *Louisiana Historical Quarterly*, XV–XVIII (October, 1932–January, 1935).

Williams, E. Russ, Jr. "Index of Private Land Claims, State of Louisiana." *Louisiana Genealogical Register*, VII–XIV (June, 1960–December, 1967).

Wright, J. Leitch, Jr. "Research Opportunities in the Spanish Borderlands: West Florida, 1781–1821." *Latin American Research Review*, VII (Summer, 1972), 24–34.

Zacharie, James S. "The Cathedral Archives." *Louisiana Historical Society Publications*, II, pt. 3 (February, 1900), 10–16.

VII. Transcriptions and Translations

A. *By Survey of Federal Archives in Louisiana, Deposited in National Archives Library and Louisiana State University Library*

Bossu, Jean Bernard. New Voyages in North America. Translated by Olivia Blanchard. New Orleans, 1940.

Dumont de Montigny, Louis François Benjamin. Settlement of the Province of Louisiana or Poèms en Vers. Translated by Henri Delville de Sinclair. New Orleans, 1940.

——. Historical Memoire on Louisiana. Translated by Olivia Blanchard. New Orleans, 1937–38.

Du Ru, Paul, Père. Extract from a Journal de Voyage in Louisiana by Père Paul de Ru 1700. From the French by Baron Marc de Villiers. Translated by Olivia Blanchard. New Orleans, 1939.

Gálvez, Bernardo de. Diary of Governor Bernardo de Gálvez during His Expedition against Pensacola, 1781. Translated by George H. Jessup. New Orleans, 1940.

Gravier, Gabriel. Relation of the Dames Religieuses Ursulines of Rouen to New Orleans with Introduction and Notes by Gabriel Gravier. Paris: Maisonneuve, 1872. Translated by Olivia Blanchard. New Orleans, 1940.

Heinrich, Pierre. Louisiana under the Company of the Indies, 1717–1731. Translated by Henri Delville de Sinclair. New Orleans, 1940.

La Harpe, Bénard de. Historical Journal of the Establishment of the French in Louisiana. Translated by Olivia Blanchard. New Orleans, 1940.

Laussat, Pierre Clément de. Memoirs and Correspondence of Pierre Clément de Laussat. Translated by Henri Delville de Sinclair. New Orleans, 1940.

Le Gac, Charles. Memoir of Charles Le Gac, Director of the Company of the Indies in Louisiana, 1718–1721. Translated by Olivia Blanchard. New Orleans, 1937–38.

Le Maire, François. Letters of Father François Le Maire, a Missionary Priest in Louisiana Describing the Country and the Habits of the Indians, 1714–1717. Translated by Olivia Blanchard and Ronald Lambert. New Orleans, 1937–38.

Louisiana, Spanish. Confidential Dispatches of Don Bernardo de Gálvez, Fourth Spanish Governor of Louisiana, Sent to His Uncle Don José de Gálvez, Secretary of State and Ranking Official of the Council of the Indies [1777–1782]. New Orleans, 1937–38.

———. Dispatches of the Spanish Governors of Louisiana (1766–1792). 5 vols. New Orleans, 1937–38.

———. Dispatches of the Spanish Governor of Louisiana. Messages of Francisco Luis Hector, El Baron de Carondelet, Sixth Spanish Governor of Louisiana, 1792–1797. 11 vols. New Orleans, 1937–41.

———. Pintado Papers; Transcripts of Land Claims and Miscellaneous Plats and Papers. 11 vols. New Orleans, 1940–41.

Pontalba, Joseph Xavier Delfan. The Letters of Baron Joseph X. Pontalba to His Wife, 1796. Translated by Henri Delville de Sinclair. New Orleans, 1939.

Survey of Federal Archives, Louisiana. Collection of Regulations, Edicts, and Decrees Concerning the Commerce, Administration of Justice and the Policing of Louisiana and the French Colonies in America with the Black Code. Typescript; New Orleans, 1940.

———. The Letters of Padre Antonio de Sedella, Curé of the San Luis Cathedral, New Orleans [1785–1816]. Typescript: New Orleans, 1940.

———. Translations of Documents in Spanish and French Relating to Padre Antonio de Sedella and His Ecclesiastical Differences with Vicar-General Patrick Walsh of the St. Louis Cathedral, 1791–1807. Typescript; New Orleans, 1937–38.

West Florida, Spanish. Archives of the Spanish Government of West Florida, a Series of 18 Bound Volumes of Written Documents Mostly in the Spanish Language Deposited in the Records Room of the 17th Judicial District Court, Baton Rouge, Louisiana. 18 vols. New Orleans, 1937–39.

————. Original Notarial Acts, Book No. 1, Bundles A, B, C, 1799 to 1816. Archives of the Spanish Government of West Florida, Vol. XIX, part 1. Translations and Transcriptions, Vol. XIX, part 2. 2 vols. New Orleans, 1940.

B. *By Survey of Federal Archives of U.S. Land Office Archives, Baton Rouge*
(Transcripts in Louisiana State University, Department of Archives and Manuscripts)

British Grants, 1768–1779, Greensburg [New Orleans], 1942.
British and Spanish Grants, Notices and Evidences in Written Claims before Cosby and Skipwith, 1819–20, Greensburg Land Claims [New Orleans], 1941.
Opelousas Land Claims, Louisiana, Book I, pts. 1–2 [New Orleans], 1939.
Greensburg Land Claims, British West Florida, Book II, (pts. 1–2). [New Orleans], 1939–40.

C. *Other Transcriptions*

Historical Records Survey, Louisiana. Transcriptions of Manuscript Collections in Louisiana, no. 1, The Favrot Papers [1695–1769]. 7 vols. New Orleans, 1940–42.

Index

Abjurations, in New Orleans, 101
Abstracts, Natchez dist. records, 186
Acadia: archival reprods. re, 46; settled by
French, 161
Acadian Coast: 9; of servicemen on, 68;
settlement of, 87, 107
Acadians: 85, 176; archival sources re, 162;
in Ascension Parish, 87, 167; in Attakapas dist., 109; built church, 177;
emigration to La., 46; guide to sources
re, 162; immigration, 57; intermarriages,
156; land grants on the Miss. R., 115;
lists, 66; marriages, 49, 107; publications
re, 48–49, 162; records of, in France, 44,
48–49; settlements in La., 87, 89, 95, 96,
97, 107, 108, 109, 177, 179; transportation
of, 48
Acadia Parish, La., land records re, 137
Account books, Spanish La., 40
Accounts: French records re, 43; La., 16; of
sailors, 7; of St. Denis, 99; at St. Louis
Cathedral, New Orleans, 174; of Spanish
La., 56
Acosta, Frederick B., 53
Acre, ———, 216
Acre, Samuel, 225
Acts of possession, 64
Adams, Cuyler, 124
Adams, Mrs. Robert M., 123
Adams, Robert M., Jr., 124
Adams County, Miss.: created, 197; land
office, 199; Spanish records at, 186–87
Adjudications, 85
Adjurations of heresy, 172, 234
Admiralty causes, 28

Agriculture: 5, 85; corresp. re, 63; Mo.,
249; promotion of, 27; records re, 18
Alabama: 19, 79; admitted as state, 215;
Anglo-Saxon inhabitants, 221; colonial
govt., 213–14; corresp. re, 79; doc.
publs., 62; land claims, 133–34, 146,
222ff.; land grants, 122, 214–15, 226–27;
land office records, 226–27; land surveys, 229–31; Pintado papers re, 123;
settlers from seaboard colonies, 208;
and Spanish records, 217–18; surv.
genl. for, 204, 230
Alabama Department of Archives and
History: 62, 219; Ala. land records, 217,
227–28, 230–31; Coffee papers, 231;
Hamilton reprods., 221; transcripts
from European archives, 191; transcripts
of Mobile church registers, 234
Alabama Historical Society, 219
Alabama History Commission, 219
Alabama-Mississippi boundary survey,
231
Alabama River, 8
Alabama secretary of state: surv. genl.'s
records delivered to, 230; translations
held by, 216, 217
Alabama Territory: created, 197, 215; land
surveys, 229–31; migration to, 215
Alcaldes, Mobile, 213
Alexandria, La., parish seat, 82
Alibamons, comdt. for, 9
Allouez, Claude Jean, 76
Almonester y Rojàs, Andrés, 171
Alsace, 172
Alsatia, 105

sus, 110; church records re, 176; families
at, 180; military post at, 169; militia, 68
Attakapas country, 96
Attakapas district: corresp. re, 77; land
records, 118; settled by Acadians, 109;
surveyor, 118–19
Attakapas Parish, La., 129, 138
Attakapas Post, La., 179
Attorney general: of La., 4, 5; of New Or-
leans, 33, 34
Aubry, Charles Philippe, 16, 25, 61, 70
Auburn University, Auburn, Ala., 220
Auctions, public, 5, 14, 107
Audiencia de Santo Domingo: 55; appeals
to, from La., 30; papers, 57; reprods.
from, 54
Augusta, Miss., 226
Austin, Moses, 245, 254
Avoyelles, La.: church, 169; confirmations,
174
Avoyelles Parish, La.: estab., 82; French
traders settle in, 88; microfilm re, 71;
records, 84, 89
Ayer, Edward E., collection, Newberry Li-
brary, 59, 76, 99

Baden, 172
Badins, M., 78
Bagby, Gov. Arthur L., 216
Baillardel, A., 72
Baldwin, ———, 74
Balize, La., 16, 31, 47, 73, 150
Baltimore Cathedral Archives, 158
Bancroft, Hubert H., 41, 63, 64
Bandelier, Mrs. Adolph, 52
Bannon, Rev. John F., 241
Baptismal registers: of Acadians, 49, 161;
of Americans on the Tombigbee River,
233; Ark. Post, 287; Baton Rouge, 165–
166; contents, 164; Donaldsonville, La.,
167; Edgard, La., 168; of Favrot family,
73; Florissant, Mo., 275; Galveztown,
La., 168–69; Mansura, La., 169; Natchez,
209; Natchitoches, La., 170–71; New
Madrid, Mo., 252; New Orleans, 171–
73; Opelousas, La., 175; Plattenville, La.,
175; Pointe Coupee, La., 176; St. Bernard, La., 169, 177; Ste. Geneviève, Mo.,

272; St. Gabriel, La., 169, 177; St. James,
La., 178; St. Martin of Tours Church, 179
Baptisms, Manchac, La., 165
Barnard, Charles, 132
Barnett, William, 201, 224
Barnó Ferrúsola, Juan B., 69
Barrière, Rev. Michael, 179–80
Barry, Edward, 249
Barton, Willoughby, 201, 224
Bastrop, Felipe E. N.: 102, 131; land grant
in Ark., 58, 138; papers, 124
Bates, Frederick, 257–59, 265, 281
Batesville, Ark., land office, 282–83
Baton Rouge, La.: 3, 83; capture of, 90, 165;
census, 66; confirmations, 174; court, 94;
Favrot at, 73, 90; genealogical library,
48, 87; govt. under the Spanish, 184;
Grand Pré at, 91; dist. land concessions,
77, 91; land offices moved to, 137; La.
Hist. Soc. at, 11; Protestant marriages at,
166; smuggling Negroes into, 59; sur-
render, 183; surv. genl. at, 144–45;
Thomas comds. fort at, 92
Baton Rouge Parish, 82
Battle plans, 40
Baudier, Roger, 157
Baudin, Nicholas, 224–25
Baume, Capt. Guillaume de la, 115
Baun, Adolph, 36
Bavaria, 172
Baynton & Wharton, 251
Bay of Biscay, 162
Bayou Bartholemew, Ark., 281
Bayou Lafourche, La.: 66, 97; church on,
175; land grants on, 115
Bayou Manchac, La., 168
Bayou Sara, La.: baptisms, 165; marriages,
166
Bayour Sara, Miss., marriages, 209
Bayou Tunica, La., marriages, 166
Beaubassin, Nova Scotia, abstracts of Aca-
dian church, 162
Beaumont, 67
Bell, William, 280
Bell and Howell, Wooster, Ohio, 190–91
Bellew, Solomon, 261
Bemis, Samuel F., 53
Benedictine friar, 273

Bent, Silas, 254, 266, 269, 270
Beranger, Sieur de, 76
Bibb, William W., 215
Bienville, Jean Baptiste Le Moyne, Sieur
de, 5, 7, 8, 17, 61, 183, 190, 213
Bienville Parish, La., land claims, 139
Biloxi, Ala., 213
Biloxi, La., 4
Biloxi, Miss.: 3, 9, 47, 183; census, 66, 192;
maps and plans, 47; marriages, 172, 268;
post at, 208
Biloxi Bay, Miss., 183, 213
Biloxi Parish, estab., 198
Biography: 14, 18, 85, 141, 146; sketches, 65
Bird, John, 128
Birth registers, 50
Bishop: of Alexandria, La., 170; of Balti-
more, 158, 233; of Cuba, 157; of Quebec,
154, 158, 274; of La., 154, 174, 179; of
Santiago de Cuba, 154
Bissell, Capt. Daniel, 251
Blache, Francisco, 37, 75
"Black Books," 15, 36
Black Code, 25, 60, 70, 78, 79
Black Warrior River, 19
Blanque, Jean Paul, 21
Blondeau, Luis, 37, 75
Bloom, Lansing B., 53
Boards of land commissioners: Ala., 222–
23; east of Pearl River, 206–207, 222ff.,
226–27; Iowa, 264; La., calendar of
corresp., 148–149; Miss. Terr., 202; Mo.,
256, 257–60, 264, 265; Orleans Terr.,
125; records, 226; reports, 133, 225, 231;
southeastern dist. La., 128–29; western
dist. La., 129, 138; west of Pearl River,
199, 201, 205–206
Bodin, George A., 160–61, 176
Bogaert, Leon, 219
Bogue, Ala., 225
Bolling, Christopher, 122
Bolton, Herbert E., 63
Bonds, 37, 147
Boone, Daniel, 260
Bordeaux, France, 16
Boré, Étienne, 22
Bossier Parish, La., land claims, 139
Bouligny, ———, 74

Boundaries: La. Terr., 91; La.-Texas, 58;
maps of, 148; microfilm re, 58; St. Louis,
269; southern, 19, 191; Spanish Flas.,
185; Tenn.-Miss., 205; western La., 131
Boundary surveys, Ark., 285
Bourbon County, Ga., 196
Bowie, Rezin P., 121–22, 286
Bowmar, Lt. Joseph, 80
Bowyer, Col. John, 216
Brand books: Attakapas dist., 109; Avoy-
elles Parish, 89; Iberville Parish, 95–96;
Opelousas dist., 109; St. Martin Parish,
110
Breach of promise suits, Mobile, 233
Brest, France, 7, 43, 49
Briand, Bp. Joseph Olivier, 274
Briggs, Isaac, 142, 195, 203, 204
Bringier, Louis, 115, 118
Bringier, Marius, 115
British: 115; in Avoyelles Parish, 89; land
claims, 127, 200, 206–207; land grants,
Ala., 222–24; transport Acadians, 161
British Museum, mss. re Acadians, 163
Broadsides, 22, 41, 62–63
Broders, Mrs. Edwin A., 93, 160
Broutin, N., 101
Brown, James, 22, 117, 118, 125–26
Brown, Joseph C., 267, 268, 270–71
Browne, Henry J., 159
Bruff, Capt. James, 246
Budreux, John Baptiste, 225
Buildings, plans for, 47
Burial records: Ark. Post, 287; Favrot fam-
ily, 73; New Orleans royal hospital, 157
Burial registers: 50, 165; Donaldsonville,
La., 167; Florissant, Mo., 273; Ft. Biloxi,
Miss., 208; Opelousas, La., 175; Ste.
Geneviève, Mo., 272; St. Louis Cathe-
dral, New Orleans, 173; See also Funeral
registers
Burials: Acadian, 49; in New Orleans,
173–74
Burnet, Edmund C., 63
Burnett, John, Jr., 205
Burr, Aaron, 71, 123
Burr, David, 123
Burrus, Rev. Ernest J., 55
Business, 18, 249

346 / Index

Catholic Life Center, Baton Rouge, 160
Catholic religion, 150
Catholics, 115
Catholic University of America, 159
Cattle: 85, 97; in Ft. Louis, Ala., 221; in
New Orleans Parish, 101; in St. James
Parish, 107; security of, 33
Cattle brands: 85; Ala., 217; Assumption
Parish, 88
Cavalry, La., 27
Cenas, Henry B., 128
Censuses: 33; Ala., 217, 221; Ark., 280; At-
takapas, La., 110; Biloxi, 192; Cabonocey,
La., 107; Carondelet, Mo., 241; Ft. Louis,
Ala., 220; Ft. Maurepas, Miss., 192; Ft.
St. Stephens, Ala., 221; La., 9, 57, 58, 65,
66, 75; La. settlements, 44; lower Miss.
R., 113; Miss., 192; Nacogdoches, Tex.,
99; Natchez, 192; Natchitoches, La., 99;
New Orleans, 22, 37, 65, 75; Ouachita
post, 102; Pointe Coupee, La., 104; St.
Charles Parish, 106; Ste. Geneviève,
Mo., 241; St. Landry Parish, 109; St.
Louis, 241; St. Martin Parish, 111; Span-
ish, 64; Spanish La., 40; Spanish W.
Fla., 93; to be conducted, 9; Upper La.,
241. See also names of places
Cerré, Jean Gabriel, 243
Chaise, Jacques de la, 7
Chalmette, La., parish seat, 82, 105
Chambers, Joseph, 222
Chambers of commerce, records re French
emigrants, 44
Champagne province, France, 150
Charente Maritime, Archives Départmen-
tales de la, microfilm on trade with
New France, 47
Charity Hospital, New Orleans, 72
Charts: Gulf of Mexico, 65; held by French
ministries, 44; La., 123; southern boun-
dary survey, 104
Chastang, Joseph, 224, 225
Chateau de Bernadets, 22
Chattahoochee River: 229; surveys west
of, 204
Chenal, La., 160
Cherokee Indians: 69, 202; field notes of
lands, 231
Cherokee River, 9

Chevalier, Andrew, 261
Chicago Historical Society, mss. held by,
75–76, 245
Chickasaw Bluffs, Memphis: 19; fort
constr. at, 8, 185
Chickasawhay River, land surveys on, 204
Chickasaw Indians: 19, 202; campaigns
against, 8, 73, 183, 213; cessions of land,
197, 205, 215; field notes of lands, 231;
publ. docs. re, 190; treaty with, 19, 79
Chico Point, Ark., 280
Chifonete district, estab., 91
Childress, Paris, 128
Chillicothe, Ohio, surv. genl. at, 267
Chimneys register, 78
Choctaw country, 76
Choctaw Indians: 19, 69; field notes of
lands, 231; land cessions, 197, 205, 215;
publ. docs. re, 190; treaty with, 19, 74
Chouteau, Auguste, 243, 254, 262
Chouteau, Pierre, 243
Chouteau, Pierre, Jr., 243
Chouteau, René, 243
Chouteaus, given trade monopoly, 277
Christy, William, 122
Churchill, Charles R., 68, 110
Church of Jesus Christ of Latter-Day
Saints, 87
Church of the Immaculate Conception,
Mobile, 225, 233
Church property: 40; inventory, 168
Church records, La.: inventory, 165; south-
west La., abstracts, 161. See also names
of individual churches
Church registers, La.: 163–65. See also
names of individual churches
Church wardens, 174, 175, 178
Cinq Hommes, Mo., 251
City hall, New Orleans. See Cabildo
City steward, New Orleans, 34
Civil suits: 34; Ala., 217; Natchitoches,
La., 98; New Orleans, 35; Spanish W.
Fla., 93
Civil War, 283
Claiborne, Ferdinand L., 80
Claiborne, La., 111
Claiborne, William C. C.: 106, 116ff., 198,
238, 251; apptd. govr. of Miss. Terr.,
193; commr. for La. transfer, 10, 20, 80;

Webb, Mary L., 194
Wells, ———, 206
West, Cato, 186
West, Elizabeth H., 53, 59
West Baton Rouge Parish, La., 111
Western land district, La., 138
Western Reserve Historical Society, 119, 188
West Feliciana, La., 119
West Feliciana Parish, La., 86, 112
West Florida: added to Orleans Terr., 83, 91; Americans occupy, 198, 215; British occupy, 90; ceded to England, 214; commerce, 28; Cuban archives re, 155; docs. re, 58; estab. by British, 26; govt. of, 26, 91; Irish priests for, 155; land grants, 115, 227; landholders, 234; land surveys, 116, 120; letters to officials of, 59; maps, 123; microfilm re, 56, 58; Papeles de Cuba re, 40; Pintado becomes surv. genl. of, 119, 123; records re conquest, 40; records transf. to Spain, 39–40; revolutionary convention records, 91, 92, 93, 186, 208; Spanish and, 19, 25, 49–50, 56, 71, 183–84, 214; Spanish land grants, 122
West Florida Republic, 58, 59, 92, 197–98
West Indies, 214
Wheless, Joseph, 249
Wherry, Mackay, 261
Whitaker, Arthur P., 56, 64
Whitbeck, A. T., 119
Whitcomb, James, 121, 131, 144
White, John R., 121
White, Joseph M., 61
White, Rev. Gregory, 209
Whitner, ———, 206
Wikoff, William, 138
Wilbur, James B., 45, 54
Wilkinson, Gen. James, 20, 23, 71, 76–80, 116–17, 197, 215, 238, 266

Wilkinson, Theodore J., 225
Wilkinson County, Miss. Terr., 197
Williams, David, 128
Williams, Guillermo, 128
Williams, Harry T., 121–22
Williams, Kemper and Leila, 23
Williams, L. Kemper, 75
Williams, Robert, 186, 200
Williams, Thomas H., 200
Wills: 5, 14, 75; Ala., 216, 227; Blondeau, 37; Concordia Parish, 90; La., 31, 85, 146; Natchez dist., 187; New Madrid, Mo., 252; New Orleans, 100; St. James Parish, 107; in St. Louis archives, 249
Wilson, John, 121
Wilson, Joseph S., 269
Winn Parish, La., land claims, 139
Winter, William, 281
Wisconsin State Historical Society, 52, 59, 240
Woodbury, Levi, 121
Work Projects Administration, 37, 100, 234
Works Progress Administration, 96
World's Fair of 1904, St. Louis, 242
World War II, 54
Wright, Irene A., 53, 68
Würtemberg, Germany, 172

Ximenes, Carlos, 9, 101, 117

Yazoo, Miss., marriage register, 268
Yazoo land grants, 172, 194, 206
Yazoo River, 8, 19, 150, 183, 184
Yazoos, 9
Yazoos district, 9
Yazoo strip, 19
Ybanez, Ferdinand, 117

Zeringue, Marlene, 174